THE
F. A. CUP
FINAL

THE
F. A. CUP
FINAL

A Post-War History
by IVAN PONTING

INTRODUCTION

What's so special about the FA Cup? The League Championship is harder to win, a more realistic mark of a team's ability; and it would be ludicrous to suggest that the European Cup doesn't carry more kudos on any honours list. Yet somehow the FA Cup remains on a glorious pedestal, in a class of its own. Even now, in the cash-crazy world that modern football has become, the Cup exercises a unique magic and romance. The excitement of sudden-death knockouts, the true democracy of giant-killing, the special atmosphere of Wembley with its famous Twin Towers, there is nothing that quite compares. The FA Cup Final continues proudly as the gala day of English soccer, an occasion which fascinates even those who don't follow football.

This book is an attempt to capture the essence of soccer's oldest senior competition by presenting, in words and pictures, a record of every post-War final to date. In fact, the story encompasses much more than the matches them-selves, taking in the finalists' paths to Wembley and reflecting footballing issues of the times. It is a thrilling tale that needs no further introduction, and I will let it speak for itself. But first I want to thank the people who have helped me: Steve Small for his brilliant design and deep fund of soccer knowledge; the great Nat Lofthouse for his gracious foreword; publisher Tony Williams for making the book possible and for his treasured memories of Birmingham City; Les Gold and Eddie Marks for the generous loan of valuable material; all at Colorsport, especially the diminutive yet dynamic Andy Cowie, a man who doesn't know the meaning of defeat when it comes to hunting down a rare picture; many people in football who shared their reminiscences, with a special mention for Ian Callaghan and Steve Perryman; Chris and Jo Forster for early support; Michael Williams and Greg Tesser for production expertise; and finally, Pat, Rosie and Joe Ponting, for everything.

Ivan Ponting

September 1993

Published by Tony Williams Publications
© Ivan Ponting

ISBN 1 869833-36-8

Designed and Typeset by Steve Small
Film Origination: Character Graphics, Taunton.
Illustrations: Colorsport, Popperfoto and Hulton-Deutsch
Printed by: Haynes Publishing Group, Sparkford
Trade Sales: Derek Searle Associates Ltd (0753) 53925
Distributed by: Little Red Witch Books (0823) 491069/490080

CONTENTS

FOREWORD

The FA Challenge Cup Final at Wembley is probably the most famous of all football occasions. These days millions of fans watch the game through television all over the world and to play in this game is the ambition of most footballers - certainly those playing in England.

I was lucky enough to play a part for Bolton Wanderers in two of the finals that seem to remain in the memories of most football fans. The first in 1953, known as 'The Matthews Final' in which Stan won his medal in a thrilling 4-3 victory thanks to a last-minute goal, and the 1958 game when Wanderers were not the most popular winners, as we triumphed 2-0 against the post-Munich Manchester United team that had fought back from their tragedy so bravely.

I will always remember both games with great pleasure. In the first I had a tremendously hard physical battle with my old friend and England colleague Harry Johnston, and although we were desperately disappointed to lose so late in the game, we were all privileged to be at Wembley on such a wonderful day.

To score in the final is, without doubt, something special and I was pleased to be able to find the net on both visits. Of the two that knocked out United, I suppose the one I bustled in from Harry Gregg will stay in most people's memories. The game was different then, the goal counted and we were thrilled to return to Wembley and this time leave as winners.

I have experienced just about every emotion during my two finals and I know that Ivan Ponting's glorious book will bring back thousands of memories to the players, managers and fans, who will recall all the elation and despair as they relive the FA Cup Finals since Derby County won the first competition after the Second World War.

Nat Lofthouse,

September 1993

IT HAPPENED THIS YEAR

Price of two-door Morris saloon car rose to £250.

New research linked smoking to cancer.

Wartime food controls relaxed, but bread still rationed.

First GI brides arrived in New York from Britain.

Nazi war criminals executed at Nuremberg.

BBC launched Third Programme.

27 April 1946

DERBY COUNTY 4

B Turner (og) 85; Doherty 91; Stamps 97, 106

CHARLTON ATHLETIC 1

B Turner 86

Half-time 0-0 Extra time played

DERBY COUNTY		CHARLTON ATHLETIC
Vic Woodley	1	Sam Bartram
Jack Nicholas (captain)	2	Harold Phipps
Jack Howe	3	Jack Shreeve
Jim Bullions	4	Bert Turner
Leon Leuty	5	John Oakes
Chick Musson	6	Bert Johnson
Reg Harrison	7	Leslie Fell
Raich Carter	8	Albert Brown
Jack Stamps	9	Arthur Turner
Peter Doherty	10	Don Welsh (captain)
Dally Duncan	11	Chris Duffy

Attendance: 98,215

Referee: E Smith, Sunderland

The War was over. Now the people of England, starved of entertainment during six years of untold misery and suffering, were determined to roll back the clouds of conflict and enjoy themselves. For countless thousands, that meant football; not the makeshift variety of the past half-decade - worthy though that was in boosting national morale - but the real thing. And in 1945/46, with the Football League not ready to replace regional competitions, that meant the FA Cup.

Few households boasted a television in those days so the only way to see the action was to go to the match. Accordingly, fans flocked to grounds all over the country, and the post-War soccer boom was under way. Indeed, the semi-final replay between Derby County and Birmingham City at Maine Road drew an astonishing 80,407 spectators, which remains the biggest midweek attendance for a club match outside Wembley. There was, though, a heinous price to be paid for such euphoria. Quarter-final day brought disaster at Burnden Park, where Bolton Wanderers were playing host to Stoke City, Stanley Matthews *et al.* So great was the demand for a place on the terraces

Left: The Rams parade their prize.
Back row (left to right): Jim Bullions, Jack Nicholas, Vic Woodley, Leon Leuty, Jack Howe, Chick Musson. Front row: Stuart McMillan (manager), Reg Harrison, Raich Carter, Jack Stamps, Peter Doherty, Dally Duncan, Dave Willis (trainer). Nearly half a century later, Derby County were still striving for a second FA Cup triumph.

that some 1,500 frustrated supporters climbed over turnstiles and the result was carnage. Thirty three died, 400 were injured and there was an impassioned plea for safer stadia, but little was to change until further catastrophes more than 40 years later. Of course, the poignancy of this tragedy was highlighted by the fact that the victims had survived the horror of war, only to perish on what should have been a harmless afternoon out.

On a sporting level, however, the Cup was a glorious success, and that despite the FA's decision to make each tie up to and including the sixth round a two-legged affair. This arrangement, while making it more likely that the best team would win through - arguably desirable in the absence of the League - struck at the very core of the Cup's allure, namely the possibility of giant-killing. In 1946 big clubs who slipped up in the first match had a second chance to crush the min-nows, and there were no real upsets. There were some stirring ties, though, notably the third-round clash between Newcastle United and Barnsley, the Yorkshiremen winning 5-4 on aggregate after losing 4-2 in the away leg. The new rule created one fascinating anomaly, too, Charlton Athletic getting to the final despite losing a match on the way; they were beaten 2-1 by Fulham in the third round second leg, but stayed on course for glory by virtue of a 3-1 first-leg win.

On a more fanciful note, it was suggested during the run-up to the final that County might as well not turn up. According to an ancient Derbyshire legend, the club had once taken over land which had been favoured by gipsies as a conve-nient encampment. Thus evicted, the enraged Romanies had cursed the club, damning them to go forever without winning League or Cup and, indeed, the Baseball Ground trophy cabinet had ever remained bare of these most prestigious baubles. To one newshound of the period, this suggested a scoop, and he took Derby captain Jack Nicholas for a meaningful discussion with an amenable mod-ern-day gipsy. That worthy, having had his palm crossed with silver in the approved manner, removed the curse and - so went the story - the two sides could then start on equal terms!

Back in the real world, Derby and Charlton were off to Wembley, which both had reached in free-scoring style. Even allowing for the double-leg innovation, the fact that the pair had netted 60 times between them on the way to the final - the Rams 32, the Valiants 28 - boded well for the big day. Happily, with the stadium resplendent for its biggest occasion in six years, the game lived up to its billing as a feast of free-flowing football, though not before a pre-match scare at the Baseball

HOW THEY GOT THERE
DERBY COUNTY
Round 3: **Luton Town** (a) 6-0, (h) 3-0.
Round 4: **West Bromwich Albion** (h) 1-0, (a) 3-1.
Round 5: **Brighton and Hove Albion** (a) 4-1, (h) 6-0.
Round 6: **Aston Villa** (a) 4-3, (h) 1-1.
Semi-final: **Birmingham City** *at Hillsborough* 1-1; *at Maine Road* 4-0.
CHARLTON ATHLETIC
Round 3: **Fulham** (h) 3-1, (a) 1-2.
Round 4: **Wolverhampton Wanderers** (h) 5-2, (a)1-1.
Round 5: **Preston North End** (a) 1-1, (h) 6-0.
Round 6: **Brentford** (h) 6-3, (a) 3-1.
Semi-final: **Bolton Wanderers** *at Villa Park* 2-0.

'The Silver Fox' in his element. Raich Carter demonstrates the assured mastery which lifted this small man head and shoulders above almost all his contemporaries in terms of pure footballing ability.

Ground. When the County players realised that their wives had been allocated inferior tickets they threatened to strike, led by Irishman Peter Doherty, then something of a shop steward among footballers. He was a proud man who railed against the exploitation by rich clubs of abysmally-paid players and his relations with authority were always uneasy. This was one confrontation he won handsomely, the directors capitulating and providing the ladies with more suitable accommodation. In fact, Doherty and fellow inside-forward Raich Carter were, as widely predicted and along with centre-forward Jackie Stamps, the stars of the show. What a combination! Carter was well-nigh the complete footballer, both play-maker and striker, whose touch was sublime and who oozed charisma. Small and prone to arrogance, he didn't suffer fools at all, let alone gladly, and was a formidable partner for the stormy petrel Doherty, who in his turn was a wonderful performer with his delightful dribbling skills, enormous work-rate and capacity for original thinking. That dull, humid afternoon the silver-haired Raich and red-headed Peter were like two marauding foxes set loose in the Charlton henhouse, their game infused with an abrasive wit that, eventually, was not to be denied, though that's not to say they had it all their own way.

Proceedings began with the contestants' nerves apparently jangling - not helped by King George VI, who exercised his royal prerogative and was late for the pre-match presentation - and both teams took time to settle. Their composure was not helped, either, by the absence through injury of regular players: Derby's right-winger Sammy Crooks (a quarter-final casualty) and left-back Jack Parr, and Charlton right-back Peter Croker, who had broken his leg ten days earlier. When a pattern did emerge it was County who took the eye, but chances were missed, Athletic 'keeper Sam Bartram made some fine saves and a Carter 'goal' was disallowed for offside.

After the break it was Charlton's turn to spurn openings, the most inviting of which was missed by skipper Don Welsh after being put through by the excellent Albert Brown. There followed a period of deadlock, enlivened by Bartram's superb deflection of a Dally Duncan shot and one exhilarating dribble past five opponents by Brown, but with five minutes of normal time remaining an injection of drama was needed. Enter Bert Turner, the Charlton right-half, who appeared to settle the destiny of the trophy when he deflected Duncan's shot into his own net. Sixty seconds later, however, Bert's world had turned upside

Left: Bert Turner, who sampled the extremes of soccer emotion within the space of a minute. First his own goal gave Derby the lead, then he made amends when his free-kick skidded off Peter Doherty and into County's net to put Charlton back on level terms.

down when his 25-yard free-kick was diverted past Derby custodian Vic Woodley by Doherty. Legend demanded that Turner went down as the first man to score for both sides in an FA Cup Final, and thus his name was entered in the records. Later County were to claim he should not appear on the scoresheet at all, with Duncan seeking credit for the first strike and Doherty admitting responsibility for the equaliser, but to no avail.

The next four minutes were played at fever pitch, highlighted by one incredible incident. A power drive from Derby marksman Stamps burst the ball, leaving the dumbfounded Bartram to catch the deflated leather and referee Smith to reflect on his remark in a recent radio interview that the odds against such an event were a million to

Above: At least they didn't start without him! King George VI, a late arrival at Wembley, is introduced to Raich Carter by Derby skipper Jack Nicholas. Next in line is the Rams' other star inside-forward, Peter Doherty.

Left: Derby's Dally Duncan, whose claim to the opening goal of the game was rejected, though poor Bert Turner would have been more than happy for Dally's name to appear on the official scoresheet.

11

Right: Derby stopper Leon Leuty, the most dominant defender on show, imperiously brushes aside the challenge of Charlton's Arthur Turner.

Opposite above: Charlton skipper Don Welsh closes in, but the ball is safely in the grasp of Derby goalkeeper Vic Woodley. Looking on are Chick Musson (centre) and Leon Leuty.

Centre-forward Jack Stamps, whose two goals in extra time set the seal on Derby's victory.

Opposite below: This is what we came for! County captain Jack Nicholas climbs down from the royal box with his hands satisfactorily full.

one! Even more amazingly, there was another burst ball when the two sides met five days later in a regional league match, and yet another when Charlton faced Burnley in the 1947 final.

Alarums and excursions notwithstanding, there were no more goals within the prescribed 90 minutes so the game moved into extra time. Now, at last, County's exuberant attacking potential revealed itself in the most devastating fashion. First the bustling Stamps dashed past a defender before unleashing a cross-cum-shot that Bartram could merely parry to the feet of Doherty, who rammed the ball into the net. That was the signal for the Irish rebel and the brilliant Carter to light up Wembley with some sparkling play, but it was the oft-underrated Stamps who was to put the trophy finally beyond Charlton's reach. First he ran through the middle, shrugged off a challenge and nudged the ball past an exposed Bartram, then he capped County's triumph by converting a Doherty pass for 4-1. Inevitably, the forwards cornered the post-match plaudits, but the performance of the Midlanders' centre-half Leon Leuty, the best defender afield, should not go unremarked.

After that extra-time blitz, and having enjoyed rather the better of exchanges during normal time, Derby could rightly claim to have deserved the spoils. However, Charlton's moment would not be long in coming.

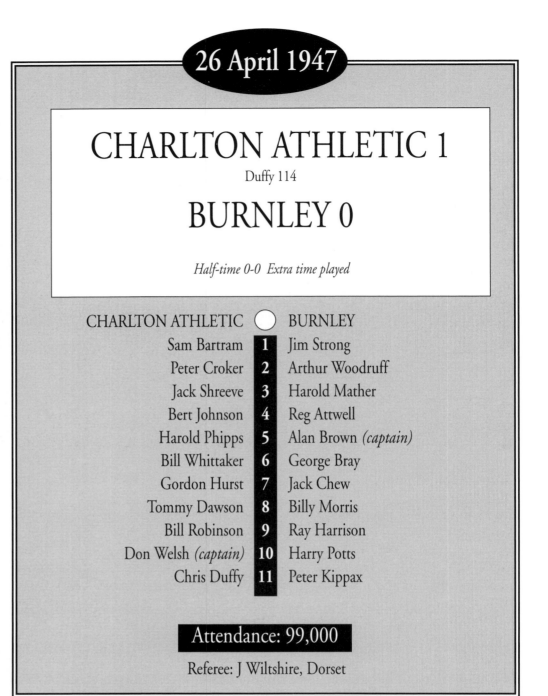

26 April 1947

CHARLTON ATHLETIC 1
Duffy 114

BURNLEY 0

Half-time 0-0 Extra time played

CHARLTON ATHLETIC	○	BURNLEY
Sam Bartram	1	Jim Strong
Peter Croker	2	Arthur Woodruff
Jack Shreeve	3	Harold Mather
Bert Johnson	4	Reg Attwell
Harold Phipps	5	Alan Brown *(captain)*
Bill Whittaker	6	George Bray
Gordon Hurst	7	Jack Chew
Tommy Dawson	8	Billy Morris
Bill Robinson	9	Ray Harrison
Don Welsh *(captain)*	10	Harry Potts
Chris Duffy	11	Peter Kippax

Attendance: 99,000

Referee: J Wiltshire, Dorset

IT HAPPENED THIS YEAR

Princess Elizabeth married Philip Mountbatten.

Partition of India, creation of Pakistan.

British coal mines nationalised.

The 31-year-old Harold Wilson joined the Cabinet.

Denis Compton finished glorious season with record 3,816 runs.

John Cobb set land speed record of 394 mph.

For Chris Duffy, the Wembley experience was proving something of a letdown. In 1946 he and his Charlton Athletic team-mates had been on the wrong end of an often masterful exhibition by Derby County; now, a year later, the chunky Scottish wingman was making precious little impact against a fearsomely efficient Burnley defence. With the end of extra time approaching and both sides seemingly resigned to a replay, Chris was looking anything but the potential match-winner he had been tagged by many pundits. The heat was stifling, the game was stagnant, most of the players were increasingly lethargic, even the crowd was listless. During the course of his two finals, Chris had scurried over the sacred turf for some 234 fruitless minutes and the prospect of glory appeared to be receding with the tantalising inevitability of a desert mirage.

Then, like a thunderclap in a cloudless sky, came the moment that transformed the afternoon from an occasion of dismal anti-climax - ironically it was the first final to be televised live and in full - to one of unbridled joy for all those who marched beneath the banner of the Valiants. Centre-forward Bill Robinson drifted wide to the right and floated a hanging cross into the Clarets' box; his skipper

Don Welsh made the subtlest of contacts with his balding pate and the ball fell to Duffy 12 yards from goal. Suddenly, all the aforementioned tedium was rendered meaningless as the little flankman smashed an instant, unstoppable volley wide of 'keeper Jim Strong and the net bulged satisfyingly. Truly it was a strike to carry forever in the memory, but as if the goal itself were not enough, Duffy contributed a celebration of such sheer unadulterated glee that it was equally unlikely to be forgotten. For several seconds he stood as if transfixed, arms above his head, and not a soul on the pitch appeared to move. Then he exploded into ecstatic motion, skipping, sprinting and leaping, until he was run to earth and engulfed by delirious team-mates. On such a day, in such a game, it had always seemed likely that a single goal would settle the issue, and despite a late rally by the Clarets, so it did.

Beforehand, the final had been seen as a confrontation between Charlton's more imaginative attack and a Burnley rearguard that was to keep 25 clean sheets and not concede more than two goals in a match all season. With the Londoners struggling near the foot of the First Division and the Lancastrians about to gain promotion from the Second - the outcome of League matters was delayed into June by a mammoth fixture backlog caused by an unprecedentedly severe midwinter freeze - there was not much to choose between the two in stature. The Valiants were the slight favourites, though, and certainly their semi-final performance had been the more convincing, an unexpectedly easy 4-0 demolition of Newcastle United, for whom Messrs Milburn, Shackleton and company were, for once, firing blanks. That win at neutral Elland Road was all the more remarkable because several members of the team were suffering from food poisoning, the legacy of a visit to a pie factory on the day before the match. Indeed, poor Sam Bartram took the field with a hot poultice strapped uncomfortably across his stomach, and even the simple act of taking a goal-kick left him doubled up in pain.

Above: The arms go up and Chris Duffy (right) has plundered a breathtaking goal to light up an otherwise rather lacklustre final.
Below: Duffy in more restrained action. The little Scot later became landlord of a Belfast pub, where customers relished his colourful memories.

Right: Put it there. Charlton's Don Welsh (left) shakes hands at the start of a second successive final, while for Alan Brown of Burnley it's a new experience.

HOW THEY GOT THERE

CHARLTON ATHLETIC
Round 3:
Rochdale (h) 3-1.

Round 4:
West Bromwich Albion (a) 2-1.

Round 5:
Blackburn Rovers (h) 1-0.

Round 6:
Preston North End (h) 2-1.

Semi-final:
Newcastle United at Elland Road 4-0.

BURNLEY
Round 3:
Aston Villa (h) 5-1.

Round 4:
Coventry City (h) 2-0.

Round 5:
Luton Town (a) 0-0, replay (h) 3-0.

Round 6:
Middlesbrough (a) 1-1, replay (h) 1-0.

Semi-final:
Liverpool at Ewood Park 0-0, replay at Maine Road 1-0.

Burnley had faced more formidable opponents in the shape of League Champions-elect Liverpool, earning their Wembley place through a late Ray Harrison winner in a tight replay at Maine Road. Incidentally their first meeting with the Reds, at Blackburn's Ewood Park, had evoked a chilling echo of the previous term's Burnden Park disaster; once again too many supporters were inside the ground but this time, though dozens departed on stretchers, there were no fatalities. As the great day approached, there was much debate as to whether or not Charlton's experience of the previous year was an advantage. Some reckoned it would stand them in good stead, others believed the pressure of avoiding a second defeat would drain them. Either way, it was inescapable that the side was weaker than 12 months earlier, with only five survivors from the clash with Derby. Furthermore, regular left-half Charlie Revell was ruled out by injury - Bill Whittaker stepped up to take his place - though Peter Croker (elder brother of Ted, later to become FA Secretary) made up for his unlucky absence in 1946 by slotting in at right-back.

When the action got under way, Charlton were quick to assume the territorial supremacy so widely predicted for them, yet apart from one heart-in-mouth moment when Harold Mather cleared off the line from Duffy, it was Burnley who created the clearest opportunities before the interval. First newly-capped Welshman Billy Morris ghosted through the Londoners' flimsy cover before shooting over from ten yards, then winger Peter Kippax twice dallied infuriatingly when in dangerous positions. Sadly for the Lancastrians, Kippax gave a lacklustre performance, confounding those who believed him capable of winning the trophy for the Turf Moor club. An England amateur international, he was superbly talented but failed to realise his potential on this, his biggest footballing occasion. Apart from those isolated thrusts, the most interesting moment of the initial period

Right: Three of Burnley's key men in their bid to take the FA Cup to Turf Moor for the first time since before the First World War. Left to right are Welsh international inside-forward Billy Morris, future Clarets boss Harry Potts and England amateur winger Peter Kippax.

came on half an hour, when the ball burst at Wembley for the second year in succession. Unlike the previous incident, this one happened well away from goal and when referee Wiltshire called for a replacement, most spectators did not realise what had happened.

After the break, the temperature took an increasing toll on rapidly tiring players. Charlton continued to dominate possession, with right-half Bert Johnson in particularly impressive form, but with mighty Alan Brown a veritable rock at the centre of Burnley's defence there seemed scant likelihood of a breakthrough. Indeed it was the Second Division outfit, once more, who came agonisingly close to taking the lead when inside-left Harry Potts - destined to lead the Clarets to the Championship as manager in 1960 - rattled the crossbar with a 20-yard drive after 67 minutes. Thereafter the game dragged, in desultory fashion, into extra time and yet again Burnley threatened an upset when Harrison was brought down in the penalty area by Harold Phipps, only for the referee to wave play on.

Then came Duffy's denouement and the Cup was on its way to The Valley for the first time. For the wee fellow from Fife, who had taken part in the D-Day landings in Normandy, it was an exhilarating highlight of a Charlton career that continued until 1952/53. Later he ran a pub in Belfast, where he would regale regulars with typically effervescent accounts of his golden day. Sadly, Chris died in 1978.

At the time most neutrals welcomed the Valiants' victory because it meant a winner's medal for one of English soccer's best-loved figures, Sam Bartram. A red-headed, Jarrow-born giant whose outsize frame was matched by his personality, he was an acrobatic performer who loved playing to the gallery, and was one of the first custodians to take free-kicks outside his area. Unswervingly loyal to Charlton - his 582 League appearances between 1934 and 1956 remain a club record - Sam must surely have displayed his talents on the international stage but for peaking in an era when the likes of Frank Swift, Bert Williams, Ted Ditchburn and Gil Merrick were in their pomp. Thus on that balmy April evening, as Charlton celebrated the greatest triumph in their history, it was appropriate that such a man - whose loss was keenly felt throughout the game when he died in 1981 - inspired many a toast far beyond his adopted homeland of south-east London.

Below: Bert Johnson, whose influential display at right-half was a significant factor in Charlton's midfield superiority.

Sam Bartram, a larger-than-life character, popular wherever he went. Left: The red-haired colossus makes one of several athletic saves that denied Burnley a Wembley breakthrough.

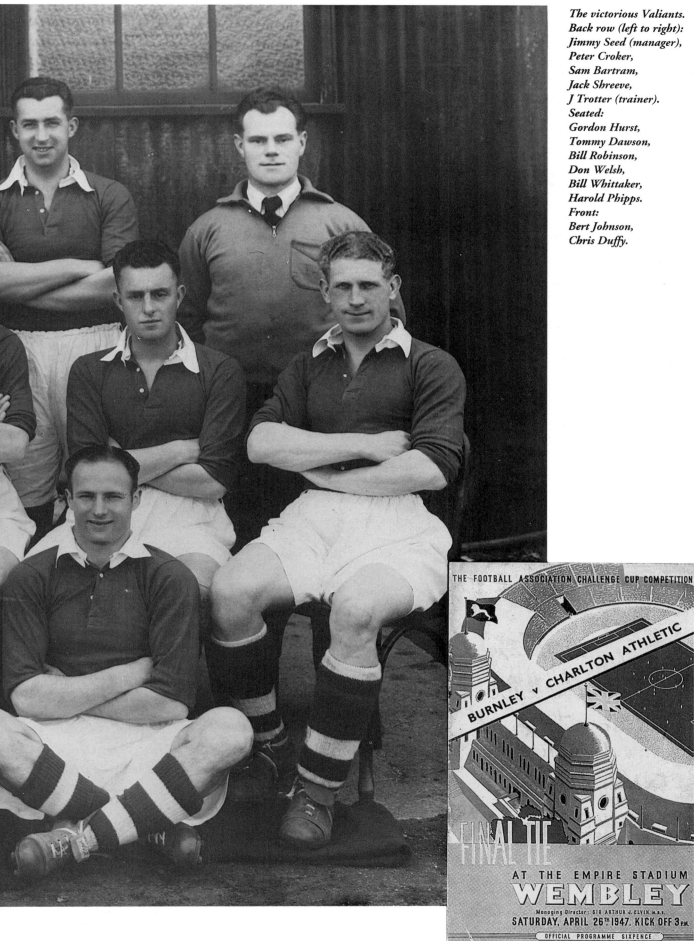

The victorious Valiants.
Back row (left to right):
Jimmy Seed (manager),
Peter Croker,
Sam Bartram,
Jack Shreeve,
J Trotter (trainer).
Seated:
Gordon Hurst,
Tommy Dawson,
Bill Robinson,
Don Welsh,
Bill Whittaker,
Harold Phipps.
Front:
Bert Johnson,
Chris Duffy.

THE FOOTBALL ASSOCIATION CHALLENGE CUP COMPETITION

BURNLEY v CHARLTON ATHLETIC

FINAL TIE

AT THE EMPIRE STADIUM
WEMBLEY
Managing Director : SIR ARTHUR J. ELVIN, M.B.E.
SATURDAY, APRIL 26TH 1947. KICK OFF 3 P.M.
OFFICIAL PROGRAMME SIXPENCE

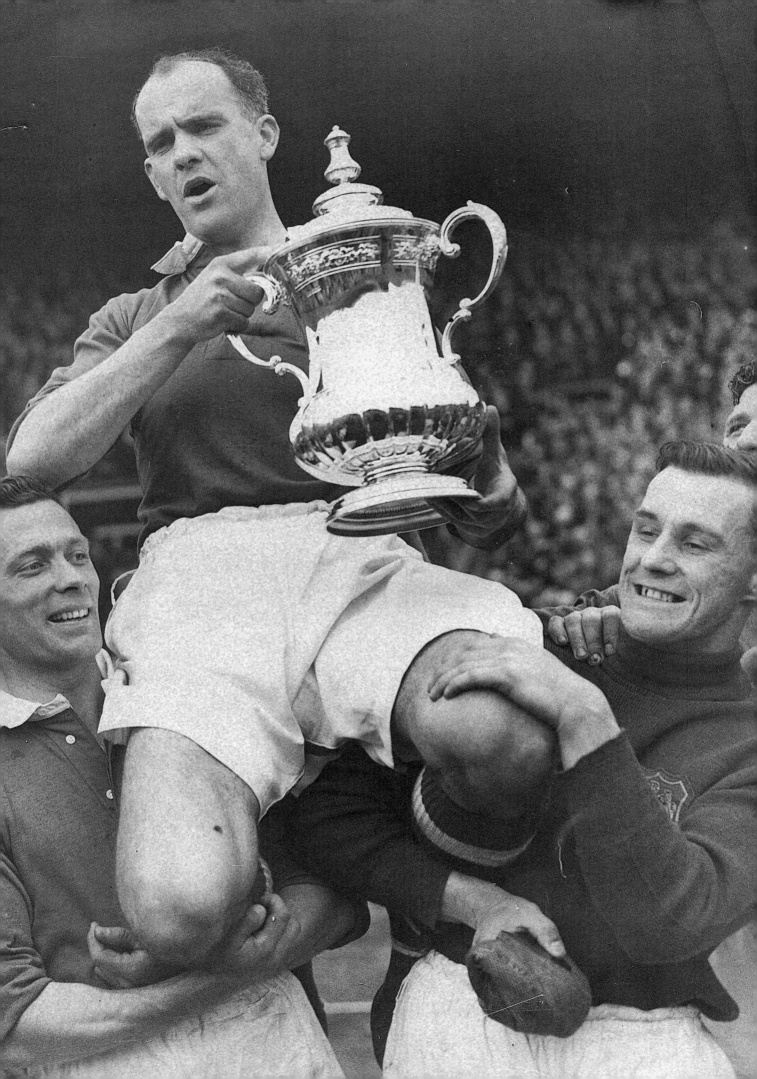

MANCHESTER UNITED 4

Rowley 28, 69; Pearson 80; Anderson 83

BLACKPOOL 2

Shimwell (pen) 12, Mortensen 43

Half-time 1-2

MANCHESTER UNITED	○	BLACKPOOL
Jack Crompton	1	Joe Robinson
Johnny Carey *(captain)*	2	Eddie Shimwell
John Aston	3	Johnny Crosland
John Anderson	4	Harry Johnston *(captain)*
Allenby Chilton	5	Eric Hayward
Henry Cockburn	6	Hugh Kelly
Jimmy Delaney	7	Stanley Matthews
Johnny Morris	8	Alex Munro
Jack Rowley	9	Stanley Mortensen
Stan Pearson	10	George Dick
Charlie Mitten	11	Walter Rickett

Attendance: 99,000

Referee: C Barrick, Northampton

1948

IT HAPPENED THIS YEAR

Mahatma Gandhi assassinated.

The birth of Israel.

Highest British birth rate for 25 years.

First operation performed inside heart.

Don Bradman finished Test career with a duck.

Emil Zatopek won 10,000 metres gold medal at London Olympics.

Here was a game that transcended hyperbole to take its place in Wembley folklore as the greatest - or at least the most aesthetically beautiful - FA Cup Final of them all. Others have equalled or even excelled it for drama and excitement, for emotion and enchantment, but - as countless contemporary observers maintain nearly half a century after it was played - for sheer skill and adventure it has never been matched. Sadly, with the modern emphasis on work-rate and defence in depth, it seems certain that we shall not see its like again.

Once Manchester United and Blackpool had reached Wembley - neither had played there before, though the Red Devils had won the Cup at the Crystal Palace in 1909 - the ingredients were in place for sumptuous entertainment. For a start, both managers were committed to free-flowing enterprise and would not allow their sides to cower back in fear of failure. Of course, United's Matt Busby went on to become one of the most successful and visionary bosses of all time, but the part played by the Seasiders' expansive, cigar-smoking Joe Smith - who helped Bolton win the first Wembley final 25 years earlier - should not be undersold.

Then there were the players - and what players they were! In terms of out-and-

Opposite: Johnny Carey, the dignified Irishman who did so much to put Matt Busby's footballing creed into practice, is hoisted on the shoulders of Charlie Mitten (left) and Jack Crompton after Manchester United's exhilarating victory over Blackpool.

21

out stars the edge rested with Blackpool, who boasted the world's finest in Stanley Matthews and, in the judgment of Busby, a marksman without current peer in Stan Mortensen. They had other influential figures too, such as skipper and wing-half Harry Johnston, who completed a potent right-wing triangle, but for quality in depth United were untouchable. There was Johnny Carey, the cool, cultured right-back and captain; the subtle, deadly inside-forward pairing of Stan Pearson and Johnny Morris; Jack Rowley, the goal machine; sparkling wingers Jimmy Delaney and Charlie Mitten, the list could go on and the weak spots were non-existent. On the way to Wembley, the two clubs took on tasks of vastly differing magnitude. While Blackpool enjoyed home advantage in three rounds and never faced a First Division club, all United's games were away from Old Trafford and all their opponents were from the top flight. In fact, Busby's men were allotted three home ties but because their own ground was still under repair following the ravages of Hitler's bombs, they were forced to play on neutral soil. One encounter that will remain vivid in the memory of all who were privileged to witness it was the Red Devils' third-round clash with Aston Villa, who took a surprise 13-second lead. Far from being stunned, United reacted by pulverising the Midlanders for the next 45 minutes to seize a 5-1 interval advantage. Then back came Villa to 5-4 before the visitors secured safe passage with a late strike by Pearson, who said afterwards: 'Today we played the best football I have seen from anybody, at any time.' Thereafter the Reds progressed emphatically, crushing Liverpool, eliminating Charlton despite a heroic show by 'keeper Sam Bartram, beating Preston on the day following the funeral of wing-half John Anderson's wife (after much heart-searching, John played in the match) and saw off Derby in the semi-final thanks to a Pearson hat-trick. Meanwhile Blackpool scored just as freely against lesser opposition, which included non-League Colchester in round five. The Seasiders' greatest scare came against Second Division Spurs in the semi, when they were a goal down with four minutes left. The irrepressible 'Morty' equalised, then grabbed two more in

*Left: The first triumph
of the Busby era - United
players and officials line up
with the FA Cup.
Back row (left to right):
Bill Petherbridge,
Alan Gibson,
George Whittaker,
Dr W McLean,
Harold Hardman (all
directors).
Middle row:
Walter Crickmer (secretary),
John Anderson,
Allenby Chilton,
Jack Crompton,
John Aston,
Henry Cockburn,
Jack Warner.
Front row:
Jimmy Delaney,
Johnny Morris,
Johnny Carey,
Matt Busby (manager),
Jack Rowley,
Stan Pearson,
Charlie Mitten.*

extra time to see his side through.

So the stage was set for a classic, though United's preparation was not ideal. Perennial arguments over ticket allocations surfaced - with the Reds having 12,000 to satisfy some 30,000 fans who wanted to travel - and the knock-on effect meant the players receiving fewer than they needed. Thus they felt hard done by, a situation exacerbated by problems over bonuses and disagreement with the press over payment for interviews. Indeed, so bitter did the last-mentioned dispute become that when the newspapers refused to cough up, the footballers retaliated by covering their faces as they left their train for their Surrey hotel, thus thwarting the photographers. Come the day, however, the United men refused to let the controversy affect their attitude. They were on their mettle because although they were going into the match as favourites - as prospective runners-up to Arsenal in the League, while Blackpool were ensconced in mid-table - they knew complacency must doom them to defeat.

The Seasiders were the people's choice, solely through a sentimental wish to see Matthews claim a winner's medal - at 33, this must be his last chance, was the theory! As the newly-crowned inaugural Footballer of the Year, he was the centre of attention as he took the pitch in white shirt and black shorts - both the Tangerines and the Reds changed colours to prevent a clash, United even more unfamiliar in royal blue - and there was no doubt that his potential threat was to the forefront of Manchester minds. Stan was so skilful and quick that the only way to deny him was to starve him of possession and Busby had instructed 'keeper Jack Crompton to direct goal-kicks towards the opposite flank. United lined up as expected, with the relatively inexperienced Anderson preferred to unlucky Jack Warner, while Joe Smith shuffled his forwards. Mortensen was

When Blackpool was well and truly on the map. An advertisement in the 1948 FA Cup Final programme uses the success of the football team to highlight the town's allure as a top-ranking holiday destination. Meanwhile the Seasiders' line-up, also taken from the programme, illustrates the eternal uncertainty of the game. Come the big day, left-back Ron Suart was sidelined by injury and forward Jimmy McIntosh was dropped.

BLACKPOOL

J. ROBINSON   E. SHIMWELL

R. SUART   H. JOHNSTON (Capt.)   L. HAYWARD

H. KELLY   S. MATTHEWS   S. MORTENSEN

J. McINTOSH   G. DICK   W. RICKETT

moved from inside-right to centre-forward to exploit stopper Allenby Chilton's so-called lack of pace; Jimmy McIntosh, who had scored five times on the Wembley trail, was axed and tiny Alex Munro was handed the number-eight shirt. One enforced absentee was the injured Ron Suart, a future Bloomfield Road boss, whose place at left-back went to Johnny Crosland.

The early exchanges appeared to vindicate Smith's decision, especially when 'Morty' nipped past Chilton and was tripped on the edge of United's area. Referee Barrick blew for a penalty and the fact that pictures proved subsequently that the foul took place outside the box was beside the point. Morally the spot-kick was deserved, and was dispatched safely by Eddie Shimwell. Now the Old Trafford side raised the tempo, their delightful passing movements gracing the grand stage,

Jack Rowley lives up to his reputation as an opportunist supreme with a brace of equalisers for Manchester United. First (below) he exploits confusion in the Blackpool rearguard and finds himself in front of an empty net; then (bottom) he dives to head powerfully past goalkeeper Robinson.

and several minutes after little Henry Cockburn had shot against the bar, Jack Rowley nipped in to score when Blackpool 'keeper Joe Robinson and centre-half Eric Hayward were involved in a mix-up following a speculative Delaney lob. So cool was the United marksman that no one could have guessed he carried a secret anxiety, the birth of his second child being well overdue. The 'Pool were not dismayed by the equaliser, and with Matthews and left-winger Walter Rickett prominent, took up the attack with thrilling gusto, reaping the reward two minutes from the break when Hugh Kelly put in Mortensen to score with a cross-shot on the turn. Thus the England man had scored in every game of that Cup campaign.

At half-time, the force was with the Seasiders but Busby and the Republic of Ireland skipper Carey - whose pre-match mail included a letter from an Irish patriot urging him to raise the question of his country's partition with the King at the presentation ceremony! - came into their own. The future Sir Matt was his usual, quietly inspirational self, while Johnny oozed confidence and composure, eschewing panic and calling for a repeat of the smooth football that had served them so well all season. Even so, Blackpool retained the ascendancy after the restart and there were only 21 minutes left when the tide turned. The wily Morris, carrying an ankle injury he had concealed from his manager, took a quick free-kick - Kelly claimed later that no offence had taken

Right: The Red Devils are rampant, but this time left-winger Charlie Mitten is thwarted by the Seasiders' right-back Eddie Shimwell and 'keeper Joe Robinson. The predatory Stan Pearson (right), scorer of United's third goal, is ready to pounce.

Below: Another near miss from the pages of the Cup Final programme.

place - and Rowley plunged forward to head a superb equaliser. However, the real turning point came ten minutes later when Mortensen was through on goal but Crompton, struggling with a back abcess, saved at full-stretch. Reporters were still scribbling about this latest slice of derring-do as the 'keeper threw to Anderson, who freed Pearson with a raking through-pass. Stan shot low across goal from 25 yards and the ball eluded Robinson's dive to go in off the far post. Now United were free to turn on the style. For the closing period they were utterly irresistible, finding each other with uncanny precision, and if Anderson's

deflected 30-yarder stretched the victory margin rather unkindly from a Blackpool viewpoint, none could deny that the Red Devils - the first team to come from behind twice to win an FA Cup Final - had earned their prize. Ironically, the Seasiders won a League encounter between the two sides four days later, and in their final match the spurned McIntosh scored five in a 7-0 annihilation of Preston. Of course, none could say he would have made any difference at Wembley and none did. The most fitting epitaph to a princely occasion was supplied by Stanley Matthews himself, who in the end had been shrewdly shepherded by John Aston: 'We were beaten by a great team and I offer them my heartiest congratulations.'

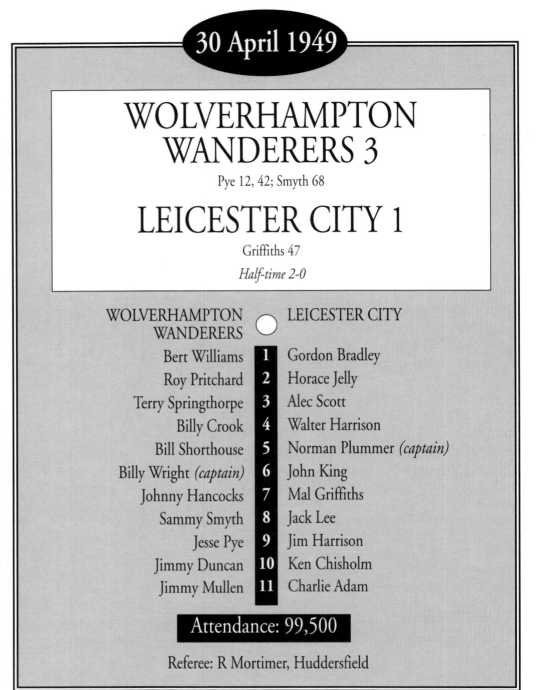

30 April 1949

WOLVERHAMPTON WANDERERS 3

Pye 12, 42; Smyth 68

LEICESTER CITY 1

Griffiths 47

Half-time 2-0

WOLVERHAMPTON WANDERERS		LEICESTER CITY
Bert Williams	1	Gordon Bradley
Roy Pritchard	2	Horace Jelly
Terry Springthorpe	3	Alec Scott
Billy Crook	4	Walter Harrison
Bill Shorthouse	5	Norman Plummer *(captain)*
Billy Wright *(captain)*	6	John King
Johnny Hancocks	7	Mal Griffiths
Sammy Smyth	8	Jack Lee
Jesse Pye	9	Jim Harrison
Jimmy Duncan	10	Ken Chisholm
Jimmy Mullen	11	Charlie Adam

Attendance: 99,500

Referee: R Mortimer, Huddersfield

When the future Queen of England advanced towards them across Wembley's lush greensward, ready for the pre-match pleasantries on her solo debut at football's equivalent of Trooping the Colour, the beleaguered men of Leicester City could be excused for reflecting that, after all, this was going to be their day. Despite toppling soon-to-be-crowned League Champions Portsmouth in the semi-final, the Filberts were seen as rank outsiders for the showdown with Wolves. Still up to their necks in a relegation battle which, if unsuccessful, would dispatch them to the *Third* Division, Leicester had lost their star performer Don Revie three days before the final and were being written off by the majority of pundits as mere cannon fodder for the Molineux side, then riding high in the First Division's top six. But now, suddenly, came what could be interpreted only as an omen, a blessed sign from above, that all was not lost.

Princess Elizabeth was decked out, most fetchingly, in City's royal blue. Admittedly she was not exactly brandishing scarf and rattle and yelling 'Come on you Filberts' at the top of her voice, but there was no escaping the hue of that smart hat and coat. So while, perhaps, the most plausible explanation was that the callow Princess had been inadequately advised on Wembley protocol, the under-dogs could, at least, afford a wry and hopeful chuckle.

In fact, fortune was *not* to smile on the gallant blue brigade in their first FA Cup Final; instead they were to experience a cruel sideswipe from Lady Luck which helped to launch the Wolves on the most glorious era in their history. Indeed, under the iron-fisted management of their former skipper, Stan Cullis, and the inspirational on-field leadership of England 'golden boy' Billy Wright, the Black Countrymen were to spend most of the ensuing decade jousting with Manchester United for the right to be called the best team in the land. For Wright, whose maturity and composure belied the fact that he was still only 25, the Leicester encounter had special overtones. Together with left-winger Jimmy Mullen, he had served City in wartime matches and made many friends among

Jimmy Mullen (below) and Johnny Hancocks (below left), the two splendid wingers so essential to the Wolves game plan.

the Filberts. It was a time for Billy to ponder, too, on the progress he had made since Wolves' previous FA Cup Final ten years earlier, when they had been victims of a shock defeat by Portsmouth. In 1939 the young Wright had been a Molineux groundstaff boy whose job it was to pre-pare the boots and shirts for Wembley. Then, after packing the kit, he was denied the pleasure and experience of watching the final, instead having to turn out for the Wolves B team. Character-forming stuff, indeed!

Of course, by 1949 the blond wing-half - later to be even more effective in the centre for club and country - was the cornerstone of a solid defence in which his international colleague, 'keeper Bert Williams, was also outstanding. The Wolves game was based on long-distance passing, fitness and stamina, with dashing wingers Johnny Hancocks, a tiny man with a savage shot, and 'Gentleman' Jimmy Mullen of prime importance. They had reached Wembley with an heroic semi-final performance against Manchester United, scrambling a 1-1 draw after being reduced to nine fit men at Hillsborough, then winning the Goodison Park replay 1-0. The only doubt about their final line-up was whether full-back Laurie Kelly,

Billy Wright (above) and Bert Williams (left), sheer quality at the heart of the Black Countrymen's defence.

injured at Sheffield, would return in place of Terry Springthorpe. He didn't, but that made little difference to the formidable proposition presented by a side which seemed inexorably on the rise.

How then could lowly Leicester hope to cope? The most popular theory was that 21-year-old schemer Don Revie, whose thoughtful approach-play was beginning already to suggest unusually deep soccer intuition, offered the only real chance of an upset. Imagine the consternation in the blue corner, therefore, when three days before the game it was announced that Revie was out, side-lined by a gushing nosebleed that left him too weak to leave hospital to watch the action, let alone

Top right: The young Don Revie, victim of a chronic nosebleed that kept him out of the final.

Above right: 'Nice of your wife to wear blue, Sir!' Leicester boss Johnny Duncan meets Prince Philip; Charlie Adam (next to Duncan) and Ken Chisholm seem well pleased.

Right: Ian McGraw, the Leicester 'keeper who missed the match because of a broken finger. Worse was to come for the unlucky Scot - complications set in and the digit was amputated.

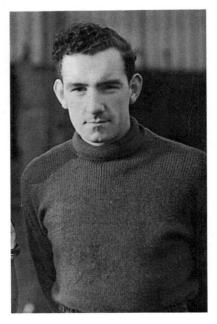

take part in it. Forced to rethink, Filbert Street boss Johnny Duncan switched Jack Lee from centre-forward to inside-right, changing the leading marksman's priorities from scoring to creating, and handed full-back Jim Harrison (an attacker in his youth) the number-nine shirt. Already deprived of first-choice goalkeeper Ian McGraw through a broken finger - Gordon Bradley deputised - Leicester were thus fearfully stretched to face such a mammoth challenge. However, there was comfort to be found in the form and fighting spirit they displayed on their way to Wembley, a somewhat tortuous trail on which two ties stood out. City's fifth-round clash with Luton was an archetypal Cup thriller which yielded no less than 18 goals - a 5-5 draw at Kenilworth Road being followed by a 5-3 home victory - while their richly deserved semi-final triumph over high-riding Portsmouth at Highbury ranked among the most accomplished displays the club had ever given. But shorn of Revie, their inspiration on that day, and haunted by the spectre of Division Three, it was undeniable that the odds were stacked against them.

Twelve minutes after kick-off, those odds mounted still further when the raven-haired Yorkshireman Jesse Pye headed home a Hancocks cross to put the favourites in front, and when he scored a second shortly before the break - a firm shot following an adroit turn just inside the box - there seemed little doubt about the destination of the trophy. It was high time for the glorious uncertainty of the FA Cup to assert itself. It duly did so five minutes into the second half when Ken Chisholm, the burly, bubbly Scot, hit a powerful drive that Bert Williams could only parry to Welsh international outside-left Mal Griffiths, who netted with an angled shot that went in off the post.

Below: The favourites forge ahead. Wolves spearhead Jesse Pye nods home the first of his two goals, converting a centre from Johnny Hancocks.

Now - as is wont to happen in such circumstances - the rhythm of the game altered radically. Leicester seized the initiative, for 20 minutes the Wolves rearguard was placed under severe pressure and midway through the half it seemed that it had cracked. The elusive Griffiths - the oldest man afield, though only just past his 30th birthday - appeared near the penalty spot to hook the ball over his shoulder to the unmarked Chisholm, who slipped the ball into goal from close range. It was a beautifully engineered strike which transported City's players and fans into raptures, but their joy was savagely curtailed, referee and linesman sharing the conviction that Chisholm had been fractionally offside when Griffiths played the ball. Later the man whose goal was ruled out reckoned that the pass had taken a slight deflection, thus playing him onside, though Wolves defender Bill Shorthouse was equally convinced that it hadn't. Either way, the Filberts could take enormous credit for the fact that they didn't contest the hairline decision on the pitch - imagine the histrionics in similar circumstances today. Subsequent examination of newsreel and photographic evidence proved less than conclusive, but tended to suggest that the officials were correct.

Above: The Filberts fight back. Billy Wright and company are helpless to prevent Mal Griffiths reducing the arrears for Leicester.

Above: Goal of the game. Sammy Smyth (also pictured right) climaxes a dazzling run past three opponents by slotting home Wolves' third. It was the end of the road for Leicester.

THE FOOTBALL ASSOCIATION CHALLENGE CUP COMPETITION

FINAL TIE

SATURDAY, APRIL 30th
1949 - KICK-OFF 3 pm

LEICESTER CITY v WOLVERHAMPTON WANDERERS

WEMBLEY
EMPIRE STADIUM

Chairman and Managing Director : SIR ARTHUR J. ELVIN M.B.E.

OFFICIAL PROGRAMME · ONE SHILLING

However, that was little consolation to poor Leicester who, understandably demoralised by the reverse, saw their dreams of glory die a minute later. Irishman Sammy Smyth, who had scored Wolves' semi-final goals, topped them both with a quite magnificent Wembley clincher, beating three men in a breathtaking 40-yard dribble which he capped with the most clinical of finishes. And that, effectively, was that, as the once-more buoyant Wolves returned to the offensive and saw out time with a spring in their collective step. Despite Leicester's brave

fight and their ill fortune at a crucial moment, Billy Wright and company had, in truth, merited the prize. As for the losers, they salvaged something from their season by taking three points from their remaining three League games to retain Second Division status by one point, thus consigning Nottingham Forest to the drop. As finals go, it had been a lacklustre affair, enlivened only rarely by either excellence or drama, and did little to conjure up the traditional, longed-for Wembley magic. But that stardust still clung to the grand old competition had been made amply evident on fourth-round day, when non-League Yeovil Town slew the First Division giants of Sunderland. That afternoon, as the mist rolled off the Somerset moors on to the famous Huish slope - one touchline was some eight feet higher than the other - the Wearsiders, complete with the great Len Shackleton, tasted the very essence of the FA Cup.

Newly-acquired silverware for the men in old gold. Back row (left to right): Billy Crook, Roy Pritchard, Bert Williams, Bill Shorthouse, Terry Springthorpe. Front row: Johnny Hancocks, Sammy Smyth, Stan Cullis (manager), Billy Wright, Jesse Pye, Jimmy Dunn, Jimmy Mullen.

The most endearing grin in football. Arsenal skipper Joe Mercer, rejected by Everton as 'past it', brandishes the FA Cup at Wembley. And he was far from finished: three years later he would lead the Gunners to the League Championship.

He was bandy-legged, lean almost to the point of scrawniness and in his 36th year, but as he led Arsenal into Wembley confrontation with Liverpool, Joe Mercer remained one of the most influential players in the land. Indeed, the night before the final he had been voted Footballer of the Year and was making Everton cringe at the mere thought of their decision, back in 1946, to release him because he was 'over the hill'. In fact, as demonstrated eloquently by genial Joe's subsequent service to the Highbury cause - which continued until he broke his leg when nearing 40 - the inspirational wing-half had barely reached his personal summit when he packed his bags and bade farewell to Goodison.

Not that Wirral-born Joe had severed his ties with that part of the world - far from it. Indeed, in his latter days as an Evertonian he had contemplated a full-time future as a Wallasey grocer, and even after becoming a Gunner, he continued to live at Hoylake and train with . . . Liverpool. Naturally enough, when the Cup Final protagonists became known, the Reds had to ponder long and hard over the desirability of having the opposition skipper in their midst as they prepared for the great day. Some clubs might have banned him instantly, but

29 April 1950

ARSENAL 2
Lewis 17, 63

LIVERPOOL 0

Half-time 1-0

ARSENAL		LIVERPOOL
George Swindin	1	Cyril Sidlow
Laurie Scott	2	Ray Lambert
Walley Barnes	3	Eddie Spicer
Alex Forbes	4	Phil Taylor *(captain)*
Les Compton	5	Laurie Hughes
Joe Mercer *(captain)*	6	Bill Jones
Freddie Cox	7	Jimmy Payne
Jimmy Logie	8	Kevin Baron
Peter Goring	9	Albert Stubbins
Reg Lewis	10	Willie Fagan
Denis Compton	11	Billy Liddell

Attendance: 100,000

Referee: H Pearce, Luton

1950

IT HAPPENED THIS YEAR

Labour won General Election with overall majority of five.

British troops joined Americans at war in Korea.

Churchill warned nation of possible Third World War.

Russia and China, Stalin and Mao, signed friendship treaty.

'The Eagle' comic launched with Dan Dare on front.

Blue moon spotted from southern England.

Liverpool were bigger than that. Instead they limited his Anfield access to the afternoons, knowing Joe was honourable enough not to seek an unfair advantage from the favour they were extending to him.

The Mercer contribution - mainly defensive alongside centre-half Les Compton, having forsaken the more physically demanding advanced role of his youth - had been as immense as ever on the road to Wembley, a road which for Arsenal had been unusually short in terms of miles travelled. They had enjoyed the rare luxury of playing every tie at home, and even their semi-final (and replay) had been at nearby Tottenham. Yet like Liverpool - who, coincidentally, reached the final without leaving Lancashire - they had made less than majestic progress. Tight encounters with Sheffield Wednesday (beaten by a Reg Lewis strike 13 seconds from time) and Swansea (unseated by a Walley Barnes penalty) were typical, and the semi-final clash with Chelsea at White Hart Lane proved even more nerve-stretching. Indeed Arsenal looked to be on their way out when Roy Bentley put the Pensioners two up, but then winger Freddie Cox scored a freak goal direct from a corner and Les Compton - spurning the instructions of his

Above: Bob Paisley, doomed to miss out on the big day as a player. Above right: Liverpool's star, the great Billy Liddell. The night before the final, Arsenal's 'iron man' Alex Forbes was castigated for arriving late at a team meeting at which ways to combat the Liddell menace were being discussed. Alex's reaction was along the lines of: 'Don't worry, I'll see him off.' Sure enough, Billy had a relatively quiet afternoon.

captain - surged forward to nod home a corner from his brother, Denis. It was left to Cox - a victim of boo-boys during his early days as a Spur before crossing North London to rebuild his career at Highbury - to score the only goal of the replay, just as his wife had dreamed the previous night! The Reds had also stuttered through the early rounds, finally convincing in a splendid quarter-final triumph over Blackpool, then seeing off Everton in the semi - how Mercer would have relished a meeting with *them* at Wembley - thanks to a speculative lob from Bob Paisley and an emphatic finish from Billy Liddell.

For the final, both teams had selection posers to settle. Arsenal boss Tom Whittaker had to choose between fiery Alex Forbes and veteran Archie Macaulay at right-half, while perming three from Peter Goring, Doug Lishman, Don Roper, Reg Lewis, Denis Compton and Ian McPherson among the forwards. In the event Forbes, Goring, Lewis and Compton got the nod and each man in his different way was to justify his selection fully. Liverpool manager George Kay - no stranger to the Empire Stadium, having captained losers West Ham United in the first final to be staged there in 1923 - faced an equally difficult choice, having two excellent candidates for the number-six shirt: Bill Jones and Bob Paisley. Agonisingly, it was semi-final hero Paisley, who had played in every game but one during the Cup campaign, to be omitted. Poignantly, his name appears in the Cup Final programme, and later a special medal was struck to commemorate his efforts, but he was never to get the chance to add to the Amateur Cup winner's gong he had earned with Bishop Auckland in 1939. Of course, Bob went some way towards making up for his disappointment in later life, managing the Reds to six League titles, three European Cups, one UEFA Cup

36

and three League Cups, though not, curiously, an FA Cup.

As the day of the game approached, the pundits expounded plentiful theories about who might win and how, but for once there were no clear favourites. Until Easter Liverpool had realistic hopes of the League and FA Cup double - indeed they started the season with 19 League games undefeated and had taken four points from the Gunners - but had since fallen away, while their North London opponents were in a respectable seventh position. If tradition counted for anything, Arsenal had been to four previous finals, winning two of them; surprisingly, it was the first time the men of Anfield had progressed so far since losing their sole previous final to Burnley at the Crystal Palace in 1914.

It was a damp afternoon at Wembley - no one was complaining, a few days earlier it had been *snowing* - as the two sides took the field with not a red shirt to be seen, Arsenal in gold, Liverpool in white. Before long the game developed a pattern which was to be decisive. Whittaker had instructed his flankmen to remain as wide as possible, leaving plenty of room through the middle for Jimmy Logie, who had inherited the play-making mantle of the great Alex James, to free Goring and Lewis for runs on goal. Meanwhile Liverpool's best and most threatening player - the brilliant, powerful and unfailingly chivalrous Liddell - was policed ferociously by both Alex Forbes and full-back Laurie Scott. Thus after an early scare, when Arsenal 'keeper George Swindin mishandled a Jimmy Payne cross on to the crossbar, the Gunners assumed the initiative and made it tell with a delightful opening goal. Walley Barnes found Logie in the inside-left berth and Goring set off on a typically selfless decoy run to the flank, taking defenders with

Liverpool did not surrender without a battle. Here grounded winger Jimmy Payne brings a goal-line save out of Arsenal 'keeper George Swindin while the Merseysiders' Albert Stubbins lurks in the hope of a rebound. The other Arsenal defenders are Joe Mercer (left) and Les Compton.

The case of the missing goalkeeper. Arsenal's George Swindin appears to be 'absent without leave' as Liverpool's Bill Jones heads against the crossbar. In fact, Swindin is obscured by centre-half Les Compton.

37

SPICER (L.B.)

SIDLOW (Goal)   LEWIS (I.L.)

Above: Reg Lewis, who broke clear of the Liverpool defence (top) to open the scoring for Arsenal. Reg, who had not been sure of his place before the match, added another in the second half.

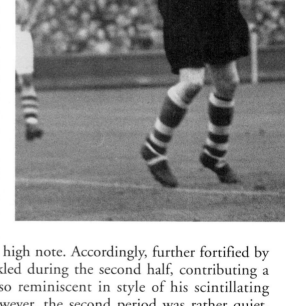

Denis Compton, boosted by a half-time pep talk from his manager and fortified by a tot of the hard stuff, put on a typically stylish show after the interval.

him; as the space opened in front of the tiny Scottish schemer, he slid the ball into it and Liverpool were undone. Reg Lewis took possession smoothly and ran towards unprotected custodian Cyril Sidlow before netting with the utmost economy. It was all so deadly simple. A little later, the popular Albert Stubbins, who once scored four successive hat-tricks for Newcastle, missed the chance of an equaliser and the interval arrived with a single goal separating the teams. Far from resting on his side's laurels, Whittaker used the break to spur on his men, especially Denis Compton, who had disappointed during the first 45 minutes. The manager urged the 32-year-old winger, about to quit the winter game because of a gammy knee and concentrate on his cricket career, to go out on a high note. Accordingly, further fortified by a nip of whisky, Denis sparkled during the second half, contributing a lovely cameo performance so reminiscent in style of his scintillating batsmanship. In general, however, the second period was rather quiet, even though the football was of a high technical quality. The Gunners remained the more controlled unit and it was nosuprise when they doubled their lead. Once more Lewis was the executioner, reacting nimbly to a subtle Cox flick and giving Sidlow no chance from ten yards. Thus a man whose very selection had been in doubt had scored twice - 17 minutes into each half, as it happened - and the trophy was as good as Arsenal's. Not that the Merseysiders wilted. Twice more Stubbins came close, Jones headed against the bar and the indomitable Liddell, making light of a succession of crunching tackles, continued to fashion openings but it was not to be enough. In the final analysis - and how easy it is to be wise after the event - the speed and tackling ability of Paisley might have proved a more effective counter to Logie's probings than the

skilful but somewhat ponderous Jones. In fairness to George Kay, every match produces its might-have-beens and he does not deserve castigation for making a brave and difficult decision.

The day's most pleasant task - that of fetching the silverware - fell to Joe Mercer, a man-of-the-match candidate alongside Forbes, Logie and Lewis, yet there was a minor shock in store for him as he arrived, with lop-sided grin working overtime, in the royal presence. After the King gave him the Cup, the Queen slipped a loser's medal into his hand, though the error was spotted before he began the descent of Wembley's famous 39 steps. The Arsenal celebrations began on the pitch and culminated that evening with a banquet at the Cafe Royal. Afterwards, Reg Lewis discovered that finding a late-night taxi in Piccadilly Circus could be more difficult than scoring the winning goals in a Cup Final. Happily, an enterprising gentleman of the press was on hand and the matter was resolved following a hasty consultation with the law. And so home rode the hero, and his wife, in a Black Maria!

Above: An aerial dogfight in the Liverpool penalty box. This time the ball was cleared, but the Merseysiders' rearguard was pierced twice without reply.

IT HAPPENED THIS YEAR

First hydrogen bomb tested.

Coloured South Africans deprived of vote.

Churchill returned to Number 10 after Tory election victory.

Briton Randolph Turpin beat Sugar Ray Robinson to win world middlweight title.

Oxford sank in University Boat Race, Cambridge won re-run.

Miss Sweden was first Miss World .

28 April 1951

NEWCASTLE UNITED 2

Milburn 50, 54

BLACKPOOL 0

Half-time 0-0

NEWCASTLE UNITED		BLACKPOOL
Jack Fairbrother	1	George Farm
Bobby Cowell	2	Eddie Shimwell
Bobby Corbett	3	Tom Garrett
Joe Harvey *(captain)*	4	Harry Johnston *(captain)*
Frank Brennan	5	Eric Hayward
Charlie Crowe	6	Hugh Kelly
Tommy Walker	7	Stanley Matthews
Ernie Taylor	8	Jackie Mudie
Jackie Milburn	9	Stanley Mortensen
George Robledo	10	Bill Slater
Bobby Mitchell	11	Bill Perry

Attendance: 100,000

Referee: W Ling, Cambridge

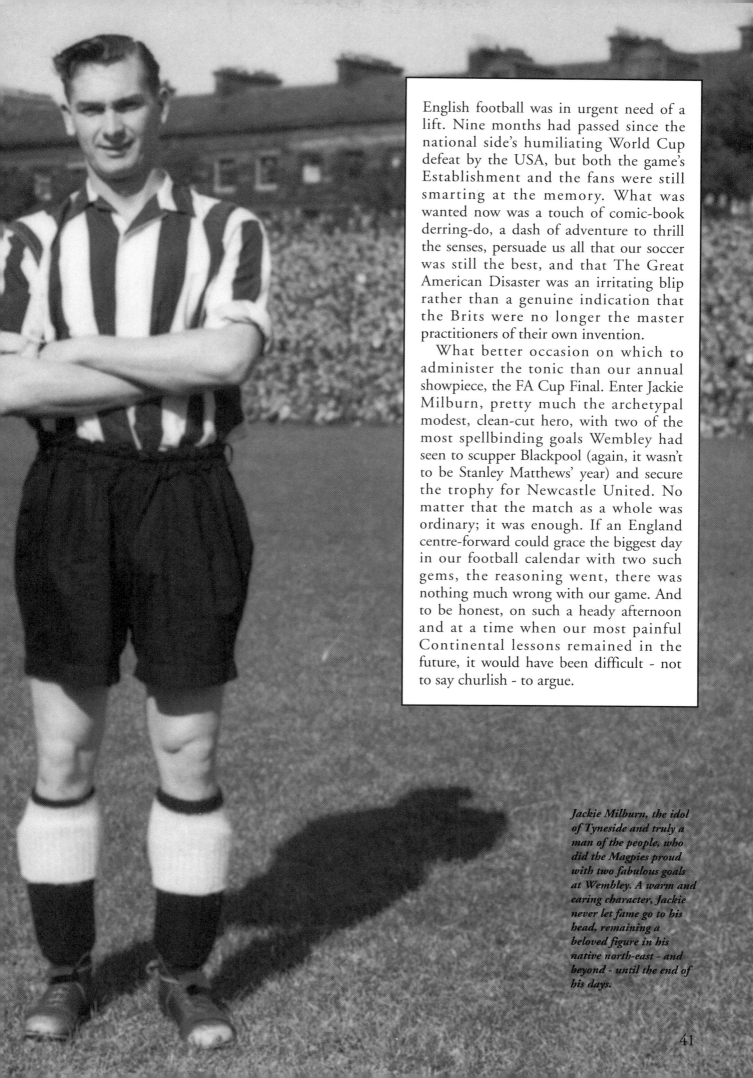

English football was in urgent need of a lift. Nine months had passed since the national side's humiliating World Cup defeat by the USA, but both the game's Establishment and the fans were still smarting at the memory. What was wanted now was a touch of comic-book derring-do, a dash of adventure to thrill the senses, persuade us all that our soccer was still the best, and that The Great American Disaster was an irritating blip rather than a genuine indication that the Brits were no longer the master practitioners of their own invention.

What better occasion on which to administer the tonic than our annual showpiece, the FA Cup Final. Enter Jackie Milburn, pretty much the archetypal modest, clean-cut hero, with two of the most spellbinding goals Wembley had seen to scupper Blackpool (again, it wasn't to be Stanley Matthews' year) and secure the trophy for Newcastle United. No matter that the match as a whole was ordinary; it was enough. If an England centre-forward could grace the biggest day in our football calendar with two such gems, the reasoning went, there was nothing much wrong with our game. And to be honest, on such a heady afternoon and at a time when our most painful Continental lessons remained in the future, it would have been difficult - not to say churlish - to argue.

Jackie Milburn, the idol of Tyneside and truly a man of the people, who did the Magpies proud with two fabulous goals at Wembley. A warm and caring character, Jackie never let fame go to his head, remaining a beloved figure in his native north-east - and beyond - until the end of his days.

HOW THEY GOT THERE

NEWCASTLE UNITED
Round 3:
Bury (h) 4-1.

Round 4:
Bolton Wanderers
(h) 3-2.

Round 5:
Stoke City (a) 4-2.

Round 6:
Bristol Rovers (h) 0-0, replay
(a) 3-1.

Semi-final:
Wolverhampton Wanderers
at Hillsborough 0-0; *replay at*
Maine Road 2-1.

BLACKPOOL
Round 3:
Charlton Athletic (a) 2-2,
replay (h) 3-0.

Round 4:
Stockport County (h) 2-1.

Round 5:
Mansfield Town (h) 2-0.

Round 6:
Fulham (h) 1-0.

Semi-final:
Birmingham City *at Maine*
Road 0-0, replay *at Goodison*
Park 2-1.

The man who sparked the euphoria, 'Wor Jackie', was the leading light not only at the climax, but throughout the Cup campaign, scoring in every round. The Magpies' progress to Wembley had been no cakewalk, with taut early clashes with Bolton Wanderers and Stoke City, followed by a narrow quarter-final escape against unfashionable Bristol Rovers. Indeed, the Pirates were unlucky not to win at St James' Park and snatched the lead in the replay, but then - as the Bristol-built Brabazon airliner took to the skies for a test flight over Eastville - a three-goal blitz by the Geordies settled the outcome emphatically. Meanwhile Blackpool had moved unostentatiously into the semi-finals, at which stage both clubs were held to goalless draws and forced to produce stirring displays to win their replays. Newcastle fell a goal behind to Wolves before two strikes in half a minute by Milburn and Mitchell saw them through, while Matthews inspired the Seasiders to victory over Birmingham City, laying on goals for Stan Mortensen and Bill Perry. The Blues were left to reflect ruefully on the fateful moment near the end of the first encounter when their popular winger Jackie Stewart had hit the post.

With the identity of the finalists decided, a public debate broke out over the seven-week wait for their Wembley meeting. Both clubs were scathing about the delay, citing the effect on players' nerves. Indeed in early spring the Geordies had been in with a realistic chance of a League and FA Cup double, but after beating Wolves they fell apart, and slumped to a disappointing fourth-place First Division finish. However, some observers felt that Magpies manager Stan Seymour had made a rod for his own back by announcing, immediately after the semi-final triumph, that there would be no team changes for Wembley. Though meant to offer peace of mind, it hardly served to motivate players who, with their final places certain, might have been tempted to ease up and take extra precautions to avoid injury. Newcastle's preparations were hampered further by disputes between players and management. With footballers across the land waking up to the fact that they were appallingly paid in relation to the income they generated, there were suggestions that now was the time for a strike. In addition, there was an internal dispute over tickets for the players' wives, who had been allocated berths away from the official party, indeed not even in the main stand. Skipper Joe Harvey and his wife Ida were especially incensed at such insensitive treatment and the players threatened to boycott the game. Seymour responded with a counter-threat to field a team of reserves, but in the end the board announced there had been an error over tickets and that potential crisis had passed. The gripe over cash remained, but with most team members convinced that the club really would send out the 'stiffs' if necessary, the matter never reached flashpoint. There followed yet another disturbance when two players broke curfew while the Magpies were staying at the spa town of Buxton for special training in Wembley week. At first it seemed they might be condemned to an instant return home and be axed from the final but, in the wider interests of Newcastle United and their loyal supporters, the sentence was commuted.

Nevertheless, there could be no whitewashing the fact that the Magpies had given a series of anaemic League displays, thus allowing Blackpool to overhaul them in the table and assume the status of fairly warm favourites. Happily, though, camaraderie among the players had not been harmed, and there was uproarious hilarity when it was discovered on arrival at the Weybridge hotel in which they were staying before the match that Milburn and Chilean international George Robledo had been given the bridal suite. Indeed, the side was full of 'characters', such as the dynamic Harvey, a leader on and off the field, and Jack Fairbrother, then the world's most expensive custodian, having cost £7,000 from Preston in 1947. Jack's trademark was a pair of white goalkeeping gloves, given to him by a North End fan, and he was also known to keep a little black book in which he noted the strengths and weaknesses of opposing marksmen.

Blackpool, of course, had even more prominent personalities in Mortensen and

NEWCASTLE UNITED FOOTBALL CLUB   F.A.CUP FINALISTS 1951
Corbett.R Cowell.R Fairbrother.J Brennan.F Crowe.C
Taylor.E Mitchell.R Milburn.J Harvey.J Robledo.G Walker.T

BLACKPOOL FOOTBALL CLUB   F.A.CUP FINALISTS 1951
Kelly.H Shimwell.E Farm.W Garrett.T Hayward.E
Matthews.S Perry.W Mudie.J Johnston.H Mortensen.S Brown.A

Matthews - whose seemingly eternal quest for that elusive winner's medal received endless press attention - while another whose importance to the Seasiders could hardly be overstated was their constructive right-half and captain, Harry Johnston, newly installed as Footballer of the Year and one of nature's gentlemen. But sadly for the Bloomfield Road team, they were deprived of another key player, the skilful sharpshooter Allan Brown, who had cost £26,500 - a record for a Scottish League player - from East Fife. His deputy was Bill Slater, an England amateur international who in 1960 was to lead Wolves to FA Cup glory but who on this occasion proved to be out of his depth. In fact it was young Bill who had the first significant opening of the game, pulling the ball

Above: Postcards of the day depicting the finalists. Such modest souvenirs were a far cry from the flashy productions of modern times but, to misty-eyed traditionalists at least, they remain infinitely more appealing.

43

wide after being set up cleverly by Matthews. After ten minutes Milburn responded by netting for Newcastle, but was judged to have handled the ball, and then it was Blackpool who stepped up the pace. Mortensen came closest to scoring when he met Bill Perry's corner perfectly to nod past Fairbrother, only to see the perfectly positioned Bobby Cowell head off the line. The scoresheet was blank at the break, but the Geordie hero's hour was at hand. During the first period the Seasiders had persisted rather tiresomely with an offside trap, but now it was sprung to spectacular effect. A Matthews cross was cleared by Robledo to Milburn on half-way; pausing only to glance at the line to check he was onside, 'Wor Jackie' set off like the Powderhall sprinter he was, leaving all and sundry in his wake as he bore down on the Blackpool goal. With some 70 yards for the Newcastle number-nine to travel, there were

several breathless moments for 100,000 fans to anticipate the outcome of this ultimate one-on-one challenge; then, some 15 yards out, Milburn shot low, hard and accurately to George Farm's right and United were in front. It was a truly magnificent goal, yet within four minutes it was to be equalled, and by the same man. Inside-right Ernie Taylor - what a superb game the tiny schemer had - found himself surrounded by markers 30 yards from goal; seeing no orthodox avenue

Above: Aerial ballet. Left to right are Blackpool rookie Bill Slater, Newcastle skipper Joe Harvey and fellow defender Bobby Cowell, and Blackpool winger Bill Perry.

Left: Blackpool's Scottish custodian George Farm fields a low shot while team-mate Hugh Kelly stands guard and Newcastle's George Robledo waits hopefully for a mistake.

Below opposite: A Stan Mortensen header is nodded off the Geordies' line by right-back Bobby Cowell, with Blackpool raider Jackie Mudie in close attendance.

of attack, he backheeled the ball impertinently into the path of Milburn, who hit it first time high into the Blackpool net. So blindingly brilliant was the execution that Jackie's team-mates were joined in their congratulations by Stan Mortensen, a warming exhibition of sportsmanship unlikely to be repeated in the modern era.

Thereafter Blackpool pressed on, but the Cup was clearly bound for the north-east and soon Harvey - with a 1901 penny carried through two final victories by previous United captains still in his pocket - led the way to the royal box. So the Magpies had lifted the trophy for the fourth time in eight finals, while poor Blackpool were yet to claim the prize once. Inevitably, public sympathy was mainly for Matthews who, though splendidly policed by Bobby Corbett, had played well. Indeed, he'd even headed the ball several times and, uncharacteristically, unleashed a series of shots in the hope of notching his first goal for nearly two and a half years. But he was unbowed: 'I'm not finished, we're a good team and there's always next year'. Those who heard the 36-year-old's brave words were moved by such supreme optimism, but they didn't believe him. In the event, of course, he was only a year out! Meanwhile, it was the Magpies' and Milburn's day, and that night the strains of 'Blaydon Races' echoed long and loud around the streets of London.

Overleaf: A goal to cherish in the memory. Ernie Taylor has duped the Blackpool defence with a cute backheel and Jackie Milburn has thundered the ball towards the top corner of the net from 25 yards. George Farm makes a noble effort to save but the airborne 'keeper is attempting the impossible.

IT HAPPENED THIS YEAR

King George VI died in his sleep.

MPs voted for equal pay for women doing the same jobs as men.

Maureen 'Little Mo' Connolly won Wimbledon at 17.

Dwight Eisenhower elected President of United States.

Last London tram ran between Woolwich and New Cross.

Headmasters condemned new GCE exam as being too stiff for many pupils.

3 May 1952

NEWCASTLE UNITED 1
G Robledo 84

ARSENAL 0

Half-time 0-0

NEWCASTLE UNITED	○	ARSENAL
Ronnie Simpson	1	George Swindin
Bobby Cowell	2	Walley Barnes
Alf McMichael	3	Lionel Smith
Joe Harvey (*captain*)	4	Alex Forbes
Frank Brennan	5	Ray Daniel
Ted Robledo	6	Joe Mercer (*captain*)
Tommy Walker	7	Freddie Cox
Billy Foulkes	8	Jimmy Logie
Jackie Milburn	9	Cliff Holton
George Robledo	10	Doug Lishman
Bobby Mitchell	11	Don Roper

Attendance: 100,000

Referee: A Ellis, Halifax

Opposite: The Prime Minister meets the Magpies. Winston Churchill is introduced to Chilean George Robledo by Newcastle skipper Joe Harvey. That afternoon Churchill, perhaps the greatest of all battlers against overwhelming odds, was to witness a valiant struggle by Arsenal.

Ever since the Gunners had dominated English soccer in the decade before the Second World War, the cry of 'Lucky Arsenal' had resounded around football grounds the length and breadth of the land. Partly, no doubt, through envy, the North Londoners were detested by rival fans, and as the club strove for the League and FA Cup double in 1951/52, the old familiar taunt rent the air with predictable frequency. Yet, in reality, it had never been less appropriate. A crippling injury crisis proved a major factor in the eventual narrow failure of the Gunners' title campaign, and the circumstances of their FA Cup Final defeat by Newcastle United would have twanged the heartstrings of all but their most curmudgeonly critics. Indeed, Arsenal's valour in the face of adversity after losing one key player early on, and having several more gritting their teeth in various degrees of pain for much of the game, must have struck a chord with Prime Minister Winston Churchill, waiting in the Wembley royal box to present the trophy. After all, he knew a thing or two about uphill struggles.

It was ironic, but testimony to the perversity of human nature, that it was only

Right: The Gunners, who showed courage above and beyond the call of duty at Wembley in 1952. Back row (left to right): Jimmy Logie, Alex Forbes, Lionel Smith, George Swindin, Walley Barnes, Peter Goring (reserve), Ray Daniel. Front row: Freddie Cox, Cliff Holton, Joe Mercer, Doug Lishman, Don Roper.

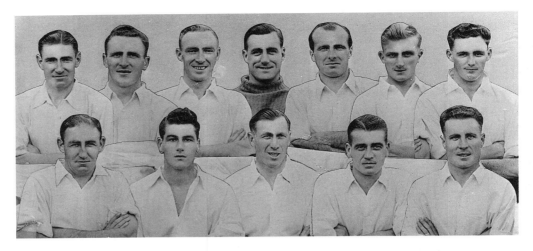

HOW THEY GOT THERE

NEWCASTLE UNITED
Round 3:
Aston Villa (h) 4-2.

Round 4:
Tottenham Hotspur (a) 3-0.

Round 5:
SwanseaTown (a) 1-0.

Round 6:
Portsmouth (a) 4-2.

Semi-final:
Blackburn Rovers *at Hillsborough* 0-0; *replay at Elland Road* 2-1.

ARSENAL
Round 3:
Norwich City (a) 5-0.

Round 4:
Barnsley (h) 4-0.

Round 5:
Leyton Orient (a) 3-0.

Round 6:
Luton Town (a) 3-2.

Semi-final:
Chelsea *at White Hart Lane* 1-1, *replay at White Hart Lane* 3-0.

Opposite page: The Magpies' Billy Foulkes heads goalwards. The newly-capped Welsh international, signed recently from Chester, was enjoying the most glorious year of his career.

in defeat that Arsenal attracted widespread warmth. Of course, back in the winter Tom Whittaker's team had enjoyed no such affection as they had progressed easily through the early rounds, rattling in a dozen goals without reply in one-sided ties with lowly Norwich, Barnsley and Leyton Orient. Meanwhile the Magpies had survived a third-round exit at home to Aston Villa, going through thanks to a three-goal burst in the last ten minutes, before crushing Tottenham Hotspur on a White Hart Lane quagmire in the fourth. That afternoon had been memorable not only for two goals from the prolific George Robledo, but also for the comprehensive chasing inflicted on Spurs full-backs Alf Ramsey and Charlie Withers by United wingers Bobby Mitchell and Tommy Walker. Most definitely, on such a gluepot, it was not a day for Arthur Rowe's men to push and run! Next Newcastle squeezed past Swansea Town before encountering formidable opposition in the shape of Portsmouth, the two sides giving fabulous entertainment highlighted by a titanic clash between England stars Jackie Milburn and centre-half Jack Froggatt. The Geordie came out on top with a stirring hat-trick, including a 20-yard screamer that equalled his Wembley effort of the previous year.

The other quarter-final was a close-run thing, too, Arsenal overcoming Luton courtesy of two goals by Freddie Cox. The veteran winger, who had reclaimed his place from young Arthur Milton, was also the Gunners' semi-final saviour, scoring in the 1-1 draw against Chelsea - played a week late because of a snowstorm on the due date - and then netting twice in the replay victory. Meanwhile Newcastle had their hands full in the other semi, gutsy Blackburn Rovers forcing a goalless draw before capitulating in a dramatic replay at Elland Road. So tense was that occasion that Milburn refused to take a penalty - admittedly he was limping with a knee injury at the time - and while skipper Joe Harvey was looking round for a replacement, Bobby Mitchell strode up and calmly dispatched the spot-kick as if he had been doing the job all his life. In fact, it was the first penalty he had ever taken!

With Newcastle and Arsenal through to Wembley, attention focused inevitably on their previous meeting there 20 years earlier in the infamous 'over-the-line' final, which the Magpies had won controversially. Indeed, film and photographs suggested that when Jimmy Richardson crossed for the first of Jack Allen's two strikes in a 2-1 victory, the ball had been well out of play. But the goal stood and the Magpies claimed the Cup if not all the credit. In that respect, at least, the 1952 rematch would offer a fascinating parallel. Many column inches were devoted also to the fact that, if successful, United - who were appearing in a record ninth final - would be the first club to lift the trophy two years in succession. Manager Stan Seymour, who had scored their winning goal against Aston Villa in 1924, left his men in no doubt what was expected of them, proclaiming: 'What we have we hold.' League form in the run-up to Wembley was not encouraging for either side, but while Arsenal had the excuse of fitness worries, the Magpies could offer scant explanation and the ire of their fans was undisguised. Certainly once again there was simmering resentment among the players over their financial rewards - match takings would be £44,000 while they would share £220 between them - but the relevance of that unrest is difficult to gauge. Newcastle went into the game with four changes from their 1951 final line-up. The newcomers were goalkeeper Ronnie Simpson, left-back Alf McMichael, left-half Ted Robledo - a makeweight in the £25,000 deal which took him and elder brother George, the sons of a Chilean father and Yorkshire mother, from Barnsley to Newcastle in 1949 - and inside-right Billy Foulkes, who was completing a season that Roy of the Rovers might have dreamed about. He began the campaign at humble Chester, made his dream move to St James' Park, scored a goal on his debut for Wales, and was now to cap it all with a Cup medal. However, the key men were seen as the free-scoring duo, Milburn and George Robledo, whom most neutrals hoped fervently would slay that nasty old North London dragon. As for Arsenal, often and unfairly dubbed 'negative', their squad was creaking under the strain of a long season. Centre-half Ray Daniel played with a plaster on his fractured wrist, schemer Jimmy Logie and leading marksman Doug Lishman were also carrying injuries, and it's possible that Reg Lewis, who had scored twice at Wembley a year earlier and netted another brace against Barnsley in the fourth round, might have won a place if Tom Whittaker had been fully confident of his fitness. As it was, young Cliff Holton came in for his first Cup tie - being given preference over Peter Goring - and, sadly, was not to do himself justice.

However, no sooner was the match under way than it became glaringly apparent that the Gunners had been best able to put their difficulties behind them. For

Ronnie Simpson, who had succeeded Jack Fairbrother and was giving a good account of himself between the Newcastle posts. But the crowning glory of his career was yet 15 years away when, on a sunny evening in Lisbon, he would help Celtic lift the European Cup.

a little more than quarter of an hour they were the slicker, brighter, more menacing team and came desperately close to taking the lead when Lishman's overhead kick flashed just past a post. But then, on 19 minutes, came the moment in which Dame Fortune frowned decisively on 'lucky Arsenal'. Their right-back Walley Barnes was on his own, going for a loose ball, when suddenly he fell to the ground, clutching his leg in anguish. It was to transpire that while turning on the lush turf, the Welsh captain had torn knee ligaments so badly that he would be out of the game for a year, in the process missing out on a Championship medal.

At first, he attempted bravely to carry on but was no more than a helpless passenger; even after leaving the field in agony, he returned with a bandage round the damaged joint, but before long was forced to withdraw permanently.

Above: Walley Barnes, whose knee injury tilted the balance of the match away from Arsenal. The full-back's misfortune was the first manifestation of the so-called Wembley jinx.

Right: The winning goal. George Robledo eludes the despairing lunge of Lionel Smith to steer his header into the Arsenal net via an upright. With only six minutes of normal time left, it was a savage blow to the outnumbered North Londoners.

The North Londoners, though, did not despair. Left-winger Don Roper took over Barnes' role, battling sensibly and with some success to contain the dangerous Mitchell. Inevitably the chances began to fall Newcastle's way, but with little going right for Messrs Milburn and Robledo, they were not being converted. Indeed the Geordies, with the honourable exceptions of Harvey and Mitchell, were giving a poor account of themselves while their depleted opponents displayed rare mettle. Marshalled by captain

Joe Mercer, who was never more inspired or inspiring, the entire defence was magnificent, with the non-stop Alex Forbes and the cultured Daniel taking the eye. The Gunners' attack was not blunt, either, and ten minutes from time Lishman might have overturned the odds but his header from a Cox corner shaved the wrong side of the crossbar. Then, four minutes later, their gallant, overworked rearguard, weakened still further by the cumulative effect of unremitting effort on various injuries, was breached at last. Mitchell skipped past Roper, one of the most recent casualties, and centred for Robledo to direct a downwards header into the net via the near post. Even then, Arsenal hit back and Forbes went close to equalising shortly before the final whistle.

Afterwards the wonderful Mercer, so fiercely proud of his fighting troops, made

sure they left the pitch at a canter with their heads held high. Later he described the day as the most emotional and honourable occasion of his career. His words found an echo from Whittaker, a man of deep humanity who exuded the same brand of quiet wisdom and integrity as Matt Busby, who said he had never been prouder of his side than in defeat that afternoon. Seymour, too, had the grace to weigh in with his own tribute: 'We have won the Cup, but the glory is yours,' he told the North Londoners.

Undeniably then, Arsenal had been unlucky, and their opponents generously admitted as much. But the bottom line was left to the milling multitude who greeted the Magpies on their return to Newcastle Central station, where a huge banner proclaimed: 'Well done, lads - it's still Wors!'

Overleaf: Acknowledging the enormous contribution of their opponents, the triumphant Magpies delay their celebrations while the gallant Gunners collect their medals. Left to right: Billy Foulkes, Alf McMichael, Jackie Milburn, Frank Brennan, Joe Harvey, Tommy Walker, Bobby Cowell and Bobby Mitchell.

53

BLACKPOOL 4

Mortensen 35, 68, 89; Perry 92

BOLTON WANDERERS 3

Lofthouse 2; Moir 40; Bell 55

Half-time 1-2

BLACKPOOL	⚪	BOLTON WANDERERS
George Farm	1	Stan Hanson
Eddie Shimwell	2	John Ball
Tom Garrett	3	Ralph Banks
Ewan Fenton	4	Johnny Wheeler
Harry Johnston *(captain)*	5	Malcolm Barrass
Cyril Robinson	6	Eric Bell
Stanley Matthews	7	Doug Holden
Ernie Taylor	8	Willie Moir *(captain)*
Stanley Mortensen	9	Nat Lofthouse
Jackie Mudie	10	Harold Hassall
Bill Perry	11	Bobby Langton

Attendance: 100,000

Referee: M Griffiths, Newport

1953

IT HAPPENED THIS YEAR

Edmund Hillary and Sherpa Tensing became the first men to climb Everest.

Coronation of Queen Elizabeth II.

Len Hutton appointed as England's first professional cricket captain.

Gordon Richards won his first Derby, on Pinza, and was knighted.

Government gave its blessing to commercial television.

Ford Popular was the cheapest car on the road at £390.

It was the day of the ultimate football fairytale, complete with its very own Peter Pan; the day the glorious game made fools of those hard-boiled sceptics who refuse to recognise its infinite capacity to express romance, beauty, indeed any number of life's finer feelings; it was the day Stanley Matthews, at long last, won the Cup.

Of course, he didn't do it on his own. After all, his great friend and Blackpool team-mate Stan Mortensen chipped in with the little matter of Wembley's first FA Cup Final hat-trick, while diminutive Ernie Taylor slaved endlessly and inspirationally to pave the great man's path to victory. Bolton Wanderers - on the day the most valiant, honourable and unlucky of opponents - contributed significantly to their own downfall, too, with an unfathomable *laissez-faire* reaction to injuries which helped to loosen their own seemingly decisive stranglehold on the trophy. And it's undeniable that Dame Fortune - after cold-shouldering the best-loved footballer in the land on his two previous appearances in the soccer showpiece - finally extended the hand of friendship. But even accepting all that, and despite Stanley's negligible contribution during the first hour or so of the action, legend

Opposite: A dream becomes reality. In the relative calm of the Wembley dressing room, Stanley Matthews brandishes the FA Cup winner's medal for which he had striven for so long.

57

dictates - emphatically and unarguably - that the game must go down as 'Matthews' Match'.

To appreciate fully the wave of euphoria that swept the nation when the balding, wiry, slightly stooped maestro - who looked, if anything, older than his 38 years - pocketed his winner's medal, it is necessary to understand both his unique place in public affection and his previous narrow failures to achieve this long-held ambition. Englishmen hailed Stanley, and not without reason, as the world's finest footballer, but also they loved his modesty, utter dedication to the work ethic and, perhaps most crucially, his apparent refusal to grow old. When Blackpool reached the final in 1948, he was 33 and it was seen as his last chance for that elusive gong; he didn't get it. His attempt in 1951, at 36, was seen as *positively* his farewell bid, and it too ended in failure. Thus, two years on, he was living every middle-aged football fan's fantasy and the weight of partisan fervour willing him to succeed projected soccer's big day into the national consciousness as never before.

Yet the early rounds of the competition offered scant clues to the remarkable climax in store. Blackpool eased through by a single goal in rounds three, four and five while Bolton's progress was less than majestic, too, especially in the fourth, in

HOW THEY GOT THERE

BLACKPOOL
Round 3:
Sheffield Wednesday (a) 2-1.

Round 4:
Huddersfield Town (h) 1-0.

Round 5:
Southampton (h) 1-1,
replay (a) 2-1.

Round 6:
Arsenal (a) 2-1.

Semi-final: Tottenham
Hotspur *at Villa Park* 2-1.

BOLTON WANDERERS
Round 3:
Fulham (h) 3-1.

Round 4:
Notts County (h) 1-1,
replay (a) 2-2,
second replay *at Hillsborough*
1-0.

Round 5:
Luton Town (a) 1-0.

Round 6:
Gateshead (a) 1-0.

Semi-final:
Everton *at Maine Road* 4-3.

which they took three games to dispose of Notts County. There was excitement elsewhere, however, with Walthamstow Avenue becoming the first amateurs for 24 years to reach the fourth round, where they lost to Manchester United only after a sensational draw at Old Trafford. Other headlines were provided by Liverpool's third-round demise at Gateshead - doomed sadly to bow out of the League at decade's end - and by Rotherham, who put paid to Newcastle's dream of three consecutive triumphs by unseating the Magpies in the fourth round.

Come the quarter-final stage, and the campaigns of the eventual finalists hotted up. Bolton were stretched to the limit by plucky Gateshead before going through by a single goal, and Blackpool won a thriller at Highbury. Unfortunately, that victory exacted a heavy price, with Allan Brown breaking his leg in a collision with Arsenal 'keeper Jack Kelsey in the very act of scoring the winner. Thus for the second time in three seasons, injury was to prevent the Scottish international's appearance in the Cup Final. The semi-finals produced two nerve-tingling finishes in the best tradition of the FA Cup, though for most of the clash between Bolton and Everton at Maine Road a close-run

THE FOOTBALL ASSOCIATION CHALLENGE CUP COMPETITION

FINAL TIE

BLACKPOOL v
BOLTON WANDERERS

SATURDAY, MAY 2nd, 1953   KICK-OFF 3 pm

EMPIRE STADIUM

WEMBLEY

Chairman and Managing Director : SIR ARTHUR J. ELVIN, M.B.E.

OFFICIAL PROGRAMME · ONE SHILLING

Above: The programme for the most famous FA Cup Final of them all, autographed by Stanley Matthews. Who else?

Left: Any one of these cars would be a collector's item now. Back in 1953 this mode of transport was still beyond the means of the average working man, yet the Wembley car park is packed.

climax seemed highly unlikely. The Wanderers had surged into a seemingly commanding four-goal lead before the Merseysiders stirred themselves, storming back to 4-3 and missing a penalty en route. Meanwhile at Villa Park there was rare melodrama in the dying seconds of Blackpool's encounter with Spurs, who had enjoyed a distinct edge throughout. With the scores level, the normally ultra-reliable Alf Ramsey released the sloppiest of back-passes to allow the sprightly Jackie Mudie to nip in and score the Seasiders' clincher.

So the final was to be an all-Lancastrian affair, though the audience was widened immeasurably as many people had recently bought their first television sets to watch the Queen's Coronation. Bolton had won the trophy three times in five previous finals and this was to be their fourth expedition to Wembley, but this time they faced a huge emotional barrier - the Matthews factor. However, they had their own star in England centre-forward and newly-crowned Footballer of the Year Nat Lofthouse, who had hit the target in every round, and despite finishing 14th in the First Division to Blackpool's seventh, were formidably rugged fighters. Manager Bill Ridding, a former England trainer, had fostered enviable team spirit, exemplified by the communal relish with which they shared their own special Cup drink - concocted from two dozen eggs and two bottles of sherry - after training before every round. Blackpool, too, were a happy unit but their season had been disrupted by Mortensen's two-month absence through cartilage trouble at the turn of the year, and in the days before the final the unthinkable reared its ugly head. Matthews himself, who had suffered intermittent knee problems for much of the campaign, had a thigh strain and was viewed as doubtful for Wembley. The uncertainty never became public - any hint of Stanley's possible absence would have provoked an unprecedented demand for sackcloth and ashes - and in the event a pre-match pain-killing injection averted the calamity. Having gambled thus on the fitness of his revered veteran, the Seasiders' boss Joe Smith was able to field eight of his 1951 side - Ewan Fenton, Cyril Robinson and Ernie

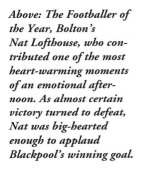

Above: The Footballer of the Year, Bolton's Nat Lofthouse, who contributed one of the most heart-warming moments of an emotional afternoon. As almost certain victory turned to defeat, Nat was big-hearted enough to applaud Blackpool's winning goal.

Right: Bolton 'keeper Stan Hanson, who like his opposite number George Farm was in embarrassingly shaky form, watches thankfully as this Blackpool attack comes to nothing.

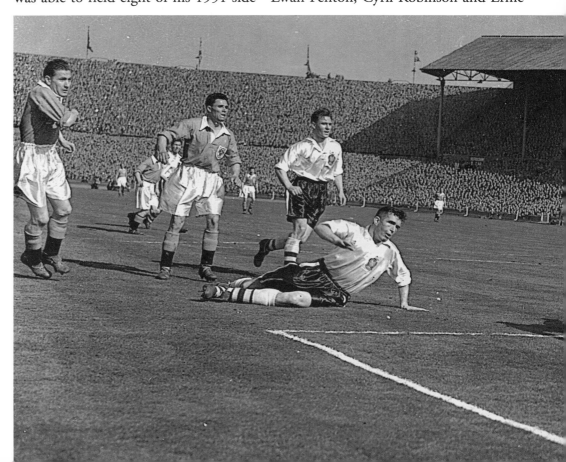

Taylor coming in for Eric Hayward, the injured Hugh Kelly and Bill Slater. Four men - Matthews, Mortensen, skipper Harry Johnston and full-back Eddie Shimwell - were turning out in their third final in six years as Blackpool sought their first FA Cup.

On a hot, sunny afternoon, the game got off to an eventful start when Lofthouse rather underhit a shot from outside the area and wrote it off momentarily as a wasted opportunity. But an instant later the ball had bobbled over the shoulder of Scottish international 'keeper George Farm and into the net for a soft opening goal. Now the Wanderers looked capable of imposing their will, but their momentum was checked on 18 minutes when left-half Eric Bell was reduced to a passenger on the left wing after pulling a hamstring. Even so, despite an enforced reshuffle that saw England inside-left Harold Hassall drop back to wing-half, they continued to pour forward and soon after Bell's injury Lofthouse stroked a shot against a post. Thus reprieved, Blackpool responded with an equaliser when Mortensen sped through a defensive gap to score with a cross-shot that took a deflection off Hassall. It seemed, though, that Bolton were not to be denied. Five minutes before the interval they regained the lead when skipper Willie Moir lunged at a speculative chip from Bobby Langton, Farm failed to make contact and the ball dropped gently over the line. The goal was credited to Moir but television replays suggest that the Scot did not get a touch. Either way, poor Farm was at fault once more, this time for not making a routine interception. Then, ten minutes after the break, the limping Bell

Left: Nat Lofthouse's innocuous shot bobbles over the shoulder of the hapless George Farm and into the net for Bolton's opener.

nodded home a Doug Holden cross to make it 3-1.

Now, surely, the Cup was destined for Burnden Park. But wait; as the match moved into its final half-hour, a transformation began. Now the wizard Matthews, who in all honesty had been a shadowy figure so far, reached decisively for

Above: Shrugging off the pain of a torn hamstring, Eric Bell rises above Eddie Shimwell to convert Doug Holden's cross and give Bolton a 3-1 lead. Now Blackpool and Matthews seem destined to be denied yet again.

Right: The model free-kick. This time Hanson is blameless as Stanley Mortensen's thunderbolt explodes in the back of his net. That levelled the scores at 3-3, setting the stage for Matthews' magical finale.

Below: Stanley Mortensen, here causing yet more mayhem in the Bolton defence, remains the only man this century to score a hat-trick in an FA Cup Final.

his wand. Understandably enough, the Trotters were tiring, and with Bell hobbling along his touchline and now left-back Ralph Banks suffering from shin cramps, it was on Stanley's flank that their weakness was most apparent. Both sides reacted to the changing situation - Blackpool positively, by feeding Matthews with possession at every opportunity; Bolton suicidally, by failing to reorganise their stricken rearguard. Ernie Taylor, in particular, supplied a steady stream of passes to his wing partner and the magic began to flow. With some 20

Above: Harold Hassall deflects Mortensen's shot into his own net for Blackpool's first equaliser. Some killjoys maintain that it should go down as a Hassall own goal, and strictly speaking they might have a case. But rarely can a man have deserved a hat-trick more than 'Morty' on this glorious day and it is morally just that the official record reads 'Mortensen 3'.

minutes remaining the old maestro, swerving and darting and evading challenges as if by alchemy, dispatched a high cross to the far post where stretching 'keeper Stan Hanson managed only to touch it into the path of Mortensen's instinctive lunge. Now it was 3-2 and belief surged through the Seasiders like life returning to a nearly-drowned man.

Yet still Bolton, on the verge of collective exhaustion, resisted heroically as Matthews created a series of chances only for Jackie Mudie, Bill Perry and Mortensen to miss them. Then, with the sanctuary of the final whistle only 180 seconds away, the Wanderers cracked. As 'Morty' lined up to take a free-kick on the edge of the box, a Bolton defender peeled away to pick up the advancing Shimwell; spotting the tiny gap in a trice, Stan drove high, hard and handsomely into the net to complete a marvellous hat-trick. More importantly the scores were level and the game was headed for extra time - or so every transfixed soul in that packed stadium and the countless thousands watching breathlessly at home could only believe. But Matthews, still bubbling with life, decreed otherwise. Deep into injury time, he received the ball level with the edge of Bolton's penalty area. Dipping his shoulder, he swerved outside the gallant Banks - who even at his utmost extremity never stooped to foul play - then deceived Malcolm Barrass with a delicate feint and reached the byline, a position described to perfection by the late Geoffrey Green as 'his most dangerous playground'. And now came the great man's most crucial decision. Looking up as ever for the marauding Mortensen, he noted that his namesake was tightly marked, so opted instead to roll the ball to the lurking Perry, slipping as he did so. The South African left winger pulled back his right foot, and cracked the ball into the corner of the net beyond two desperate Bolton sentinels who straddled the line.

Pandemonium broke out - not only at Wembley but all over

Above: In all the euphoria over Stanley Matthews, the man who scored the winning goal tended to be overlooked. Here he is, Bill Perry, the most successful of several South Africans who joined Blackpool after the War.

Right: Ours at last! After their Wembley defeats of 1948 and 1951, Blackpool finally took the Cup in Coronation Year. Skipper Harry Johnston and folk hero Stanley Matthews are carried shoulder-high to receive the adulation of the fans.

England - and the tangerine shirts danced a victory jig. With only seconds left, the game was up for Wanderers, who became the first side to lose an FA Cup Final after leading by two goals, and yet - what a moving sight - the lion-hearted Lofthouse, all effort spent, still found strength to applaud the goal that shattered his hopes. Thereafter, that longed-for medal safely secured, Stanley Matthews was hoisted shoulder-high alongside his captain Harry Johnston and the nation, indeed the whole of the footballing world beyond the boundaries of Bolton, rejoiced long and loud. If subjected to technical analysis, the game did not stand comparison with, say, the 1948 final; but for sheer, straight-from-the-heart emotion and late, late drama, there could hardly be another Wembley occasion - arguably, not even England's 1966 World Cup triumph - to touch it.

Inset left: The unlucky Allan Brown (left) and Hugh Kelly, who both missed the final through injury, get their hands on the Cup. Nursing the trophy is skipper Harry Johnston.

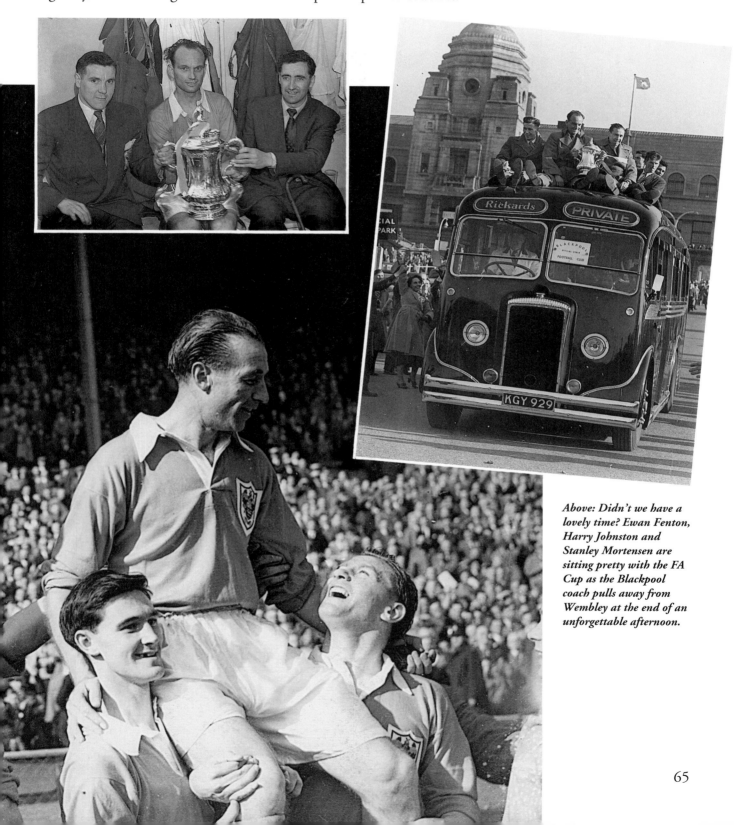

Above: Didn't we have a lovely time? Ewan Fenton, Harry Johnston and Stanley Mortensen are sitting pretty with the FA Cup as the Blackpool coach pulls away from Wembley at the end of an unforgettable afternoon.

65

1 May 1954

WEST BROMWICH ALBION 3

Allen 21, 63 (pen); Griffin 88

PRESTON NORTH END 2

Morrison 22; Wayman 51

Half-time 1-1

WEST BROMWICH ALBION	○	PRESTON NORTH END
Jim Sanders	1	George Thompson
Joe Kennedy	2	Willie Cunningham
Len Millard *(captain)*	3	Joe Walton
Jimmy Dudley	4	Tommy Docherty
Jimmy Dugdale	5	Joe Marston
Ray Barlow	6	Willie Forbes
Frank Griffin	7	Tom Finney *(captain)*
Reg Ryan	8	Bob Foster
Ronnie Allen	9	Charlie Wayman
Johnny Nicholls	10	Jimmy Baxter
George Lee	11	Angus Morrison

Attendance: 100,000

Referee: A Luty, Leeds

For Matthews, read Finney; for the second season in succession, the FA Cup Final provided the opportunity for a national footballing treasure to win his first major club honour. But unlike the evergreen Stanley - to whom he was compared favourably by many, perhaps a majority, of the game's shrewdest judges - Tom Finney was to be thwarted. Indeed, the 'Preston Plumber', born within sight of his beloved Deepdale and a North End man in every fibre of his being, endured the most frustrating afternoon of his career. Losing to West Bromwich Albion at Wembley, just a year after being pipped for the League title on goal average by Arsenal, was bad enough; offering such an uncharacteristically lacklustre personal performance compounded the misery to a merciless degree. With the peerless benefit of hindsight, there appeared to be obvious reasons for the failure - quite apart from the admirable skill, spirit and enterprise of Albion - and though the faultlessly sportsmanlike Finney would be the last man to seek excuses, they do bear the examination which follows in due course.

The Cup campaign had begun in the shadow of one of the rudest shocks ever inflicted on our domestic soccer, the 6-3 humbling of England by Hungary at

Footballer of the Year Tom Finney, who was expected to win the Cup for Preston. For a variety of reasons, it didn't turn out like that and poor Tom felt he had let down himself, his team and his town. In fact, he was being unduly self-critical, but no matter what the verdict on his disappointing day, it could not besmirch his reputation as perhaps the finest player of his generation.

Wembley. For those with eyes to see, the 'Magnificent Magyars' had exposed the myth of British supremacy and signalled the beginning of a new era in which enlightened managers, the likes of Manchester United's Matt Busby and Stan Cullis of Wolves, would seek to learn from their Continental counterparts. Even so, it would take more than the humiliation of the national team to deflate enthusiasm for the oldest club competition, and come the day of the third round - when the giants entered the fray - the post-War attendance boom was maintained.

For the Throstles, who saw off Chelsea's challenge with the only goal of the match, it was the start of a sequence of home ties up to and including their emphatic quarter-final beating of Spurs. Arguably their most significant achievement was the unseating of Newcastle, then in the process of a run which saw them lift the trophy three times in five years. Preston's trail began at the Baseball Ground, where a narrow-angled Finney strike clinched victory over Derby, but he was not at his irresistible best until the fifth-round clash with Ipswich. The North End skipper, unperturbed by the over-abrasive attentions of his opponents, lacerated the East Anglians with his skill and pace, and it was at this stage that the

Above: Just this once . . . West Bromwich Albion skipper Len Millard fails to prevent Tom Finney from delivering a cross. It was one of the few occasions that the 'Preston Plumber' managed to get the better of his clam-like marker.

Deepdale Cup dream began to take shape. Leicester provided a severe test in the last eight, forcing a second replay before Preston claimed their place in the semi-finals, where they faced Sheffield Wednesday. Once more, Finney was magnificent as North End poured forward, forcing 22 corners and a 2-0 victory. Meanwhile Albion, still not obliged to leave the Midlands as their semi-final with Port Vale was at Villa Park, found themselves locked in a tense struggle. No matter that the men from the Potteries played their football in the Third Division North - in fact, they were to finish champions by 11 points - they had dumped holders Blackpool from the FA Cup and were not about to be overawed by anyone else. At the end, West Bromwich were thankful to go through, courtesy only of a flukey lob by Jimmy Dudley and a penalty by Ronnie Allen against his former team.

At the time, there were high hopes at the Hawthorns that the Throstles could take the League and Cup double. They had started 1953/54 with a nine-game unbeaten run, and though they had fallen away in mid-term, they had gone into their semi-final as table-toppers. However, injury problems were mounting - goalkeeper Norman Heath and full-back Stan Rickaby were invalided out of the final - and a depressing record of three points from their last seven games allowed Wolves to pip them for the title. Mid-table Preston found themselves under pressure of a different sort, all to do with the newly-installed Footballer of the Year, Tom Finney. His presence created an overwhelming weight of expectation which, in the weeks before the grand occasion, proved ever more burdensome on his shoulders. Not a man to shirk his duty to the public, he gave unstintingly of himself, fulfilling practically every demand on his time and energy, ever unwilling to say 'no'. In later years, clubs would not dream of leaving their players thus exposed, instead hiding them away in country retreats where they could compose

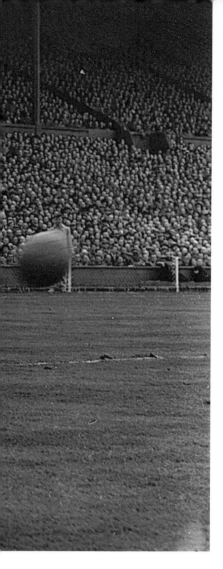

themselves for the trial ahead. Admittedly, the mid-1950s media were nothing like as hysterical as their 1990s counterparts - as Paul Gascoigne would testify - but constant requests for tickets and personal appearances, which modern managers would not countenance, took an inevitable toll. To be fair, boss Scot Symon did take his team to a London hotel for the last few days before the match, though some players felt that preparation made them lethargic and encouraged them to brood. In addition, Finney was not fully fit, suffering with a long-standing groin strain that was to prove a debilitating handicap on Wembley's lush turf. Though every word ever written about his modesty was true, the Preston captain looked a proud man as he led his side out to face Albion. He was the star performer, the focal point, the talisman of his hometown club - here seeking their third victory in their sixth final appearance - and perhaps not even his stirring achievements for his country had prepared him for such an emotional moment. Tom started the game brightly enough, but soon it became apparent that Albion planned to starve him of possession, and when he did get the ball he was confronted not only by Throstles' full-back and skipper Len Millard, but also that accomplished, frequently underrated left-half Ray Barlow. Accordingly, and remembering his physical condition, Finney laboured to negligible effect and it was left to West Bromwich to make the first decisive impact. That came when George Lee seized on a loose ball and squared it firmly for Allen - whose combination of touch, guile and speed might have won him more than his five England caps - to sidefoot into the net. Within a minute, though, North End were level when winger Angus Morrison headed home a lob from Tommy Docherty, the workaholic wing-half who had recently returned from a lengthy lay-off.

Soon after the interval it seemed that Finney might get his winner's medal after

HOW THEY GOT THERE
WEST BROMWICH ALBION
Round 3: **Chelsea** (h) 1-0.
Round 4: **Rotherham United** (h) 4-0.
Round 5: **Newcastle United** (h) 3-2.
Round 6: **Tottenham Hotspur** (h) 3-0.
Semi-final: **Port Vale** *at Villa Park* 2-1.
PRESTON NORTH END
Round 3: **Derby County** (a) 2-0.
Round 4: **Lincoln City** (a) 2-0.
Round 5: **Ipswich Town** (h) 6-1.
Round 6: **Leicester City** (a) 1-1, replay (h) 2-2, second replay *at Hillsborough* 3-1.
Semi-final: **Sheffield Wednesday** *at Maine Road* 2-0.

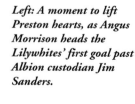

Left: A moment to lift Preston hearts, as Angus Morrison heads the Lilywhites' first goal past Albion custodian Jim Sanders.

all. When Docherty dispatched a raking through-ball into Albion territory it seemed that 'Cheeky Charlie' Wayman was offside by several yards, but there was no whistle and the centre-forward went on to round 'keeper Jim Sanders before giving Preston the lead, thus maintaining his record of scoring in every round. Many of the players on both sides were convinced that Wayman's goal should have been ruled out, but to the Throstles' undying credit they refused to whinge, instead knuckling down to seek an equaliser. They found one just after the hour when the ubiquitous Docherty ended a surging run by Barlow, who had left two opponents in his wake, by felling him inside the box. Allen took the penalty, but not before he had stretched his own

Above: The Throstles flock round the Preston goal, but this time 'keeper George Thompson is equal to the situation.

nerves and those of every Albion fan in the ground to breaking point. Twice a divot on the spot caused the ball to roll away, and twice the referee ordered it to be re-spotted. Then, when Ronnie did send his shot goalwards, he miscued and it crept over the line via the fingertips of 'keeper George Thompson, who had made a noble effort to turn it away. Later the scorer described the moment as the most anxious of his career: 'The ball seemed to take an hour to reach the net,' he added. It was all too stomach-churning for Sanders, between the posts at the other end; he averted his eyes as the kick was being taken! Thereafter, with Finney a marginal figure and West Bromwich marksman Johnny Nicholls hampered increasinly by a pulled muscle, an extra period seemed likely. But two minutes from the end of normal time, the hitherto disappointing Throstles flankman Frank Griffin escaped his faithful marker, Joe Walton, for one of the few times that afternoon, and scored the winner, deceiving the unfortunate Thompson with an innocuous-looking cross-shot from the right angle of the area which stole inside the far post. There was no time for any reply and the Midlanders had won an entertaining, well-balanced, though far-from-classical

Right: 'Tell me when it's all over!' Albion 'keeper Jim Sanders can't bear to look as Ronnie Allen nets the Throstles' equaliser from the penalty spot.

Above: The puff of dust at the feet of Ronnie Allen tells the agonising story. The England centre-forward has scuffed his shot from the penalty spot and he said later that the ball seemed to take an age to creep into the net.

Left: Griffin's grubber wins the Cup. There is little time for Preston to reply as Frank Griffin's low shot eludes George Thompson and squeezes into the net for the Albion winner.

West Bromwich Albion just missed out on the League title, but the FA Cup offered rich consolation.
Back row (left to right): Joe Kennedy, Jimmy Dugdale, Ray Barlow, Jim Sanders, Jimmy Dudley, Len Millard, George Lee.
Front row: Reg Ryan, Ronnie Allen, Frank Griffin, Johnny Nicholls.

Below: Had there been a 'man of the match' award in 1954, then a fitting recipient would have been Albion captain Len Millard, who shadowed Tom Finney faithfully and effectively throughout the 90 minutes.

encounter to claim the Cup for the fourth time in their nine finals. All credit to their flamboyant boss Vic Buckingham, and an attractive all-round side in which Barlow, Allen and Millard, who had policed the 'Preston Plumber', had been outstanding. And what a wonderful day for Sanders and full-back Joe Kennedy, brought in for their first ties of the season because of the injury crisis.

But the heart of the football world was heavy on behalf of Tom Finney, who felt he had let down himself, his team and his town. It was a poignant admission from a truly great player, and his team-mates were angered by general criticism of his display. After all, he had been heavily marked and they had failed to capitalise on the extra space afforded to them. Docherty, in particular, was outraged, writing: 'You'd have thought he was a pygmy, not a giant having an off-day.' Not for the last time, 'The Doc' had contributed the final and most telling word.

7 May 1955

NEWCASTLE UNITED 3

Milburn 1; Mitchell 53; Hannah 60

MANCHESTER CITY 1

Johnstone 44

Half-time 1-1

NEWCASTLE UNITED		MANCHESTER CITY
Ronnie Simpson	1	Bert Trautmann
Bobby Cowell	2	Jimmy Meadows
Ron Batty	3	Roy Little
Jimmy Scoular *(captain)*	4	Ken Barnes
Bob Stokoe	5	Dave Ewing
Tom Casey	6	Roy Paul *(captain)*
Len White	7	Bill Spurdle
Jackie Milburn	8	Joe Hayes
Vic Keeble	9	Don Revie
George Hannah	10	Bobby Johnstone
Bobby Mitchell	11	Fionan Fagan

Attendance: 100,000

Referee: R Leafe, Nottingham

Newcastle's Jimmy Scoular, a worthy successor to Joe Harvey both as inspiring captain and dynamic wing-half, is held aloft with the trophy that the Magpies were beginning to regard as their personal property.

Rarely can the oldest Cup cliche of them all have been more apt than in 1955, when Newcastle United lifted the glittering prize for the third time in five seasons. The Geordie hordes who raised the Wembley rafters with their joyous rendition of 'The Blaydon Races' might beg to differ - maintaining that their heroes were the ultimate knockout experts, pure and simple - but any reasoned examination of the campaign points to one irresistible conclusion: from the first kick of their first game on the road to the final, the Magpies' name was etched indelibly on the famous trophy. After all, they had baulked and stuttered at nearly every hurdle on the way to Wembley, where they came face to face with a side capable of enchanting football. Indeed, in many ways Manchester City, with their enterprising espousal of the Hungarian-influenced 'Revie Plan', were the team of the moment.

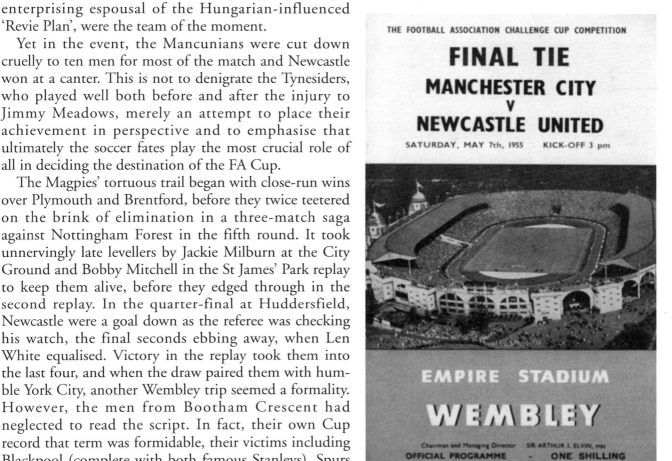

THE FOOTBALL ASSOCIATION CHALLENGE CUP COMPETITION

FINAL TIE
MANCHESTER CITY
V
NEWCASTLE UNITED

SATURDAY, MAY 7th, 1955   KICK-OFF 3 pm

EMPIRE STADIUM
WEMBLEY

Chairman and Managing Director   SIR ARTHUR J. ELVIN, MBE
OFFICIAL PROGRAMME   -   ONE SHILLING

Yet in the event, the Mancunians were cut down cruelly to ten men for most of the match and Newcastle won at a canter. This is not to denigrate the Tynesiders, who played well both before and after the injury to Jimmy Meadows, merely an attempt to place their achievement in perspective and to emphasise that ultimately the soccer fates play the most crucial role of all in deciding the destination of the FA Cup.

The Magpies' tortuous trail began with close-run wins over Plymouth and Brentford, before they twice teetered on the brink of elimination in a three-match saga against Nottingham Forest in the fifth round. It took unnervingly late levellers by Jackie Milburn at the City Ground and Bobby Mitchell in the St James' Park replay to keep them alive, before they edged through in the second replay. In the quarter-final at Huddersfield, Newcastle were a goal down as the referee was checking his watch, the final seconds ebbing away, when Len White equalised. Victory in the replay took them into the last four, and when the draw paired them with humble York City, another Wembley trip seemed a formality. However, the men from Bootham Crescent had neglected to read the script. In fact, their own Cup record that term was formidable, their victims including Blackpool (complete with both famous Stanleys), Spurs (whose purchase of York's star Dave Dunmore a year earlier had financed, with delicious irony, the rebuilding programme that resulted now in the North Londoners' Cup exit) and Notts County. Having thus become only the third Division Three side to reach the semi-final, City were not about to roll over and expire without doughty resistance and, to be fair, United expected a fight. But hardly were they ready for the battle royal mounted by the Minstermen, who forced a 1-1 draw at Hillsborough and were denied a sensational last-minute upset only by 'iron man' Jimmy Scoular's desperate interception. Scoular, who had replaced Joe Harvey as Newcastle skipper, had seen plenty in an illustrious Portsmouth career, but rarely can he have experienced quite such melodrama. Predictably, York had given their best shot and succumbed 2-0 in the replay, going on to pay a high price for their Cup exploits through the resultant fixture pile-up which arguably cost them promotion.

Meanwhile, Manchester City's progress to Wembley, though exciting enough, was comparatively smooth, though it owed much to a series of magnificent displays by their German goalkeeper Bert Trautmann. Their most satisfying achievement had been knocking out neighbours United in the fourth round, and after seeing off Sunderland in a semi-final mudbath at Villa Park they were slight favourites to take the trophy. City's eminence during a season which had seen them emerge as Championship challengers was due hugely to the playing influence of centre-forward Don Revie, who was the key man in manager Les McDowall's bold and commendable attempt to adapt the methods of the 'Magnificent Magyars' to the English game. Instead of leading the line in traditional fashion, Revie was deployed in a deep-lying role, a roaming schemer calculated to confuse defenders brought up to understand that number-nines pounded towards goal through the middle of the pitch. It was a fluid, attractive style which involved playing the ball to feet and was suited admirably to the talents of skilful operators such as Revie and his fellow play-maker, the emerging Ken Barnes. Inevitably the new system attracted scathing criticism from xenophobes and traditionalists, but more enlightened commentators applauded City's initiative and Revie was voted Footballer of the Year.

At one point, the title was a feasible target, but as so often happens when the League/FA Cup double appears tantalisingly on the horizon, there was a springtime slump. One significant factor in the loss of form was the broken leg suffered by inside-left Johnny Hart in March, and Wembley preparations were hampered further by injury to Welsh winger Roy Clarke, whose diving header against Sunderland had secured City's

final place. The side had been strengthened, however, by the recent signing of Scotland inside-forward Bobby Johnstone from Hibernian, and it was felt that the wide open spaces of Wembley would suit their passing game.

There was a minor row in the Maine Road camp over the standard of tickets allocated to the players' wives - Revie and skipper Roy Paul insisted successfully that changes were made - but that was nothing to the discontent bubbling beneath the surface at St James' Park. United players, it seemed, were being given a dozen tickets each (compared with 40 per head for the City men), but that was merely a symptom of deeper problems over wages that would not reach crisis point until Newcastle's George Eastham took his historic stand at the end of the decade, revolutionising the pay and conditions of all English footballers in the process. Perhaps even more disruptive at the time was a private pantomime - the news didn't leak out till later - in which manager Duggie Livingstone dropped Jackie Milburn, the idol of all Tyneside, for the final, only for his selection to be overturned by the board. Livingstone, former boss of Eire and Belgium, never quite regained his

Proving a point. Jackie Milburn, who had been dropped for the final by his manager and then reinstated by the board, opens the scoring for the Geordies with an adroit header after only 45 seconds.

stature at the club after this incident and left the following year. Unavoidably absent from the Wembley line-up were left-half Charlie Crowe, who had twisted his ankle, and laryngitis victim Reg Davies, whose place at inside-right was taken by Milburn, with Len White - Livingstone's original choice in place of Jackie - coming in on the right wing. The absence of the popular Crowe, who had played in the 1951 final but lost out to Ted Robledo in 1952, was seen as such a blow by some team-mates that they offered to 'carry' his disability so he could play, but the sensible Charlie knew that would be wrong and stood down.

All things considered, probably Manchester City arrived at Wembley enjoying the greater peace of mind, but if so, Newcastle - now so experienced at dealing with big-day nerves - were not long in shattering it. Some 45 seconds, in fact! That's how long it took United to open the scoring, and if their directors had glanced a trifle smugly towards Duggie Livingstone, then who could have blamed them? White lifted a corner into the box, the City defence stood as if petrified and Jackie Milburn - who else? - soared to head high into the net. It was a

77

Above: 'Hoodoo' victim Jimmy Meadows of Manchester City and England, whose burgeoning career was ended by the knee injury he suffered at Wembley.

Top: Head to head. Newcastle spearhead Vic Keeble is policed by Manchester City's Dave Ewing and the ball flies wide of Bert Trautmann's goal.

majestic contribution, and the only notable one of the match from 'Wor Jackie', who was to labour with a strained stomach muscle. Now the Geordies looked capable of a gala performance, with the lanky, tricky Mitchell beginning to sparkle on the left wing, but the real turning point in their favour was to come in a most unwanted manner. After 18 minutes, City right-back Meadows - newly capped by England - overstretched and wrenched knee ligaments so badly that he never played again. Occurring on almost the same spot where Walley Barnes had fallen three years earlier, and bearing in mind Eric Bell's accident in 1953, it fuelled the theory of a Wembley hoodoo, which was to grow ever-more persuasive following a sequence of mishaps lasting into the 1960s.

For the present, however, the question was: how would it affect a City side already under considerable pressure? Perversely, after the Geordies had forced Trautmann into two superb saves, the Mancunians - with winger Bill Spurdle filling in for Meadows - began to blossom, their posse of gifted creators making repeated inroads into the Newcastle defence. Most prominent was little Johnstone, who on one run outwitted four opponents only to be thwarted at the last, and it was he who snatched the against-the-odds equaliser, heading in a short cross from Joe Hayes just before the break. Could they continue to defy logic and carry the game to United in the second half? The answer was not long in coming, and it was devastating. During the interval Livingstone had called for a possession game, which would make their extra man count, and they played it to perfection. Soon, with City being made to toil, Scoular freed Mitchell who gulled Trautmann to net from the narrowest of angles. Seven minutes later, Mitchell turned creator as the big German could only push his firm cross to the feet of George Hannah, who scored with ease. Thereafter Newcastle cruised, enjoying their numerical advantage and entertaining splendidly. What if Meadows not been injured? None can know, but Manchester's attacking spell before half-time suggests the outcome would have been closer, at the very least.

For City it was their fifth final and their third defeat, while Newcastle were firmly in the record business. Now they joined Blackburn and Aston Villa with the most FA Cup wins - six - and became the first club to play in ten finals. Milburn, Mitchell and right-back Bobby Cowell each claimed their third winner's medal in five years, though they would have been the first to spare a thought for poor Jimmy Meadows, hobbling up the royal-box steps in his blazer to claim the loser's gong that signalled the end of his career.

Left: The point of no return for ten-man City. Bobby Mitchell's acute-angled shot puts the Magpies in front and Ken Barnes (right) is understandably dismayed.

Below: 'This is getting to be a habit.' Bobby Mitchell, who played in all three of Newcastle's FA Cup victories, is about to slake his thirst from the coveted trophy, flanked by fellow goalscorers George Hannah (left) and Jackie Milburn. Wing-half Tom Casey (right) waits his turn.

**IT HAPPENED
THIS YEAR**

Suez crisis
threatened to cause
Third World War.

Russians crushed
Hungarian revolution
against Soviet rule.

England's Jim Laker
took 19 wickets
against Australia at
Old Trafford.

Rocky Marciano
retired unbeaten as
world heavyweight
champion .

Film star Grace Kelly
married Prince
Rainier of Monaco.

First premium bonds
went on sale.

5 May 1956

MANCHESTER CITY 3

Hayes 3; Dyson 66; Johnstone 69

BIRMINGHAM CITY 1

Kinsey 15

Half-time 1-1

MANCHESTER CITY	◯	BIRMINGHAM CITY
Bert Trautmann	1	Gil Merrick
Bill Leivers	2	Jeff Hall
Roy Little	3	Ken Green
Ken Barnes	4	John Newman
Dave Ewing	5	Trevor Smith
Roy Paul *(captain)*	6	Len Boyd *(captain)*
Bobby Johnstone	7	Gordon Astall
Joe Hayes	8	Noel Kinsey
Don Revie	9	Eddy Brown
Jack Dyson	10	Peter Murphy
Roy Clarke	11	Alex Govan

Attendance: 100,000

Referee: A Bond, London

*A promise kept. the
Mancunians' skipper
Roy Paul, who pledged
that City would be back
a year later after tasting
defeat in the 1955 final,
descends from
Wembley's royal box
with the Cup safely in
his keeping.*

*Far right: Trautmann's
trauma. No one knew it
at the time but
Manchester City's groggy
'keeper, supported by
the arm of centre-half
Dave Ewing and sur-
rounded by anxious
team-mates, had just
broken his neck.*

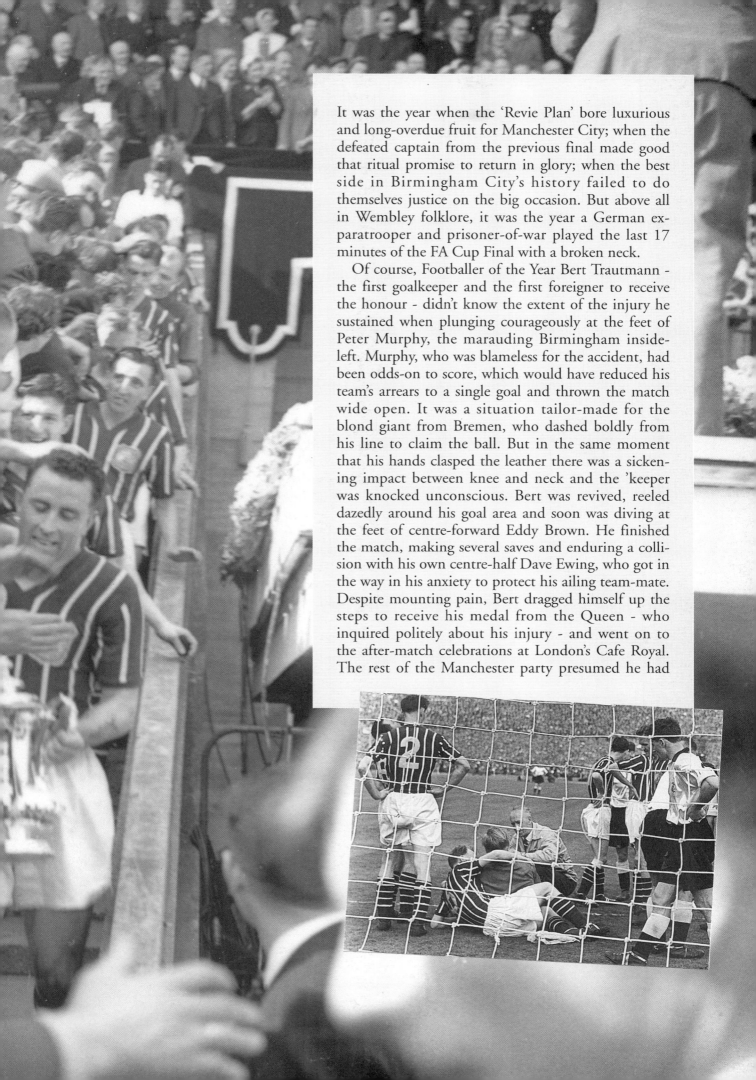

It was the year when the 'Revie Plan' bore luxurious and long-overdue fruit for Manchester City; when the defeated captain from the previous final made good that ritual promise to return in glory; when the best side in Birmingham City's history failed to do themselves justice on the big occasion. But above all in Wembley folklore, it was the year a German ex-paratrooper and prisoner-of-war played the last 17 minutes of the FA Cup Final with a broken neck.

Of course, Footballer of the Year Bert Trautmann - the first goalkeeper and the first foreigner to receive the honour - didn't know the extent of the injury he sustained when plunging courageously at the feet of Peter Murphy, the marauding Birmingham inside-left. Murphy, who was blameless for the accident, had been odds-on to score, which would have reduced his team's arrears to a single goal and thrown the match wide open. It was a situation tailor-made for the blond giant from Bremen, who dashed boldly from his line to claim the ball. But in the same moment that his hands clasped the leather there was a sickening impact between knee and neck and the 'keeper was knocked unconscious. Bert was revived, reeled dazedly around his goal area and soon was diving at the feet of centre-forward Eddy Brown. He finished the match, making several saves and enduring a collision with his own centre-half Dave Ewing, who got in the way in his anxiety to protect his ailing team-mate. Despite mounting pain, Bert dragged himself up the steps to receive his medal from the Queen - who inquired politely about his injury - and went on to the after-match celebrations at London's Cafe Royal. The rest of the Manchester party presumed he had

Above: Peter Murphy, the Birmingham inside-left whose accidental collision with Bert Trautmann broke the German's neck.

Right: Blues winger Alex Govan, the bathtime songster who inspired a new Brummie battle hymn.

aggravated an old muscle strain and it was not until several days later - after various examinations had revealed nothing untoward - that an x-ray in a Manchester hospital told the frightening truth. His second vertebra was broken in two and jammed against the third, which held the fragments in place and thus saved his life. An operation which involved drilling into his skull was needed, and he was out of the game until December, but he did make a full recovery. Anything less would have been tragic for a man who had risen above inevitable post-War anti-German prejudice to become one of British soccer's best-loved personalities.

Trautmann's tale is one of gripping human drama, as opposed to the usual sporting variety, but it must not be allowed to overshadow totally the exploits of Revie and his team-mates (of which more later), or the deeds of Birmingham City, who that season had excelled themselves. Newly-promoted from the Second Division, the men from St Andrews had taken the top flight in their stride, finishing a highly creditable sixth in the table after running third in late winter. Their game was based on power, notably a half-back line comprising skipper Len Boyd, Young England stopper Trevor Smith and the tenacious Roy Warhurst, while up front they fielded a quick-moving quintet which included the effervescent, eccentric Eddy Brown at number nine. Though hardly the classiest of operators, he toiled unceasingly and scored his share of goals, but it was as a larger-than-life character that he was adored by the Birmingham faithful. On scoring, his celebrations might encompass a brisk hand-shake with a corner-flag, perhaps a swift chat with an admirer in the crowd, or he might even offer a comic cuddle to a policeman. A sharp-witted individual who once considered a career in the priesthood and later taught for a time, Eddy would sprinkle his post-match pronouncements with quotations from Shakespeare, introducing welcome and hilarious variety into many a routine press conference. Left-winger Alex Govan was a popular figure, too, and he it was who inspired the adoption of Blues' 1956 Cup anthem, Keep Right On To The End Of The Road, after a group of fans heard him singing the grand old song in the bath.

Though they had plenty of *good* players, what Birmingham lacked was true class, a quality that was limited to veteran Gil Merrick, one of the League's finest post-War goalkeepers, and the quick, skilful right-back Jeff Hall, who within three years was to lose his life to polio at the age of 29. In human terms, of course, Jeff's death was an unbearable tragedy; football-wise, too, it represented a chronic loss to the St Andrews cause. At the time of the 1956 final, he was in the course of a 17-match England run alongside Manchester United's Roger Byrne, also doomed to die young, in the Munich air disaster.

Such horrors, which place the game in its true perspective, were well in the future as the Cup campaigns got under way. From the third round up to the semi-final, Birmingham's was one of barely diluted delight, with 18 goals scored - seven of them by Brown - and only two conceded, and that despite becoming the first side to reach Wembley without a home tie. The annihilations of Torquay and Leyton Orient were followed by a sweet local derby triumph over West Bromwich Albion and then a convincing quarter-final defeat of Arsenal. Highlight of that

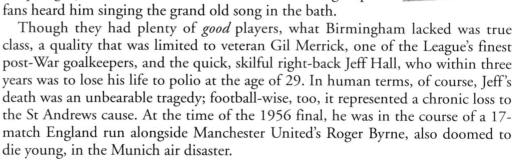

Two of the classiest operators afield. Manchester City's Don Revie (left) was the dominant influence on the match, his tactical acumen and skills a delight to behold. Meanwhile Jeff Hall, the Birmingham City and England full-back, gave a characteristically polished performance; his early death through polio was a chronic loss to the game.

Highbury encounter was an athletic diving header by winger Gordon Astall, the definite lowlight being a leg muscle injury to Warhurst that ruled him out for the rest of the season. When moneybags Sunderland were thumped comprehensively in the semi-final, the in-form Brummies were installed in the novel position of Cup favourites, even though their Wembley opponents were to finish two places above them in the League.

Those odds were based on a combination of the Lancastrians' faltering Cup progress, well-publicised difficulties between star schemer Don Revie and manager Les McDowall, and several injuries. In truth, Manchester City were as well-served by fortune in reaching the final as had been Newcastle in 1955. They scraped by Blackpool at the second attempt after fog had caused the first game to be abandoned, then only a superb display by Trautmann saw them past Southend, where the game was played in a quagmire studded with cockleshells - which had been added to aid drainage but which played havoc with the players' knees. Next up were Liverpool, who were dispatched in a replay only after the referee disallowed a Billy Liddell goal because he had blown for time fractionally before the ball crossed the line. Everton were distinctly unlucky not to earn at least a quarter-final replay, and the semi-final victory over Spurs - which, to be fair, the Mancunians did deserve - was achieved amid loud controversy. Late in the second half, with City one up through Bobby Johnstone, Tottenham winger George Robb appeared to be on the point of equalising when Trautmann grabbed his leg. Amazingly, there was no penalty and the Maine Road side were through. It was a particularly satisfying moment for captain Roy Paul, who after the 1955 defeat had promised supporters 'We'll be back next year.' It's something most losers say, but a pledge that few manage to keep. Astonishingly enough, a previous City

Manchester City boss Les McDowall, whose stormy relationship with Revie did not prevent him calling 'The Don' into his side at the 11th hour.

Above: The final nail. The subtly skilful Scot Bobby Johnstone tucks home Manchester City's third goal following a precise lay-off from Jack Dyson.

Opposite top: The pride of Maine Road.
Back row (left to right): W Griffiths (secretary), A Douglas, R Smith, W Smith, F Jolly, E Gill (all directors).
Middle row: Laurie Barnett (trainer), Ken Barnes, Bill Leivers, Bert Trautmann, Dave Ewing, Roy Little, Les McDowall (manager).
Front row: Bobby Johnstone, Joe Hayes, Roy Paul, Don Revie, Jack Dyson, Roy Clarke.

skipper, Sam Cowan, had mouthed similar words after losing in 1933 - and led his team to triumph a year later.

Meanwhile, the Maine Road camp had other problems. The gifted, but strong-willed Revie had missed half the League programme and had played in only one Cup match because of strife between him and the management. It was believed his future lay elsewhere - he was to join Sunderland that summer - and that McDowall was in the process of adapting the 'Revie Plan', involving a constructive, deep-lying centre-forward, to become the 'Johnstone Plan', with the gifted little Scot at its hub. Some three hours before the final, there was no place for Revie, but when Bill Spurdle withdrew with an attack of boils, the Maine Road boss - after much agonising and bearing in mind that Johnstone was carrying a calf strain - opted for Don's experience rather than recall Johnny Hart. So eight of Manchester's class of '55 lined up for a second final, Wembley 'hoodoo' victim Jimmy Meadows, Spurdle and Fionan Fagan being replaced, after a slight reshuffle, by Bill Leivers at right-back, Lancashire cricketer Jack Dyson up front, and

Typical Trautmann. The courageous German throws himself headlong at the feet of Birmingham centre-forward Eddy Brown while defender Bill Leivers attempts to intervene. In a similar act of derring-do, Bert broke his neck.

Roy Clarke, absent with injury a year ago, on the left wing. Birmingham were one man short of full strength, John Newman taking the Warhurst role that had been filled by Jack Badham in the semi-final.

The northerners, assaulting the eyeballs in their Continental-style maroon-and-white-striped change strip, got off to a perfect start, and one which questioned their wisdom in ever contemplating the exclusion of Revie. Three minutes into the action, the 'thinking man's footballer' slid the ball to Clarke on the left flank, ran forward to take the return, then executed an exquisite sole-of-the-boot lay-off that left the Brummies' defence hopelessly wrong-footed and set up Joe Hayes for an emphatic close-range opener. Now Manchester City, beautifully orchestrated by Revie, threatened to get on top of opponents who simply never played to their potential.

However, Brown had other ideas, dashing dynamically down the right before crossing for the canny Noel Kinsey to convert with a firm shot that went in off a post. Now the excellent Boyd, playing with a corset to support a long-standing back weakness, drove his colleagues on, but the Mancunians slowly assumed mastery. In truth, they were claiming their just deserts when the perceptive Ken Barnes freed Dyson for their second goal midway through the second half and, three minutes later, Dyson flicked on a Trautmann punt for Johnstone to become the first man to score in successive finals. Now there was no way back for Birmingham - apart from a brief sally during Trautmann's period of trauma - and they finished runners-up in their second final as they had been in their first. Thus the Cup went back to Maine Road for the third time (the product of six finals) and suddenly for City fans, Manchester United's recent League title triumph was not quite so difficult to bear.

Don Revie takes a well-earned draught from the Cup he did so much to secure. And yet if it hadn't been for poor Bill Spurdle's boils, he would not have made the team for Wembley.

4 May 1957

ASTON VILLA 2

McParland 65, 71

MANCHESTER UNITED 1

Taylor 83

Half-time 0-0

ASTON VILLA	○	MANCHESTER UNITED
Nigel Sims	1	Ray Wood
Stan Lynn	2	Bill Foulkes
Peter Aldis	3	Roger Byrne *(captain)*
Stan Crowther	4	Eddie Colman
Jimmy Dugdale	5	Jackie Blanchflower
Pat Saward	6	Duncan Edwards
Les Smith	7	John Berry
Jackie Sewell	8	Liam Whelan
Bill Myerscough	9	Tommy Taylor
Johnny Dixon *(captain)*	10	Bobby Charlton
Peter McParland	11	David Pegg

Attendance: 100,000

Referee: F Coultas, Hull

Above right: The man who made Manchester United steps out at the head of his most irresistible combination. Matt Busby leads the Babes, left to right, Roger Byrne, Johnny Berry, Jackie Blanchflower, Ray Wood, Bill Foulkes, Bobby Charlton, Tommy Taylor, Liam Whelan, Duncan Edwards and David Pegg. Little Eddie Colman is obscured by the colossus Edwards.

Often during the 20th century there had been careless talk of the League and FA Cup double. Almost every year the claims of one or more candidates to attain what was then the holy grail of English football were advanced, only for them to wither and die with seeming inevitability in the spring sunshine. But now, for the first time since Queen Victoria was on her throne, there was a team hailed widely as both worthy and capable of achieving the Herculean feat. Manchester United's Busby Babes were the first newly-crowned League champions for 60 years to reach the FA Cup Final. They were the best side in the land by a long way and one of the finest in the world; indeed, it had taken the incomparable Real Madrid to end their hopes of a *treble* in the European Cup semi-final nine days before Wembley. Now only mid-table Aston Villa, a solid team of modest pretensions, stood between the Red Devils and the ultimate accolade. It seemed nothing less than an act of God, a collective brainstorm or some monstrous misfortune could stop them now. And sure enough it did. In fact, the emissary of fate was clad in claret and blue stripes and answered to the name of Peter McParland. Excellent and honest player though he was, the Irish winger was to be the instrument of possibly the

1957

grossest miscarriage of natural sporting justice seen on a football field for many a day.

As Matt Busby, who had shown such insight in breaking up his ageing 1952 title-winning combination to give youth its fling, led United out at Wembley, it was an appropriate moment to reflect on his latest creation. Leading the attack was England's ebullient Tommy Taylor; at inside-forward were the shuffling Irish artist Liam Whelan and Bobby Charlton, an explosive new talent who was to mature into one of the all-time greats, yet was playing now only because of a groin injury to the subtly incisive Dennis Viollet; on the wings were young David Pegg and the more experienced Johnny Berry. That sparkling quintet plied their wares in front of a half-back line comprising Eddie 'Snakehips' Colman, the cultured Jackie Blanchflower and the young leviathan, Duncan Edwards, while 'keeper Ray Wood and right-back Bill Foulkes offered defensive dependability alongside their masterly skipper, Roger Byrne. Weaknesses there were none, and as United got off to a confident start the destination of the Cup appeared as certain as anything in soccer can ever be. But then, after six min-

Above: A split second after this picture was taken, the Red Devils' hopes of lifting the League and FA Cup double lay in tatters. United custodian Ray Wood had the ball securely in his hands but Villa winger Peter McParland continued his headlong charge, heads crashed together and the 'keeper played no effective part in the remaining 84 minutes of the match.

utes, the contest was transformed. Ray Wood gathered a straightforward header by McParland, then took a step forward with the ball in his arms as the Villa winger charged towards him like a runaway bulldozer. It seemed certain that the Irishman must draw back at the last instant, but he kept coming and barged into the United man at full throttle. There was a sickening clash of heads and both players stretched their length on the Wembley turf; soon McParland sat up but Wood remained motionless, blood trickling down his cheek. After a cursory examination, the stricken Ray was stretchered off - Bert Trautmann's broken neck a year earlier had made the spectre of a potentially fatal injury especially vivid - and with him went the Red Devils' dreams of the double. No one other than outraged United fans suggested the challenge had been malicious, but what upset most people - including neutral observers - was the utter needlessness of it. For all practical purposes, the ball was dead the moment Wood had caught it; there was no danger to the goal, four yards away, and no legitimate advantage to be gained by following through. Unless there was some reckless intention to test the 'keeper's resolution, it

must be put down as a rush of blood to McParland's head. Referee Frank Coultas, who did not punish the assailant, could offer little enlightenment, telling the press later: 'McParland wasn't trying to harm Wood. He was just too robust, too emphatic at playing the British game of getting stuck in.' As if that made it all right!

Of course, 84 minutes of the match remained and with the scoresheet blank there was still, at least in theory, everything to play for. Charlton, who often went between the posts in training, expected the job now, but the green jersey was tossed to Blanchflower, who wore it with a distinction none could have expected. United's enforced reshuffle saw Edwards move to centre-half and Whelan drop back to left-half, and it's a remarkable tribute to their all-round ability that they both vied with the emergency custodian to be popular choice as man of the match. For ten minutes after the accident, the game became extremely physical, with several Mancunians seemingly intent on revenge, but as the half wore on the venom subsided and the footballing exchanges proved pretty even. Blanchflower dealt coolly with everything that came his way and shortly before the interval United were boosted by the return of Wood, albeit as a virtual invalid on the right wing.

But as the second period progressed, Villa - for whom skipper Johnny Dixon gave an outstanding display at inside-left - gradually wore down their overtaxed opponents and began to dominate.

Above: After the impact. Wood and McParland are stretched out on the turf as anxious teammates and officials cluster around. Inset left: United captain Roger Byrne examines the disorientated Wood, watched by Bobby Charlton and Duncan Edwards (right). Below: Ray Wood wanders forlornly at the shoulder of United physio Ted Dalton after a test behind the Wembley stands has revealed him unfit to continue in goal.

Main picture: Bobby Charlton, a dazzling new star in the Old Trafford firmament, shoots explosively but his effort is blocked by Villa's Jimmy Dugdale.

Inset: Beaten at last. The gallant Jackie Blanchflower, who performed heroically as emergency 'keeper, can only stand and stare as McParland's bullet header gives Aston Villa the lead.

Ironically their liveliest attacker - and ultimate match-winner - was the sinewy, speedy McParland, who proved a constant menace cutting inside Foulkes, and when he fashioned the breakthrough, just after the hour, it was no surprise. Having issued fair warning by hitting a post from a Jackie Sewell pass, McParland went one better when he met a Dixon cross with a magnificent header which rocketed high into the net from near the penalty spot. Then, six minutes later, McParland struck again, running back from an offside position to volley home from six yards after a shot from his ubiquitous captain had rebounded from the

angle of bar and post. Since half-time Tommy Taylor and his depleted line had been held comfortably by stopper Jimmy Dugdale and company, but now Roger Byrne urged his men on to another desperate effort. Villa were forced to defend in depth as United's superior quality began to assert itself despite the odds, and with seven minutes left, Taylor spawned new hope when he found the net with a looping header from an Edwards corner. That was the signal for one last gamble, the disorientated Wood returning to his goal to free Blanchflower to support a do-or-die blitz on the Midlanders' stronghold. Now the Red Devils forced a string

Inset left: McParland strikes again, cracking home a searing volley after Johnny Dixon had rapped United's woodwork. Inset right: Defiant to the end. Tommy Taylor (hidden) nets with a header to give the Red Devils late hope.

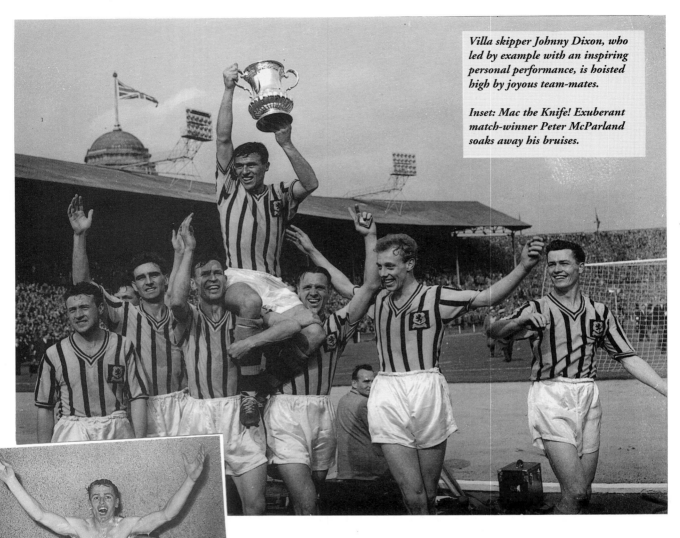

Opposite: The Aston Villa underdogs who defeated the Busby Babes, albeit with a little help from that most fickle of mistresses, Dame Fortune. Back row (left to right): Peter Aldis, Stan Lynn, Nigel Sims, Stan Crowther, Peter McParland. Middle row: Eric Houghton (manager), Jackie Sewell, Bill Myerscough, Johnny Dixon, Les Smith, W Moore (trainer). Front row: Jimmy Dugdale, Pat Saward.

of corners, Whelan netted only to be judged unarguably offside, and the Cup went to Villa Park for a record seventh time. No one on the pitch had outshone Tynesider Dixon and it was fitting that he should be the man to receive the trophy from the Queen. Excelling alongside him throughout the game had been McParland, who showed admirable temperament to rise above the controversy and play so well, and right-half Stan Crowther, whose hard, industrious display made him a target when United needed urgent reinforcements in the horrific situation that overtook them the following season.

Most observers believed that but for the loss of Wood, the Old Trafford side would have completed the double at their ease, but that is unfair to Aston Villa. FA Cup history is littered with shock results and the spirited underdogs might well have triumphed in normal circumstances. Busby's tactical reaction to the central incident provoked heated debate, some pundits maintaining that he should have reinstated Wood earlier and relied on the team's outfield superiority to protect him. But that is an unworthy, unfeeling argument, placing the result of a game - no matter how significant - above an individual's future welfare. At half-time, United physio Ted Dalton had taken Ray behind the stand and tested his capabilities; suffering from double vision and periodic blackouts as he was, they were negligible. No, Matt Busby was right to take the only humane decision possible. It was to his utmost credit, too, that he never made the injury an excuse for defeat, though he did use it to press for a rule-change that had long been dear to his heart - the introduction of substitutes. As the Wembley 'hoodoo' continued, more and more people in the game echoed his cry - it was, after all, the voice of reason - but still the diehards claimed that unscrupulous clubs would abuse such a system by replacing players who were not injured, and substitutes were not allowed until the mid-1960s. In this, as in so much else, the future Sir Matt was way ahead of his time.

So dramatic were the events of the 1957 final that little space remains to do justice to the exciting campaigns enjoyed by both clubs in reaching it. Villa's progress was a tribute to their doggedness, which enabled them to come from behind to beat Luton, Middlesbrough, Burnley, then local rivals West Bromwich Albion in the semi-final. They needed three replays and owed much to McParland, whose brace of Wembley goals took his Cup tally to seven, and the clever Sewell, who scored the winner against Bristol City. (Incidentally, it was a telling sign of the times that Jackie remained the League's most expensive player more than six years after his record-breaking £34,500 move from Notts County to Sheffield Wednesday). United's Cup conquests had included minnows Hartlepools, who fought back from a 3-0 deficit to level the scores only for Liam Whelan to spoil their celebrations with a late winner, and Bournemouth, who had beaten Wolves and Spurs already and led at half-time before bowing out to the odd goal in three. In the last four they faced a resolute Birmingham, whose presence completed a trio of 'Second City' semi-finalists, winning through with goals from former St Andrews favourite Johnny Berry and Bobby Charlton.

Come the end of their stirring season, the Babes were disappointed by such a frustrating failure to take the double - oddly enough, the last double-winners were Aston Villa in 1897, aided by a considerably less crowded fixture list - but as the Cup Final programme noted, for such a young team the best years must surely lie ahead. In the light of the calamity that befell Manchester United on a snowbound German runway ten months later, those words were to prove heart-rendingly poignant.

IT HAPPENED
THIS YEAR

West Indian Gary
Sobers' highest score
in Test history, 365
not out against
Pakistan.

Britain's motorists
confronted by first
parking meters and
yellow lines.

Opening of Britain's
first stretch of
motorway, the
Preston bypass.

Race riots flared in
London's Notting Hill
Gate.

Formation of
Campaign for
Nuclear
Disarmament.

3 May 1958

BOLTON WANDERERS 2

Lofthouse 3, 55

MANCHESTER UNITED 0

Half-time 1-0

BOLTON WANDERERS	○	MANCHESTER UNITED
Eddie Hopkinson	1	Harry Gregg
Roy Hartle	2	Bill Foulkes *(captain)*
Tommy Banks	3	Ian Greaves
Derek Hennin	4	Freddie Goodwin
John Higgins	5	Ron Cope
Bryan Edwards	6	Stan Crowther
Brian Birch	7	Alex Dawson
Dennis Stevens	8	Ernie Taylor
Nat Lofthouse *(captain)*	9	Bobby Charlton
Ray Parry	10	Dennis Viollet
Doug Holden	11	Colin Webster

Attendance: 100,000

Referee: J Sherlock, Sheffield

'The fact that you have got this far is a miracle. All I want to say is "Thank you" from the bottom of my heart for all you have done. Win, lose or draw, I am proud of you.' The words came from Jimmy Murphy, assistant manager of Manchester United, addressing his patchwork side before they went into battle against Bolton Wanderers at Wembley. His sentiments were echoed not only by football fans everywhere, but by millions of people normally without the slightest shred of interest in the game, whose emotions had been captured by the catastrophe of Munich.

It was the sporting tragedy of the age. The League champions had been on their way home from a European Cup quarter-final in Belgrade when their plane had stopped to refuel at the snowy German airport; two attempts at take-off had been foiled by the weather, the third ended in the crash that claimed 23 lives and left others scarred forever. Among the eventual death toll were six of the 1957 FA Cup Final team - skipper Roger Byrne, Eddie Colman, Duncan Edwards, Liam Whelan, Tommy Taylor and David Pegg - together with centre-half Mark Jones

and reserve full-back Geoff Bent. Club secretary Walter Crickmer, coach Bert Whalley and trainer Tom Curry also perished, as did two crew members, two other passengers and eight journalists, including Frank Swift, the former Manchester City and England goalkeeper. Johnny Berry and Jackie Blanchflower were so badly injured they would never play again. Matt Busby, manager and inspiration of his club, hovered between life and death in an oxygen tent, his chest crushed.

It was against such a background that Jimmy Murphy led Manchester United from the fifth round to the final of the FA Cup, borne along by an unprecedented groundswell of public sympathy which gripped the nation and reached near-hysterical intensity on the terraces for the remainder of the campaign. But before examining that monumental achievement, it is right to make one thing clear. Despite a Wembley controversy reminiscent of the previous term's Wood-McParland episode, Bolton were worthy winners of the trophy. Having been engulfed by a tidal wave of euphoria over Stanley Matthews in 1953, it was hard

Above: Dennis Viollet, recalled to the United side for Wembley despite having played only twice since Munich, meets Prince Philip, watched by (left to right) Alex Dawson, Bobby Charlton and Ernie Taylor. Come the game Viollet, who had missed the previous final through injury, was understandably subdued.

*Above: Rough-and-ready
wing-half Stan Crowther,
the emergency signing
from Aston Villa who had
helped defeat United in
1957. He never had the
class for a long-term Old
Trafford career and after
plugging a temporary gap
he moved to Chelsea a
few months later.*

*Right: Harry Gregg, the
second United 'keeper to
be embroiled in FA Cup
Final controversy in
successive seasons. To
his credit, the fiery
Irishman never held a
lasting grudge against
Nat Lofthouse for his
violent barge and today
the two men are the best
of friends.*

lines, indeed, that when they next reached the final they should be cast again in the role of 'the other team'. They coped with a difficult situation professionally and with dignity, and deserve enormous credit. However, it would be idle to deny that the spotlight rested almost exclusively on United.

Though the Football Association gave the club an extra four days to prepare for their fifth-round tie against Sheffield Wednesday at Old Trafford, it was asking a superhuman effort of Murphy and his back-up staff to put out a team just two weeks after the disaster. Not only was he shorn of seven dead, the dying Duncan Edwards and the two whose careers were finished, but also the likes of Bobby Charlton, Dennis Viollet, Albert Scanlon and Kenny Morgans were not yet ready for action. With only two survivors from Munich - goalkeeper Harry Gregg and full-back Bill Foulkes - to call on for that first match, how did Jimmy do it? Later he confessed he had been at his wits' end, but managed somehow through a combination of hasty dips into the transfer market and the promotion of youngsters from the reserves and even the third team. At one stage, the shrewd little Welshman had toyed with the idea of going for the great Hungarian Ferenc Puskas, but that proved unrealistic and he lowered his sights. Even so, he did well in acquiring the services of veteran schemer Ernie Taylor - a Wembley winner with Newcastle in 1951 and Blackpool two years later - and combative wing-half Stan Crowther, who had impressed for Aston Villa in the 1957 final. So with Foulkes as captain, the brave new United ran out to face a Wednesday side who must have wished they were somewhere else. They simply never had a chance against a make-do-and-mend outfit buoyed up by the sea of raw feeling that Old Trafford had become that night. United won 3-0, with two of the goals supplied by 20-year-old Shay Brennan, later to win top honours at right-back but then turning out as a makeshift left winger. Any celebrations, though, were savagely curtailed two days later with the news that the incomparable Duncan Edwards had succumbed in hospital to multiple injuries received in the crash. He, more than any other player, had been the symbol of the Busby Babes, and a more bitter blow was impossible to imagine.

Nevertheless, United had pledged to go on, and now Murphy's mixture of men and boys faced a quarter-final clash away to one of the leading League sides, West Bromwich Albion. Public opinion was that while they had won once through sheer emotion, reality would now reassert itself. However with Taylor - irreverently but affectionately christened 'Uncle Ernie' by his young team-mates - at his creative peak, and with Bobby Charlton - more mature and serious since his ordeal - back in the side, the Reds

managed to earn a replay. At Old Trafford, Albion pounded them mercilessly but without piercing a rearguard in which young centre-half Ron Cope was outstanding, and three minutes from time Charlton dashed down the right flank to lay on a simple winner for Colin Webster. Incredibly, the 'impossible dream' of battling through to Wembley was still alive; indeed, with the prospect of meeting Second Division Fulham in the semi-final, it had become a definite possibility. By now the Cup adventure of Murphy's gallant remnants was making front-page news as well as supplying headlines for the back pages but, quite rightly, the Cottagers were not going to surrender their own ambitions to speed the Reds' ever-more-romantic progress. Accordingly the match at Villa Park was desperately close with Fulham, inspired by Johnny Haynes, leading until a Charlton thunderbolt near the end forced a draw. Such was the popular support for United that the replay, though played at Highbury, might have been a home match for the Mancunians, who won an exhilarating tussle 5-3. Charlton, increasingly influential, scored another brilliant goal and 18-year-old Alex Dawson plundered a hat-trick, though it must be admitted that Fulham 'keeper Tony Macedo endured a 'stinker'.

Nothing, however, could detract from United's prodigious feat, certainly not the exploits of poor, unsung Bolton, who merited high praise for the way in which they had disposed of Tom Finney's Preston, survived a scare and a replay against courageous little York City, defeated Second Division Stoke City with comparative ease and then unseated League Champions-elect Wolves in the quarter-final. Wanderers went into their all-Lancashire semi-final against Blackburn Rovers deprived of their trump card, England centre-forward Nat Lofthouse, who had broken his shoulder. As it happened, they needn't have worried, as Nat's stand-in - reserve winger Ralph Gubbins - scored both goals in a 2-1 win. Thus the Trotters were back at Wembley, though with only two of the side that had faced Matthews five years earlier - the fit-again Lofthouse and winger Doug Holden. They were known as the '£110 team', as each member had cost only a £10 signing-on fee; yet with defenders who tackled like man-traps and everyone capable of doing the simple things well, they were not to be taken lightly as they strove towards their first trophy since lifting the Cup three times in the 1920s.

Meanwhile Murphy had a considerable selection problem. With the classy Viollet back in contention, despite having played only twice since the crash, Jimmy had to choose between him and young Mark 'Pancho' Pearson, who had done so well on the road to the final. In the end he opted for the older man's

The men of Bolton who were on a hiding to nothing as United rode a tide of public sympathy. In fact, the Trotters' Wembley win was fully merited.
Back row (left to right): Bill Ridding (manager), Roy Hartle, Derek Hennin, Eddie Hopkinson, Gordon Edwards John Higgins, Bryan Edwards, Bert Sproston (trainer).
Front row: Brian Birch, Dennis Stevens, Nat Lofthouse, W H Warburton (chairman), Ray Parry, Doug Holden, Tommy Banks.

Left: The pain and the pride. Still suffering from the terrible injuries he received at Munich, Matt Busby (left) sits on the Wembley bench alongside his faithful lieutenant Jimmy Murphy. The ebullient Welshman had been in sole charge since the disaster and had worked wonders in taking his patchwork side to the FA Cup Final.

Three minutes gone at Wembley and 'The Lion of Vienna' roars. Nat Lofthouse prods home Bolton's opener with United 'keeper Harry Gregg and defender Stan Crowther powerless to intervene.

experience, bringing anguish to Pearson and also disappointing gallant contributors such as Shay Brennan, Kenny Morgans and Wilf McGuinness. United's cause received a massive pre-match boost when it was announced that Matt Busby would attend, though he had been advised he was not fit enough for the exertion. Nothing could keep him from such an occasion, however, and, looking heartachingly frail, he took his place on the bench alongside his faithful lieutenant.

After such a hectic build-up - the Reds had been forced to clear the backlog of fixtures caused by the tragedy, playing 13 times between March 22 and April 26 - the final was always likely to result in something of a letdown from a United viewpoint, and so it proved. They had come so far on fervour and fortune, and now came the day of reckoning. It started badly when, after three minutes, a speculative pass from Bolton wing-half Bryan Edwards was deflected into the path of Lofthouse, who netted simply from five yards. Thereafter the Wanderers always looked the more controlled and powerful unit, though Charlton did bring one superb first-half save from Eddie Hopkinson. The dramatic sequence of events that decided the outcome came shortly after the interval. First Taylor, for once escaping the ruthless markers who had stymied most of his promptings, set up Charlton for a blistering 15-yard drive that left Hopkinson leaden-footed, only to cannon off the inside of a post into the arms of the grateful custodian. Then the action switched to the other end where Dennis Stevens - a cousin of Duncan Edwards - unleashed a stinging shot which Gregg could only push into the air; as the Irishman caught the ball, Lofthouse bore down and barged into him with all his might; goalkeeper and ball were sent flying into the net and the referee signalled a goal. Today such a challenge would be penalised instantly, and even in 1958 - when 'keepers enjoyed far less protection - many observers were convinced it was a blatant foul. Nevertheless, it stood and it proved the killer for the over-stretched Reds. Now no-frills Bolton were able to cruise through the rest of the

Left: The infamous clash that infuriated and puzzled many Manchester United supporters, though to their eternal credit, the club never whinged. In the main picture Nat Lofthouse, left elbow extended, bundles Harry Gregg over the line to put Bolton two goals in front. Above: the goal already given, a shaken Gregg is treated where he fell.

Main picture: There is a spring in the Lofthouse stride as he leads his men towards the royal box.

Inset right: Time for a cuddle. Nat celebrates with Trotters boss Bill Ridding, while United skipper Bill Foulkes takes a more sombre view.

Below: 'If you can't look on . . . look in.' Sound advice from an advertisement in the match programme.

match and Lofthouse duly collected the silverware from Prince Philip.

Hard though it was for United supporters to take at the end of such a grievous season, Nat was claiming his just reward, both on the day and as the crowning glory of a magnificent career. Matt Busby reacted in the only way he knew how - with consummate grace - by limping into the Bolton dressing room, supported by his walking stick, and congratulating each man in turn. It was the climax of an afternoon of pain, distress and pride which drained the ailing Scot to an overwhelming degree, yet those close to him maintained that it rekindled some

inner flame which had seemed in danger of being extinguished forever. For now it
seemed all that remained was the return to Manchester, where tears fell
unashamedly among the countless thousands of men, women and children who
lined the streets to greet the heroes who had given so much over the past three
months. Yet staggeringly, just five days later, the Red Devils roused themselves
once more to beat AC Milan 2-1 in the first leg of the European Cup semi-final at
Old Trafford. A 4-0 defeat at San Siro followed, but the message to the football
world was loud and clear: Manchester United would rise again.

2 May 1959

NOTTINGHAM FOREST 2
Dwight 10; Wilson 14

LUTON TOWN 1
Pacey 62

Half-time 2-0

NOTTINGHAM FOREST		LUTON TOWN
Chick Thomson	1	Ron Baynham
Bill Whare	2	Brendan McNally
Joe McDonald	3	Ken Hawkes
Jeff Whitefoot	4	John Groves
Bobby McKinlay	5	Syd Owen *(captain)*
Jack Burkitt *(captain)*	6	Dave Pacey
Roy Dwight	7	Billy Bingham
John Quigley	8	Allan Brown
Tommy Wilson	9	Bob Morton
Billy Gray	10	George Cummins
Stuart Imlach	11	Tony Gregory

Attendance: 100,000

Referee: J Clough, Bolton

Asked to name a selection of the most memorable post-War FA Cup Finals, few people would give a second thought to a clash between two unfashionable teams from the wrong half of the First Division, mustering between them only one player - Billy Bingham - who might qualify for the 'star' category. Yet Nottingham Forest's meeting with Luton Town contained half an hour of the brightest attacking football Wembley had witnessed that decade, an infusion of drama as the injury 'hoodoo' struck again, a stirring rearguard action and a pulsating finish. Admittedly, it was by no means a fully-blown classic, yet it was anything but humdrum and deserves an honourable niche in the history of English soccer's annual showpiece.

Neither club was rich in Cup tradition - Forest had won the trophy in 1898 but had never been to Wembley, Luton had never progressed beyond the quarter-final stage - but both, in their contrasting ways, were monuments to the worthiest values of the Football League. The

Top: Men of substance.
Veteran captains Jack
Burkitt of Nottingham
Forest (left) and Luton
Town's Syd Owen, the
reigning Footballer of the
Year, perform the ritual
pleasantries watched by
referee J Clough of
Bolton. Mr Clough had
been in the running to
officiate at each of the
previous six finals but
each time his chance had
been scuppered by a
Lancashire team
reaching Wembley.

Below: Bobby McKinlay,
whose massive authority
at centre-half helped
Forest survive a late
Luton onslaught.

Trentsiders, in their 20th year of Billy Walker's management, were renowned for their attractive approach - some things never change! - while the Hatters stood for hard graft and solidity. Indeed, since joining Division Three in 1920 they had never been relegated, rising eventually to the top flight in 1955.

Remarkably, both sides were to remain unchanged throughout their Cup runs. Forest owed much to a splendid half-back trio comprising skipper Jack Burkitt, stopper Bobby McKinlay and former Busby Babe Jeff Whitefoot. Inside-forwards John Quigley and Billy Gray laboured constructively in midfield, with most of the goals coming from centre-forward Tommy Wilson and right winger Roy Dwight. Managerless Luton - Dally Duncan had left for Blackburn in October - relied heavily on Syd Owen, their 37-year-old centre-half, skipper and coach. Shortly before facing Forest, Syd was named as Footballer of the Year, a fitting end to a distinguished playing career of which the final would be his last match before putting aside his boots to take over as Luton boss. Other important figures were the Northern Ireland and ex-Sunderland winger Bingham, former Scotland inside-right Allan Brown, England 'keeper Ron Baynham and the versatile Bob Morton, who during 1958/59 was called into the England squad himself, only to lose international impetus when the Hatters shifted him from wing-half to centre-forward.

Neither club enjoyed comfortable paths to Wembley. Indeed, Forest survived an embarrassing third-round scrape against non-League Tooting and Mitcham, who were leading their supposed betters by two goals with only 40 minutes of the game left. Then fortune frowned on the minnows, their 'keeper being beaten by a wicked bounce on an icy surface which transformed a sedate back-pass into a fluke own-goal, and then a hotly-disputed penalty. Back at the City Ground,

*Opposite: Lone star.
Billy Bingham of Luton
Town and Northern
Ireland, the only 'big
name' on display.*

HOW THEY GOT THERE

NOTTINGHAM FOREST
Round 3:
Tooting and Mitcham (a) 2-2, replay (h) 3-0.

Round 4:
Grimsby Town (h) 4-1.

Round 5:
Birmingham City (a) 1-1, replay (h) 1-1, second replay *at Filbert Street* 5-0.

Round 6:
Bolton Wanderers (h) 2-1.

Semi-final:
Aston Villa *at Hillsborough* 1-0.

LUTON TOWN
Round 3:
Leeds United (h) 5-1.

Round 4:
Leicester City (a) 1-1, replay (h) 4-1.

Round 5:
Ipswich Town (a) 5-2.

Round 6:
Blackpool (a) 1-1, replay (h) 1-0.

Semi-final:
Norwich City *at White Hart Lane* 1-1, replay *at St Andrews* 1-0.

Forest duly dispatched the Isthmian League side 3-0, then swept confidently past Grimsby Town, before coming perilously close to elimination at the hands of Birmingham City. Late strikes by Wilson at St Andrews and Dwight at the City Ground earned them a second replay, in which they finally trounced the Brummies 5-0, with Dwight notching a hat-trick. Wilson was the hero again, his two goals seeing off holders Bolton in the quarter-final, then Quigley snatched the only goal of a taut semi-final victory over Aston Villa.

While Forest were fretting against Tooting, Luton made a convincing start to their campaign, crushing Leeds United 5-1, but Leicester City proved less accommodating in the fourth round. At a frost-bound Filbert Street, the hosts took the lead and looked to be on their way through when Bingham, having switched to centre-forward, prodded an equaliser. However, back home the Town won convincingly, as they did at Ipswich in the fifth round, but two infinitely more daunting obstacles lay between them and their ultimate objective. First came Cup favourites Blackpool, whom Allan Brown had helped to reach the final in 1951 and 1953, only to miss both games through injury. Now he was to take a decisive step towards Wembley at the expense of his former employers, netting the winner at Kenilworth after a 1-1 draw at Bloomfield Road. That Allan should be the Seasiders' executioner was ironic, but at least it enabled their more charitable supporters to congratulate a former hero on his change of luck. Now Luton faced Norwich in the semi-final, and for all the Canaries' valiant deeds in dumping Manchester United and Spurs out of the competition, it would have been a faint-hearted Hatter who was not anticipating a relatively straightforward passage. But

Above right: Allan Brown, who as a Blackpool man had been forced to sit out two FA Cup Finals with injury, finally made it on to the pitch with Luton.

Right: Winger Roy Dwight (arms raised, left) salutes his tenth-minute opener for Nottingham Forest, a crisp drive from Stuart Imlach's cross.

the East Anglians were to decree otherwise, taking thousands of fanatical followers to the White Hart Lane confrontation, then scaring the living daylights out of Luton by coming from behind to grab a well-earned second chance. With Syd Owen finding his hands full in mastering Norwich's prolific marksman Terry Bly, the Canaries gave a good account of themselves once more and it took a Bingham goal against the run of play - Billy scored in every round - to book his side's Wembley ticket.

Ron Baynham, whose international career was curtailed by the plethora of outstanding English goalkeepers in the 1950s, watches a Forest shot whistle high and wide.

The identity of the finalists did little to excite the pundits, who were predicting a drab match. To be fair, the springtime form of Forest and Luton gave the snipers plenty of ammunition as they both slumped down the table, and tales of internecine strife in the two camps over Cup Final 'perks' exacerbated the situation. With the Hatters playing 14 games and the Trentsiders 13 between semi-final and final, there was ample opportunity to analyse strengths and weaknesses, with a particular opportunity afforded by the meeting of the two at Kenilworth Road. That ended in a swingeing 5-1 victory to the home side, with Brown scoring four, but as a portent for the future it could hardly have proved more inaccurate.

Come the day of the match, there were no selection surprises, though those who had clamoured for the recall of Luton's out-of-favour goal-scorer Gordon Turner were to claim some vindication. As the opening exchanges got under way, the Hatters appeared to have no attacking ideas and Forest swarmed all over them, passing sweetly and tearing gaping holes in their defence. So one-sided was the action that a Nottingham goal seemed only a matter of time, and after several close calls, the inevitable occurred, Quigley freeing outside-left Stuart Imlach, whose pull-back into the stride of Dwight was driven emphatically into the roof of the Luton net. Still the red tide did not abate, and five minutes later Forest struck again when Wilson nodded home Gray's delightfully weighted diagonal cross. Now the floodgates were poised to open and only some elastic saves by the lanky Baynham kept his tormentors at bay.

But suddenly, on 33 minutes, the whole tenor of the contest changed in

Below: Spot the likeness? Roy Dwight, Elton John's uncle, who experienced the extremes of emotion at Wembley. After scoring a splendid goal, he was carried off with a broken leg (inset below) and watched the climax of the match on a hospital television.

Bottom: New hope for the Hatters. A posse of Forest defenders are powerless to prevent Dave Pacey pulling back a goal for Luton, setting up an exciting last half-hour.

distressing, though wholly accidental circumstances. Dwight seemed slightly unbalanced as he went into a tackle with Brendan McNally, and the awkward impact fractured the winger's shin. As he left on a stretcher, Roy - who was to watch the closing stages of the game on a hospital television - was sporting enough to exonerate the Irish defender from blame, but the damage had been done. Forest faced the prospect of surviving for almost an hour with ten men, though it should be pointed out that McNally, too, had suffered in the collision and was unable to move freely for the remainder of the game. Now Luton sniffed salvation for what had looked for all the world like a lost cause, and began to move forward with renewed purpose. It was the signal for Forest, earlier so ebullient on the offensive, to display their mettle at the back. The greatest danger came from the skill and pace of Bingham and Brown on the Hatters' right flank, but full-back Joe McDonald was adroit in combating the wiles of his former Roker Park team-mate while Burkitt and company shackled Brown intelligently.

After the break Luton advanced resolutely and both Burkitt and right-back Bill Whare needed treatment after heavy challenges. Afterwards some critics felt Syd Owen's men had been too cautious during this period, but that was hardly true after Dave Pacey had halved the arrears by hammering home a Ken Hawkes pass from ten yards. With a little less than half an hour remaining, Luton committed themselves to attack, yet no matter how strenuous their efforts became, they lacked inspiration. The Forest rearguard, with McKinlay majestic, retained its composure, endeavouring to play their way out of trouble with measured football, and it paid off handsomely. Clear-cut chances were scarce and when one finally presented itself to Brown, just four minutes from time, he headed Bingham's centre narrowly wide. So Forest took the Cup with an excellent all-round performance, leaving Luton to rue a display that was disappointing from the outset. Sadly, it was to prove an isolated peak for that particular Nottingham combination, which was never to play together in its entirety again. Indeed, after a poor 1959/60, Billy Walker was to retire and a City Ground era was to end. For Luton the future was even more traumatic, Owen leading them to relegation in his only term in charge, and then resigning. On a wider front, the injury to Dwight - incidentally the uncle of one Reg Dwight, later to become rather better known as rock star and Watford chairman Elton John - produced the ritual calls for substitutes and the equally ritual negative response from the authorities. Happily, though, more enlightened counsels were making themselves heard; the days of the dinosaurs were numbered.

Twelve years after joining Forest from non-League football, 33-year-old Jack Burkitt crowns his career by lifting the FA Cup.

7 May 1960

WOLVERHAMPTON WANDERERS 3

McGrath (og) 41; Deeley 68, 88

BLACKBURN ROVERS 0

Half-time 1-0

WOLVERHAMPTON WANDERERS		BLACKBURN ROVERS
Malcolm Finlayson	1	Harry Leyland
George Showell	2	John Bray
Gerry Harris	3	Dave Whelan
Eddie Clamp	4	Ronnie Clayton *(captain)*
Bill Slater *(captain)*	5	Matt Woods
Ron Flowers	6	Mick McGrath
Norman Deeley	7	Louis Bimpson
Barry Stobart	8	Peter Dobing
Jimmy Murray	9	Derek Dougan
Peter Broadbent	10	Bryan Douglas
Des Horne	11	Alastair MacLeod

Attendance: 100,000

Referee: K Howley, Middlesbrough

It was the sourest, most tawdry climax to a season English football had seen since the War. Indeed, the clash between Wolverhampton Wanderers and Blackburn Rovers made a mockery of the FA Cup Final's traditional role as soccer's annual showcase. Marred by injury, negative tactics, some over-physical tackling and ungracious fans, it could hardly have been more disappointing for anyone but the most devoted of Molineux partisans. Nevertheless the Cup campaign, the preparations for Wembley and the action on the big day lacked neither drama nor controversy.

In differing fashions, both clubs had experienced a traumatic run-up to the final. Wolves had been on the brink of completing a rare hat-trick of League Championships until a home defeat by Spurs had given Burnley the chance to pip them in the title race. Even after the Tottenham reverse, Stan Cullis' side bounced back with a 5-1 thrashing of Chelsea on the last League Saturday, only for the Turf Moor men to claim the prize by a point with a 2-1 triumph at Manchester City two days later. Having their hopes of becoming the first team this century to claim the League-FA Cup double flattened so agonisingly duly increased the

Wembley pressure on the Black Countrymen, and it was an indication of the disarray in their opponents' camp that they remained hot favourites. Blackburn's problems were diverse. As well as the springtime loss of form so familiar to many winning semi-finalists - one that saw them slither into the relegation zone to finish only three points ahead of doomed Leeds United - there was an impression abroad that manager Dally Duncan was not universally popular among directors, and also an outcry from supporters over ticket allocation. But potentially more devastating were difficulties involving two key players, skipper Ronnie Clayton and centre-forward Derek Dougan. Despite the boost of succeeding Billy Wright as England captain, Ronnie had contributed a series of below-par displays recently, not least because of a bout of tonsillitis which refused to be shaken off. Though one of the classiest and most industrious wing-halves in the land, he was beginning to attract widespread flak to the extent that his England place was rumoured to be in doubt - indeed, he was to lose it for good following a lacklustre display against Yugoslavia a few days after the Wolves encounter. Not surprisingly, team morale was sapped, although those closest to Clayton were convinced that the talented 25-year-old, a born leader, would overcome his travail. Eventually, of course, they were proved right; he served Blackburn nobly through nine further seasons and today the name of Ronnie Clayton is perhaps the most honoured in the club's history.

The Dougan situation was altogether more combustible. An outspoken, intelligent Ulsterman who had arrived at Ewood Park from Portsmouth in March 1959, he was less than enamoured at the way the club was run and was not slow to make his feelings known, especially regarding what he saw as woefully unimaginative training methods. His unrest culminated in a transfer request,

disastrously timed on the very eve of the FA Cup Final. As it turned out, Derek hindered the cause still further by declaring himself fit after rigorous tests on a pulled muscle, only to break down five minutes into the game.

Early in the season Blackburn had topped the First Division, then made up for a League decline by an exhilarating, sometimes cliff-hanging Cup campaign. They needed a replay to dispose of Sunderland in the third round, then a late equaliser from Mick McGrath saw them scrape a home draw against Blackpool in the fourth. A thumping 3-0 victory at Bloomfield Road set up a taxing tie at White Hart Lane against a Spurs side fresh from the 13-2 annihilation of Crewe Alexandra. Two goals from strapping marksman Louis Bimpson, a recent signing from Liverpool, and one from stopper Matt Woods completed a splendid victory against Danny Blanchflower and his lovely team, whose own crowning glory remained a year ahead. Now Blackburn faced Burnley, destined to be Champions and with their own designs on the double. In front of their own fans, Harry Potts' team overran Rovers at first and built up a three-goal lead. But a rousing comeback capped by another late leveller from McGrath earned an unlikely replay at Ewood, where Blackburn won the day. In the semi-final it was the turn of Dougan, playing like some mettlesome but mercurial charger, to make the decisive contribution, taking his club to Wembley with two perfectly-judged shots from awkward angles. Wolves, meanwhile, had progressed less eventfully, their closest calls being a third-round draw at Newcastle and a single-goal semi-final triumph against Joe Mercer's Aston Villa, the spirited Division Two champions.

The Wembley selections threw up one major surprise. Wolves inside-right Bobby Mason, who had played in every Cup round and 37 of that term's 42 League games, was axed in favour of 21-year-old Barry Stobart, who had only five

HOW THEY GOT THERE

WOLVERHAMPTON WANDERERS
Round 3:
Newcastle United (a) 2-2.
replay (h) 4-2.

Round 4:
Charlton Athletic (h) 2-1.

Round 5:
Luton Town (a) 4-1.

Round 6:
Leicester City (a) 2-1.

Semi-final: Aston Villa *at The Hawthorns* 1-0.

BLACKBURN ROVERS
Round 3:
Sunderland (a) 1-1.
replay (h) 4-1.

Round 4:
Blackpool (h) 1-1,
replay (a) 3-0.

Round 5:
Tottenham Hotspur (a) 3-1.

Round 6:
Burnley (a) 3-3.
replay (h) 2-0.

Semi-final:
Sheffield Wednesday *at Maine Road* 2-1.

Left: A restless spirit. Derek Dougan, who stunned Blackburn with a transfer request on the eve of the final.

A surprise omission. Unlucky Bobby Mason, a Wolves regular throughout the season who was axed for Wembley. Not surprisingly after that, he never fully recovered his confidence.

senior appearances to his name. For the skilful, hard-working Mason, who had scored twice in the fifth-round defeat of Luton Town, it was a devastating blow, and one from which many Wanderers fans believe his confidence never recovered; for Stobart it was a dream opportunity, which he made the most of with a bright display at Wembley, yet failed to make it the springboard for a major career. As ever, Wolves would lean heavily on an iron-clad defence, in which England wing-half Ron Flowers and Bill Slater - their centre-half and captain and the new Footballer of the Year - were outstanding, though not enough credit went the way of Dover-born schoolchums Peter Broadbent and Jimmy Murray. Without being able to oust the brilliant Johnny Haynes, schemer Broadbent did win a handful of full caps, but the unlucky Murray was limited to under-23 and Football League honours. In fact, he was a marvellous leader of his line, blessed with guile and control as well as the speed and strength needed for Wolves' traditional long-ball style. As for Rovers, they were a yeoman team enlivened by Clayton, the thrustful Peter Dobing at inside-right, the unpredictable Dougan and, best of all, by Bryan Douglas, who had succeeded Stanley Matthews on England's right wing. Standing only 5ft 5in, he was a captivating ball artist whom many pundits believed was best employed at inside-left, where he lined up for the final.

However, on the day there was precious little artistry on show from any quarter, the least hint of delicacy being stifled relentlessly by a combination of offside traps and bone-jarring challenges from both sides. Against most predictions, it was Blackburn who started most positively, and Wolves 'keeper Malcolm Finlayson was forced to make two smart saves. But soon the Midlanders seized the initiative and as the half wore on Rovers were engaged mainly in holding and frustrating

their opponents, hoping the legendary Molineux vigour had been worn down by the title quest. Fate, however, was not prepared to deal another hammer blow to Cullis' team, instead letting not one, but two, fall on the Lancastrians in the space of two minutes shortly before the interval. First Stobart crossed low and hard from the left, but as the ball arrowed towards the lurking Norman Deeley, it struck Mick McGrath and was deflected into the unguarded net. Then, with Rovers still reeling, Deeley and his marker Dave Whelan met in a distinctly brisk but fair challenge. While Norman was able to limp away and play on, the full-back was going nowhere without a stretcher; there had been an audible crack, poor Dave's leg had snapped and was left bent like a boomerang.

Half-time brought little respite for beleaguered Blackburn, and with an inconsolable McGrath standing head-in-hands, their dressing-room did not present an uplifting scene. However, with Mick withdrawing to left-back and feisty left-winger Alastair MacLeod - one day destined to march at the head of 'Ally's Army' as Scotland boss - moving to left-half, Rovers were determined to go down battling. So they did, too, and with Woods in dominant form at the heart of defence, they held out until three-quarter time, when little Deeley converted a Des Horne centre from 12 yards. Then Wolves were in full cry, Flowers and Murray both having goals disallowed before Deeley wrapped up proceedings when he

Top: The anguish on the face of Blackburn's Mick McGrath is plain to see as he deflects the ball into his own net to put Wolves ahead. Norman Deeley is about to celebrate.

Above: Rovers' Dave Whelan is stretchered off with a broken leg after challenging for the ball with Norman Deeley, who appears distressed as he walks alongside.

Right: Rovers' goalkeeper Harry Leyland gropes at thin air but Peter Broadbent just misses a cross with the goal gaping.

Below: Wolves parade the FA Cup. Standing (left to right): Gerry Harris, Malcolm Finlayson, Ron Flowers, Bill Slater (shoulder-high), Peter Broadbent, Eddie Clamp and George Showell. Kneeling: Barry Stobart, Des Horne, Jimmy Murray and Norman Deeley.

capitalised on a rare error from Woods to drive home from a Stobart cross.

The last whistle brought merciful release at the end of a depressingly poor match, which had seen the old-gold-and-black brigade collect the Cup for the fourth time in eight finals while Rovers recorded only their second defeat in eight. Even then, a thoroughly wretched occasion was not yet complete. As Slater - making up for his disappointment as a loser with Blackpool nine years earlier - held aloft the trophy, the stadium echoed to the boos of Blackburn supporters, despite valiant efforts from the marching

Above: Young Barry Stobart examines the medal he could hardly have expected to win. It was the high point of a career which tailed off disappointingly.

Left: Skippers Ronnie Clayton of Blackburn and Bill Slater of Wolves offer their post-match verdicts to a youthful BBC reporter by the name of David Coleman.

band, who increased their volume in a bid to drown the jeers. Then the Lancastrians, who felt the victors had been allowed to get away with unfair play, showered orange peel and other rubbish on the Wolves players and referee Kevin Howley - at 35, the youngest man to take charge of a Cup Final - as they left the arena. Still the bile wasn't spent, as Dally Duncan learned at Blackburn's banquet that evening, when his chairman, Norman Forbes, referred to him in less than glowing terms. Shortly afterwards Dally was asked for his resignation; he refused to give it and was sacked that July.

Meanwhile as the recriminations flew, Dave Whelan - only the previous year described by Matt Busby as one of the League's most improved performers - was in hospital being treated for that hideous break. He had played his last game in the top flight, seeing out his career with Crewe, but there was a silver lining for the shrewd Yorkshireman. After leaving football he set up a foodstore chain and became a millionaire; money can't buy a winner's medal, but it has its consolations!

Above: Who wants to be a millionaire? Dave Whelan, the Blackburn left-back whose top-flight career was ended by the shattered leg he suffered at Wembley. Awaiting him a few years hence was huge success in business.

IT HAPPENED
THIS YEAR

Soviet Yuri Gagarin
became the first man
in space.

Birth Pill went on
sale in the United
Kingdom.

Work began on
building the Berlin
Wall to stop East-
West refugee deluge.

Russian ballet dancer
Rudolf Nureyev
defected to the West.

Angela Mortimer beat
fellow Brit
Christine Truman in
Wimbledon final.

6 May 1961

TOTTENHAM HOTSPUR 2

Smith 66; Dyson 75

LEICESTER CITY 0

Half-time 0-0

TOTTENHAM HOTSPUR		LEICESTER CITY
Bill Brown	1	Gordon Banks
Peter Baker	2	Len Chalmers
Ron Henry	3	Richie Norman
Danny Blanchflower *(captain)*	4	Frank McLintock
Maurice Norman	5	Ian King
Dave Mackay	6	Colin Appleton
Cliff Jones	7	Howard Riley
John White	8	Jimmy Walsh *(captain)*
Bobby Smith	9	Hugh McIlmoyle
Les Allen	10	Ken Keyworth
Terry Dyson	11	Albert Cheesebrough

Attendance: 100,000

Referee: J Kelly, Chorley

Opposite page: That irrepressible imp Terry Dyson capers under the silverware his goal had helped to secure. The hands on the Cup belong to skipper Danny Blanchflower, who had predicted at the start of the season that Spurs would win the double, and Bobby Smith, who netted the opener against Leicester.

It was all so desperately inappropriate. After decades of near misses, the elusive League and FA Cup double had been achieved for the first time in the 20th Century, and by a side to whom the descriptions 'great' and 'glorious' could be applied with little fear of contradiction. Yet on the bleak May afternoon at Wembley when the name of Tottenham Hotspur earned an immortal niche in football folklore, there was an unavoidable sense of anti-climax. Bill Nicholson's men had done what many pundits had believed was impossible in modern times, but only after their movingly gallant opponents, Leicester City, had been reduced to ten men early in the game by the latest incidence of the Cup Final injury jinx. In addition, the North Londoners had performed for much of the match with a caution that was utterly uncharacteristic; skipper Danny Blanchflower seemed off-colour and tense, many of his colleagues appeared sluggish with anxiety and the usual flowing accuracy that had turned the title race into a procession was conspicuous by its absence.

Afterwards Nicholson, the ultimate soccer perfectionist, expressed frustration

that Spurs, in the hour of their greatest triumph, had not appeared before the world in their full splendour. Happily, with the perspective of history, there is no doubting the wonder of his creation.

Like Manchester United four years earlier, Tottenham travelled to Wembley as universally-lauded Champions, and deservedly so. Led by the intellectual Blanchflower, as articulate in his midfield promptings as in his often-outspoken pronouncements, they fielded a veritable cornucopia of talent. There was Dave Mackay, the inspirational, warrior-like wing-half; Cliff Jones, as penetrative a winger as any in the world; John White, the subtlest of schemers; Bobby Smith, who combined a bullish physique with deceptively delicate skills; and if the rest of the side boasted less extravagant gifts, each man contributed richly to a well-nigh perfect blend.

When the players had gathered for pre-season training, the skipper had predicted to chairman Fred Bearman that Spurs would win the double, and little had happened during the campaign to dent Danny's confidence. Yet inevitably there were uncomfortable interludes, few more so than in the White Hart Lane encounter with Charlton Athletic in the third round of the Cup. After leading 2-0, then 3-1, Tottenham had appeared to be cruising to victory, only for the Second Division Valiants to justify their nickname with a furious late onslaught that yielded another goal and came perilously close to earning a replay. That hurdle overcome, albeit shakily, fourth-round opponents Crewe were crushed 5-1 - an honourable effort by an Alexandra team determined to improve on the 13-2 humiliation of the previous season, which they managed thanks largely to a terrific display by their goalkeeper, Brian Williamson. Aston Villa offered little resistance in the fifth round, then Sunderland proved inordinately obstinate quarter-final opposition, forcing a well-merited draw at Roker Park before succumbing 5-0 at the Lane. The semi-final at Villa Park threw Tottenham against reigning champions Burnley, whom many observers expected to be at a low ebb after losing

When Danny met Jimmy. Tottenham's Blanchflower (left) and Leicester's Walsh shake hands under the genial gaze of referee J Kelly.

a two-goal lead and being ejected from the European Cup in Hamburg only three days earlier. In fact, though Nicholson's men won 3-0, such a margin was a travesty of justice with the Lancastrians dominating long spells of the match and the result offered a telling illustration that even the finest teams need their fair share of luck to win the double. But what of Leicester City; were they mere cannon fodder for the aristocratic Lilywhites? Not a bit of it. The Filberts had demonstrated their mettle by finishing a highly creditable sixth in the League table, and anyone who doubted their capacity to cope with Spurs had only to recall that in February they had become the first visitors to win at White Hart Lane that term. Admittedly their line-up was considerably less stellar than Tottenham's, but in young goalkeeper Gordon Banks and right-half Frank McLintock they had two men destined for the heights, and the rest of their side boasted considerable ability and vitality. Their most potent attackers were England under-23 outside-right Howard Riley and recently-capped Welsh marksman Ken Leek, who had scored in every round on the way to Wembley. Not that their progress had been easy. True, Oxford United and Bristol City - dispatched at the second attempt after the first game had been abandoned in a quagmire - had caused few problems, but thereafter Leicester became bogged down, needing replays to dispose of both Birmingham City and Barnsley, and overcoming Sheffield United in the semi-final only after three grim struggles.

Of course, Spurs were the heavily-backed favourites, but in the weeks before the final there was no shortage of respected judges who reckoned the Midlanders were just the sort of workmanlike, no-nonsense outfit to play on the North Londoners' inevitable nerves and cause an upset. However, Wembley week brought a selection bombshell from Filbert Street that seemed to stack the odds even more overwhelmingly in Tottenham's favour. Leicester boss Matt Gillies announced that he had dropped Leek in favour of rookie Hugh McIlmoyle, and speculation became rife over the reasons for leaving out a man who had netted 25 times that season, including once in each of his last three outings. The manager maintained there was no personal rift and that it was merely a matter of form - McIlmoyle had netted four times in seven games, though was goalless in his last two - but to most fans it remains a mystery to this day. Certainly the man most relieved by Gillies' decision was Spurs stopper Maurice Norman. 'Monty' dreaded facing Leek, who was particularly lethal in the air and against whom he seldom excelled. Not surprisingly the Welshman never played for Leicester again, joining Newcastle United that summer.

Above: Ken Leek, who was a shock absence at Wembley after scoring in every previous round of the Cup. Below: Leek's replacement, Hugh McIlmoyle, is introduced to the Duchess of Kent. The inexperienced Scot never let Leicester down but the feeling that the free-scoring Welshman might have been more productive was unavoidable.

The day of the final was grey and inhospitable, but as the teams stood in line to meet the Duchess of Kent, the royal visitor discovered that the Blanchflower charm and wit were as sunny as ever. She remarked to the Spurs captain that the City players carried their names on their tracksuits, to which he replied: 'Ah yes, but *we* know each other!' As the action got under way, Spurs began purposefully and before long Mackay was demonstrating a delicate touch - his 'iron-man' image tended to obscure the fact of his superb ball control - as he tricked his way past a defender on the left. The Scot crossed sweetly, only for his countryman, White, to blaze over the bar when he seemed certain to score. Had that effort

Above: Spurs shall not pass. Leicester left-back Richie Norman clears for a corner as goalkeeper Gordon Banks stands guard at the post.

gone in, Spurs might have relaxed and served up a football feast worthy of the occasion; as it was, paused precariously on the precipice of achievement, they became tentative and Leicester bustled efficiently into contention. With Riley notably thrustful and young McIlmoyle roaming enterprisingly, the chances began to arrive, only to be spurned by Howard and Hugh themselves, as well as their captain Jimmy Walsh and left-winger Albert Cheesebrough, who might not have been playing but for Gordon Wills' long-term injury.

But just as an intriguing encounter was shaping up, it was sabotaged on 17 minutes by that old 'hoodoo'. City right-back Len Chalmers reeled out of a tackle with Les Allen and fell to the turf writhing in agony. He had suffered serious injury to knee and shin and would be a passenger, limping pathetically and dragging his leg behind him, for the remainder of the proceedings. As he sat up being tended by trainer Alec Dowdells, surrounded by dismayed team-mates, he wagged an admonishing finger towards Allen, but later admitted the gesture had been

Insets above: Leicester casualty Len Chalmers, whose serious injury early in the first half unbalanced what promised to be a fascinating contest.

121

Below: Was it a goal? Not according to the record books. Cliff Jones strikes but a linesman flagged for offside.

Bottom: A goal of sheer quality. Having wrong-footed his marker with a delicate dummy, big Bobby Smith slams the ball past Gordon Banks.

made in the heat of an extremely stressful moment. Len accepted graciously that there was no ill intent in the challenge, which in fact had visibly upset the Tottenham inside-left, who apologised after the match and told the press: 'The incident spoiled the game for me.' Unfortunately the seventh major mishap in nine finals ruined the contest for Leicester, too, though they battled on bravely enough to stretch Spurs' defence at times without quite regaining their former impetus. Walsh set a splendid example, beavering energetically alongside the deeply-lying McIlmoyle, who did enough to show why Gillies considered him worthy of a Wembley berth without wiping out the impression that the more experienced and direct Leek would have been more likely to snatch a goal.

Faced with a depleted force, Tottenham might have been expected to shift up a gear, yet with the stakes so high they restricted themselves to an essentially safety-first approach, with Mackay placing more than usual emphasis on defensive duties and the mighty Norman venturing forward only rarely for set pieces. Unusually (and significantly), the Spurs players who took the eye were defenders, especially left-back Ron Henry, whose display of tackling, intercepting and passing was practically flawless. Also excellent was 'keeper Bill Brown, sometimes denigrated for his technique at taking crosses, but apparently wearing adhesive gloves on this occasion. The only Tottenham forward to do himself justice during the first three-quarters of the match was Jones, whose incisive runs made deep inroads into Leicester territory and also relieved pressure on his own rearguard. Indeed, after 38 minutes Cliff found the net, only for the 'score' to be wiped out by a marginal offside decision which many fans believed to be mistaken, maintaining the linesman had been deceived by the Welshman's speed.

In the circumstances, however, a breakthrough seemed inevitable, though with City's ten toiling like men possessed, it did not come until just after the hour. Then Allen fed Terry Dyson in the inside-right position, and the ball was played through to Smith, standing in front of his marker, Ian King, near the penalty

spot. Belying his bulk, the England centre-forward feinted one way, then swivelled the other to wallop an unstoppable drive past Banks, who nevertheless made a valiant, flying attempt to keep it out. Bobby tumbled as he shot, and didn't know the ball had gone in until his back was pounded by ecstatic team-mates. That goal was the signal for Tottenham to relax, at least partially, and it was no surprise when they doubled their lead nine minutes later. Poor Chalmers surrendered possession, the ball reached Smith on the right flank and he floated a perfect centre beyond the far post where the irrepressible little Dyson rose to nod it emphatically into goal.

Thereafter Spurs were able to show brief snatches of their best form but, as if unwilling to needlessly pound a stricken opponent, did not add to their tally. At the end Leicester, beaten as much by tiredness as by Tottenham, formed a guard of honour for their conquerors and it was unfortunate that Blanchflower and company - in all innocence - failed to notice it as they were ushered away for TV and radio interviews. During the post-match inquest, it was difficult not to reflect that posterity deserved a more fitting performance from one of the finest club sides of all time. But in the long run, nothing should be allowed to detract from the greatest day in Spurs' history and one of the most memorable in the annals of English football.

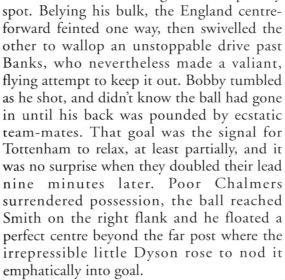

Even at full stretch Gordon Banks, then a promising youngster, cannot prevent Terry Dyson's header from sewing up the game, the Cup and the double. Looking on are Cliff Jones and Frank McLintock.

As Tottenham celebrate with understandable euphoria, it is appropriate to consider the contribution of one of their unsung heroes. On a day when the team as a whole did not touch their supreme best, full-back Ron Henry (bottom left) played one of the finest games of his life. Never showy, invariably effective, Ron was a veritable nugget throughout a long and distinguished White Hart Lane career. His fellow double-winners are (left to right) Bill Brown, Cliff Jones, Peter Baker, Terry Dyson (foreground), Danny Blanchflower (with Cup), Bobby Smith, Les Allen, John White, Dave Mackay and Maurice Norman.

Inset: Sartorial contrast for Spurs' scorers. Little Terry Dyson faces the camera in his undies, while Bobby Smith is resplendent in shirt and tie.

THE FOOTBALL ASSOCIATION CHALLENGE CUP COMPETITION

FINAL TIE
BURNLEY
v
TOTTENHAM HOTSPUR
(Holders)

SATURDAY, MAY 5th, 1962   KICK-OFF 3 p.m.

EMPIRE STADIUM
WEMBLEY

OFFICIAL PROGRAMME   ·   ONE SHILLING

Main picture: Men at the helm. Managers Harry Potts of Burnley (left) and Tottenham's Bill Nicholson return to Wembley. It was Harry's first official engagement at the national stadium since he appeared for the Clarets in the 1947 final. Bill, of course, had paid a profitable visit just a year earlier.

Right: Period piece. The match programme shows Wembley before the all-round roof was completed in 1963.

TOTTENHAM HOTSPUR 3

Greaves 3, Smith 51, Blanchflower (pen) 80

BURNLEY 1

Robson 50

Half-time 1-0

TOTTENHAM HOTSPUR	○	BURNLEY
Bill Brown	1	Adam Blacklaw
Peter Baker	2	John Angus
Ron Henry	3	Alex Elder
Danny Blanchflower *(captain)*	4	Jimmy Adamson *(captain)*
Maurice Norman	5	Tommy Cummings
Dave Mackay	6	Brian Miller
Terry Medwin	7	John Connelly
John White	8	Jimmy McIlroy
Bobby Smith	9	Ray Pointer
Jimmy Greaves	10	Jimmy Robson
Cliff Jones	11	Gordon Harris

Attendance: 100,000

Referee: J Finney, Hereford

1962

IT HAPPENED THIS YEAR

Threat of nuclear war receded as Cuban missile crisis was resolved.

Marilyn Monroe died of sleeping pill overdose.

Nelson Mandela jailed for inciting strike in South Africa.

James Hanratty hanged for murder, protesting innocence to the last.

Sonny Liston won world heavyweight crown from Floyd Patterson.

In the spring of 1962, two clubs of vividly contrasting stature shared the English soccer limelight. On the one hand were Tottenham Hotspur, mightiest of the mighty and glamour personified, who were seeking an unprecedented second successive League and FA Cup double; indeed, boosted by the signing of goal-scorer supreme Jimmy Greaves, they were out to add the European Cup to their list of conquests and so complete a stupendous *treble*. On the other hand were hitherto humble Ipswich Town who, under the guidance of former Spurs favourite Alf Ramsey, had stunned the football world by tilting for the title with a team which, with all due respect, consisted largely of rejects and bargain buys - and all in their first term since winning promotion from the Second Division. It was the classic confrontation between haves and have-nots and, understandably, it monopolised media coverage.

Jimmy McIlroy of Burnley, whose silky touch and incisive vision made him one of the most entertaining and effective schemers English football has seen.

Fair enough, except in one respect: it ignored the magnificent campaign being enjoyed by Burnley, who were to face Tottenham in an FA Cup Final which was to be greeted with scorn by blood-and-thunder addicts, but which won joyful acclaim among connoisseurs of a more thoughtful, technically excellent brand of football. In fact, the men from Turf Moor were to come agonisingly close to the much-coveted double themselves, yet they attracted the merest fraction of the attention heaped on their apparently more newsworthy rivals.

Burnley, run with imperious disdain for opposing opinions by controversial chairman Bob Lord, were a remarkable club. Hailing from an East Lancashire cotton town of no more than 80,000 inhabitants, they had taken on the big-city battalions to win the League Championship in 1960, then consolidated by performing admirably in all competitions the following season. Come 1961/62, with substantially the same personnel, they appeared ready to scale new heights. The heart of the team was the midfield pairing of Ulsterman Jimmy McIlroy, who remains one of the most complete play-makers the British game has seen since the War, and skipper Jimmy Adamson, destined to pip his creative partner for the 1962 Footballer of the Year accolade. Up front the main cutting edge was provided by two England internationals, the direct, skilful winger John Connelly, and roving leader of the line Ray Pointer, as industrious a number-nine as could be found anywhere in the First Division. Underpinned by a steady defence, in which full-backs John Angus and Alex Elder and wing-half Brian Miller were outstanding, and managed by Harry Potts - who had pocketed a loser's medal with the Clarets in 1947 - they were a well-equipped all-round side. Accordingly, Burnley started the season in fine fettle, surging zestfully to the top of the table, and when they crushed West Ham 6-0 in early March the title seemed theirs for the taking. But then came an inexplicably abysmal run in which they managed only 11 points out of a possible 26, thus allowing Ramsey's East Anglians to sneak past them at the death, leaving only the Cup in their sights.

Meanwhile the White Hart Lane 'aristocrats' had been hogging the headlines through their heroic exploits in the European Cup - they were desperately unlucky to lose their semi-final to Benfica, the eventual winners - and by combining a late bid for the Championship with a formidably convincing march on Wembley. The superb double-winning combination remained essentially intact, with Danny Blanchflower rendering meaningless the evidence of his birth certificate - which revealed him to be 36 that February - and Jimmy Greaves adding his peerless marksmanship to the North Londoners' cause. Indeed, though Jimmy Adamson fully merited his award from the Football Writers Association, there was no doubt that by public consent, the perky ex-Chelsea prodigy was soccer's personality of the season. On returning to Britain in December from his unhappy four-month sojourn with AC Milan - the deal cost Spurs £99,999, Bill Nicholson stubbornly refusing to part with a six-figure fee - Greaves had struck sensational form, commencing with a hat-trick on his League debut against Blackpool and finishing the season with 30 goals in 31 outings. Naturally, he played a central part in Spurs' Cup progress, beginning with a brace in their closest brush with elimination, a 3-3 draw with Birmingham City at St Andrews in the third round. There followed a goal in the replay victory over the Blues, a pair in the crushing of Plymouth and two more in a splendid win at West Bromwich, before he failed to hit the mark in the quarter-final against Aston Villa. Jimmy was back on target at Hillsborough in the semi-final, sealing the spoils against a Manchester United side showing signs that Matt Busby's post-Munich rebuilding programme was on the right track; that made eight of Tottenham's 18 Cup goals to date - with Wembley still to come.

Meanwhile Burnley's road towards the Twin Towers had started smoothly, with a 6-1 drubbing of Queen's Park Rangers, but then almost ended at home to Leyton Orient, who had the better of a 1-1 draw at Turf Moor. Brian Miller's

Above: The Duke and Greavsie. Danny Blanchflower introduces Jimmy, evidently in typically chirpy form, to Prince Philip. Dave Mackay and John White await the royal handshake.

Left: The coin is in the air and Danny Blanchflower, referee Jim Finney and Burnley captain Jimmy Adamson await the outcome.

strike saw the Clarets scrape through at Brisbane Road, though not before the O's had showed the pedigree that was to see them rise from the Second Division at season's end. Then came an all-Lancashire clash with Everton (3-1 at the Moor) and a battle of the Roses with Sheffield United (won by Pointer's goal at Bramall Lane) to set up what proved to be a taut semi-final encounter with Fulham. The Cottagers gave the lie to their lowly First Division placing - they were to finish just one point better off than relegated Cardiff City - with a spirited display at Villa Park from which Burnley were thankful to escape with a draw, courtesy of a goal by Connelly. The replay at Filbert Street was tight, too, with a double strike by Jimmy Robson securing a final place. Thus the stage was set for an encounter which has been described as the 'Friendly Final' by outsiders who perceived, perhaps wrongly, a lack of passion among the combatants. Certainly there was less tension in the Tottenham camp than a year earlier, probably because nine of the team already had winner's medals at home and were accustomed to the Wembley experience, while the remaining two - Jimmy Greaves and the genial Welsh wingman Terry Medwin, who replaced Les Allen and Terry Dyson respectively - were both seasoned internationals. Almost inevitably it was Greaves - as irrepressible in his playing days as he was later as a TV pundit - who

129

had the first say in deciding the destination of the trophy. Beforehand he had joked about scoring in the fourth minute; in the event he was to open his account with 60 seconds to spare, and in a decidedly bizarre manner. Goalkeeper Bill Brown punted downfield and Bobby Smith nodded the ball into Jimmy's path, but as the ace poacher moved into the penalty box he overran it. The chance might have eluded him, yet even in the act of stumbling he managed a half-hit shot which wrong-footed four defenders, crept 15 yards along the ground and nestled snugly in the back of Adam Blacklaw's net. Having taken the lead in somewhat fortunate circumstances, Tottenham now appeared to relax and enjoyed a period of marked superiority, with Dave Mackay and John White prominent in a series of fluid midfield manoeuvres. Nevertheless, there were chances at either end and after Brown sprang to divert a long-range effort from Miller, Blacklaw had to be equally nimble to tip a Greaves rasper over the bar. Gradually Burnley regained

territorial parity, and it was no more than they deserved when they equalised five minutes into the second half. The opening arrived when the workaholic Pointer robbed Mackay and released Gordon Harris on the left. The blond flankman beat Peter Baker before crossing hard and low to Robson, who allowed the ball to cannon from his shins between Brown and the upright for the 100th goal in Wembley finals. But just as the balance of power might have shifted, Tottenham responded like the great side they were. White slipped away from Angus and McIlroy on the left and floated a pass to Smith. The England centre-forward, who had lost his place to Allen for a spell in mid-season, confirmed his re-emergence with an act of pillage similar to his opening goal in the 1961 final. Controlling the ball adeptly, he spun away from Miller and crashed a shot high into the net from 15 yards. Burnley had been level for no more than a minute.

Smith's strike was a brutal blow to Burnley's aspirations, and although they con-

Inset top: One of the afternoon's key battles. Maurice Norman in aerial combat with Burnley's Ray Pointer. Inset centre: Though the ball is agonisingly close, Spurs' keeper Bill Brown cannot prevent Jimmy Robson from equalising. Inset below: Within a minute, Bobby Smith has swivelled superbly and beats Blacklaw with an unstoppable shot to restore Tottenham's lead.

131

Right: The perfect penalty. Danny Blanchflower sends the ball one way, Burnley 'keeper Adam Blacklaw goes the other. The score is 3-1 and Spurs have retained the Cup.

tinued to play high-quality football, there was a feeling that they would never quite match their opponents. Nevertheless they had their moments: Robson ran through to find the net a second time but was clearly offside; Pointer shot narrowly wide and Connelly brought spectators to their feet with a darting run past several defenders. Then, ten minutes from time, came the incident that sealed the Clarets' fate. A loose ball fell to Medwin whose attempt at goal was saved by the hand of centre-half Tommy Cummings, who had endured a rather harrowing afternoon in trying to contain the ebullient Smith. Though Burnley claimed there had been a foul on Blacklaw - a theory to which a linesman's flag added credence - the referee gave a penalty. Blanchflower, unphased by a delay while Medwin received treatment for a knock, stepped up to dispatch his low spot-kick with ultimate precision, sending Blacklaw one way and the ball the other.

Thus Spurs retained the FA Cup and went on to inspire further choruses of 'Glory, Glory, Hallelujah' by winning the European Cup Winners' Cup in 1963, before their wonderful team declined. For Burnley, who had not lifted the trophy since 1914, there was no silverware on the horizon. Indeed, though they finished third in the League in 1962/63, their fine side, too, was on the verge of breaking up. The influential Adamson - who after the '62 final faced a busy summer as assistant to England boss Walter Winterbottom as well as a playing member of the party that travelled to Chile for the World Cup finals - was passing his peak and would never play another complete season before retiring. Even sooner, McIlroy would depart to join the Stanley Matthews-inspired renaissance at Stoke, and the ageing Cummings would move into management. Within two years even their remaining star, Connelly, would leave the Moor to win a Championship medal with Manchester United and take his place in England's victorious 1966 World Cup squad. And for those who wonder what happens to players when they leave the game, here's a clue in John's case. If you're ever in Bury and fancy some fish and chips, look out for . . . wait for it . . . Connelly's Plaice!

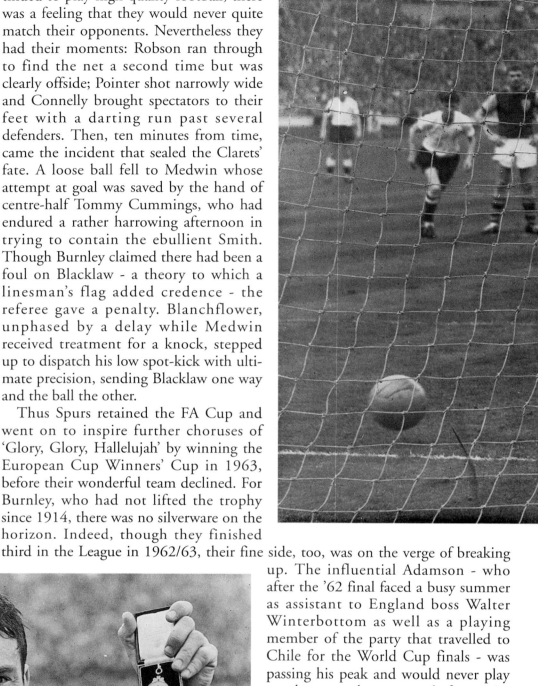

That familiar cheeky grin is still working overtime after the match, and no wonder. Jimmy Greaves has just won his first major club honour.

Contrasting contributors to the Spurs success story brandish the famous trophy. The slender playmaker John White, all subtlety and invention, and the mountainous, prodigiously strong centre-half Maurice Norman. Stark tragedy was awaiting John, who was killed by a bolt of lightning on a golf course in 1964.

1963

Main picture: The splendid David Herd, so often overshadowed by Old Trafford's galaxy of stars, enjoys an afternoon in the spotlight. Here David (left) prods home United's second after Gordon Banks failed to hold a Bobby Charlton rasper. Five minutes from time he clinched the Cup with a second and similar goal. Inset: Matt Busby, whose new side was on the verge of great things.

MANCHESTER UNITED 3

Law 29; Herd 57, 85

LEICESTER CITY 1

Keyworth 80

Half-time 1-0

MANCHESTER UNITED		LEICESTER CITY
David Gaskell	1	Gordon Banks
Tony Dunne	2	John Sjoberg
Noel Cantwell *(captain)*	3	Richie Norman
Pat Crerand	4	Frank McLintock
Bill Foulkes	5	Ian King
Maurice Setters	6	Colin Appleton *(captain)*
Johnny Giles	7	Howard Riley
Albert Quixall	8	Graham Cross
David Herd	9	Ken Keyworth
Denis Law	10	David Gibson
Bobby Charlton	11	Mike Stringfellow

Attendance: 100,000

Referee: K Aston, Ilford

As British football emerged from the Big Freeze that paralysed everyday life for several months, so Manchester United awoke from the hibernation that had gripped the club since a dream had died at Munich. The Arctic conditions had thrown fixture lists into chaos and made the FA Cup Final three weeks late, but come the end of May, the onset of the Red Devils' own personal spring was irresistible. After surviving a winter as bleak in terms of League results as the weather - the spectre of relegation had receded only a week earlier - Matt Busby's expensively assembled collection of stars gelled gloriously at last.

Against Leicester City at Wembley, after a predictably fitful opening, they delighted the eye, their moves flitting like sunshine across a velvet green carpet that for so long had been obscured beneath a straitjacket of ice. There were individual triumphs aplenty: Pat Crerand controlled the midfield with an attacking wing-half display that was a study in near-perfection; Bobby Charlton gave notice that he was on the verge of harnessing his wayward genius; the underrated David Herd scored two vital goals - and then there was Denis Law. The skinny, blond Aberdonian inside-forward was everywhere, his talent flashing across the afternoon like a sudden outbreak of summer lightning. As one-off entertainment, it was spellbinding; as a taster for United's scintillating spell of success in the mid-1960s, it was exhilaratingly prophetic.

And yet, perversely, the Old Trafford side had gone into the final as undoubted underdogs. After all, the Filberts were a formidably solid outfit who had enjoyed one of the best seasons in their history. In April they had led the League and though they slipped away to finish in fourth place, that was still 15 rungs higher than United could manage. Their method was based on a sound defence and swift counter-punching, with most of their moves involving the Scottish midfield pairing of wing-half Frank McLintock and inside-forward Davie Gibson. There were seven survivors from the 1961 FA Cup Final - 'keeper Gordon Banks (a recent transfer target of Arsenal), left-back Richie Norman, the half-back line of McLintock, Ian King and skipper Colin Appleton, and forwards Howard Riley and Ken Keyworth. The newcomers - right-back John Sjoberg, utility man Graham Cross, winger Mike Stringfellow and Gibson - did nothing to weaken the combination, and plenty to strengthen it. Unspectacular and unfashionable they might have been, but they were a credit to the team-building skills of manager Matt Gillies and were in with a wonderful chance of lifting Leicester City's first top honour. City had reached Wembley economically, professionally, fully in keeping with their image of grindingly effective stolidity. Grimsby, Ipswich, Leyton Orient and Norwich were removed methodically from their path before they became involved in a passionate semi-final encounter with Liverpool at Hillsborough. In territorial terms, Bill Shankly's men dominated proceedings, but City were used to soaking up pressure which they did to great effect, then nabbed the spoils with a Stringfellow header. The Kopites were bitter afterwards, but they should not have been surprised.

In contrast, the Mancunians had blown hot and cold on their Cup journey. They began by hammering Huddersfield, for whom United's 1957 'hoodoo' victim Ray Wood was in goal, then edged narrowly past Aston Villa and Chelsea

before playing their finest football of the campaign to date - albeit against Third Division opposition - in disposing of Coventry in the quarter-final. Their last-four clash with Southampton at Villa Park was a desperately dour affair in which the Saints gave as good as they got, but were unable to prevent Law from poking home a late winner. Running parallel with this fitful progress was an inglorious struggle to pull away from the lower reaches of the First Division, a position that made a mockery of the ability at Matt Busby's disposal. Between Boxing Day and April 22, the Red Devils had managed only one League

Below: A flash of summer lightning. Denis Law, whose Wembley display was one of the most brilliant in any final since the War, challenges for a cross with Gordon Banks.

win - admittedly not as bad as it sounded, with all of January and much of February being written off by the Big Freeze, but a tally of six points from a possible 22 had made United prime candidates for the drop.

Since Munich, Busby had bought, chronologically, the likes of inside-forward Albert Quixall (£45,000), wing-half Maurice Setters (£30,000), full-back and now skipper Noel Cantwell (£29,000), marksman David Herd (£32,000), Denis Law (£115,000) and Pat Crerand (£55,000). So what had gone wrong? Clearly, the right on-the-field blend had proved elusive, but also there were disquieting rumours of dressing-room strife over training methods and of the players splitting broadly into two camps. True or not, by May the situation was approaching crisis point and it was not until a tense draw in a relegation dogfight at Maine Road on the 15th - City were destined to go down - and a home victory over already-doomed Leyton Orient a week before the final that United were safe. Busby had used 22 players in securing a First Division future, and three of them were particularly unfortunate not to get a place at Wembley. Full-back Shay Brennan had missed only six League and Cup games all season, wing-half Nobby Stiles had played 35 times and poor Harry Gregg, the best goalkeeper at the club, had failed to regain his place from young David Gaskell after injury. Thus it was not the most contented group of footballers, officials and fans who headed south for the final, yet as events turned out, Manchester United were on the brink of a crucial turning point in their fortunes. Indeed, in retrospect, the greatest scare of the day was to be when Pat Crerand went missing as the team prepared to take the field. It transpired that the Glaswegian, the possessor of a perpetually inquiring mind, had wanted to hear the crowd's rendition of 'Abide With Me' and slipped out into the tunnel, where he was discovered wearing nothing but his jockstrap!

For the rest of the day, just about everything went according to plan. Bobby Charlton, a regular visitor to Wembley with England, had made the point that the lush turf played havoc with stamina, so it was decided to push the ball around in the early stages and let Leicester set the pace. This the Midlanders did, and came perilously close to sabotaging the Manchester design in the 14th minute when Cantwell almost turned a cross from the dangerous Stringfellow into his own net. With the skittish Gaskell failing to command his area, City fashioned several chances but failed to take them and slowly, inexorably, as United began to switch

Opposite page: The 'nearly men' of Leicester City, destined to finish another fine season empty-handed. Back row (left to right): Gordon Banks, Graham Cross, Ian King, John Sjoberg, Richie Norman, Ken Keyworth, Colin Appleton. Front row: Howard Riley, David Gibson, Frank McLintock, Mike Stringfellow.

Denis the deadly. Inset above: Having controlled the ball and swivelled in one smooth movement, Law slots in United's first goal.

Inset above right: A header from the scintillating Scot rebounds from the post into the custody of Gordon Banks.

the ball slickly from man to man, an irreversible change came over the game. Now United grew in confidence and they took the lead with a sweet goal that summed up their gathering supremacy, involving as it did the two men of the match. Banks gathered the ball and threw it towards Gibson, but with typically canny anticipation Crerand nipped in to intercept before striding forward regally down the inside-left channel. Having infiltrated the City box, Paddy rolled the ball square to his compatriot, Denis Law; spinning on the spot like a scarlet top, the Reds' record signing wrong-footed two defenders and struck a perfectly angled, low 15-yard shot across and beyond Banks into the corner of the net. Suddenly Law was uncontrollable; shortly after his goal he wriggled past two opponents like some audacious eel, exchanged passes with Herd and slid the ball goalwards even as Banks dived at his feet, only to see McLintock and Norman scramble it to safety.

Now the mantle of favourites looked ill-fitting and inappropriate on the shoulders of Leicester. After the break United continued to play beautiful football, with flankmen Charlton and Johnny Giles - soon to seek (and find) his fortune as a play-maker with Don Revie's Leeds United after differences of opinion at Old Trafford - finding acres of space in which to ply their wares. Indeed, the two of them combined to set up the second goal: Giles freed Charlton on the left with a superb crossfield ball, the prematurely balding England star unloosed a low piledriver which Banks could not hold and Herd touched the rebound over the line. But to their considerable credit, Matt Gillies' well-drilled, tenacious team refused to lie down. With

Left: The slide-rule precision that was to serve Johnny Giles so magnificently at Leeds is in evidence as Leicester's Richie Norman fails to cut out the Irishman's cross.

Below: Down but not yet out. Ken Keyworth sprawls beneath the weight of Tony Dunne but is oblivious to the pain as his superb diving header eludes David Gaskell to revive the Filberts' hopes with only ten minutes to go.

Graham Cross prominent in all areas of the action, the Filberts began to ask belatedly searching questions of the United rearguard. (In fact, by this time of the year, as one of the dying breed who made their living from football *and* cricket, Cross really should have been playing for Leicestershire rather than Leicester City, but we digress). Ten minutes from time the pressure paid off when McLintock volleyed into the box and Ken Keyworth flung himself horizontal to head the ball off Tony Dunne's toecap and wide of Gaskell's dive. It was a brave and brilliant strike, but could it set up a genuine Leicester recovery? Certainly not if Law had any say in the matter. Just moments after Keyworth's goal, the dazzling Scot clipped the ball to Herd, then scampered some 45 yards to meet the return with a coruscating corkscrew of a header that flashed against a post only to rebound into the arms of the immobile Banks. Denis sank to his knees in sheer disbelief; it would have been a jewel of a goal to crown a princely performance. Instead the final act was left to Herd, who turned home his second and United's third after the unhappy Banks had dropped a Giles cross.

Lapping up the adulation, left to right, are Maurice Setters, Noel Cantwell and the inspirational Pat Crerand.

For Leicester, it was a debilitating anti-climax. After all, for the past nine months they had been a far more effective unit than the Reds, yet at what should have been their finest hour they were eclipsed by the artistry of opponents who, for much too long, had been failing to fulfil their potential. As for United, they celebrated with an unsuppressed glee that told not only of their delight at winning the FA Cup for the third time in five finals, but also of their relief at emerging from the pit into which their season had descended. When Cantwell hurled the Cup high into the air - fortunately, he caught it neatly - it was as though he was casting off the cares of that dark miserable winter. And so it proved. That Wembley triumph heralded the dawn of a wondrous period of glamour and achievement at Old Trafford, one in which Law, Charlton, Crerand and company would play starring roles. Yet for Matt Busby, the work of reconstruction that had begun five years earlier in the shadow of Munich was not quite complete. To finish the job he would need the

What goes up . . . Noel Cantwell tosses the Cup skywards, and proves to have a safe pair of hands.

help, the inspiration, of a mere slip of a lad who would be only 17 when he made his senior debut that autumn. The boy would be both the spark to light the touchpaper of United's ambitions and the flame to keep them burning brightly until the decade grew old. His name, of course, was George Best.

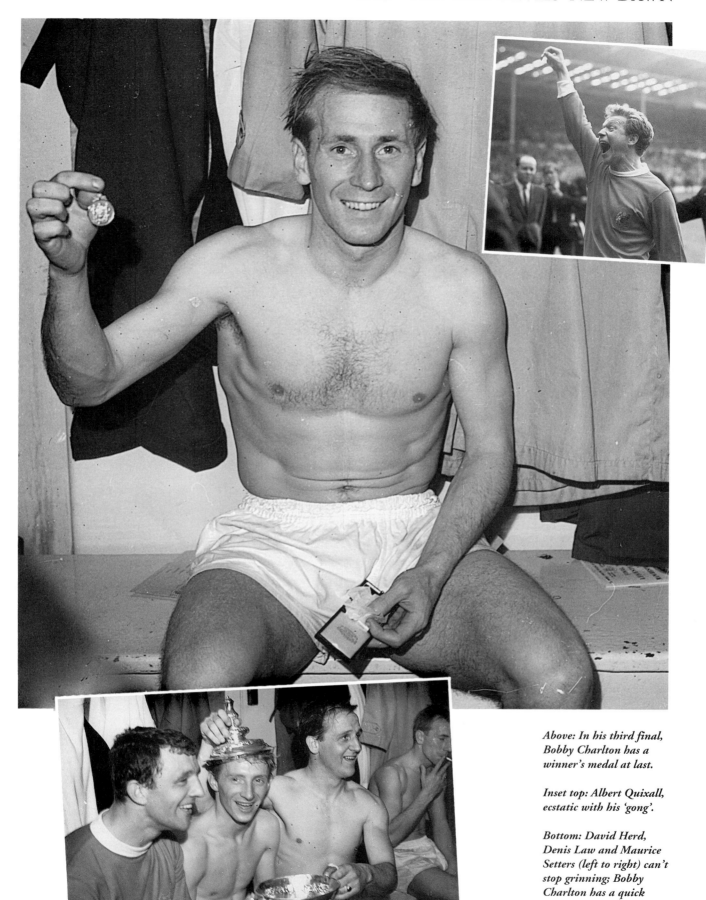

Above: In his third final, Bobby Charlton has a winner's medal at last.

Inset top: Albert Quixall, ecstatic with his 'gong'.

Bottom: David Herd, Denis Law and Maurice Setters (left to right) can't stop grinning; Bobby Charlton has a quick drag.

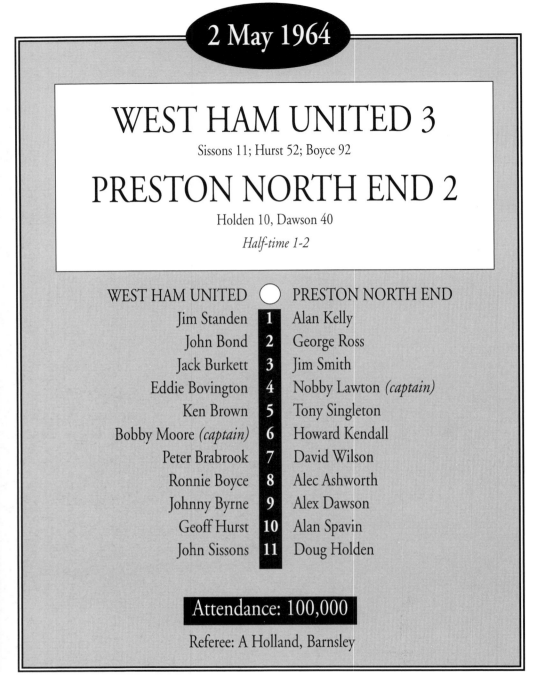

2 May 1964

WEST HAM UNITED 3
Sissons 11; Hurst 52; Boyce 92

PRESTON NORTH END 2
Holden 10, Dawson 40

Half-time 1-2

WEST HAM UNITED		PRESTON NORTH END
Jim Standen	1	Alan Kelly
John Bond	2	George Ross
Jack Burkett	3	Jim Smith
Eddie Bovington	4	Nobby Lawton *(captain)*
Ken Brown	5	Tony Singleton
Bobby Moore *(captain)*	6	Howard Kendall
Peter Brabrook	7	David Wilson
Ronnie Boyce	8	Alec Ashworth
Johnny Byrne	9	Alex Dawson
Geoff Hurst	10	Alan Spavin
John Sissons	11	Doug Holden

Attendance: 100,000

Referee: A Holland, Barnsley

One man's loss is another man's windfall: one of life's more poignant truisms that football, being a team game with only so many places up for grabs, illustrates vividly time and time again. Consider, for example, the cases of Ian Davidson and Howard Kendall as their team, Preston North End, prepared for the 1964 FA Cup Final. Davidson was a hard-working wing-half who had arrived at Deepdale from Kilmarnock in December 1962 and in 1963/64 played a full part in Preston's progress to Wembley. A week before the match, against West Ham United, manager Jimmy Milne wanted to field his strongest side for a League match against Northampton Town, but had been unable to do so because Davidson had requested compassionate leave to attend a funeral in Edinburgh. Fair enough, until Milne discovered holes in the Scot's story, and that actually he had travelled north to help a relative who was in debt. In the circumstances, Jimmy elected to axe Ian from his Wembley team, replacing him with the promising Howard Kendall, who had filled the number-six shirt against Northampton and had distinguished himself already when called up through injuries for three Cup matches.

The first Howard knew of his shock inclusion was when the line-up was posted on the club noticeboard. There followed a team photograph, the rather embarrassed Kendall offering his chair to Davidson and the older man declining with thanks. It was an emotional moment for both of them. Davidson, a competent performer but one who must have known he would never scale the heights, was missing out on what would have been the greatest day of his career; indeed, the following year he left Deepdale to see out his League days with unremarkable spells at Middlesbrough and Darlington. Contrastingly, Kendall was on the verge of becoming the youngest player to appear in an FA Cup Final - at 17 years and 345 days - and had the ability to forge a glittering future, as his subsequent achievements with Everton were to demonstrate.

If the 1964 final was to prove a watershed for Davidson and Kendall, it was no less so for the two clubs who met at Wembley. The Hammers, a trifle fortunate to win an open encounter in which fortunes seesawed thrillingly, went on to European glory and to establish themselves as a high-profile 'personality' team. In stark contrast, for poor Preston - whose Cup defeat was coupled with a narrow failure to gain promotion to the First Division - the future contained only a dismal decline into mediocrity from which they had not emerged nearly 30 years later. Managed by the thoughtful Ron Greenwood, West Ham were emerging as one of the most attractive sides in the First Division, always a threat in knockout competitions but whose League aspirations, like the bubbles in their theme song, were all too prone to vanish and die.

The two men at the heart of the Deepdale drama in Wembley week. Left: Ian Davidson, who was dropped sensationally after his request for compassionate leave from a League match proved to be based on a false story. Below: Howard Kendall, who became the youngest man to turn out in a final, meets the Earl of Harewood.

Their best-known player, one who was destined for fame the world over, was skipper Bobby Moore, who but for his position of wing-half might have been Roy of the Rovers incarnate. Tall, blond and handsome, assured in every move he made, he was a ready-made hero for a generation of young fans growing up in the early 1960s. United's outstanding attacker at this time was Johnny Byrne, as skilful a centre-forward as might be found anywhere in England, but whose international career was never commensurate with his enormous ability. Nevertheless 'Budgie' - so dubbed because he never stopped talking - refused to be despondent and lived life to the full.

Geoff Hurst and Martin Peters, the two men whose names will go down in history alongside Moore's as 1966 World Cup heroes, were rising stars in 1964, though utility man Peters missed the FA Cup Final after losing his regular place to Eddie Bovington in the second half of the season. The East Londoners' route to Wembley was an entertaining one, with three goals scored in each round. The narrowest margin of victory was 3-2 against Burnley in the quarter-final, but by far the most stirring occasion was the 3-1 semi-final disposal of Manchester

Above: Preston boss Jimmy Milne, who had picked up a loser's medal with North End in 1937 and was sidelined by injury when they won the Cup in 1938.

143

HOW THEY GOT THERE

WEST HAM UNITED

Round 3:
Charlton Athletic (h) 3-0.

Round 4:
Leyton Orient (a) 0-0, replay (h) 3-0.

Round 5:
Swindon Town (a) 3-1.

Round 6:
Burnley (h) 3-2.

Semi-final:
Manchester United *at Hillsborough* 3-1.

PRESTON NORTH END

Round 3:
Nottingham Forest (a) 0-0, replay (h) 1-0.

Round 4:
Bolton Wanderers (a) 2-2, replay (h) 2-1.

Round 5:
Carlisle United (h) 1-0.

Round 6:
Oxford United (a) 2-1.

Semi-final:
Swansea Town *at Villa Park* 2-1.

Defeated Preston skipper Nobby Lawton, whose personal display was worthy of a winner's medal.

United in a Hillsborough mudbath. It was an epic contest for which the Hammers were hyped up after the northern press had written them off as having little chance against Matt Busby's multi-talented combination. As it turned out, Greenwood's men adapted better to the quagmire and thoroughly deserved their win, which was gained courtesy of two goals by Ronnie Boyce and a cracker by Hurst. Afterwards, amid the general euphoria, the West Ham coach almost left for the railway station minus the manager, who was giving an interview. Sadly the train journey south was to be marred by boorish gatecrashers who infiltrated the club's carriage.

Preston's passage was more laboured - every triumph was gained by a one-goal margin - but no less exciting. Their first victims were Nottingham Forest, caught unawares by a long-range drive from the young Kendall. Local Lancastrian passions were aroused by the fourth-round derby against Bolton Wanderers, which had special significance for North End's veteran winger Doug Holden - he'd played for the Trotters in the 1953 and 1958 finals. Next came a relatively routine meeting with Carlisle United before media attention intensified for the quarter-final, not least because the opponents were Oxford United, the first Division Four side to reach that stage of the competition. The semi-final, at Villa Park, was an all-Second Division clash with struggling Swansea Town, settled by an astonishing 40-yard shot by centre-half Tony Singleton, his first senior goal for the club. Thus the men from Deepdale had reached Wembley, and although they were not blessed with

illustrious names, they were a sparky, resilient outfit containing several individuals capable of match-winning performances. Two of them, right-half and captain Nobby Lawton and centre-forward Alex Dawson, were former Busby Babes who had failed narrowly to make the grade at Old Trafford, and both had been in splendid form as Preston had challenged Leeds and Sunderland for a promotion spot. The pair offered a remarkable contrast: Lawton the cool, blond, creative prompter, Dawson the swarthy, muscular dreadnought known forbodingly as 'The

Black Prince of Deepdale'. North End were admirably served, too, by manager Milne, a North End man through and through, who had been a Wembley loser with the club in 1937 and missed the 1938 triumph because of injury.

It had been predicted freely that the final would underline a chasm in class between the two sides, yet as the game began, it was the underdogs who looked the more impressive. With Lawton and fellow schemer Alan Spavin bestriding the midfield and with the rookie Kendall showing no trace of nerves, pressure built

'The Black Prince' in all his pomp. Preston's Alex Dawson, as physically fearsome a specimen as the English game possessed, outjumps Hammers centre-half Ken Brown.

145

Right: Veteran winger Doug Holden, playing in his third FA Cup Final, is on hand to give Preston an early lead with a tap-in.

Below: A minute later and West Ham are level as John Sissons (second left) beats Preston 'keeper Alan Kelly with a low shot to become the youngest scorer in a Wembley final.

up on the Hammers' defence. Alec Ashworth missed a presentable chance, but after ten minutes Doug Holden made no such mistake, prodding home from close range after goalkeeper Jim Standen had failed to hold a shot from Dawson. However, Preston were given no chance to savour their advantage. Only 60 seconds later, West Ham were level after a slick move involving Moore and Byrne culminated in Johnny Sissons

netting with a well-placed effort from the edge of the box. Thus the 18-year-old winger, a close chum of Kendall in the England youth team, became the youngest scorer in an FA Cup Final. After their bright start, the equaliser was an undeserved setback to North End, but they refused to wilt and continued to enjoy the better of exchanges until they were rewarded with another goal five minutes before half-time. It came from the broad forehead of the implacable Dawson, who brushed aside the challenge of centre-half Ken Brown to head firmly into the net from a corner by David Wilson.

Above: Rising to the occasion. Alex Dawson wins another aerial battle to give North End the lead shortly before the interval.

However, the interval gave Greenwood, that enterprising tactician, the chance to think again, and he implemented crucial changes. Now Moore was switched from sweeper to become Brown's twin stopper, freeing Bovington to mark Spavin, and Boyce to take responsibility for the influential Lawton. From the restart the Londoners looked far more cohesive and they regained parity when Brabrook's corner was turned on by Brown to Hurst, who headed against the underside of the bar. As the ball bounced down it hit grounded goalkeeper Alan Kelly and bobbled over the line. That was the signal for Byrne and company to strike something like their true form and West Ham assumed the upper hand, though chances were scorned at either end as the likelihood of an extra 30 minutes increased.

In the event, no extension was needed. After 90 seconds of injury time, Hurst battled past a tackle near half-way and found Brabrook on the right, even as Boyce began to drift forward from a deep position. Socks around his ankles to ward off cramp, the former England flankman swept a tempting cross into the middle, a posse of tired Preston defenders were guilty of ball-watching and Boyce stole into space to nod precisely past poor Kelly, who was limping from a knock received ten minutes earlier. As the stadium erupted, the beaming scorer - known as 'Ticker' for his ceaseless midfield work - ran behind the goal, where he was engulfed by partying team-mates. Even then, gallant Preston would not bow their heads and forced a free-kick on the edge of the Hammers' box, but the ball was scrambled to safety and the final whistle blew. Lawton, Dawson and any number of their colleagues

hardly deserved to be on the losing side, but at least they had let no one down. Indeed when they went home to a civic reception, the mayor of Preston told them: ' You didn't win the Cup but you won the admiration of the country. It was one of the finest sporting shows ever seen at Wembley.' The fans, too, were in no doubt that their men had done them proud, singing, in the idiom of the times: 'We love you, yeah, yeah, yeah!'

Above: The Hammers' second equaliser. Geoff Hurst's header hits the bar (top) and bounces over the line off prone 'keeper Alan Kelly with Jim Smith helpless.

Perfect timing from 'Ticker'. Workaholic midfielder Ronnie Boyce nods home the winner in the 92nd minute. Heady stuff for the Hammers but, in truth, Preston did not deserve such savage fortune.

A whole gamut of expressions from the happy Hammers, with manager Ron Greenwood (clutching the Cup) displaying the most abandon. The players pictured are (standing, left to right): John Bond, Jim Standen, Bobby Moore, Geoff Hurst, Ken Brown, Peter Brabrook and Ronnie Boyce. Kneeling: Jack Burkett, John Sissons, Johnny Byrne and Eddie Bovington. Opposite: The golden boy, destined for fame beyond measure. Bobby Moore, whose premature death in 1993 saddened the sporting world, holds high his first major trophy.

Naturally, West Ham's joy was unconfined, though they found time to reflect on the past as well as anticipate an exciting future. Among the guests at their official celebration was Billy Moore, a player in the club's only previous FA Cup Final, in 1923, which was lost to Bolton Wanderers. It is renowned on two counts, as the first to be played at Wembley, and as 'The White Horse Final'. That day the gate was recorded as 126,047 but unofficial estimates put the figure at more than 150,000; the pitch was invaded and policemen on horseback were called in to disperse the multitude. For the Hammers' modern Moore, Bobby, the Cup victory capped a wonderful season in which he had been voted Footballer of the Year and confirmed his status as a world-class performer. Indeed, it was no surprise when Spurs attempted to acquire his services in mid-term, after their own great wing-half, Dave Mackay, had broken his leg. West Ham, wisely, were not to be tempted and reaped the benefit as Bobby led them to triumph in the 1965 European Cup Winners' Cup. But arguably the Hammer with most reasons to celebrate in 1964 was 'keeper Jim Standen: not only did he collect a winner's medal at Wembley, that summer he went on to help Worcestershire lift the county cricket championship and completed an *Annus Mirabilis* by topping the national bowling averages, claiming 64 wickets with his brisk medium pace!

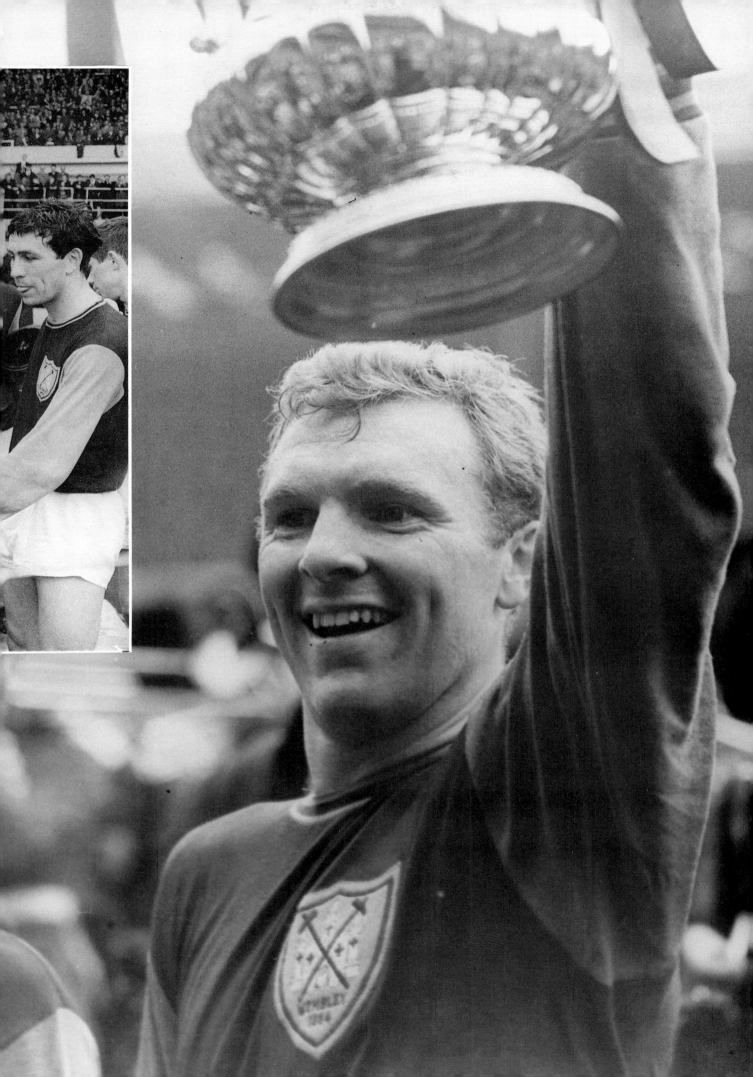

IT HAPPENED
THIS YEAR

Death of Sir Winston
Churchill.

Beatles awarded
MBEs, many other
recipients outraged.

Ted Heath succeeded
Lord Home as
Conservative leader.

Mary Whitehouse
launched campaign to
'clean up TV'.

Soviet Alexei Leonev
became first man to
walk in space.

Goldie the Eagle
escaped from London
Zoo, attracted huge
crowds of supporters.

1 May 1965

LIVERPOOL 2
Hunt 93; St John 111

LEEDS UNITED 1
Bremner 101

Half-time 0-0 Extra-time played

LIVERPOOL		LEEDS UNITED
Tommy Lawrence	1	Gary Sprake
Chris Lawler	2	Paul Reaney
Gerry Byrne	3	Willie Bell
Geoff Strong	4	Billy Bremner
Ron Yeats (captain)	5	Jack Charlton
Willie Stevenson	6	Norman Hunter
Ian Callaghan	7	Johnny Giles
Roger Hunt	8	Jim Storrie
Ian St John	9	Alan Peacock
Tommy Smith	10	Bobby Collins (captain)
Peter Thompson	11	Albert Johanneson

Attendance: 100,000

Referee: W Clements, West Bromwich

Some called it the 'Bore of the Roses'; during the match, even Bill Shankly likened it to a game of chess that had reached stalemate . But for once, perhaps, the greatest of all Liverpool managers - and what an accolade *that* is - was selling his men short. To most observers, despite the tightness of the scoreline, the 1965 FA Cup Final was one of the most one-sided in living memory. Quite simply, the Reds poured forward virtually non-stop for 120 minutes, while Don Revie's Leeds United adopted an utterly sterile approach that destroyed the game as a footballing spectacle. But what it could not do was rob it of drama. With both mighty clubs seeking their first FA Cup - it was the Yorkshiremen's first final and Liverpool's third - there was too much at stake for the action to be anything but riveting. And although the massed ranks of Reds partisans did not know it at the time, in the performance of their left-back Gerry Byrne - who played for 117 minutes with two edges of a broken collarbone grinding together - they were witnessing one of the most heroic displays in Wembley history.

But let's be fair to Leeds, and place their effort in context. Just three years earlier they had been within an ace of dropping into the Third Division - then came

Revie, who brought about salvation, followed by renaissance. In 1964 the Elland Roaders were promoted, and only a week before their Wembley date with Liverpool they had completed their first campaign back in the top flight by conceding the title to Manchester United on goal average alone. All this had been achieved on the back of superb defensive organisation combined with the midfield dynamism of Bobby Collins and the increasingly influential Billy Bremner. But come the final, with Footballer of the Year Collins rendered less effective than usual by the Reds' non-stop surge, Leeds were to give a convincing impression of a spent force.

It was hardly surprising if they were tired; the latter stages of their Cup campaign were severely draining, both physically and mentally. Their quarter-final clash with Crystal Palace was remorselessly rough, though it was nothing compared to the semi-final collison with Manchester United. In fact, the 0-0 draw at Hillsborough degenerated into little better than a brawl at times and reflected no credit on either club. Happily the replay, at the City Ground, Nottingham, was more of a footballing contest, and like the first it was dominated by the Red

The long and the short of it. Liverpool's colossus Ron Yeats greets his fellow Scot, the diminutive Bobby Collins. Despite his lack of inches, however, the Leeds skipper and Footballer of the Year was every jot as hard as Big Ron. As one opponent once said, while reflecting ruefully on Bobby's biting tackle: 'That wee fellow, he's half-man, half crocodile!'

Devils. However, it remained scoreless until near the end when a Bremner header from a Johnny Giles free-kick - how sweet that moment must have been for the former Busby Babe - stole the spoils.

Liverpool's passage to Wembley had lacked any such epic struggle, but it had been eventful all the way. Victory in the third round at West Bromwich came only after a bizarre incident when Reds skipper Ron Yeats had picked up the ball in his own penalty area, believing he had heard the referee blow. In fact, it had been a rogue whistler in the crowd and Albion were awarded a spot-kick, only for Bobby Cram to miss the target. There was another fright lurking at the next stage: Stockport, bottom of the Fourth Division, held the reigning League champs to a draw at Anfield, courtesy of a goal from Len White, who had played for Newcastle in the 1955 final. There was no shock at Edgeley Park, though, or at Burnden Park in the fifth round, where Liverpool beat Bolton thanks hugely to a courageous display by the injured Yeats against the aerial might of Wyn 'The Leap' Davies. Now the Merseysiders were paired with Leicester, whose scalp they were especially keen to claim in view of the spoiling tactics the Filberts had employed in the 1963 semi-final. This time Shankly's men prevailed but only just, with Roger Hunt's replay goal the only strike during two immensely tight contests. In the last four, Liverpool were paired with Tommy Docherty's bright young Chelsea side, and coming only four days after the Reds finally won their three-match European Cup marathon against FC Cologne, it was a daunting prospect. But a brilliant solo goal by winger Peter Thompson and a penalty from wing-half Willie Stevenson produced the result that transported Kopites into ecstasy.

By now, Liverpool had given up hopes of retaining their title but with two trophies still in their sights, the closing weeks of the campaign could hardly have been more uplifting for their legions of fans. How they relished their unique rapport with Bill Shankly, which he demonstrated so warmly on the radio programme Desert Island Discs, revealing that his favourite tune was - surprise, surprise - You'll Never Walk Alone! As the Reds' public profile grew ever more prominent, and with the Beatles at the peak of their popularity, 'Scouseness' was never more fashionable. It had even taken over the London Palladium, where Merseyside comedian Ken Dodd was entertaining the masses with his 'Diddy Men from Knotty Ash' routine, and the Liverpool squad caught a performance during Cup Final week.

I have written earlier how, in the anxiety of the moment, Bill Shankly might have underestimated the superiority his side was exerting at Wembley, but before kick-off he was in more characteristically bullish mood. Rasping every word with fervent belief, he told his players: 'You're going to win because you're the best team. Leeds are honoured to be on the same field as you. *and* you're not going to disappoint the greatest supporters in the world. If necessary - and it won't be - you should be prepared to die for them.' It was a moving call to arms, and as the two sides emerged from the tunnel, it would have been impossible to take issue with Shanks' assessment of the Liverpool following. Having upset many traditionalists by 'amending' most of the lyrics during the pre-match community singing, now the fans made the stadium's rafters rattle as never before with a fusillade of thunderous chants.

Both teams lined up as expected, with Leeds at full strength and with Geoff Strong replacing the injured Gordon Milne in the Liverpool midfield. The absence of Gordon, hurt at Chelsea in a League match two weeks earlier, was particularly unfortunate as it echoed the experience of his father Jimmy, who had been invalided out of Preston's 1938 final victory over Huddersfield. Mercifully, since 1961 the English soccer showpiece had been free of the so-called Wembley hoodoo, but now it was to strike again within three minutes of kick-off. The casualty was Gerry Byrne, who fell to the ground after a tackle with Collins and appeared to be treated for a leg injury. But as he resumed, he noticed a numbness in his shoulder and when trainer Bob Paisley returned to the field to give further attention, he was quick to realise that the combative defender had broken his collarbone. Bob warned Gerry that if he remained in the fray there was a risk that the bone might pierce his lung. Gerry asked the older man what *he* would do, and Paisley - who had been omitted from Liverpool's previous Cup Final team, in 1950 - informed him that he would have played on, even if he'd needed a wooden leg! Thus Byrne took up his position and continued

Left: After delivering a call to arms that would have done credit to Attila the Hun, Bill Shankly leads out his troops to face a Leeds team which he described as 'honoured to be on the same field' as Liverpool. Looking understandably tense in their leader's wake are Ron Yeats, Tommy Lawrence, Gerry Byrne, Ian Callaghan and Willie Stevenson.

Below: Bulwarks of a formidable Leeds barrier. Recently capped England centre-half Jack Charlton and Welsh goalkeeper Gary Sprake clear their lines for the umpteenth time.

Right: The Great Escape (continued). Norman Hunter (left), Jack Charlton and the prone Gary Sprake breath again as the ball scrapes past the Leeds post. Willie Stevenson, who gave an immaculate performance in Liverpool's midfield, sighs for what might have been.

Below: Jim Storrie, whose immobility after an early injury did much to disarm the Leeds attack.

Inset top: The moment the Kopites died a thousand deaths. Billy Bremner hits a scorcher past Tommy Lawrence to put Leeds level.
Below: 'Sir Roger' stoops to conquer. After an afternoon of utter frustration, Hunt nods Gerry Byrne's cross calmly and precisely into the Leeds net.

unflinchingly, doing his utmost to disguise his pain from Leeds. Revie's team were renowned for their ruthlessness and surely must have been quick to capitalise on the plight of their stricken opponent, if only they'd realised it. Even his team-mates did not know the extent of Gerry's difficulty until the interval, after which they did their best to protect him without giving away his secret. Only once was there an awkward moment, when Ian St John urged him to take a quick throw, before he realised what he'd said. Even then, though, Leeds didn't notice. Remarkably, not only did Gerry remain in the action, he played a full part, even making tackles at high speed, a stupendous display of raw courage.

In fact, Leeds also suffered a first-half injury setback when front-runner Jim Storrie pulled a muscle that left him little more than a passenger, and his virtual non-participation had a significant bearing on his side's anaemic showing in attack. Even so, it hardly explained Liverpool's almost total domination. With the constructive Stevenson in magnificent passing form, the red tide was incessant, but repeatedly it broke on the white rock of the Yorkshiremen's rearguard. Jack Charlton, Norman Hunter and company were as unyielding as granite, and goalkeeper Gary Sprake, sometimes maligned as a weak link, was inspired, pulling off a string of fine saves to deny Thompson on three occasions and Strong on two. United's much vaunted 'Black Flash', speedy winger Albert Johanneson, was played out of contention by Chris Lawler, and Yeats blunted any vestige of threat from spearhead Alan Peacock. With one side apparently bent only on survival, there was precious little to savour on a bleak, rainy afternoon and the prospect of the first added time in a final since 1947 was greeted with dismay by many neutrals.

However, the extra period brought relief. Three minutes in, Stevenson went past two men and passed to the incredible Byrne; he surged down the left and crossed from the byline for Roger Hunt to stoop and place a header neatly into the net. There was a veritable explosion of joy

and released tension from the Liverpool support; now, surely, lacklustre Leeds were dead and buried - yet eight minutes later, they struck back. In a rare attack, Hunter hoisted
a high pass into the Liverpool box, Charlton got a touch
and the ball fell to Bremner some 20 yards out. The diminutive Scottish fireball
hit it perfectly on the half-volley and it arrowed into the top corner of the Reds'
net, leaving hitherto unemployed 'keeper Tommy Lawrence open-mouthed in
horror. The unfairness of it all struck the Kopites momentarily dumb, and suddenly, with Bremner bristling with renewed menace, there was the threat of robbery in the air. But with only nine minutes separating the teams from a replay,

Saintly intervention. An airborne Ian St John heads the Reds' dramatic winner from Ian Callaghan's perfect cross, and justice is done.

Below: Pity poor Gordon Milne (centre), a regular member of the Liverpool side who was forced by injury to sit and soak on the sidelines as his team-mates won the Cup. With him, left to right, are Ron Yeats, Gerry Byrne, Willie Stevenson and Ian St John.

justice was done. Ian Callaghan was fed by the redoubtable Tommy Smith, then hared down the right wing, went past Willie Bell and delivered a low, raking cross. St John met it with a flying jack-knife header that punctured Leeds' hopes as it sped past the helpless Sprake. The 'Saint' said later that the goal had yawned before him as wide as the Mersey Tunnel, but he was too modest; it was an expert finish, one fit to win any prize, and in this case it secured the FA Cup.

Later, while the rest of the team were bound for a banquet, Gerry Byrne went to hospital, eventually joining the celebrations white-faced and with his arm in a sling. Shankly had never been prouder of anyone and announced: 'All the lads should give their medals to Gerry, he deserves the lot.' Some 250,000 Merseysiders lined the route from Lime Street station to the town hall to greet the returning heroes and 90 needed treatment after being caught in the crush, prompting Bill to reflect: 'A great welcome, but it really put the wind up me.' Even then, Liverpool's season went on. On Tuesday, the day after Chris Lawler's wedding, they outplayed Inter Milan at Anfield in the European Cup semi-final first leg, giving what many maintain is still the club's greatest display in any competition. Sadly they were to bow out controversially at San Siro, but nothing could dim the satisfaction of a fabulous campaign.

Left: As brave as they come. Gerry Byrne lifts the lid of the FA Cup after playing for 117 minutes with a broken collarbone. Note the stiffness of his right arm, though he is able to clutch that precious medal! Alongside Gerry are goal-scorer Roger Hunt and ever-dependable 'keeper Tommy Lawrence (with plinth).

157

IT HAPPENED
THIS YEAR

116 children killed as coal tip collapsed on school in Aberfan.

Labour won election with increased majority, then introduced pay freeze.

Freddie Laker offered first cheap flights for package holidays.

Arkle won Cheltenham Gold Cup for third year in succession.

Bob Dylan 'went electric' and pushed back boundaries of popular music.

14 May 1966

EVERTON 3

Trebilcock 58, 63; Temple 80

SHEFFIELD WEDNESDAY 2

McCalliog 4, Ford 57

Half-time 0-1

EVERTON		SHEFFIELD WEDNESDAY
Gordon West	1	Ron Springett
Tommy Wright	2	Wilf Smith
Ray Wilson	3	Don Megson *(captain)*
Jimmy Gabriel	4	Peter Eustace
Brian Labone *(captain)*	5	Sam Ellis
Brian Harris	6	Gerry Young
Alex Scott	7	Graham Pugh
Mike Trebilcock	8	Johnny Fantham
Alex Young	9	Jim McCalliog
Colin Harvey	10	David Ford
Derek Temple	11	Johnny Quinn

Attendance: 100,000

Referee: J Taylor, Wolverhampton

Mention Wembley '66 to most English football fans and the next few minutes are likely to be spent wallowing in World Cup nostalgia - Geoff Hurst's historic hat-trick, the magnificent eyesight of that splendid Russian linesman, the evocative commentary of Kenneth Wolstenholme. But talk to an Evertonian and the images will be different - he'll recall an heroic fightback, an unlikely Cornish saviour, one of the coolest pieces of finishing the old stadium has seen. Then, like as not, the discussion will turn to policemen and their helmets, which for those who do not remember one diverting incident when the tension was at its height, I shall explain in due course. A Sheffield Wednesday supporter, too, might recall the occasion with pride, albeit rather ruefully. After all, the Owls were only the second side since the War to lose an FA Cup Final in which they had led by two goals, but they walked off at the end with their heads held high, having played a stirring part in a truly memorable contest.

For one of Everton's top stars, though, his club's triumph was distinctly bittersweet. Centre-forward Fred Pickering, an England international, had scored four times during the 1966 Cup campaign, only for a knee injury to force him out of the first of the Blues' three quarter-final clashes with Manchester City and the semi-final against Manchester United. During the run-up to Wembley, Fred pronounced himself fully recovered and played in three League matches; but his game was off the boil, Harry Catterick harboured doubts about his ability to last the distance on Wembley's springy turf and he was dropped for the final. In the last season in which substitutes were not to be allowed, the manager's decision was understandable - an early breakdown might have cost his club the trophy - but it was heart-breaking for Pickering, whose face as he watched the action from the trainer's bench was a study in misery. Harry's gamble in replacing such a prolific marksman with the inexperienced Mike Trebilcock might easily have backfired; in the event, it succeeded so spectacularly that it emphasised the poignancy of Pickering's plight. At 25, Fred was young enough to have many productive years at Goodison ahead of him, but sadly, it was not to be. After one more injury-ravaged season and with the young Joe Royle pushing for recognition, he departed to Birmingham City. For Everton he had scored 70 goals in 115 outings, a strike rate to compare with the very best.

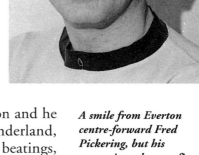

A smile from Everton centre-forward Fred Pickering, but his expression when confined to the Wembley bench was rather less sunny.

Back in January 1966, the clouds were yet to drift across Fred's horizon and he was playing an integral part in the Toffeemen's FA Cup progress. Sunderland, non-League Bedford Town and Coventry City were each handed 3-0 beatings, and belief grew that this could be Everton's year. In the sixth round, however, they encountered sterner resistance and were decidedly lucky to survive in a goalless Maine Road encounter with Manchester City. That was followed by another blank scoreline at Goodison before the matter was settled, thanks to goals by Pickering and Derek Temple, at Molineux. In the last four, the Blues met even more formidable opponents in the shape of Manchester United, but the soccer fates rarely looked kindly on the Red Devils' exertions at this stage of the competition. Indeed, after defeat here, they had reached four semi-finals in five years and won only one of them. This time they put the Merseysiders under heavy pressure, but lost to a rare goal by Colin Harvey. Thus

Joy for Wednesday after their semi-final win over Chelsea. But for Vic Mobley (extreme left with blond hair) injury despair was imminent.

Everton became the first club since Bury in 1903 to get to the final without conceding a goal. Wednesday, on the other hand, had failed to return a single clean sheet, going through by a one-goal margin in every round until the semi-final, when strikes by Graham Pugh and Jim McCalliog overturned the much-fancied Chelsea. For Tommy Docherty's men, it was a second successive semi-final defeat; next year, at last, they would go one better.

The teams lined up at Wembley each shorn of a regular member. Ironically, the player joining Pickering among the absentees was the one who would have been marking him, England under-23 centre-half Vic Mobley, who had damaged ankle ligaments against Chelsea. He was replaced by 19 year-old Sam Ellis, who was

*Above: The underrated
Johnny Fantham, whose
brilliant run created
Wednesday's second goal
for David Ford (top).*

*Right: No way to treat
'The Golden Vision'.
Ron Springett fells Alex
Young but no penalty was
given.*

making his FA Cup debut and further lowering the experience quota of a side containing six players aged 21 or under. Not that the underdog Owls looked like greenhorns when the game got under way. A fast, fit, direct combination, as

Above: Wednesday are one up after four minutes and scorer Jim McCalliog takes off. Everton 'keeper Gordon West can't believe it, while Brian Harris seems in a hurry to put the setback behind him.

any team prepared by martinet manager Alan Brown was sure to be, they tore into the attack from the outset and reaped a nearly dividend. David Ford received the ball on the left from a Peter Eustace throw-in and crossed into the path of the in-rushing McCalliog. The young Scot hit a first-timer from the edge of the box, it took a slight deflection off England full-back Ray Wilson and gave 'keeper Gordon West no chance as it zipped into the net. Thereafter Wednesday, with Eustace dictating midfield affairs, looked capable of building on their enterprising start, although it was a strangely punchless Everton who came closest to adding to the scoreline. That was after 18 minutes when Alex Young, the 'Golden Vision' himself, appeared to be brought down in the box by Sheffield custodian Ron Springett, only for referee Jack Taylor to wave play on.

The Owls had fully deserved their interval advantage, and after the break, apart from a Young effort that brought a smart save from Springett, continued to hold sway. Soon their ascendancy paid off when the excellent Johnny Fantham, perhaps unlucky to win only one England cap, picked up the ball in a deep position, ran past three defenders and shot low from 20 yards. There was beef in the effort but a 'keeper of West's calibre might have expected to gather it; instead the ball bounced from his chest into the path of Ford, who slipped it past him - 2-0 to Wednesday and surely the Cup was on its way to Hillsborough.

Here beginneth the fairytale of Mike Trebilcock. Until now he had looked like

Above: Ron Springett's fingertips are not enough to keep out Mike Trebilcock's half-volley and the Toffeemen are level at 2-2.

Above: Panto time, starring Everton's Gordon West and Brian Labone, two officers of the law and a man in braces

what, essentially, he was: a young striker out of his depth in the highest class of British club football. But just a minute after Ford had pounced, Brian Harris chipped into the Wednesday box, Temple nodded down and Mike popped up to ram a searing 12-yard volley just inside the post. Five minutes later Alex Scott floated in a tantalising free-kick from the right, Ellis' mistimed clearance fell to Trebilcock on the edge of the box and the little opportunist dispatched a waspish half-volley to which Springett got a hand but could not repel. For two Everton fans, the emotions engendered by such a dramatic transformation were too wild to contain and they dashed on to the pitch. One was detained almost instantly by the forces of law and order, but the second, having engulfed Trebilcock in an embrace that deposited the hero on the turf, set off as if to sprint to the far end of the stadium. As he did so, he was grabbed from behind by a policeman, but escaped from custody by shrugging himself free of his jacket. However, the moment of reckoning was at hand: now a second bobby appeared at high speed and brought the exuberant interloper to earth with a flying rugby tackle. With helmets now littering the pitch, reinforcements arrived and the miscreant was borne away by six officers. Several players, apparently urging mercy over what had been a non-malicious intrusion, retrieved the displaced headgear and the offender's coat, only pausing to try them on for size before passing them to the appropriate authorities.

When the decks were cleared for action, the game resumed with its rhythm altered irrevocably. Where the Toffeemen had been tentative and pallid, now - with Jimmy Gabriel returning to something like his usual dynamic best in midfield - they were fired with certainty of purpose, driving forward at every opportunity. After 77 minutes Trebilcock spurned a good chance to complete his hat-trick, but the decisive moment was at hand. Ten minutes from time, Harvey loosed a long ball out of defence and it dropped to Gerry Young near the edge of the centre circle. There was no aparent danger, but somehow the ball squirmed under the left-half's foot and skidded past him into the path of Derek Temple. The next few moments are enshrined in the memory of every Blues fan privileged to be present. With no opponent between himself and Springett, the speedy wing-man carried the ball some 35 yards; there was plenty of time to panic, but as the England 'keeper advanced, Derek kept his cool and, with exquisite timing and placement, struck a low 20-yard shot into the corner of the net. Poor Ron, who had done everything right, managed to get a slight touch and came agonisingly close to making a stunning save. But it is on fractions of inches that the destiny of the most glittering prizes can often hinge - as Geoff Hurst was to demonstrate controversially some two months hence - and this time the fraction favoured the Merseysiders. Even then the gallant Yorkshiremen, having seen the Cup dangled in front of their eyes only for it to be yanked brutally away, were not finished. Though weary beyond belief, they launched a swift break down the left which was halted only after Everton full-back Tommy Wright, ignoring the agonies of cramp, made a desperate interception at the last ditch.

And then it was all over. Unusually for that time, the losers did a lap of honour, the very least they merited for their spirited display. Harry Catterick, renowned as a stern, unbending disciplinarian, wore a happy face now as his players bore him shoulder-high in celebration. For Harry, there had been a radical turnabout in recent fortune; earlier in the season, as Everton had disappointed in the League and he had dropped Alex Young, he had been shoved and threatened by his own club's angry fans. Having managed Wednesday before moving to Goodison, he

Below: Derek Temple's sweetly-struck winner, as viewed from either side of the goal. For England 'keeper Ron Springett there could not be a shred of blame; for the scorer of such a clinical goal under intense pressure, no praise could be too high.

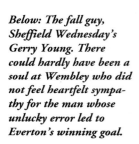

knew many of their players well, and took the Cup into their dressing room to offer a consoling draught of Champagne. First swig went to the dejected Young, an impeccable professional who simply did not deserve the humiliating stroke of ill-luck that came his way. As he said later, 99 times out of 100 he would have trapped and cleared the ball, and the hearts of all true sportsmen went out to him in his distress. The other side of the Cup Final coin was illustrated by the beaming countenance of Mike Trebilcock, whose name was not listed in the match programme but would be plastered over the back pages of newspapers for days to come. Unfortunately, the genial Cornishman who had been signed from Plymouth five months earlier was not to make the Goodison grade, and before long slipped back to the Second Division with Portsmouth. Still, he'd had his wonderful day and no one could ever take that

Left: Mike Trebilcock, whose career never hit the heights again but who had enjoyed the day of a footballing lifetime.

away from him. His goals had been instrumental in keeping the Cup on Merseyside, and the undercurrent of humour that moderated the tension between Liverpool and Everton was evident as the Toffeemen made their ten-mile triumphal procession through their home city on an open-topped bus. As they passed one fan, decked out defiantly in red amidst a sea of blue, he had a message for them, passed on in a spirit of healthy one-upmanship and in reference to his team's Cup victory of a year earlier. It consisted of one word - 'Copycats!'

20 May 1967

TOTTENHAM HOTSPUR 2

Robertson 45; Saul 68

CHELSEA 1

Tambling 86

Half-time 1-0

TOTTENHAM HOTSPUR		CHELSEA
Pat Jennings	1	Peter Bonetti
Joe Kinnear	2	Allan Harris
Cyril Knowles	3	Eddie McCreadie
Alan Mullery	4	John Hollins
Mike England	5	Marvin Hinton
Dave Mackay *(captain)*	6	Ron Harris *(captain)*
Jimmy Robertson	7	Charlie Cooke
Jimmy Greaves	8	Tommy Baldwin
Alan Gilzean	9	Tony Hateley
Terry Venables	10	Bobby Tambling
Frank Saul	11	John Boyle

Attendance: 100,000

Referee: K Dagnall, Lancashire

It was the first all-London FA Cup Final of the professional era and - in the interests of posterity, at least - might have been expected to produce a match worthy of the occasion. But to everyone except Tottenham Hotspur and their supporters, the encounter with Chelsea was low-key and predictable, the 2-1 scoreline preposterously flattering to the losers. In the weeks before the game, as if sensing the onset of ennui, the nation at large refused resolutely to become excited by the 'capital clash' in a manner quite unprecedented for the English game's gala day. Perhaps there was an element of pique in the north that their finest, the likes of Manchester United, Liverpool and Leeds, had all fallen by the wayside, but more fundamental was the contrasting state of the two finalists. Spurs were unbeaten in 23 games and, but for an equally impressive run by Matt Busby's United, might have sneaked up to take the title; having been rebuilt comprehensively by Bill Nicholson since the 'Glory, Glory' days of the early 1960s, they positively exuded confidence. In comparison, Chelsea were a mess; riven by strife between manager Tommy Docherty and the board, and with the

players mutinous over Wembley bonuses and ticket allocation, they had lost five of their last seven matches and could hardly have been more ill-prepared for their biggest match of the decade. So often in football, foregone conclusions have a beguiling way of transforming themselves into earth-shaking upsets, and therein lies a huge part of the game's undying attraction. But not this time.

For several seasons now, the Tottenham reconstruction programme had been under way. Its radical nature was illustrated by the fact that only Dave Mackay remained of the 1961 League/FA Cup double side (indeed, only he and Jimmy Greaves of the present team had taken part in the 1962 Cup triumph), with another survivor, Cliff Jones, getting a seat on the Wembley bench in this first year that substitutes were allowed. Of course, to apply the qualification 'only' to Mackay or Greaves was a contradiction in terms. Though a tad slower in his 33rd year than at his peak, Dave, now the skipper, remained a formidable operator, and his recovery from two shattered legs bore eloquent testimony to his apparent indestructibility. Meanwhile the Greaves goal-machine was back in top order after jaundice had interrupted normal service the previous term (even then he had struck 16 times in 31 outings - some malfunction!).

Around these two stalwarts was assembled a high-quality collection of new talent, including goalkeeper Pat Jennings, centre-half Mike England, Cyril Knowles at full-back, Alan Mullery and Terry Venables in midfield, and Alan Gilzean up front. On paper, Nicholson's expensive combination appeared irresistible - and, to be fair, for the second half of 1966/67 it had been - yet several recruits had endured traumatic settling-in periods. It's hard to imagine in view of later achievements, but Jennings made a shaky start in North London and was barracked by the notoriously demanding White Hart Lane crowd, while Mullery, too - saddled with the impossible task of emulating Danny Blanchflower - took

Men apart. Managers Tommy Docherty of Chelsea (left) and Tottenham's Bill Nicholson lead their teams out for the first all-London final of the modern era. The public personae of the abrasive, ever-controversial 'Doc' and the quiet Nicholson offered a vivid contrast.

167

HOW THEY GOT THERE

TOTTENHAM HOTSPUR
Round 3:
Millwall (a) 0-0, replay (h) 1-0.

Round 4:
Portsmouth (h) 3-1.

Round 5:
Bristol City (h) 2-0.

Round 6:
Birmingham City (a) 0-0, replay (h) 6-0.

Semi-final:
Nottingham Forest *at Hillsborough* 2-1.

CHELSEA
Round 3:
Huddersfield Town (a) 2-1.

Round 4:
Brighton and Hove Albion (a) 1-1, *replay* (h) 4-0.

Round 5:
Sheffield United (h) 2-0.

Round 6:
Sheffield Wednesday (h) 1-0.

Semi-final:
Leeds United *at Villa Park* 1-0.

Cigarette advertisements remained much in evidence in 1960s match programmes. This one unwittingly presages the advent of shirt advertising in the 1980s.

CADETS

The NOW cigarette for the NOW people

some time to be accepted. As for Venables, the man destined to manage and become part-owner of the club, he never really won a place in the fans' affections as a player, eventually fulfilling rather more of his potential with Queen's Park Rangers.

Terry had, of course, been signed from Chelsea, where his deteriorating relationship with Docherty had been but a single strand of the discontent which appeared to permeate Stamford Bridge. Having revived an ailing club in the early 1960s and put together a bright young side that came close to winning the Championship in mid-decade, 'The Doc' was running into the type of stormy patch that was to characterise his career. Arguably the seeds of his problems were sown several months *before* Chelsea's 1964/65 title tilt, when coach Dave Sexton left to manage Leyton Orient. Much of the credit for Chelsea's re-emergence belonged to Dave and although the Pensioners - as they were still nicknamed then, before opting for the less distinctive 'Blues' - continued to be a major force over the next two-and-a-half seasons, a crucial influence had been lost. A further blow to stability had been the sudden death in 1966 of chairman Joe Mears, with whom Docherty had worked happily and productively. Mears' successor, Charles Pratt, was less amenable to his manager's individualistic style and a catalogue of morale-sapping disputes ensued. One flashpoint occurred in February 1967 over players' free tickets for the fourth round FA Cup tie at Brighton. After the two men had disagreed, Tommy aired his views in the media and received a public reprimand for his pains.

In such an appalling atmosphere, it was amazing that Chelsea should have reached Wembley at all, but they did so by demonstrating that whatever travails afflicted them off the field - and such was the players' ire over what they considered a hopelessly inadequate Cup Final bonus that they mooted boycotting the after-match banquet - they could pull together impressively when they crossed that white line. Apart from the tie with Brighton, settled after a replay, they progressed by waging a one-club war on Yorkshire, disposing of Huddersfield in the third round, overcoming stiff challenges from Sheffield United and Wednesday in the fifth and sixth, and then seeing off Leeds United, thanks to a marvellous header from Tony Hateley, in the semi-final. That goal was the one memorable act in the short Stamford Bridge sojourn of the big centre-forward, an emergency signing from Aston Villa the previous October after the infinitely more creative Peter Osgood had broken his leg. Still, it *was* a vitally important contribution. Not only did it earn the club's first appearance at Wembley - their only previous final, which they lost to Sheffield United in 1915, had been at Old Trafford - it also staved off a wholly insupportable hat-trick of semi-final reverses, following defeats by Liverpool in 1965 and Sheffield Wednesday in 1966. Chelsea's other major newcomer that term, Scottish schemer Charlie Cooke, had bedded in much more promisingly alongside such admirable performers as striker Bobby Tambling, midfielder John Hollins, defenders Ron Harris and Eddie McCreadie and 'keeper Peter Bonetti, and despite Osgood's continued absence, there was no sound *footballing* reason why Docherty's young team - McCreadie and centre-half Marvin Hinton were the 'old men' at 27 - should fear Tottenham. Indeed, they had taken three League points off Nicholson's side that season, and had

dumped them out of the Cup in both 1964 and 1965.

Untroubled by such factors, Spurs' thoroughbreds had shown on their own road to Wembley that they could battle at need - and certainly the need was there in their third round clash with Second Division Millwall. Fresh from creating a League record of 59 home games without defeat, the Lions were not to be trifled with at the Den and forced their classy visitors to settle for a draw before bowing out to a single goal at the Lane. Portsmouth and Bristol City presented few difficulties, but then Birmingham City were unlucky not to earn more than a replay in a tense quarter-final at St Andrews. Having had their wobble, Tottenham won the rematch 6-0 before facing high-flying Nottingham Forest at Hillsborough in the last four. The Trentsiders, who were to finish runners-up in the League, were threatening to take control when Greaves turned the tide with a sensational piece of opportunism. England punted upfield, Gilzean nodded on and Jimmy, though off balance and with the Forest defence apparently not expecting a shot, hit an instant 25-yard grubber that crept into the net via the foot of a post. The game was made safe by another excellent individual effort by Frank Saul and Spurs, who had won all four of their previous finals, were through to their fifth. In the run-up to the Wembley showdown, as more tales of turmoil leaked from the Chelsea camp, an overwhelming feeling of inevitability about the outcome had gathered, and the opening exchanges did little to alter the impression. With the Pensioners nervy and off-key, Tottenham were playing the smoother football, and with

Prolific marksman Bobby Tambling, still the holder of Chelsea's goal-scoring record, rises above Tottenham's Dave Mackay in this aerial duel. Mike England stands guard at his captain's shoulder.

Gilzean enjoying almost total aerial superiority over Hinton - who had lined up as traditional stopper rather than sweeper, the role in which he had dominated the wily Scot in previous meetings - a swift breakthrough was on the cards. But even when the pendulum swung further in Spurs' favour after McCreadie injured a shoulder, severely restricting his efforts to tame the speedy Jimmy Robertson, there was no early goal. Saul missed one chance, Bonetti moved athletically to deny Robertson, then Greaves failed to capitalise on two openings. At the other end, Hollins tried a shot and then, in one of Chelsea's better moments, Cooke capped a captivating run by forcing a fine save from Jennings. Thus the stalemate persisted until shortly before the interval, and it needed an element of fortune to lift it. Taking possession after a free-kick, Mullery surged through centre-field before unleashing a powerful drive; the ball cannoned against right-back Allan Harris and

fell to Robertson, who netted firmly from 15 yards.

As the second half began Tottenham maintained the upper hand, with only a 58th-minute Hateley header - with which he might have done better - offering a hint of retaliation. Ten minutes later, the result was decided beyond all reasonable doubt when Saul, in the box, received the ball with his back to goal and swivelled adroitly to hook it inside Bonetti's near post. Thereafter Spurs cantered to victory, a situation in which their forwards might have been expected to take the eye. In fact, the major honours went to two members of the rearguard: the majestic England, who rendered Hateley well-nigh ineffective, and right-back Joe Kinnear, who had started the season as a reserve and owed his place in the side to the broken arm suffered in February by his chum, Phil Beal. Four minutes from time, Tambling notched a consolation - his sixth goal of the competition - when Jennings misjudged a centre from John Boyle and Bobby, seemingly surprised to be presented with the opportunity, nodded in. The final margin was a travesty of justice, and it is a measure of the North Londoners' dominance that even after Tambling's strike, Chelsea - for whom only Hollins and Ron Harris approached their best form - could not muster a meaningful late assault.

The next day more than 100,000 people jammed Tottenham High Road as the Cup was paraded on an open-topped bus. Fathers held up babies to see the conquering heroes, players wept with emotion and the prospect of a return to the European Cup Winners' Cup, which Spurs had won in 1963, was savoured. For Chelsea, the short-term future was turbulent, the longer-term full of good things. That October, after further commotion at the Bridge, Docherty resigned. Nineteen days later he was replaced by his former lieutenant, Dave Sexton, and the club embarked on the most sustained period of success in their history.

Left: Master of the unorthodox. Tottenham goalkeeper Pat Jennings performs one of the one-handed takes for which he was renowned and Chelsea centre-forward Tony Hateley's leap is in vain.

Below left: Another fine custodian, Chelsea's Peter Bonetti, is beaten by Frank Saul's shot which put the result beyond reasonable doubt.

Overleaf: Terry Venables (second left) savours the highlight of his playing career as a Spur. Other revellers, left to right, are Cyril Knowles, Joe Kinnear, Dave Mackay (at back), Jimmy Robertson, Alan Gilzean (partly obscured), Frank Saul and Mike England.

WEST BROMWICH ALBION 1

Astle 93

EVERTON 0

Half-time 0-0 Extra time played

WEST BROMWICH ALBION		EVERTON
John Osborne	1	Gordon West
Doug Fraser	2	Tommy Wright
Graham Williams *(captain)*	3	Ray Wilson
Tony Brown	4	Howard Kendall
John Talbut	5	Brian Labone *(captain)*
*John Kaye	6	Colin Harvey
Graham Lovett	7	Jimmy Husband
Ian Collard	8	Alan Ball
Jeff Astle	9	Joe Royle
Bobby Hope	10	John Hurst
Clive Clark	11	Johnny Morrissey
*(sub Dennis Clarke)		

Attendance: 100,000

Referee: L Callaghan Merthyr Tydfil

Right: A bevy of Baggies show off their prize. Left to right are Graham Lovett, Dennis Clarke, Doug Fraser, Tony Brown and Bobby Hope. Both sides wore change strips, Albion donning all white and Everton switching to amber shirts and blue shorts.

IT HAPPENED THIS YEAR

Martin Luther King and Robert Kennedy assassinated.

Richard Nixon elected President of the United States.

Czechoslovakia invaded by Soviet tanks.

Enoch Powell stoked racial tension with 'rivers of blood' speech.

Manchester United became first English club to win European Cup.

Jim Clark, world's top racing driver, killed in Germany.

The sheer, unadulterated joy of a man who has scored what turns out to be the Cup-winning goal. Albion striker Jeff Astle gives full vent to his feelings after passing Everton goalkeeper Gordon West with a fearsome shot.

The time: nearly twenty minutes to five on a murky January afternoon. The place: Layer Road, a relatively little-known outpost of professional football, some 65 miles from Wembley yet worlds away from the national stadium in terms of atmosphere and grandeur. The occasion: a third-round FA Cup tie between humble Colchester United, struggling for survival near the foot of the Third Division, and mighty West Bromwich Albion, one of the game's elite. Improbably, with only 90 seconds of the game remaining, the minnows are holding their illustrious visitors to a draw and for the plucky Essex outfit the dream of a lucrative replay at the Hawthorns is close to becoming reality. Yet suddenly, something even more sensational is in the air; the ball reaches United marksman Peter Bullock, the next instant it is beyond the grasp of 'keeper John Osborne and nestling in the Throstles' net. Colchester fans erupt, their players celebrate, the Albion men are downcast for there will be no time to fight back. But wait. Yes, the referee has blown his whistle but he is not pointing to the halfway line; he has spotted a handball and signalled for a free-kick. The 'goal' is ruled out, the game ends and the 'giants' have not been killed after all.

By such a narrow thread did the Cup ambitions of West Bromwich hang, and the fact that they went on to win at Wembley underlines the enduring attraction of senior football's oldest knockout competition. After the fright at Colchester, Albion skipper Graham Williams was the first to concede that he'd believed Bullock's strike to be valid, and might have pondered that but for the vigilance of an unsung official, the greatest day in the club careers of himself and his colleagues would never have come to pass. As it was, the Baggies (the more colloquial of the Midlanders' two nicknames) accepted their second chance against the underdogs with relish, crushing them 4-0 and leaving Colchester to spend the rest of the season waging an unsuccessful campaign to avoid relegation. However, their own supreme moment of Cup glory was only three years away, as any Leeds supporter might need a deal of persuading to recall!

Meanwhile Albion's progress continued thanks to a late Jeff Astle winner in a replay against Southampton and a narrow victory at Portsmouth, earning the dubious reward of a quarter-final confrontation with Liverpool. Draws at home and away were attained without the services of injured Scottish schemer Bobby Hope, whose return in the concluding sector of a gripping trilogy proved decisive as he plotted the Reds' downfall in front of more than 56,000 people at Maine Road. Also significant was the switch of John Kaye from front line to back in the absence of sidelined central defender Eddie Colquhoun; indeed, so successful was the move that it became permanent. The semi-final threw up a local derby against Birmingham City, then in Division Two but as combative as ever as they demonstrated with a resolute performance against an Albion side considerably below their best. However, though the Blues missed several inviting chances, the Baggies' bandwagon rolled on thanks to goals from Tony Brown and the prolific Astle.

The Midlanders had taken nine games to reach the final, while their opponents, Everton, had managed with the statutory minimum of five, the most taxing of which had been the first and last. On paper the campaign opener at Haig Avenue, the headquarters of their Third Division neighbours Southport, should not have represented a major obstacle, but there was more at stake than a place in the next round. The Sandgrounders were managed by Billy Bingham, a former Goodison star (and future boss) whose team was studded with would-be Toffeemen who hadn't made the grade with Everton and were burning to prove a point. Therefore, on a windy day (aren't they all at Southport?) and a hard pitch, the likes of Arthur Peat, Stuart Shaw and Ambrose Clarke were on their mettle, stretching Harry Catterick's men to the limit before a single goal from young Joe Royle settled the issue.

Albion 'keeper John Osborne foils Jimmy Husband (left) in one of many frustrating moments for the Everton raider. Fellow Toffeemen Joe Royle and John Hurst (right) are in attendance, John Kaye is the airborne defender and skipper Graham Williams guards the post.

Thereafter Everton's passage was comparatively tranquil as they disposed of Carlisle United, Tranmere Rovers and Leicester City - but tranquillity was never going to be on the agenda for their semi-final meeting with Leeds United at Old Trafford. Already Don Revie's side had won the League Cup, reached the semi-final of the UEFA Cup and retained aspirations in the title race; a titanic clash was in prospect. The Toffeemen's cause was weakened significantly by the absence of the rampantly dynamic Alan Ball, who was suspended, and the cultured, unassuming central defender cum midfielder John Hurst - 'Gentleman Jack' to his friends and one of the most underrated operators in the top flight - who had contracted hepatitis. The game was as tight as predicted, being decided by a Johnny Morrissey penalty, Jack Charlton having handled a goalbound chip by Jimmy Husband after a mistake by goalkeeper Gary Sprake.

Having finished fifth in the First Division (three places above Albion) and exhibited the telling signs of a genuinely potent force on the rise, Everton were favourites to win the final. Often their critics had labelled them disparagingly as 'moneybags', yet now, with six home-grown players in the side, the tag was hardly appropriate. Admittedly Catterick had the resources to recruit from the top drawer and had done so with the likes of Ball, his fellow midfielder Howard Kendall and England left-back Ray Wilson, but also had nurtured such talents as Colin Harvey, the third member of that superb engine-room, right-back Tommy Wright and the richly promising centre-forward Royle. Ranged against the Merseysiders was a team that had benefited enormously from the organisation of Alan Ashman in his first term as Hawthorns boss. Having given up chicken farming to become manager of Carlisle United, Alan had impressed at Brunton Park before taking the Albion job, but must have been jolted by a chronic start to the 1967/68 season which saw the Baggies slump to the foot of Division One. He reacted by calling the players together, calmly imparting a few home truths and outlining a basis for improvement. His young squad responded positively, and the result was a compact, mobile, tactically aware side that climbed the table and battled dauntlessly all the way to Wembley.

Poacher turned gamekeeper. Albion's erstwhile striker John Kaye demonstrates his newly-employed defensive capabilities, clearing his lines despite the attentions of Everton's John Hurst.

As Albion took the field for their tenth FA Cup Final - equalling the record held by Newcastle United - one player in particular might have been reflecting on the topsy-turvy nature of life in general and football in particular. Some 17 months earlier, a car crash had left midfielder Graham Lovett with such severe injuries to his neck and spine that doctors had feared he might never walk again. Sadly, the after-effects of the accident eventually precepitated his early retirement, but for now, at least, here he was striding on to soccer's grandest stage. For those in search of omens, Everton had thumped the Throstles 6-2 in March, with Ball netting four times, but anyone anticipating another goal feast was to be sorely disappointed. What the two teams served up on a greasy, rain-soaked surface was a grim, relentless, occasionally over-physical struggle that offered meagre entertainment to supporters uncommitted to either camp. As expected, Everton made most of the initial running, with Albion content to absorb pressure and threaten on the break. Perhaps an early goal might have sparked the contest to life, but with the ageing Alex Young now confined to the Goodison sidelines, there appeared to be no Toffeeman with the guile to penetrate a defence in which stopper John Talbut and his partner John Kaye were outstanding. Predictably, the two best chances of the first half fell to the Merseysiders: on 12 minutes, Jimmy Husband shot wide from a dangerous position after Osborne had dropped a cross, then three minutes before the break, the 'keeper saved well from Morrissey. Thereafter, the proceedings became slightly more eventful, with Astle - clearly the Midlanders' main hope of a breakthrough - heading narrowly wide after 51 minutes; then at the other end Kaye cleared off the line from Royle and Husband delayed his shot when an instant strike might have pierced the Albion armour. As the second half wore on and Everton became increasingly frustrated at their inability to convert territorial supremacy into goals, the underdogs, with Hope probing cleverly at their hub, grew in confidence. Yet as extra time became ever more inevitable, their burgeoning hopes should have been terminally dashed. Morrissey crossed for the umpteenth time, but for once found an unmarked man, the unfortunate Husband, who sent a free header tamely over the bar. It was the last meaningful move of normal time.

The redoubtable Kaye, who had soldiered on effectively with an ankle damaged early in the game, was replaced by Dennis Clarke for the extra period, in the first FA Cup Final substitution, the newcomer in at right-back and Doug Fraser switching to the centre. Now the sun shone at last, the sodden turf glistening in its welcome rays as the day's decisive act unfolded. Foraging in a deep position, the industrious Astle rode a vigorous challenge by Kendall and carried the ball forward, only to scuff a disappointing right-foot shot. However, instead of going wide, the leather rebounded from Harvey into the path of the still advancing Astle; he hit it fiercely from the edge of the box with his unfavoured left foot and it screamed unstoppably into the net, high and to West's left. Later Jeff - now, in the best traditions of Mortensen and Lofthouse, a scorer in every round - told the press: 'I saw this huge gap, the white net and the yellow ball streaking for the corner. It was a fantastic moment, nothing will ever match it.' West, who until then had hardly been called on to make a save, confirmed his utter helplessness: 'I saw it coming all the way, but could do nothing about it. You can't make excuses for a goal like that.' Still 27 minutes remained, and with the deadlock broken the action became less inhibited. Royle and Hurst went close for Everton, as did Brown for Albion before Lovett spurned a wonderful chance to cap his comeback with a goal. In the final analysis, it didn't matter: West Bromwich had won the Cup. A tracksuited Kaye, the wounded warrior, joined his team-mates for the 39-step climb to the royal box, then limped back down to the pitch clutching proudly the medal his

Above: That most combative of wingmen, Everton's Johnny Morrissey, rides a challenge from Ian Collard.

Everton 'keeper Gordon West and captain Brian Labone combine to deny winger Clive Clark.

Inset top: A brief respite. Everton ready themselves for extra time.

Inset above right: Everton's Gordon West is gracious with his congratulations to match-winner Jeff Astle.

courage had done so much to earn. Alan Ball's loser's gong was not as well received, the fiery little competitor hurling it to the ground in disgust. Indeed, there were tears from several young Evertonians, but older hands such as skipper Brian Labone and Gordon West urged them to get their heads up and run round the track to acknowledge their fans. To their credit, they reacted well and even the mortified Ball admitted later to being grateful that his medal had been retrieved for him. As for Albion captain Graham Williams, he might have permitted his thoughts to drift briefly from the euphoria of victory, back to Layer Road and that late, late effort from Peter Bullock . . .

'I saw this huge gap, the white net and the yellow ball streaking for the corner . . .' Jeff Astle (second white shirt from right) supplies the decisive finish.
Inset: A long way from the chicken farm! Albion boss Alan Ashman greets his players after the final whistle.

A glorious chemistry. Together Joe Mercer (left) and Malcolm Allison transformed the sagging fortunes of Manchester City, creating an upliftingly attractive side that won trophies and, so vital to their fans, ended the local dominance of United.

Whisper it softly at Old Trafford, where a time of severe trial was awaiting the Red Devils, but by the tail-end of the 1960s they were no longer top dogs in their own backyard, let alone in the wider world of the First Division. United's European Cup triumph notwithstanding, it was City who led the way in Manchester for the first time since the War. Another City, another story. Leicester, having endured a decade of missed opportunity in which they had lost two FA Cup Finals already and who recently had been riddled with internal strife, had been fighting an increasingly desperate battle against relegation to Division Two. Thus did the 1969 Wembley combatants line up in vividly contrasting circumstances.

The Maine Road revolution had been effected by the unlikely but inspired combination of two men who, for differing reasons, had both been at a footballing loose end: Joe Mercer, so affable and avuncular but with the wits and heart of a tiger, and Malcolm Allison, the game's playboy prince, whose raffish public persona masked one of the shrewdest coaching brains in the land. In 1964 ill health had forced Joe into premature retirement as Aston Villa boss, and the fol-

IT HAPPENED THIS YEAR

Neil Armstrong was the first man to walk on the moon.

British troops deployed in Northern Ireland as violence escalated.

Maiden flights of Concorde, the Anglo-French supersonic airliner . . .

. . . and of Monty Python's Flying Circus, the satirical TV programme.

26 April 1969

MANCHESTER CITY 1
Young 24

LEICESTER CITY 0

Half-time 1-0

MANCHESTER CITY		LEICESTER CITY
Harry Dowd	1	Peter Shilton
Tony Book *(captain)*	2	Peter Rodrigues
Glyn Pardoe	3	David Nish *(captain)*
Mike Doyle	4	Bobby Roberts
Tommy Booth	5	Alan Woollett
Alan Oakes	6	Graham Cross
Mike Summerbee	7	Rodney Fern
Colin Bell	8	David Gibson
Francis Lee	9	Andy Lochhead
Neil Young	10	Allan Clarke
Tony Coleman	11	Len Glover*
		(sub Malcolm Manley)

Attendance: 100,000

Referee: G McCabe, Sheffield

lowing year Plymouth Argyle sacked Malcolm. Against the advice of friends who feared for his life if he returned to the relentless business of soccer management, Mercer accepted the Moss Side hot seat in the summer of 1965 and made unemployed Allison his first signing. They inherited a Second Division club so far in the shadow of their illustrious neighbours that they were no longer perceived as a threat. But now a unique chemistry began to take effect. Pulling together, one's commonsense tempering the other's audacity, they built a lovely, exhilarating side, albeit one prone to inconsistency, and before long Manchester was blessed with a new glorious trinity, no longer red-hued, in the form of Lee, Bell and Summerbee.

The light-blue revival - which was to bring four major trophies in the space of three seasons, starting with the Championship in 1968 - reads something like a fairytale, yet it pales in comparison with the Boys' Own-type fantasy that attended the personal rise of their skipper. Throughout what might have been his prime years, Tony Book divided his time between laying bricks and playing Southern League football for his hometown club, Bath City . . . whose manager was a

The red-and-black men of Maine Road. Back row (left to right): Heslop, Doyle, Oakes, Dowd, Mann, Pardoe, Booth, Coleman. Front row: Connor, Owen, Bell, Book, Lee, Summerbee, Young.

certain Mr Allison. Soon after Malcolm took over at Plymouth, he sent for Tony and the speedy full-back made his League debut at the age of 28. Later, when Big Mal had moved in at Maine Road, he persuaded Joe Mercer that Book would be a priceless asset and so, one month short of his 31st birthday, the former brickie stepped into the top flight. He was an instant success, soon became captain, managed to throw off an Achilles tendon injury that threatened to wreck his career and led City through their golden age. Quite incredible, but it gets better! In 1969, shortly before the FA Cup Final, Tony Book was voted joint Footballer of the Year along with Derby County skipper Dave Mackay. The honour spoke for itself, yet somehow it was enhanced still further by the fact that he was bracketed with one of the greatest players British football had known since the War.

How the long-suffering Leicester fans would have relished the sort of success that had transformed Manchester City. Instead, they had lived with anti-climax - losing to Spurs in the 1961 FA Cup Final, watching their 1963 Championship challenge falter at the death before capitulating to Wembley underdogs Manchester United, subsisting thereafter on a diet of unrelieved mediocrity in the League - with only triumph in the 1964 League Cup, which then carried little kudos, to comfort them. Now, as their team took time off from struggling against demotion to prepare for their fourth FA final in 21 seasons, the Filbert Street faithful could only pray it would not end in a fourth defeat.

However, they could not claim that the current campaign had been dull. Manager Matt Gillies had signalled Leicester's ambition during the preceding summer by breaking the League transfer record with the £150,000 import of striker Allan Clarke from Fulham, beating off competition from Manchester United in the process. The fans' delight was tempered slightly by the fact that one of their favourites, Frank Large, was released as a makeweight in the deal, but if that was the price of success, they reasoned, then so be it. Soon Clarke had endeared himself to his new followers with a classy hat-trick against Manchester City, but overall results were poor and tales of discontent in the camp began to leak out. Gillies attempted to stop the rot in October with the purchase of Andy Lochhead as a striking partner for Clarke, but there was no instant turnaround and in November the board precipitated a crisis by sacking coach Bert Johnson. Matt, City's longest serving team manager, could not countenance that and resigned, to be replaced by Torquay boss Frank O'Farrell. Some of the players were

upset - precociously talented 19-year-old goalkeeper Peter Shilton had a transfer request turned down - but the quietly-spoken O'Farrell restored calm and turned his attention to two battlefronts. In the League, Leicester showed little sign of escaping from their dire predicament, but the Cup brought welcome diversion. Their early victims were Barnsley, after a replay, and Millwall, with popular left winger Len Glover netting in all three games. Then, after a month-long weather-enforced lay-off, they met Liverpool twice in three days, following a goalless draw at Filbert Street with an uplifting, unexpected 1-0 victory in front of the Kop. City's heroes on a stirring night at Anfield were Lochhead, who scored with a characteristic header, and Shilton, who sprang athletically to save a Tommy Smith penalty. Then they scrambled past gallant Mansfield Town, recent conquerors of West Ham, to confront the holders, West Bromwich Albion, in the last four.

Above: Frank O'Farrell and his prodigiously gifted young goalkeeper Peter Shilton. The new Leicester boss managed to smooth the rookie's ruffled feathers and a transfer request was withdrawn.

At this stage, with Everton facing Manchester City in the other semi-final, a repeat of the previous year's Wembley meeting was a possibility, and so it remained until late in both games. But then with three minutes left at Hillsborough, Clarke snatched a winner for Leicester, while at Villa Park, the Mancunians' 19-year-old centre-half Tommy Booth left it even later, sinking the Toffeemen with a goal in the last minute. Mercer's men, who had begun the season as Champions, had progressed in the Cup against a background of frustrating League results and a disastrous first-round elimination from the European Cup at the hands of the unfancied Turks, Fenerbahce. On the way they had disposed of Luton Town courtesy of a Francis Lee penalty, Newcastle United after a replay, Blackburn Rovers with ease and Tottenham thanks again to a single strike from Lee. Despite being known as thrilling attackers prone to defensive frailties, they had conceded only one goal in six matches.

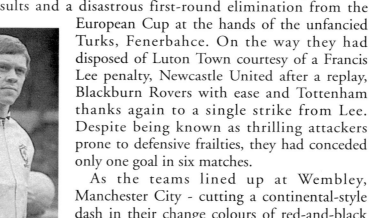

As the teams lined up at Wembley, Manchester City - cutting a continental-style dash in their change colours of red-and-black striped shirts and black shorts - remained warm favourites, despite losing four of their previous five League games. Leicester, led by David Nish, at 21 the youngest FA Cup Final skipper, were presumed to be feeling the strain of their travail in the bread-and-butter competition. In addition, they had suffered an injury crisis which had threatened to deprive them of Glover, who never looked fully fit and was to be replaced by 18-year-old substitute Malcolm Manley, and Clarke, who had strained a leg muscle. If experience in the final counted for anything, though, Leicester had the edge, with both Graham Cross and David Gibson surviving from the 1963 side.

Above: Teenage stopper Tommy Booth, a semi-final goal hero and one of Manchester City's most impressive performers at Wembley.

Left: Breaking new ground. Leicester's David Nish becomes, at 21, the youngest captain in an FA Cup Final. He was to lead his men to both Wembley defeat and relegation, an unwanted double last suffered in 1926 - by Manchester City.

In tune with majority opinion, it was the Lancastrians who started the brightest, their enterprising assaults flowing smoothly towards

Right: One of the misses that Leicester were to rue. Peter Rodrigues (second right) miscues and the Mancunians escape. Others players, left to right, are Maine Roaders Glyn Pardoe, Harry Dowd and Tommy Booth, and Filbert Len Glover.

the Leicester goal. Pressure mounted and early in the second quarter it paid off. Mike Summerbee took possession on the right, evaded Nish and Alan Woollett, then reached the byline before pulling the ball neatly into the path of Neil Young. The lanky inside-left, so often underrated in the stylish company he kept, hit a devastating 15-yarder with the outside of his left foot; the ball rose high beyond Shilton's dive and the net billowed. Now, with the Manchester machine purring along so sweetly, a rout was on the cards, but the plucky Filberts were having none of it. Instead of folding they elected to fight, and only an alert save by 'keeper

Striking with snakelike venom and accuracy, the left foot of Neil Young deals the killing blow to Leicester. Graham Cross tumbles and Bobby Roberts lunges to no avail.

Below: One of many intriguing personal duels was fought out between Manchester's feisty winger Mike Summerbee (left) and Leicester full-back David Nish.

Harry Dowd prevented Clarke's 30-yard effort from levelling the scores. Then shortly before the interval, with the balance of play on an increasingly even keel, the ball was played across the face of the Manchester goal towards Leicester full-back Peter Rodrigues. It seemed he only had to slam it into a yawning net but he was defeated by the bounce and the chance had gone. Rodrigues, of course, was not ultimately to be denied his moment of Wembley glory; that would come as skipper of Southampton, seven years hence. However, in the absence of a crystal ball, he looked suitably distraught.

Words of wisdom from the resourceful Mercer and Allison during the break might have been expected to tighten their side's precarious hold on the game, but far from it. Though they never matched their opponents' elegance, with the

Top: Men of the match. Allan Clarke of Leicester, who was voted the outstanding performer on display, and Neil Young, scorer of the northerners' winning goal.

Above: Two tough nuts. Tony Coleman attempts robbery on Andy Lochhead.

notable exception of Clarke, the Midlanders continued to surge forward and created the two best chances of the second half. Both fell to Lochhead, who drove over when well placed following a Clarke knock-down and then was crowded out in the act of shooting after appearing to pierce a decidedly stretched rearguard. So Manchester City had claimed the Cup for the fourth time in seven finals, but though their performance had been good enough (just) it had been far from vintage. They had their stars, though, especially young Booth, who had handled the warlike Lochhead with both skill and courage, and Colin Bell, whose non-stop running and precise distribution had evoked memories of one of his club's former luminaries, Peter Doherty.

But to Leicester went many of the plaudits - Clarke, for instance, won the journalists' Man of the Match award, an idea borrowed from the Rugby League Cup Final - and all of the sympathy. Though the nation rejoiced for Joe Mercer, a Wembley winner again 19 years after lifting 'the old tin pot' (as he called it) as a player with Arsenal, it felt for the Filberts. With the season having been distorted by midwinter postponements, over the next three weeks they were required to take seven points from five games to stay up, and they managed only five. After excelling themselves to no avail at Wembley, it was a crushing blow made more poignant by the realisation that if they had reproduced their Cup Final form in the League they must have survived. For Manchester City, meanwhile, the future glowed. Though not consistent enough for League success, they lifted both the European Cup Winners' Cup and League Cup in 1970. And Leicester? In the summer they sold the unsettled, ambitious Clarke to Leeds United for £165,000, then missed out on promotion by two points!

Ex-brickie Tony Book sits in triumph on the shoulders of Mike Doyle, flanked by Francis Lee (left) and 'keeper Harry Dowd.

IT HAPPENED
THIS YEAR

United Kingdom age
of majority dropped
from 21 to 18.

Edward Heath led the
Tories to a surprise
election victory.

Bobby Moore arrested
on trumped-up theft
charge in Bogota.

Rock stars Jimi
Hendrix and Janis
Joplin died after using
drugs.

Beatles broke up
acrimoniously in the
High Court.

South African cricket
tour to England can-
celled over apartheid.

11 April 1970

CHELSEA 2

Houseman 41; Hutchinson 86

LEEDS UNITED 2

Charlton 21; Jones 84

Half-time 1-1 Extra time played

CHELSEA	○	LEEDS UNITED
Peter Bonetti	1	Gary Sprake
David Webb	2	Paul Madeley
Eddie McCreadie	3	Terry Cooper
John Hollins	4	Billy Bremner *(captain)*
John Dempsey	5	Jack Charlton
*Ron Harris *(captain)*	6	Norman Hunter
Tommy Baldwin	7	Peter Lorimer
Peter Houseman	8	Allan Clarke
Peter Osgood	9	Mick Jones
Ian Hutchinson	10	Johnny Giles
Charlie Cooke	11	Eddie Gray
*(sub Marvin Hinton)		

Attendance: 100,000

Referee: E Jennings, Stourbridge

Chelsea fans could hardly be expected to agree, but Leeds United were unlucky not to win the FA Cup in 1970. That's not to say the Blues, who showed inspirational resilience under heavy bombardment, were not worthy of lifting the trophy; they earned it honourably and were a credit to themselves and their excellent manager Dave Sexton. But despite all the sniggers about Elland Road boss Don Revie, his obsessive dossiers on opposing teams and his almost comic intensity, there is no doubt that his side could play beautiful football - and for long periods at Wembley and in the Old Trafford replay, they did so to breathtaking effect. Indeed, the incandescent display by 22-year-old Leeds winger Eddie Gray in the first encounter lives in the memory as one of the most thrilling individual performances in post-War finals, and certainly merited better than a loser's medal. Yet neither for the first nor last time, Revie's men were not only frustrated by unexpected defeat, but also afflicted by the infinitely more awful feeling that they had been the better team and still lost - and that, somehow, the world in general knew this and rejoiced. In fact, for once at least, they were mistaken; their plight in winning nothing after tilting for an unheard-of treble - the League, FA Cup and European Cup - attracted considerable public sympathy.

During their rise to eminence under Revie, Leeds had been lambasted by countless critics - sometimes unfairly, sometimes not - for play that was dour and over-physical. But after winning the Championship in 1968/69, it was as if 'The Don' had made a conscious decision to show the disbelieving populace just how good his side really were. Accordingly, while retaining every scrap of their ruthless hardness and professionalism, they played with a new fluency and verve that deserved greater recognition. That was witheld, at least in part, due to an unfortunate public perception of their manager as brooding, cynical, even mean, a distorted picture of the man that upsets and offends those who knew him best. Nevertheless, as his achievements became ever more undeniable, there were personal plaudits too, and in New Year 1969 Don was awarded the OBE. Thus feted, he led Leeds into an FA Cup campaign that began quietly with a narrow home victory over Swansea City, then moved to the unlikely theatre of Gander Green Lane. There, in the heart of the Surrey commuter belt, the elite force from the north took on non-League Sutton United, affording Revie new horizons on which to indulge his passion for detail. Sure enough, a bulging folder was prepared on the part-timers and come the day of the match the Leeds boss fuelled his eccentric reputation by expressing dismay that his hosts had installed temporary seating - and that there was no reference to it in his file! He needn't have worried, however, as Leeds cantered through 6-0, and there was a bonus. Despite the scoreline, Sutton centre-half John Faulkner had performed nobly against England man Mick Jones, and a few weeks later John was signed as cover for Jack Charlton. In the event, his Elland Road career was not a distinguished one - encompassing just four senior appearances - but Revie's judgement was vindicated as Faulkner went on to serve Luton Town with credit. Leeds'

A stroll in the Wembley sunshine for 'Whispering Dave' and 'The Don', two of the most respected managers in the game. Chelsea's Sexton (left) would retain his serenity until the final was decided, but Revie of Leeds would be unable to contain his feelings.

Cup campaign continued at the expense of Mansfield and Swindon, before the earth began to shake in anticipation as Manchester United were announced as semi-final opponents. Though the extent of their problems were not yet fully apparent, the Red Devils were in decline, yet that did not prevent them rising to the occasion against their bitter rivals from across the Pennines. In a confrontation that evoked memories of the two 1965 Cup clashes, the two Uniteds tussled titanically but goallessly at Hillsborough, then Villa Park, before Billy Bremner settled matters with a single strike (just as he did five years earlier) at Burnden Park.

In the meantime, though the Yorkshiremen had garnered the lion's share of the headlines, Chelsea had been enjoying no lean season either. They finished third in the First Division, only two points behind Leeds, and were a credit to Dave Sexton, one of the most astute coaches in the business, a quiet, intelligent man with a penchant for poetry, but one who did not revel in media attention. Under Tommy Docherty in the early 1960s, he had helped lay the foundations of the current attractive side, and was now reaping the benefit. Dave took over in

Soft goal number one. An uncharacteristically feeble header from Jack Charlton (left) deceives Chelsea's Eddie McCreadie (number three) and Ron Harris to put Leeds in front.

Eddie Gray of Leeds, who wasn't billed to play in the match programme but whose tormenting of Dave Webb earned him a place in Wembley folklore.

October 1967, five months after Chelsea's Wembley reverse against Spurs, and retained the essence of the team he'd inherited. Peter Bonetti, skipper Ron Harris, Eddie McCreadie, John Hollins, Charlie Cooke, Peter Osgood (who missed the Tottenham final through injury) and Marvin Hinton (destined to be substitute this time round) were all integral to his plans, with defenders David Webb and John Dempsey, and forwards Ian Hutchinson, Peter Houseman and Tommy Baldwin being added. In fact, there was one other significant newcomer, though he was to be denied the chance to parade his silky talents before the nation. Back in August, a precocious 18-year-old play-maker, name of Alan Hudson, had profited from an injury crisis to claim a regular place. He proclaimed his ambition to pass like Johnny Haynes and score like Jimmy Greaves, and if he never came close to the second aspiration, there were days when he achieved the first. But cruelly, in March, he damaged ankle ligaments, and after playing in every preceding round was forced out of the final. Of course, there was still time for Alan to have his day, and he went on to play for England, yet throughout a career that took in Stoke (twice), Arsenal and Chelsea for a second time, he came into that infuriating category of individuals who could not translate bountiful gifts into match-winning displays consistently enough to fulfil their full potential. However in January 1970 the name of Hudson was synonymous with rich promise, and he played a central part in the third-round defeat of Birmingham. Chelsea were buoyant as they faced Burnley in the fourth, but received a rude shock, allowing a two-goal home lead to disappear in the last ten minutes. Maintaining their momentum, the Lancastrians were close to a one-goal replay victory, but they had reckoned without Peter Houseman. The oft-unsung Londoner stepped

in with a brilliant late equaliser, then set up the Blues' second and scored their third in extra time. Peter netted again in an emphatic fifth round win at Crystal Palace, but allowed Peter Osgood to take the quarter-final limelight with a hat-trick against Queen's Park Rangers. Then, in the semi-final thrashing of Watford (shock conquerors of Liverpool), it was Houseman who led the way once more, with two of Chelsea's five goals. Surrounded by star names, Peter seemed rather unobtrusive but his contribution was immense. He was a popular man, too, and the soccer world was appalled when he and his wife Sally died in a car crash in 1977.

As the final began, the scene at Wembley, where both clubs were attempting to win the Cup for the first time, was dominated somehow neither by the teams nor the fans, but by the *pitch*. The smooth, verdant bowling green of years gone by had been replaced by something more reminiscent of a grubby beach, the legacy of recent equestrian events. The term 'cabbage patch' comes to mind, but it would have been an insult to any self-respecting gardener, with areas of sand and mud engulfing what little grass there was. With Gray (named as substitute in the programme) replacing broken-leg victim Paul Reaney - after a reshuffle in which Paul Madeley was switched to right-back - and Tommy Baldwin filling the void left by Hudson, both sides were shorn of one regular, but before long it became evident that to Leeds the enforced change might prove a blessing in disguise. All afternoon, United's Scottish flankman ran at poor David Webb, turning him this way and that, stranding him helplessly time and again with sorcerous trickery that gave (temporary) credence to extravagant comparisons of Eddie with George Best. But if Gray's skills demanded particular attention, it was Leeds' all-round excellence that proclaimed that the Cup must be on its way to Elland Road. Thus when the breakthrough came, albeit scrappily, it seemed inevitable. Gray swung over a corner, Charlton beat Bonetti's clutch with a weak header and the ball bounced low in the sandy morass, evading the despairing lunges of goal-line guardians Harris and McCreadie to creep in. Now, surely, the Yorkshiremen would change gear and put the match beyond Chelsea's reach, but not so. As Leeds poured forward, Sexton's spirited braves resisted nobly, and Osgood forced Charlton to clear off his line before Houseman struck a bizarre equaliser four minutes before the break, his speculative 20-yarder squirming under Gary Sprake's dive to give the Welshman perhaps the most excruciating moment of his career. But as Revie's men turned on the second-half style, few observers can have

Left: Soft goal number two. Leeds 'keeper Gary Sprake, not unknown to drop the occasional clanger, allows a weak shot from Peter Houseman to slip past him for Chelsea's first equaliser. Tommy Baldwin, waiting for a rebound more in hope than expectation, can hardly believe the Blues' luck.

Above: Peter Bonetti is on his knees and Allan Clarke celebrates as Mick Jones restores United's lead.

Right: Against most expectations, Chelsea claw themselves level for the second time as Ian Hutchinson outmanoeuvres Jack Charlton to head home from John Hollins' cross.

Right: Gary Sprake mulls over what might have been as Leeds regroup for extra time.
Far right: Full-back Eddie McCreadie appears content with the first Wembley FA Cup Final still unresolved after extra time. In contrast, a chastened-looking Dave Webb seems keen to reach the refuge of the dressing room.

believed that Peter had done more than postpone execution. But Leeds, for whom the rampant Gray had hit the bar, were not to regain the advantage until six minutes from the end when Allan Clarke, their record-breaking £165,000 signing from Leicester, headed against a post and Jones converted the rebound with an accurately drilled daisy-cutter. Mick ran to the touchline to be embraced by his ecstatic manager, who was led back to the bench by two officers of the law. That should have been that, but still the Blues would not lie down, and two minutes later Hutchinson outjumped Charlton to net at the near post from a Hollins chip. That brought extra time during which, though both teams were on the point of exhaustion, Leeds continued to hold sway. Clarke rapped the woodwork once more, a Giles effort was bludgeoned off the line by Webb and then it was all over until the Old Trafford replay in 18 days time. Before then, United had a European Cup semi-final with Celtic, and after defeat at Hampden Park, there were pundits

29 April 1970

Replay at Old Trafford

CHELSEA 2
Osgood 78; Webb 104

LEEDS UNITED 1
Jones 35

Half-time 0-1 Extra time played

CHELSEA		LEEDS UNITED
Peter Bonetti	1	David Harvey
Ron Harris *(captain)*	2	Paul Madeley
Eddie McCreadie	3	Terry Cooper
John Hollins	4	Billy Bremner *(captain)*
John Dempsey	5	Jack Charlton
David Webb	6	Norman Hunter
Tommy Baldwin	7	Peter Lorimer
Charlie Cooke	8	Allan Clarke
*Peter Osgood	9	Mick Jones
Ian Hutchinson	10	Johnny Giles
Peter Houseman	11	Eddie Gray
*(sub Marvin Hinton)		

Attendance: 62,078

Referee: E Jennings, Stourbridge

who reckoned they could not pick themselves up, that narrow failure in Europe and the League was too much for flesh and blood to stand. They had, of course, reckoned without Revie, who rallied his troops stirringly and brought in David Harvey for Sprake, who had suffered a knock and was thus deprived of the chance to redeem himself. But Sexton, too, had not been idle. He switched Harris and Webb, thus giving 'Chopper Ron' the task of policing Gray while Webb shifted to central defence. The move did not eradicate Eddie's menace by any means, but it lessened it; meanwhile Webb gave a solid performance - and ultimately won the Cup for Chelsea.

In a physically bruising but highly skilful contest at the home of Manchester United, Leeds again assumed

early ascendancy, but with Gray shaving the wrong side of a post and McCreadie making a goal-line clearance from Peter Lorimer, the all-whites did not make the pressure tell until ten minutes before half-time. Then Clarke swayed past three challenges in the deep and fed Jones, who slipped between two defenders before beating Bonetti - by then handicapped by a heavy knock to his knee - with a fierce, rising shot. Now Giles and Bremner were imperious in midfield, and with Bonetti's knee so swollen that there was talk of Webb replacing him for the second half, only one result seemed possible. But Peter soldiered on, and as the game grew old and there were no further goals, a change came over the action. Suddenly Chelsea were stringing together incisive passing movements, invariably with Cooke at their heart, and Charlie it was who chipped into space for Osgood to equalise with a sensational horizontal header 12 minutes from the end of normal time. With an extra period necessary, the tension mounted unbearably and, against all probability, it was Leeds who cracked. Hutchinson arched his back to launch a 35-yard throw from the left touchline, Charlton could only deflect it

Above: Chelsea's star talents combine to sensational effect. Charlie Cooke has delivered a tantalising chip and Peter Osgood dives thrillingly to head past Gary Sprake.

Opposite: For most of the contest it didn't look likely, but now Chelsea skipper Ron Harris brandishes the FA Cup.

across goal and Webb bundle-headed it into the net at the far post, his subsequent leap of joy threatening to take him over the stand.

Thereafter, with 16 minutes left and Osgood withdrawn for defender Hinton, Leeds attacked frenziedly. There were several last-ditch clearances, but the Blues survived and the Cup was bound for the Bridge for the first time. As they surveyed the ashes of their season, Leeds were less than gracious; perhaps understandably, perhaps not. Whatever, the Londoners' victory was a tribute to perseverance and organisation, spiced with flair at vital moments. On their triumphal bus ride along Chelsea High Road, as the players whooped it up exuberantly on the open upper-deck, Dave Sexton sat quietly in a corner downstairs. Perhaps he was mulling over the drama, maybe he was reciting a favourite poem, but one thing could be taken for granted: had his team lost he would have been as serene and dignified in defeat as he was in victory.

Left: Perhaps not the prettiest of winning goals but Chelsea were hardly going to agonise over that! Putting his earlier trials behind him, Dave Webb rises to bundle the ball into the Leeds net.

Below: After his unholy chasing at Wembley, Dave Webb was an unlikely hero, yet the last laugh was his. Resplendent in a swapped Leeds shirt, he manages to retain hold of both the FA Cup and a much-needed cigarette.

IT HAPPENED
THIS YEAR

Decimal Day herald-
ed end of shilling,
florin and half-crown.

Sixty six people died
after barriers
collapsed at Ibrox.

Postal strike crippled
communications in
Britain.

Australian Evonne
Goolagong won her
first Wimbledon title.

Idi Amin became
President of Uganda
in military coup.

Princess Anne won
Sportswoman of the
Year award.

8 May 1971

ARSENAL 2

Kelly 101; George 111

LIVERPOOL 1

Heighway 92

Half-time 0-0 Extra time played

ARSENAL	◯	LIVERPOOL
Bob Wilson	1	Ray Clemence
Pat Rice	2	Chris Lawler
Bob McNab	3	Alec Lindsay
*Peter Storey	4	Tommy Smith *(captain)*
Frank McLintock *(captain)*	5	Larry Lloyd
Peter Simpson	6	Emlyn Hughes
George Armstrong	7	Ian Callaghan
George Graham	8	Alun Evans*
John Radford	9	Steve Heighway
Ray Kennedy	10	John Toshack
Charlie George	11	Brian Hall
*(sub Eddie Kelly)		(sub Peter Thompson)*

Attendance: 100,000

Referee: N Burtenshaw, Great Yarmouth

When star-spangled Spurs won the League and FA Cup double in 1961, they did it with uplifting, often lyrical football that thrilled the senses; understandably, Bill Nicholson's creation was hailed as his supreme master-piece and a national treasure. But when North London neighbours Arsenal emulated the feat ten years on, there was open season on Gunner-baiting. Subjected to an unprecedented fusillade of flak, or at best, damned by the faintest of praise, they were dismissed widely as functional, physical dullards, unworthy to be mentioned in the same breath as their double-winning predecessors. The majority of pundits admitted the excellence of manager Bertie Mee's organisation, the effectiveness of coach Don Howe's tactics and the ultra-professionalism of everyone involved, but the overrid-ing message seemed to be along the lines of 'If this is really the cream of our beloved game, then forget it!' In fact, most of the criticism amounted to little more than self-righteous cant. Of course Arsenal were not as artis-tic as that truly exceptional Spurs side; yes, they were hard (but no more so than almost any other First Division team); no, their line-up was not studded with household names. But their goal tally was the third highest attained by any League Champions of the 1970s, their players were *not* lacking in individual technique and their strength of character - which enabled them to come from behind to lift both trophies - was second to none.

Surprisingly enough, Arsenal had risen to the heights without adding to the squad which the previous term had been unable to lift the club into the top half of the table and had fallen at the first FA Cup hurdle, though there had, of course, been the little matter of triumph in the European Fairs Cup. The point was that several key players had switched positions under the guidance of Don Howe - Frank McLintock from midfield to centre-back, George Graham from striker to play-maker, Peter Storey from full-back to midfield ball-winner - and that had the same enlivening effect as bringing in new faces. Accordingly, come the

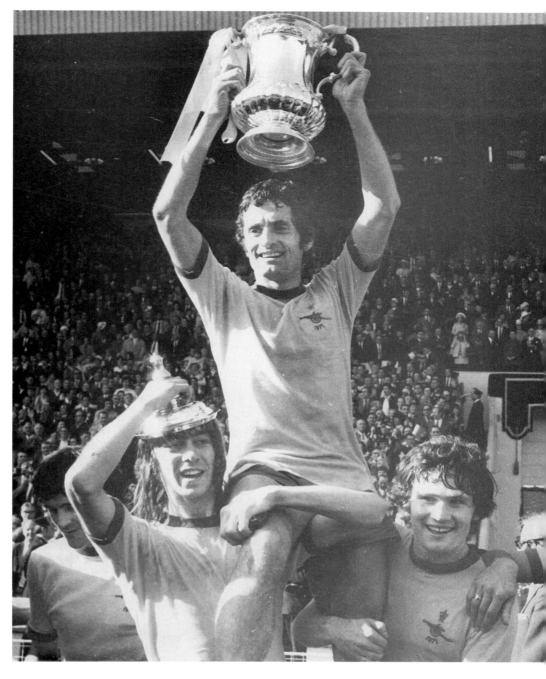

Above: The moment that makes up for everything. Frank McLintock, four times a Wembley loser during the 1960s, experiences that winning feeling at last. Lending a shoulder are Charlie George (left) and Pat Rice.

Opposite: Charlie is the Gunners' darling. Match-winner George with appropriate headware.

spring of 1971, the team had a pleasingly well-balanced look: Bob Wilson was a brave, solid custodian, Pat Rice and Bob McNab a tough, intelligent full-back pairing, while in McLintock and the chronically underrated Peter Simpson, the Gunners boasted good footballers at the heart of their rearguard. In midfield was an ideal combination of the combative Storey, the elegant Graham and the workaholic wide-man George Armstrong; up front Ray Kennedy and John Radford matched their obvious strength with frequently unlauded skills, and roaming dangerously was the brilliant but volatile Charlie George, a man who could (and did at Wembley) win a match in the twinkling of an eye. With the versatile, workmanlike Eddie Kelly on the bench, the Gunners were splendidly equipped to cope with the climax of an increasingly demanding campaign.

Their FA Cup Final opponents, Liverpool, possessed players of equal calibre, but had been undergoing a period of radical transition. As the new decade dawned, Bill Shankly broke up his first great team, bidding farewell to Kop favourites such as front-men Ian St John and Roger Hunt, his colossus of a centre-half Ron Yeats and goalkeeper Tommy Lawrence. Of the side that lifted two titles and an FA Cup in the mid-1960s, only right-back Chris Lawler, tank-like defender Tommy Smith and evergreen winger Ian Callaghan retained regular slots, with Ian's fellow flankman Peter Thompson still on the fringes. Midfielder Emlyn Hughes had been in situ for several seasons, but the others - the likes of Ray Clemence in goal, stopper Larry Lloyd, left-back Alec Lindsay, midfielder Brian Hall and front-runners Alun Evans, John Toshack and the refreshing Steve Heighway were all comparative newcomers. Even so, they had finished an honourable fifth in the First Division, and no team of Shankly's could ever be dubbed true underdogs. Their Cup success had been thanks largely to a parsimonious defence that had not conceded a goal until the semi-final, though there had been awkward moments, of which the most potentially embarrassing came in the third round against lowly Aldershot. Directed shrewdly by Jimmy Melia, a former Liverpool schemer, the Shots restricted their hosts to a single goal and came close to forcing a rematch. Next Swansea were brushed aside and Southampton beaten 1-0 before Spurs provided the opposition in the Reds' fourth successive home tie. However a White Hart Lane replay was needed to settle the issue and set up the meeting all Merseyside had prayed would be delayed one more stage. The derby with Everton, down the East Lancs road at Old Trafford, was a thriller. Early on, the Reds conceded their first goal of the competition (scored by Alan Ball) but came back superbly to win through Evans and Hall. Arsenal's journey towards the Twin Towers had begun on a Somerset hillside - well, the famous Yeovil Town slope! - but all fears that they would go the way of Sunderland in 1949 were allayed to the tune of 3-0. In the fourth round Portsmouth forced a replay, thanks to a late strike by Mike Trebilcock (who knew a bit about scoring Cup goals) and a Peter Storey spot-kick clinched victory in the second clash. Next, in the round that saw Leeds toppled by humble Colchester, Manchester City proved a formidable obstacle at Maine Road but were removed by Charlie George's marvellous double-strike, then Leicester offered doughty quarter-final resistance, Arsenal progressing by the only goal over two matches. But if the Gunners, who had been drawn away in every round, thought *that* had been hard work, there was yet more arduous toil in store. Indeed there was a time, with Stoke two up in the Hillsborough semi-final, that Highbury's interest in the Cup appeared to be in terminal decline. Even when Storey's 20-yarder

Ray Clemence, very much a part of Bill Shankly's new Liverpool, clutches the ball safely to his chest. Ray was to taste defeat this time, but his share of glory would follow in due course.

pegged back the Potters in the second half, the cause appeared to be lost but Mee's men kept going and won a penalty in injury time. To Storey fell the duty of dispatching it, which he did coolly, and from that moment the notion of the League and Cup double grew ever less fanciful.

Having won the rematch at Villa Park, the Gunners faced a daunting League programme. Six points behind Leeds United but with three matches in hand, they had ten games before their Wembley date with Liverpool, and it was during this congested period that they proved their mettle beyond doubt. They racked up

eight victories and a draw, claiming 17 points from a possible 20, and clinched the Championship in the closing minutes of the last match, at White Hart Lane of all places, when Kennedy headed the night's only goal. Even in those closing moments, Arsenal had to fight: though a win or a 0-0 draw was good enough, a 1-1 draw would have seen the title slip away to Elland Road, so a late equaliser would have been disastrous.

Duel in the sun. Left to right are Ray Kennedy (a Liverpool star of the future), Alec Lindsay, Larry Lloyd and Bob McNab.

Naturally, that victory lifted some of the pressure from the Gunners' shoulders - at least they could not finish the season empty-handed - but realisation that the double was within touching distance brought renewed tension. Though the final was only five days away, the Champions were allowed to celebrate into the early hours of Tuesday morning and take the rest of the day off. Then it was back to work at their London Colney training ground, where a pitch had been marked out to exact Wembley dimensions, complete with extra-long grass to match the lushness of the national stadium's surface (happily restored since the previous year). As they prepared, McLintock in particular must have been wondering if he was ever going to be a Wembley winner. He had been on the losing side in two FA Cup Finals with Leicester (1961 and 1963) and two League Cup Finals with Arsenal (1968 and 1969). Five defeats in a row would be a blow for which not even his title medal and newly-awarded Footballer of the Year statuette could compensate wholly. On the eve of the match, the Reds and the Gunners bumped into each other while both were sampling the stadium's atmosphere, and the incorrigible Shankly tried a typical piece of psychology on Bob Wilson. Venturing an apparently informed opinion that there was thunder about, Bill predicted rain for the morrow, adding: 'Och, it'll be a nightmare for 'keepers, son.' This time, though, he had picked on the wrong fellow. Bob - who would have been helping to cover the match for BBC television had he not been playing in it - refused to

Above: Extra time beckons and Bill Shankly rouses his Reds. Helping out are former stars Tommy Lawrence and Ron Yeats in the centre, while Joe Fagan attends to Larry Lloyd (right).

Below: It hardly matters whether the last touch comes from Eddie Kelly (light shirt, left) or George Graham (centre). Arsenal are level and the game turns.

rise to the bait and remained as unruffled as ever.

In fact, Shanks' weather forecast was way off the mark, the temperature hovering in the eighties as the game got under way. The opening period was tactically cagey and physically bruising, with Storey - who represented a gamble by Bertie Mee, as he was by no means fully fit - especially prominent. For most of the first half Liverpool were the more sprightly side without managing to trouble Wilson, and as the match wore on the exchanges became more even. Midway through the second half, Storey was replaced by Kelly and Liverpool brought on the experienced Thompson for Evans, and the action - which admittedly would have been less than riveting had the stakes not been so high - became more open. Even then, goalmouth incidents

were few, with most of the shots being made from a distance, though the long-awaited breakthrough almost came on 78 minutes when Graham nodded against the bar from Radford's long throw, then Lindsay scrambled the ball off the line.

Extra time arrived with some inevitability, and within two minutes the score-sheet was no longer blank. Thompson fed Heighway on the left, and the unorthodox raider pranced past Rice and Armstrong to shoot from 12 yards out, close to the byline. Wilson, who had moved out in anticipation of a cross, was deceived and the ball fizzed past him at his near post. After so long without a goal, it seemed Liverpool thought they had won - and so did just about everybody else in the ground. But not Arsenal. They bent to their task with a will, pushing Graham forward and withdrawing the exhausted George to midfield, and not long after Wilson had made amends for his error by making a point-blank save from Hall, their efforts were rewarded. Radford, who'd had a wonderful game, hooked the ball hopefully over his shoulder and into a crowded Liverpool box, where Kelly poked it towards goal. It bobbled over a succession of feet, Graham swung at it and might or might not have got the slightest of touches; either way, it was enough to deceive Clemence, who missed it and it rolled unchecked into the net. At the time, pressmen awarded the goal to Graham - and he believes still that

Two minutes into extra time Steve Heighway (number nine) gulls Bob Wilson at his near post to break the deadlock towards the end of a long, hot afternoon. Now the Cup seems bound for Merseyside, but the real drama is yet to unfold.

Inset above: Bob Wilson, unphased by Shanks' weather forecast, made up for his one error with a sound all-round display.

Inset above right: Tommy Smith (left) congratulates John Radford, who had played nobly throughout.

it was his - but on the basis of inconclusive television evidence it was officially given to Kelly, who thus became the first substitute to score in the final.

At this juncture, the Gunners looked ready to settle for a draw, and George and Graham swapped places again, Charlie going forward out of harm's way. But suddenly, in a burst of renewed vitality, he exchanged passes with Radford and struck a superb rising drive from 20 yards which took a slight deflection off Lloyd and left Clemence helpless. The drained hero threw himself flat on his back, holding his arms aloft to receive the embraces of converging team-mates. Eight minutes later, Norman Burtenshaw blew the final whistle and Arsenal had done it.

Main picture: Charlie George shoots, the ball takes a slight deflection off the lunging Larry Lloyd and scorches towards the Liverpool net. In that moment, the double was won.

Below: 'We've really done it!' Full-back Bob McNab and coach Don Howe converge for a cuddle.

Inset left: Doubly delighted are, left to right, Peter Simpson, Charlie George, George Graham and manager Bertie Mee.

'Stroller' Graham, who had lived up to his nickname while contributing his share of sweat, was voted Man of the Match, though many thought the accolade should have gone to Radford, who'd had a huge hand in both goals and exemplified all that was best about his club. On such a day, it was the merest of details, and the down-to-earth John would have been the last man to cavil. By Sunday, with vitriolic criticisms of the Gunners' style in common currency, some 250,000 fans lined their heroes' route from Highbury to a reception at Islington town hall. As far as they were concerned, the carping pundits could say what they liked - Arsenal had won the double, and Spurs supporters could lord it no more.

6 May 1972

LEEDS UNITED 1
Clarke 53

ARSENAL 0

Half-time 0-0

LEEDS UNITED	○	ARSENAL
David Harvey	1	Geoff Barnett
Paul Reaney	2	Pat Rice
Paul Madeley	3	Bob McNab
Billy Bremner (captain)	4	Peter Storey
Jack Charlton	5	Frank McLintock (captain)
Norman Hunter	6	Peter Simpson
Peter Lorimer	7	George Armstrong
Allan Clarke	8	Alan Ball
Mick Jones	9	Charlie George
Johnny Giles	10	John Radford*
Eddie Gray	11	George Graham. (sub Ray Kennedy)*

Attendance: 100,000

Referee: D Smith, Gloucester

In the spring of 1972, respected soccer judges the length and breadth of the land were queueing up to pay homage to Leeds United. If their renowned consistency had slipped a fraction, not even their most rabid followers - the type who had gloried for years in the Elland Road camp's iron-fist image - were cavilling about the occasional blip as Don Revie's side ran into a vein of form that verged on the sublime. After seasons of cold, dour, sometimes cynical struggle for success, Leeds had blossomed into a team worthy of the nation's embrace, one of which English football could be proud. Significantly, among those most vociferous in singing the Yorkshiremen's praises were their victims. Pat Jennings - after Spurs had been outclassed in an FA Cup quarter-final yet somehow limited the margin to 2-1 - described them as the best club combination he had ever known; Terry Paine - a member of the Southampton side annihilated 7-0 in what many considered to be the most thrilling exhibition of team play seen in Britain since the War - reckoned Johnny Giles, Billy Bremner and company had approached perfection that day and added: 'They did us a favour by keeping it down to seven.'

So, with the side once ridiculed as 'Revie's Robots' being compared in some quarters to Real Madrid at their peak, what a desperate shame that they should take part in arguably the drabbest, tetchiest, most forgettable FA Cup Final of the modern era. Of course their opponents, Arsenal, shared the blame and in Leeds' mitigation it should be pointed out that they *were* battling to win the trophy for the first time in their history, having lost their only other finals in 1965 and 1970. But if the public felt let down by such a shabby show at Wembley, it was nothing to the anti-climax experienced by Leeds themselves two days later. Needing only a draw at Molineux to complete the League and Cup double, they stumbled to infuriating defeat against mid-table Wolves.

But what of the 1971 double-winners? On paper the Gunners should have been stronger than ever after manager Bertie Mee had reinforced an already formidable squad with the world-class midfielder Alan Ball, whose £220,000 acquisition from Everton had broken the British transfer record. The diminutive, ultra-competitive redhead had arrived in December to find Arsenal in comparatively lacklustre condition, and he took a few matches to become acclimatised. Initially Ball was frustrated by the North Londoners' tendency to bypass midfield, but with characteristic vigour he asserted his own beliefs, changes were made and before long there was a marked improvement in results. Indeed, until a run of League defeats in March, ambitious hopes of a second double remained alive.

For both Leeds, who beat Bristol Rovers, and Arsenal, who saw off Swindon, the Cup campaign began gently enough, with the third-round headlines being monopolised by non-League Hereford United, who ousted top-flight Newcastle in a replay on an Edgar Street mudheap. Hereford's equalising goal, a phenomenal 35-yard drive by carpenter Ronnie Radford, will remain forever in the memories of all those lucky enough to witness it. Goal of the season? Goal of a lifetime, more like. In the fourth round, the Gunners won at Reading while Leeds clashed mightily with Liverpool at Anfield, going through only at the second attempt, courtesy of two Allan Clarke goals. The fifth saw the Yorkshiremen enjoy the easier passage, at Cardiff's expense, Arsenal needing a three-match engagement with Derby County before progressing. In the first game of the trilogy, Charlie George scored twice at the Baseball Ground, where he was destined to become a favourite in the middle and late 1970s. At the quarter-final stage, Leeds played their most irresistible

Centenary celebrations. Top: The programme cover bearing the names of all the previous winners. Above: Young Gunners join in the pre-match procession, led by Richie Powling and a certain Liam Brady.

football of the competition in the encounter with Spurs that so impressed Pat Jennings; certainly, that day at Elland Road, their fluid, one-touch passing movements were a wonder to behold. Arsenal - drawn away in every round for the second successive year - were involved in an altogether earthier contest with Second Division Orient, who had already beaten Leicester and Chelsea, and the Gunners were happy to leave Brisbane Road with a single-goal victory. In the last four, Revie's team - by now shorn of England left-back Terry Cooper, who was out for the season after breaking his leg - swept aside Birmingham City, who would gain compensation in the form of promotion to Division One, while Arsenal faced Stoke City, who had given them so much trouble in the 1971 semi-final. Fresh from beating Chelsea to lift the League Cup - the first trophy in their 100-year history - the Potters constituted no mean threat, and it was with considerable relief that Gunners fans saw George Armstrong secure the lead. But then 'keeper Bob Wilson was injured, a soft goal was conceded and centre-forward John Radford took Bob's place between the posts for the past 15 minutes. As cool and efficient in this emergency role as in everything he undertook, 'Raddy' remained unbeaten, Geoff Barnett was called up for the replay and Arsenal went through 2-1. Wilson did not regain fitness in time for Wembley, thus being restricted to organising the players' perks pool, an increasingly onerous task as potential earnings from the media began to mushroom. The Gunners' other absentee from their 1971 starting line-up was striker Ray Kennedy, a young man whose form had dipped in the aftermath of the previous term's peak. This time he was reduced to the role of substitute, and despite being blessed with apparently limitless potential, Ray would not regain full impetus until he moved to Liverpool in 1974.

Back to '72, and it was the FA Cup Final's centenary year - not the hundredth final, that was not until 1981 - and due pageantry was laid on to mark the milestone. Before kick-off there was a procession in which all previous

Above: The General considers his options. Leeds' Johnny Giles, as so often, appears master of the situation.

Top: Arsenal's George Armstrong, one of the finest uncapped players of his era.

winners were represented, with the likes of The Wanderers, Oxford University and Royal Engineers leading the way in an assortment of lurid hooped shirts and jaunty knickerbockers. It was a light-hearted, colourful curtain-raiser to an unremittingly sour main event. Clarke set the tone by fouling Ball within three seconds of the start, then within a minute Bob McNab was booked for a challenge on Peter Lorimer. As niggly confrontations flourished all over the pitch, the football was relegated to a poor second place, and it was a wonder that only three more names - those of Norman Hunter, Billy Bremner and Charlie George - were entered in the notebook of referee David Smith. The majority of what positive first-half enterprise there was came from Leeds, with Clarke heading against the bar, and Bremner and Giles gradually establishing ascendancy over Ball and company in midfield. Nevertheless, there were occasional menacing moments from the North Londoners, a deflected shot by Frank McLintock forcing a smart save from David Harvey and Paul Reaney clearing a Ball effort off his line.

The second period began marginally more brightly, with Peter Simpson turning an Eddie Gray centre into his own net, only for the linesman to signal that the ball had gone over the byline before the Scot had crossed. Then McNab wasted a rare opening with an inaccurate header at Leeds' far post and George, having run through a gap in the Yorkshiremen's rearguard, hesitated unaccountably. Spurning these opportunities were to prove costly, indeed, for Arsenal. Not long after Charlie had surrendered that initiative, the ball reached Mick Jones on the right, he nipped past McNab and delivered his cross perfectly into the path of Clarke some 15 yards out and slightly to the left of goal. 'Sniffer' needed no second invitation: leaning his slim frame forward, he measured his angle before directing a powerful header into the far corner of the net; the placement was perfect and the diving Geoff Barnett had no vestige of a chance to keep it out. It was the strike of a cold-eyed, professional assassin, slipping a stiletto between the Gunners' ribs and into their heart.

Thereafter George rattled the Leeds crossbar and Lorimer thumped a shot against Barnett's near post, but there were no more goals and the northerners were deserving victors. Pick of the Arsenal contingent was Peter Simpson, who must qualify alongside his team-mate Armstrong in that unfortunate category comprising the finest players never to win an international cap. Clarke picked up his second Wembley Man of the Match award - his first came with Leicester three years earlier - though Revie maintained that the star man was Norman Hunter whom he dubbed, admittedly while consumed by the emotion of triumph, as the

Below: The assassin's thrust. Allan Clarke (out of picture) has guided a precision header towards the corner of the net and Geoff Barnett - replacing the injured Bob Wilson in the Gunners' goal - is powerless to repel it.

Above: Mick Jones gasps in agony as he is treated by Leeds trainer Les Cocker.

Top: Minded by a thoughtful Norman Hunter (in front), the plucky Jones makes his painful way back to the pitch from the royal box.

'best player who ever lived.' In fact, there had been a last-minute drama, though amid the elation and despair which naturally attends the final whistle at Wembley it was relegated to something of a sideshow. Mick Jones, having rounded McLintock, tripped over the advancing Barnett and fell awkwardly, dislocating his elbow in the process. He was still receiving treatment, writhing in agony, as his colleagues advanced towards the royal box, and he opted to rise painfully from his stretcher to follow them. The considerate Norman Hunter returned to help his fallen comrade, who was by now swathed in bandages, and together they climbed those 39 steps, normally the most exhilarating of journeys for a Wembley winner, but now, for the plucky Mick, it must have seemed a never-ending trek.

Of course, Jones had no chance of recovering in time for the Wolves game on the Monday, which was a more debilitating loss to the Leeds cause than might have been imagined. The doughty Midlander rarely garnered the bouquets accorded to more spectacular performers, but he was a noble and not unskilful forager and marksman whose contribution would be sorely missed. With Clarke also nursing an injury which would prevent him from completing the match at Molineux, it was surprising that Jones' replacement was midfielder Mick Bates rather than the combative young striker Joe Jordan, who had been used as a substitute in recent League matches. With another midfielder, Terry Yorath, on the bench, it prompted the thought that with only a draw needed Revie was erring unduly on the side of caution. In the event Wolves, with nothing to play for but their own self-esteem, excelled themselves and after an hour were two goals to the good. Still game for the fight, Bremner pulled one back, but with more than 53,000 fans spellbound by the dramatic climax to the title race, Leeds could not conjure up an equaliser. Not unexpectedly, Revie being Revie, he voiced claims that his team should have had three penalties, and there was widespread sympathy within the game that the Cup winners should have to fulfil such an important fixture only two days after the final. On the same night, Liverpool had been playing at Highbury and, with Leeds losing, two points would have taken the Championship to Anfield. However they could manage only a draw, so the crown went to Brian Clough's Derby County, who had completed their programme and were on holiday in Majorca, awaiting events more in hope than expectation. Meanwhile, Revie's men had the Cup for consolation; but for such a wonderful side at the peak of their powers, it was hardly enough.

Billy Bremner holds aloft the Cup that Leeds have just won for the first time. His fellow revellers (left to right) are: substitute Mick Bates (who was not used), Paul Madeley, Paul Reaney, Allan Clarke, Johnny Giles and Peter Lorimer.

IT HAPPENED THIS YEAR

Ceasefire declared in Vietnam, American death toll set at 50,000.

VAT came into effect in Great Britain.

Watergate hearings began in the United States.

Princess Anne married Captain Mark Phillips.

50mph speed limit introduced to conserve fuel.

John Conteh beat Chris Finnigan to become world light-weight champion.

5 May 1973

SUNDERLAND 1
Porterfield 31

LEEDS UNITED 0

Half-time 0-0

SUNDERLAND		LEEDS UNITED
Jim Montgomery	1	David Harvey
Dick Malone	2	Paul Reaney
Ron Guthrie	3	Trevor Cherry
Mick Horswill	4	Billy Bremner *(captain)*
Dave Watson	5	Paul Madeley
Richie Pitt	6	Norman Hunter
Bobby Kerr *(captain)*	7	Peter Lorimer
Billy Hughes	8	Allan Clarke
Vic Halom	9	Mick Jones
Ian Porterfield	10	Johnny Giles
Dennis Tueart	11	Eddie Gray*
		(sub Terry Yorath)*

Attendance: 100,000

Referee: K Burns, Stourbridge

It might have been a prophet reciting from tablets of stone: 'There is no way Sunderland can beat Leeds.' The words came with characteristic emphasis on the eve of the 1973 FA Cup Final from that most astringent of TV pundits, a certain Brian Clough, though in fairness to the Derby County boss it should be stressed that his opinion was shared by just about everyone else in football. Of course, there *was* a way - a glorious, uplifting, romantic way - and it was discovered by the joyful Wearsiders to bring about the most improbable upset yet witnessed at Wembley.

Leeds United were a team of stars dripping with quality, white-hot favourites on whom a bet would be wasted, while Sunderland, who started the campaign as 250-1 outsiders, had spent much of the winter levering themselves away from the trap door that opens on to the Third Division. The confrontation was given added edge by an absence of affection between the two managers, Don Revie of Leeds and Sunderland's Bob Stokoe. The pair had crossed swords at Wembley once before, in 1955, when they had been in direct opposition. That day Stokoe,

Displaying all the sartorial elegance of the early 1970s - the players, that is, not Bobby Stokoe! - Sunderland greet their fans before the match. Sporting bell-bottoms (left to right) are Billy Hughes, Richie Pitt and Vic Halom.

playing as a traditional stopper for victorious Newcastle United, had done much to negate the subtle scheming of Revie, who operated as a deep-lying centre-forward and was the much-lauded fulcrum of Manchester City's attack. As managers of their current clubs, too, they were polls apart. Revie, with so much to lose and his excellent team's narrow failures continuing to outnumber their successes, seemed to draw tension about him like a cloak; Stokoe, having arrived at Roker Park in November and lifted his new charges from 21st to sixth in Division Two, was positively carefree and exuberant by comparison. Where Don appeared tight-lipped and gave an impression of deviousness, Bob was expansive and candid, exuding a folksy north-eastern bonhomie that endeared him to the uncommitted.

Of course, the Sunderland manager was no wide-eyed innocent, and was canny indeed in the ways of soccer psychology. Not for nothing did he express confidence before the game that Wembley referee Ken Burns would be able to handle the Yorkshiremen's loquacious skipper Billy Bremner, recently criticised for battering the eardrums of match officials; then there were his protests that Leeds had been allotted the 'best' dressing room and their fans the tunnel end of the stadium, as if to underline that the Wearsiders were *not* to be put upon; and he it was who urged his men to run out eagerly for the second half, passing their trudging opponents on the way. But his most significant pre-match achievement - aside from footballing considerations, for which coach Arthur Cox deserved a share of the credit - was to ensure that a light-hearted (though thoroughly determined) attitude pervaded the Sunderland party that arrived in London for the final. The difference in the atmosphere of the two camps was illustrated vividly in front of the TV cameras, the Leeds players responding to questions with taut monosyllables, while the Wearsiders, quite palpably, were out to enjoy themselves - as the BBC's Barry Davies found when he asked centre-half Dave Watson about his attacking talents. The response was an explosion of maniacal cackling, not from the mildly embarrassed Watson but from effervescent team-mate Billy Hughes,

The side that Wearside will never forget. Back row (left to right): David Young (substitute not used), Vic Halom, Dave Watson, Jim Montgomery, Dick Malone, Richie Pitt. Front row: Mick Horswill, Bobby Kerr, Dennis Tueart, Billy Hughes, Ian Porterfield and Ron Guthrie.

HOW THEY GOT THERE

SUNDERLAND
Round 3:
Notts County (a) 1-1,
replay (h) 2-0.

Round 4:
Reading (h) 1-1,
replay (a) 3-1.

Round 5:
Manchester City (a) 2 -2,
replay (h) 3-1.

Round 6:
Luton Town (h) 2-0.

Semi-final:
Arsenal *at Hillsborough* 2-1.

LEEDS UNITED
Round 3:
Norwich City (a) 1-1,
replay (h) 1-1,
second replay *at Villa Park* 5-0.

Round 4:
Plymouth Argyle (h) 2-1.

Round 5:
West Bromwich Albion
(h) 2-0.

Round 6:
Derby County (a) 1-0.

Semi-final:
Wolverhampton Wanderers
at Maine Road 1-0.

who had activated his new toy, a laughing box. Clearly, the Sunderland men were great friends - most of them remain so to this day - partly because many of them had been together since winning the 1969 FA Youth Cup during the managerial reign of Alan Brown, but partly, also, because Stokoe encouraged them to pull together in any situation.

That all-for-one spirit had been evident throughout the Rokerites' Cup journey, which had almost foundered at the earliest possible juncture. A goal down just 15 minutes from the end of their third-round tie at Notts County, only a stupendous save by 'keeper Jim Montgomery averted what must have been a fatal second strike; thus reprieved, they battled on, Watson was thrown forward and he grabbed a late equaliser. It was not the last time during the campaign that Montgomery and Watson would be the heroes of the hour. The replay posed few problems, but then Stokoe's men could manage only a draw at home to Reading, needing a rousing performance at Elm Park to progress. Next as the standard of opposition increased, Sunderland were not found wanting. In front of the first of four successive crowds of 50,000-plus, they chiselled a memorable draw against Manchester City at Maine Road, before ousting Malcolm Allison's star-laden combination 3-1 on Wearside. Out went Luton in the quarter-final, and then - incredibly - so did Championship runners-up Arsenal in a thrilling semi-final at Hillsborough, in which goals from Vic Halom and Hughes spared the nation what many described as the ultimate footballing agony - a repeat of the dire 1972 Leeds-Gunners final. For their part, the Elland Roaders had enjoyed no easy path to Wembley, needing three games to dispose of First Division strugglers Norwich City, then inching past Plymouth Argyle, beating West Bromwich Albion rather more comfortably and winning by the only goal in a predictably tight sixth-round clash at Derby's Baseball Ground. Their semi-final at Maine Road offered the chance of vengeance over Wolves for inflicting the last-match defeat that deprived them of the title a year earlier, and they took it thanks to a single strike by Bremner.

For the second successive final, Leeds were without the services of the splendid Terry Cooper at left-back - he had been out for 13 months now with a broken leg - but that was hardly expected to affect the result. Popular wisdom had it that United left-winger Eddie Gray, who had so embarrassed David Webb in 1970, would do the same and worse to Sunderland's unsung Dick Malone and that

Leeds would win by a hatful. In the event, the industrious Malone would neutralise the Scot's threat so efficiently that Eddie would be withdrawn in favour of defensive midfielder Terry Yorath, though it should be pointed out that the flankman had been struggling for fitness for much of the season.

But that is getting ahead of the narrative. As the teams emerged from the tunnel, it was apparent immediately that Leeds were facing an 'away' match. The cheers from their 20,000 fans would surely have been drowned anyway by the 'Roker Roar', transported to Wembley by an equal number of rabidly fervent north-easterners, out to savour their club's first Cup Final since their only triumph in 1937. But it was the almost unanimous support of the 60,000 so-called neutrals that tipped the decibel level so overwhelmingly in the underdogs' favour. Nevertheless, the Yorkshiremen were accustomed to concerted unpopularity, and set about justifying their status as one of Europe's finest sides. But somehow, though they were playing in their eighth major final in nine seasons, they seemed ill at ease on the slippery, rain-soaked surface. With the Wearsiders' central defenders Watson and Richie Pitt tackling like mantraps to ensure that the predatory Allan Clarke, in particular, was not allowed in the vicinity of goal, Revie's men were passing to opponents with disconcerting regularity.

Meanwhile the red-and-white stripes moved forward purposefully, and soon

One for all and all for one. With his defenders sorely stretched, Sunderland centre-forward Vic Halom heads clear from Leeds' Trevor Cherry.

after Mick Horswill - a study in perpetual motion in his successful midfield combat with Bremner and Johnny Giles - went close with a smartly-struck 20-yarder, Sunderland took a deserved lead. Skipper Bobby Kerr slightly overhit his cross from the right, but it forced 'keeper David Harvey to play safe and concede a corner. As Hughes' deep kick from the left soared beyond the six-yard box, Watson lunged towards it; he missed but took two defenders with him and the ball cannoned from Halom's knee to Ian Porterfield, standing some eight yards out and unmarked. In one smooth movement, the lanky, left-footed midfielder controlled

Left: Leeds' armour is pierced. Ian Porterfield (on the left, hidden behind United full-back Trevor Cherry) cracks the only goal of the game past 'keeper David Harvey. Vic Halom is the other Sunderland atacker.

Above: Porterfield leaps skywards and Wearside joy is uncontained. But surely it couldn't last . . .

it on his thigh and half turned to smash a fierce *right*-foot volley high into the net, giving two men on the line no chance of keeping it out. Later he was ribbed mercilessly by team-mates who believed he reserved his right 'peg' for standing only, but in the circumstances Ian could hardly have cared less. With an hour of the match remaining, Porterfield's strike might have been little more than a warning shot across Leeds' bows, but as half-time came and went it began to assume increased significance. However, during the middle period of the second half the First Division 'aristocrats' ran into a vein of improved form, and began to

Right: Hero at work. Sunderland 'keeper Jim Montgomery parries a header from Trevor Cherry (seen grounded beyond him). The rebound ran to Peter Lorimer and the game, surely, was up. But somehow the grounded Monty corkscrewed backwards to make the save of his life. It was at that moment, perhaps, that Leeds lost their grip on proceedings.

mount attacks with ominous smoothness. Several chances were spurned before Leeds carved out the opportunity which seemed certain to bring them the equaliser, setting in motion a sequence of action which has been even more extensively documented than Porterfield's goal. Paul Reaney sent a long ball from the inside-right channel into space at the far post and Trevor Cherry dashed forward to launch a diving header goalwards. Montgomery threw himself to his left, parrying brilliantly but only to the feet of Peter Lorimer six yards out. With the Sunderland custodian grounded 'The Lash' opted for placement rather than power and sidefooted firmly towards the beckoning net. Somehow Montgomery twisted backwards and upwards to get a hand to the ball, deflecting it on to the bar before it bounced to the feet of Malone, who effected a hasty clearance. It all happened so quickly that TV commentators David Coleman and Brian Moore were not alone in their initial reaction that the ball had gone in, but action replays revealed clearly that it had not crossed the line. The Wearsiders were still in front, and though 20 or so minutes remained, it was a crucial turning point. After that, how could Leeds *believe* they could score,

Below: Sheer ecstasy for Sunderland boss Bob Stokoe as he hugs goal-scorer Ian Porterfield. Dennis Tueart (left) and Billy Hughes await their turn.

and though they continued to probe it was the north-easterners who came closest in the later stages when Halom's 15-yarder brought a superb save from Harvey.

When the final whistle went, it was the prelude to some of the most joyous, emotional scenes that even Wembley has witnessed. Leaping from the bench, a beige raincoat covering his red tracksuit and a pork-pie hat perched on his head, Bob Stokoe hit the pitch running and accelerated like some ageing, spidery sprinter in the direction of the goal his 11 heroes had been defending. As he ran his grin broadened, his arms spread wide and then he engulfed Jim Montgomery in a gigantic bear-hug that said more eloquently than any words: 'Thanks for giving me the sweetest moment of my career.' Later Bob explained: 'That run was pure instinct. I wanted to pay tribute to Jimmy's contribution throughout the whole competition, not just in the one match.' Montgomery, generally recognised as the League's most accomplished uncapped 'keeper, admitted that it was not until he had watched film of his double save that he realised its significance; at the time, it was just one of countless incidents in which he was involved as Leeds

Sitting jauntily atop Dennis Tueart, Sunderland skipper Bobby Kerr shows off the FA Cup. Alongside, left to right, are Jim Montgomery, Ian Porterfield and Ron Guthrie. The Rokerites, who had lifted the trophy for the second time, were the first Second Division side to triumph at Wembley since WBA in 1931.

A study in dejection. Leeds' Allan Clarke (left), Billy Bremner and manager Don Revie can hardly believe that the worst has happened.

piled on the pressure. Of course, it was no one-man triumph; some made Watson their man of the match, others went for Horswill, but above all it was a victory for matchless teamwork.

In the aftermath, as poor Don Revie bravely mouthed the platitudes expected of the vanquished manager, he was grey with shock and distress, utterly crushed by the outcome. Traumatically for 'The Don', there was another helping of sackcloth and ashes just around the corner. Eleven days later Leeds were beaten in the final of the European Cup Winners' Cup by AC Milan to complete a mortifying

Left: A moment of quiet satisfaction for Bob Stokoe, who rejoiced in telling the world that he hadn't needed a lucky suit to win the Cup. This was a wicked reference to one of the many superstitions of Don Revie, a man with whom he had never seen eye to eye.

Above: A Wearside welcome for the shock conquerors of Leeds.

season. Meanwhile the ripples from that dramatic Wembley afternoon continued to spread happiness throughout the rest of the football-conscious community. Fans all over the country, without the slightest allegiance to the Rokerites, rejoiced at the triumph of the 'little man' over the big battalions; the north-east, that beleaguered, unemployment-riddled region, had, at least temporarily, a new spring in its collective step and pride in its heart; and the English game as a whole, then going through a lacklustre period with Alf Ramsey's national side struggling in the World Cup qualifiers, received a much-needed tonic.

LIVERPOOL 3

Keegan 58, 88; Heighway 75

NEWCASTLE UNITED 0

Half-time 0-0

LIVERPOOL	○	NEWCASTLE UNITED
Ray Clemence	1	Iam McFaul
Tommy Smith	2	Frank Clark
Alec Lindsay	3	Alan Kennedy
Phil Thompson	4	Terry McDermott
Peter Cormack	5	Pat Howard
Emlyn Hughes *(captain)*	6	Bobby Moncur *(captain)*
Kevin Keegan	7	Jimmy Smith*
Brian Hall	8	Tommy Cassidy
Steve Heighway	9	Malcolm Macdonald
John Toshack	10	John Tudor
Ian Callaghan	11	Terry Hibbitt
		(sub Tommy Gibb)*

Attendance: 100,000

Referee: G Kew, Amersham

Two great clubs, each with their larger-than-life personalities and outstanding performers; two sets of fiercely partisan supporters whose pride and passion were second to none; the ingredients for the 1974 FA Cup Final were enough to stir the senses of any red-blooded lover of the English game. On the one hand were Liverpool, League Champions a year earlier, runners-up this time around, managed by that unique, irrepressible soccer sage Bill Shankly; the Anfield Reds boasted class in every position and in the still-maturing Kevin Keegan they had arguably the most special talent on the current domestic scene. On the other hand were Newcastle United, the Tynecastle Magpies, who were going for a record seventh FA Cup victory, whose boss Joe Harvey had captained them to Wembley triumph twice in the early 1950s, and whose current goal-scoring idol, Malcolm 'Supermac' Macdonald, had whipped up a storm with a swaggering line in pre-match braggadocio. For every cool head who maintained that the quality gap in Liverpool's favour was so vast that there could be only one result, there was a misty-eyed romantic who pointed to the heroic deeds of Sunderland 12 months

1974

IT HAPPENED THIS YEAR

Labour won two elections by narrow margins.

IRA bombs caused carnage in Birmingham and Guildford pubs.

President Nixon resigned over Watergate, replaced by Gerald Ford.

Disappearance of Lord Lucan.

Muhammad Ali beat George Foreman to regain world heavyweight crown.

earlier and declared that a Geordie win would constitute far less of an upset. Come the day, however, it was more one-sided than even the most fervent Kopite might have dreamed. It was an occasion that catapulted Keegan to fully-fledged superstar status, left Macdonald with an oversized dollop of egg on his face and caused poor Joe Harvey to shake his head in embarrassed disbelief that his team had played so badly. And though no one knew it at the time, the final was to earn a poignant place in football folklore as the last game - begging the Charity Shield's pardon - in which Shanks was to guide the fortunes of his beloved Liverpool.

Such a scenario would have been deemed unthinkable back in January when the two clubs embarked on respective roads to Wembley that both proved long and winding, and in the case of the Magpies, unexpectedly dramatic. Harvey's men began at home to the Isthmian League amateurs of Hendon, who stunned the St James' Park faithful by forcing a draw. The replay, held in a quagmire at Watford's Vicarage Road, saw Newcastle cruise through 4-0, no doubt feeling more relieved than euphoric. Their next opposition were Scunthorpe United,

Above: Well played, son. Bill Shankly shakes the hand of Kevin Keegan, who contributed brilliantly to what turned out to be the Liverpool chief's farewell triumph. Tommy Smith (centre) and Emlyn Hughes share the moment.

Opposite: Kopites Pete and Arthur in suitable Wembley attire. After the match, two equally demonstrative fans kissed Bill Shankly's feet.

then floundering in the lower reaches of Division Four, and they too flourished in the rarified atmosphere of Tyneside, earning a second match at the Old Showground. Once again the Geordies won comfortably, as they did in the fifth round at Second Division West Bromwich to set up a quarter-final home clash with Nottingham Forest that was to raise a difficult moral question. Midway through the second half, with Forest 3-1 up, there was a pitch invasion, apparently in protest at the sending-off of Newcastle defender Pat Howard. Referee Gordon Kew took the teams off and the match was held up for a quarter of an hour. Then, with some 20 minutes remaining and many supporters still highly incensed, the Geordies surged back to finish 4-3 winners. There was a predictable outcry, with some folk claiming United should be expelled from the competition on grounds of intimidation, others saying the result should stand. The FA opted for a re-match at neutral Goodison Park, which ended goalless and it was not until a third encounter, also at the home of Everton, that Newcastle squeezed through thanks to a single goal by Macdonald. 'Supermac' then maintained his record of scoring in every round - shades of Jackie Milburn - with a semi-final brace against Burnley, and began waxing loud and lyrical about how he would slaughter the opposition at Wembley.

While the Geordies were struggling against Hendon, Liverpool were having 'minnow trouble' themselves, trailing at half-time in their Anfield encounter with Doncaster Rovers, then propping up the Fourth Division. It took a goal from Keegan to earn a replay in his hometown, where the Reds won 2-0, only to face more toil in the fourth round. This time it was Carlisle United, one of the Second

Division's leading lights, who had the temerity to hold the Reds in front of the Kop before capitulating at Brunton Park. Ipswich Town were disposed of in more routine fashion, then plucky Bristol City found that the 'miracle' they had wrought against mighty Leeds in the previous round was not to be repeated, though Liverpool only scraped through 1-0 at Ashton Gate. The semi-final pitted them against Leicester City, old Cup adversaries who took the Merseysiders to two games before bowing out.

Having led his men to Wembley, Shanks picked what was clearly his best side, but that did not insulate him from discontent within his camp. Two players, centre-half Larry Lloyd and utility forward Phil Boersma, were dismayed at their absence from the 12 selected for the big day. Their cases differed in that England international Lloyd was a victim of circumstance, while Boersma, though a whole-hearted trier, was never quite good enough. Big Larry had been ever-present that term until an injury in February had seen him replaced as Emlyn Hughes' partner by Phil Thompson; the new pairing gelled instantly, playing the ball out of defence in the Continental style that became such a feature of the Reds' subsequent success, and there was no way back for Larry. Understandably, he left the club that summer and, to his immense credit, went on to further his England career while serving Nottingham Forest. Poor Boersma probably felt his omission even more keenly, having played throughout most of the Cup campaign. He expected only the role of substitute, but when that was given to veteran Chris Lawler, it was just too much for Phil to take and he walked out on the Wembley party. Shankly, moved by the depth of Phil's hurt, demonstrated his wisdom by patching up their differences, and the curly-haired Merseysider remained at Anfield for a further 18 months.

More to the point, as far as the game was concerned, who *was* playing for Liverpool? The cast was as starry as ever, but one man deserves a special mention. Ian Callaghan, like Tommy Smith and Lawler a survivor from the 1965 Cup triumph, was now 32 and, having been converted from conventional winger to industrious midfielder, was playing better than ever. Indeed, he had just been voted Footballer of the Year, and his all-pervading presence at the heart of almost every attacking move was to have a profound, if characteristically unspectacular influence on the final outcome. The Reds' eye-catcher, of course, was Kevin Keegan, who had joined them as an unknown quantity from Scunthorpe in the Cup Final week of 1971, and watched his new side lose to Arsenal. A little later, as Kevin's prodigious talent was blossoming, Shankly recalled that day: 'He looked so downhearted that we had lost. He probably thought that if he had played we would have won - and we would have done!' Three years on, the little man's hour was at hand.

Newcastle's only selection worry was caused by an injury to full-back David Craig, but with richly promising 19-year-old Alan Kennedy stepping in, Geordie fans had no reason to fear a weakness. In any case, there was relatively little public focus on their team make-up, such was the media attention accorded to Mr

Main picture: After almost constant Liverpool pressure, the Tynesiders' defences are breached at last as Keegan cracks the ball into the net from just inside the area.

Inset below: One of the game's crucial contests - Tommy Smith of Liverpool versus the Magpies' Terry Hibbitt. Until he injured a knee, the Newcastle schemer was doing well.

Inset below right: The screamer that didn't count. Alec Lindsay nets but his cross-shot was ruled out for offside.

Above: Terry McDermott, who left the pitch wearing a swapped Liverpool shirt. Before long he would be wearing one on a regular basis.

Macdonald, christened 'Supermouth' on Merseyside. If Malcolm was to be taken at his word, it was hardly worth Liverpool's while turning up at Wembley, but if he believed he was striking a psychological blow for the Magpies he was sadly mistaken. Instead of making the experienced Reds quail, it merely motivated them to deliver retribution where it was most effective - on the pitch. Of course, that wily old bird Shankly could not resist a few barbs of his own, pronouncing the north-easterners as 'frightened to death', though his most effective was allegedly accidental. At the end of a TV debate with his old friend Joe Harvey, Bill thought the microphones had been turned off and ventured the aside: 'Christ, Joe's a bag of nerves, he's beaten already.' Though Shanks was left protesting his innocence, the remark was heard by millions! The war of words was taken up with a vengeance by the fans, with the travelling Kopites holding all the aces. One huge banner proclaimed 'No way the lads!' and as the match progressed, with the Newcastle attack manifestly impotent, the refrain rattled round the stadium: 'Supermac, Superstar, How many goals have you scored so far?' The answer, of course, was none; indeed, it was 78 minutes before Macdonald managed a shot and that went hopelessly wide. To be fair, the Geordies had begun in fairly sprightly fashion with two midfielders, the fetcher-and-carrier Terry McDermott and the creative Terry Hibbitt, in good form. But after Hibbitt had twice ghosted past Smith on the left flank, Brian Hall was pushed into a wider position to close down the space and

228

Liverpool gradually gained an ascendancy they were never to relinquish. Even so, they didn't manage a goal in the first period, and had Hibbitt not wrenched his knee in the 40th minute, thereby severely restricting his mobility, there just *might* have been surprises in store. As it was, the Reds began the second half at a gallop and seemed to have taken the lead when Alec Lindsay played a slick one-two with the ubiquitous Keegan and netted with a scorching cross-shot. But the straw-haired left-back had been marginally offside and the scoresheet remained blank. Not for long, though. Thirteen minutes after the break Smith crossed from the right and the ball bounced to Keegan, just inside the box; with a posse of defenders stranded helplessly by his deft control, he flipped it up and volleyed home via diving 'keeper Iam McFaul's left hand. And that, effectively, was that. Liverpool were now rampant and a quarter of an hour from time - three minutes after the Magpies first corner! - Heighway seized on a Toshack back-header, evaded two opponents and scored with a firm, low drive from 15 yards. Thereafter the Reds moved the ball around at will and the third goal - tucked in from close range by Keegan after a Smith pull-back from the byline - was the culmination of a delightful 13-touch sequence. For Liverpool,

Inset above left: Steve Heighway skims past Bobby Moncur and Frank Clark to put the Reds two up.

Above: Tommy Smith's cross eludes Peter Cormack, 'keeper Iam McFaul and Pat Howard to reach Kevin Keegan, who is about to prod home Liverpool's third at the far post.

229

Left: Setting off on a lap of honour are, left to right, Peter Cormack, John Toshack, Chris Lawler (unused substitute), Tommy Smith and Emlyn Hughes.

Opposite page: A seat on the fence and egg on his face. Newcastle's Malcolm Macdonald, whose pre-match predictions proved rather embarrassing.

Opposite page inset: How would he have looked if Liverpool had lost? Kevin Keegan, perhaps exhausted by his non-stop display, shows his medal to the fans.

'KK' had scintillated, Thompson had bottled up Macdonald with almost ridiculous ease and everyone else had contributed admirably. For United the pick of the bunch had been McDermott and Kennedy - ironically, both were destined to serve the Anfield cause with distinction - while skipper Bobby Moncur and fellow stopper Pat Howard had offered brave resistance. Beyond that, and Hibbitt's early touches, the Geordies' performance had been abysmal, leaving Harvey to mutter despairingly: 'We didn't even do the simple things well.' At the end of the uneven contest, Shankly showed his innate compassion by finding time for a word of commiseration with each Newcastle player. In contrast, Liverpool skipper Hughes was ready to rub salt into wounds, telling the press: 'They did all that talking, then what did they do? Nothing.'

When Liverpool went home with the trophy, an emotional Shanks told the assembled throng of supporters, the people whom he prized so dearly: 'It was *you* who won the Cup.' But as he revealed later, he was 'tired with all the years' and in the summer stunned the football world by resigning. Though his successor Bob Paisley was to outstrip his tally of honours, when Bill Shankly walked away from Anfield, the game he had graced for so long had suffered an irreplaceable loss.

'Do you think stripes suit me?' Liverpool's Toshack (in Newcastle shirt) and Lindsay pause for photographers en route to the dressing room.

IT HAPPENED
THIS YEAR

Margaret Thatcher
replaced Ted Heath as
Tory leader.

Sex Discrimination
Act came into force.

Britain welcomed first
oil from North Sea.

Dutch Elm Disease
wiped out 6.5 million
trees in Britain.

West Indies beat
Australia at Lord's to
win cricket's first
World Cup.

Czechoslovakian ten-
nis star Martina
Navratilova defected
to the West.

3 May 1975

WEST HAM UNITED 2
A Taylor 60, 65

FULHAM 0

Half-time 0-0

WEST HAM UNITED		FULHAM
Mervyn Day	1	Peter Mellor
John McDowell	2	John Cutbush
Frank Lampard	3	John Fraser
Billy Bonds *(captain)*	4	Alan Mullery *(captain)*
Tommy Taylor	5	John Lacy
Kevin Lock	6	Bobby Moore
Billy Jennings	7	John Mitchell
Graham Paddon	8	Jim Conway
Alan Taylor	9	Viv Busby
Trevor Brooking	10	Alan Slough
Pat Holland	11	Les Barrett

Attendance: 100,000

Referee: P Partridge, Durham

The scene was set for romance and drama on the grand scale. But while the principal actors, two illustrious veterans and a callow rookie, did themselves proud, it must be admitted reluctantly that the production as a whole was an artistic flop. West Ham United, renowned for their classical approach and adherence to skill, had just finished yet another First Division campaign in mid-table, seemingly their natural habitat, while dear old friendly Fulham occupied a similar position in the second flight. Nothing remarkable there, perhaps, but special ingredients abounded. At the quarter-final stage, injuries had forced the Hammers to draft in Alan Taylor, a recent recruit from the League's basement level, and his goals unseated mighty Arsenal. In the semi-final, the 21-year-old Lancastrian force-fed Ipswich Town the same medicine; could he pre-scribe another dose for the Cottagers? As for Fulham, their campaign had been led by skipper Alan Mullery, who had begun his soccer life at the homely Thames-side club, then won fame and glory with Spurs and England before returning to his roots. That he was not content to play out the autumn of his career in the carpet-slipper manner of some ageing professionals was borne out by his recent election as Footballer of the Year at the age of 33, a fitting tribute to an ever-dynamic competitor. But the crowning, irresistible attraction of the second all-London final - Mullery had also played in the first, for Tottenham against Chelsea in 1967 - was the identity of the underdogs' number-six, the peerless former England captain and the greatest figure in the history of West Ham themselves, none other than Bobby Moore.

Bobby, now 34, had moved to Craven Cottage in March 1974 and combined with Alan to rid the dressing room of a certain inferiority complex, pumping up colleagues to believe in their own abilities. On the pitch, he remained an inspiration, cool and cultured, strong and skilful, the best possible example. The team was run by Alec Stock, more experienced than any current

Above: Has veteran Fulham skipper Alan Mullery asked for a breather? If so, referee Pat Partridge insists on timing it!

Left: Immaculate as ever, the incomparable Bobby Moore clears the Fulham lines and launches another attack on his former club's goal.

League manager and one of the most respected men in football. Back in 1949 he had been skipper and boss of the Yeovil Town side that had pulled off one of the biggest shocks of all time in dumping Sunderland out of the FA Cup, and it afforded immense pleasure to countless people in the game that such a wise and doughty campaigner at all professional levels should now walk with the elite at his country's premier venue.

True, Alec had led Queen's Park Rangers out at Wembley for the 1967 League Cup Final, but this was the real thing. It was the first time Fulham had reached the Twin Towers, and the road had been devilishly hard. It had taken them 11 games - including seven in resolving their first two ties - and some 18 hours of playing to earn the right to face the Hammers. As Bobby Moore pointed out drily, that should have been enough football to take them through to the following season's European Cup Winners' Cup Final! The trail began, uneventfully enough, with a home draw against Hull City, neighbours in the middle reaches of the Second Division, and

Victorious Hammers, left to right, are man of the hour Alan Taylor, Mervyn Day and Trevor Brooking.

the Tigers' teeth were not drawn until a third match at Filbert Street. But an even more protracted saga was in prospect against Nottingham Forest, also of Division Two. Two meetings at Craven Cottage and one at the City Ground failed to settle the issue, so it was back to Trentside for a fourth match in which two goals from Viv Busby finally put Fulham through. In view of the struggles to date, there appeared few reasons for optimism among the Londoners' fans when their side was drawn away to Championship contenders Everton in the fifth round but, with the endearing unpredictability that is part of the club's heritage, the Cottagers responded with a stirring victory, courtesy of another Busby brace. More top flight opposition awaited in the quarter-final, this time struggling Carlisle United, who failed to reply to a single Les Barrett strike, mainly due to a magnificent display of goalkeeping by Peter Mellor. Now only First Division Birmingham City barred the way to Wembley, and they were removed by two goals from John Mitchell, one earning a draw at Hillsborough, the other clinching victory at Maine Road, with Moore marshalling his forces majestically on both occasions. In the winners' dressing room a beaming Alan Mullery climbed on to a table, raised a glass of champagne and proclaimed a toast to his young team-mates 'for taking two old men back to Wembley.'

For their part, West Ham clocked up far fewer miles on their team coach, never venturing farther north than Swindon until the semi-final stage. Success at Southampton was followed by a win over the Wiltshiremen at the second attempt, then a dazzling show by the gifted Trevor Brooking inspired victory over Queen's

Poor Les Strong, who missed the final through injury but received a special medal from the FA.

Park Rangers in the mud of Upton Park. Enter Alan Taylor, the blond marksman signed from Rochdale for a mere £40,000 in November. With several more senior forwards unfit, the speedy youngster - already he had proved himself the quickest man at the club - was pitched in for his full Hammers debut against Arsenal in the quarter-final. Anything but over-awed, he repaid team boss John Lyall's faith with both goals in a pulsating triumph in front of more than 56,000 supporters at Highbury. Not surprisingly he retained his place for the Villa Park semi-final encounter with Bobby Robson's high-riding Ipswich, who outplayed West Ham but could not claim the spoils. In the replay at Stamford Bridge, the East Anglians again dominated long spells of the action, but were put to the sword by Taylor, who scored another pair in a 2-1 victory. Dubbed 'Sparrow' for his spindly, almost scrawny build, Alan had come a long way in a short time - only two years earlier he had been a motor mechanic who played his football part-time for non-League Morecambe. Now he was on the threshold of Wembley.

The Hammers were to contest the final with an all-English team for the second time - the first was in 1964 - and remained the only club to do so at Wembley. Again they would face Second Division opposition, though with Moore and Mullery among the Fulham ranks, the Cottagers would not be feeling there was a gulf in class. Ecstatic at reaching their first final after losing a quartet of semis, most recently in 1962, they could rejoice in the happy precedent of having knocked West Ham out of the League Cup back in October.

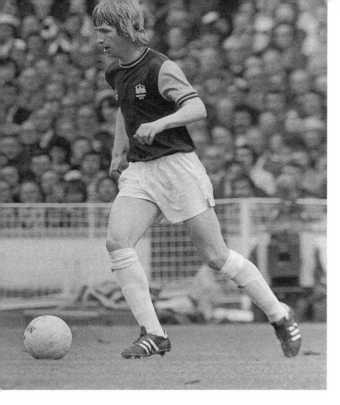

Not that their horizon was cloudless as they approached the most prestigious game in their history. One minor irritation arose when the players became caught up in a legal wrangle over contracts with boot manufacturers, the problem being solved by blacking out the footware trademarks before taking to the pitch. Far more serious was the injury suffered by left-back Les Strong, who had not missed a match all season, at home to Portsmouth just two weeks before the big day. Sadly, he was ruled out of contention, and right-back John Fraser switched flanks with John Cutbush taking the number-two shirt. It was a

Left: West Ham's Kevin Lock dribbles the ball out of defence, keeping a wary eye on the predatory Viv Busby, the Cottagers striker who netted six times on the way to Wembley.

shattering blow to poor Les, who received some consolation in the form of a medal specially minted by the FA. West Ham had injuries to contend with, too, sidelined forward Keith Robson being replaced by Patsy Holland, though there was better news of skipper Billy Bonds. Helped by painkilling injections, he overcame the effects of long-term groin trouble to undertake his important midfield role.

Before the game, Moore was in the dressing-room corridor in good time to greet his former team-mates from Upton Park, his charismatic presence offering them an awesome reminder of his capabilities. Though good-natured in the extreme, he was supremely professional, too, and it was as if he was saying to them 'I'm the man you've got to beat, and I've been here one or two times before!' Bobby's next job was to join with Stock and Mullery in ensuring a calm atmosphere among his current colleagues, which was achieved to splendid effect, though clearly someone in the Fulham party had been suffering from jangling nerves. The shin-pads had not been packed and a set had to be bought from a near-by sports shop; they turned out to be too big and assistant manager Billy Taylor had to trim then to size with a hacksaw.

That 'crisis' over, the action got under way and far from being outdone by their supposedly more sophisticated rivals, the Cottagers settled first. While the overall standard of play was decidedly scrappy (and would remain so for far too long), it was the Second Division outfit who contributed the smoothest movements. Despite one uncharacteristic early slip that allowed Billy Jennings to bring an excellent save from Mellor, Bobby Moore exerted a significant influence, now dominating the rearguard, then sailing forward to prompt his forwards, while his fellow elder statesman was equally effective. For the Hammers, who were disappointingly disjointed at this stage, only the occasional immaculate touch from Brooking took the eye, though they did create the lion's share of half-chances. However, it was Fulham who almost broke the stalemate just before the interval when Mitchell beat Kevin Lock adroitly, only to see his shot on the turn saved capably by Mervyn Day. After the break, West Ham

Below: Jim Conway, who survived Fulham's drop from the top flight to the Third Division, then helped them back up to the Second. Now he was relishing his chance on the big stage.

235

Above: Alan Taylor's FA Cup goal-rush continues as he pounces to open the scoring after Peter Mellor has blocked Billy Jennings' shot.

Right: 'Sparrow' strikes again. The unfortunate Mellor has dropped Graham Paddon's shot at the feet of Taylor, who nets for the second time in five minutes.

Inset top right: These Hammers know that, barring accidents, they have won the Cup. Returning to their positions after the second goal are, left to right, Graham Paddon, scorer Alan Taylor, Frank Lampard and Billy Bonds.

seemed determined to limit Moore's input by starving him of the ball, and gradually the favourites grew more incisive. Even so, they could not assert superiority until, on the hour, Holland dispossessed Cutbush on the left and passed inside to Jennings. The sprightly, former Watford marksman drilled the ball netwards, Mellor could only parry it and Alan Taylor - who else? - was on hand to drive it past the stricken custodian. Five minutes later, Holland was involved again, setting up Graham Paddon for a strike which the unhappy Mellor dropped at the feet of Taylor, who capitalised ruthlessly on the error by shooting high into the net. Of course, nobody mentioned it at the time, but it was a fitting moment to recall that but for the goalkeeper's brilliance at Carlisle, Fulham might never have reached Wembley in the first place. Thereafter, as might have been expected, West Ham cast off their tension and began to play more like their true stylish selves. Fulham, too, raised their game, with Busby looking particularly dangerous and Mitchell pulling another fine stop from Day. But it was too late, both for the Cottagers to loosen the Hammers' ever-tightening grip on the trophy and for the game to be saved as a spectacle.

The final whistle was the signal for street parties to break out all over the East End, some of them continuing for the rest of the weekend, while for Bobby Moore there was an unpleasant jolt in store. Tired after Fulham's after-match function, he headed home and went straight to bed, not discovering until the next morning that his house had been burgled. At first examination, it was apparent that treasured football trophies and mementoes were among the missing property, but on opening the front door he found them piled neatly on the lawn. Presumably the thief, on discovering the nature of his swag, had suffered a pang of conscience. Meanwhile that Sunday, Bobby's former club celebrated victory with a drive through packed streets to a reception at East Ham town hall. One notable absentee was general manager Ron Greenwood, who had guided the Hammers to their 1960s triumphs. This time, he maintained, it was team boss John Lyall's day.

Left: They know it's all over. Pat Holland (left) and Billy Jennings with the FA Cup.

IT HAPPENED
THIS YEAR

Britain sizzled
through the hottest
summer of the
century to date.

Punk movement
caught on with
British youngsters.

Harold Wilson
resigned as British
Prime Minister,
replaced by Jim
Callaghan.

Jimmy Carter elected
President of United
States.

Bjorn Borg beat Ilie
Nastase to win his
first Wimbledon title.

1 May 1976

SOUTHAMPTON 1

Stokes 83

MANCHESTER UNITED 0

Half-time 0-0

SOUTHAMPTON		MANCHESTER UNITED
Ian Turner	1	Alex Stepney
Peter Rodrigues (captain)	2	Alex Forsyth
David Peach	3	Stewart Houston
Nick Holmes	4	Gerry Daly
Mel Blyth	5	Brian Greenhoff
Jim Steele	6	Martin Buchan (captain)
Paul Gilchrist	7	Steve Coppell
Mick Channon	8	Sammy McIlroy
Peter Osgood	9	Stuart Pearson
Jim McCalliog	10	Lou Macari
Bobby Stokes	11	Gordon Hill*
		(sub David McCreery)*

Attendance: 100,000

Referee: C Thomas, Treorchy

There was a distinct and unexpected edge to the habitually soft, rounded Wiltshire burr. Surrounded by celebratory mayhem in the Stamford Bridge dressing room after Second Division Southampton's FA Cup semi-final victory over Crystal Palace, Mick Channon took a break from the badinage to sound a chilling warning to all who believed Manchester United were in for a Wembley walkover. Glancing indulgently at his euphoric team-mates, partly musing to himself and partly responding to an interviewer's questions, the England forward declared: 'It's no good just *getting* to the final. Now we've got to *win* the bloody thing!' Countless thousands of United fans around the country, themselves savouring a famous triumph over Derby County that afternoon, must have caught the broadcast and greeted it with varying degrees of derision. Even Gordon Hill, the Red Devils' gifted winger whose two superb strikes had knocked out the Rams, was moved to remark to the cameras: 'Who are Southampton?' Indeed, it was tempting to dismiss Channon's words as hot air, the inevitable bravado of an underdog who was having his day and was enjoying it to the full, knowing it couldn't last.

Having marched all over Manchester United, the Saints settle back to enjoy themselves, presided over by shoulder-high captain Peter Rodrigues.

But those who thought a countrified accent plus a lop-sided grin added up to a quaint but essentially harmless adversary - after all, didn't Wiltshiremen spend their Saturday nights trying to fish the moon out of a duckpond? - were in for the rudest of May Day awakenings.

Of course, United did have due cause for confidence. Freshly returned to the First Division, Tommy Docherty's exhilarating young side had administered a sorely-needed injection of dash and adventure to a rather sterile top-flight scene. Attacking for all they were worth, leading the way with a pair of captivating wingers - 'Merlin' Hill and Steve Coppell - the Old Trafford side had contested the Championship race memorably with Liverpool and Queen's Park Rangers, trading win for win with their more mature rivals until four games in eight days on the last lap had proved too much for them and they had finished third. Their line-up dripped with quality, notably the cool Martin Buchan in central defence, the dynamic, skilful Lou Macari in midfield and quicksilver striker Stuart Pearson, who all contributed royally to a stirring Cup campaign. It had begun routinely

239

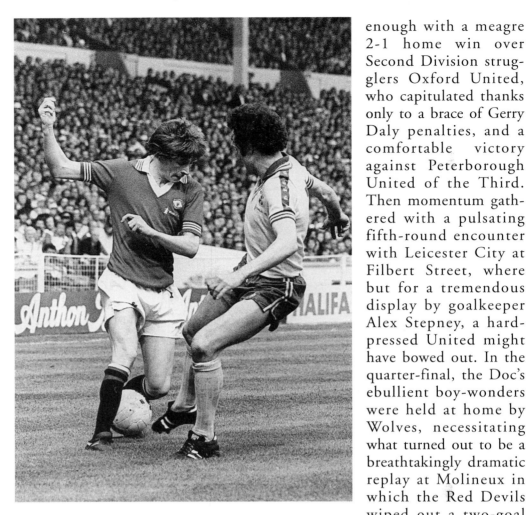

Above right: Shall we dance? United's Gerry Daly is in the mood but Paul Gilchrist of Southampton is intent on ruining his rhythm.

Lawrie McMenemy. As Tommy Docherty put it, success couldn't have happened to a nicer man.

enough with a meagre 2-1 home win over Second Division strugglers Oxford United, who capitulated thanks only to a brace of Gerry Daly penalties, and a comfortable victory against Peterborough United of the Third. Then momentum gathered with a pulsating fifth-round encounter with Leicester City at Filbert Street, where but for a tremendous display by goalkeeper Alex Stepney, a hard-pressed United might have bowed out. In the quarter-final, the Doc's ebullient boy-wonders were held at home by Wolves, necessitating what turned out to be a breathtakingly dramatic replay at Molineux in which the Red Devils wiped out a two-goal deficit to win in extra time. That set up a titanic semi-final clash at Hillsborough with reigning League champions Derby, who fell victim to United at their irresistible best, prompting match-winner Hill's rash comment.

Meanwhile, comparatively free of the publicity that accompanied the Mancunians' every spit and cough, Southampton were progressing steadily, if not without moments of difficulty. Shortly after marksman Bobby Stokes had refused to join neighbouring Portsmouth in exchange for defender Paul Went - what an inspired decision *that* turned out to be come May the 1st - the Saints began their Cup journey against Aston Villa at The Dell, and came within 60 seconds of elimination. Reprieved by a last-minute equaliser from midfielder Hugh Fisher, they upset the odds by winning at Villa Park, then faced successive Second Division opponents. First a mediocre Blackpool were overcome with no alarums or excursions, but high-flying West Bromwich Albion at the Hawthorns presented an altogether more taxing prospect. Yet despite a stomach bug afflicting four Saints, they earned a draw, taking the promotion aspirants back to the south coast where a Channon hat-trick sunk them without trace. In the last eight, Lawrie McMenemy's men were paired with one of the League's basement clubs, Bradford City, who outraged public opinion by drastically increasing their admission prices for the tie. The Yorkshiremen were rewarded by the lowest quarter-final crowd since the War, only 14,195 fans filing into the 23,000-capacity Valley Parade to see their team fall to the only goal of spirited contest. Southampton's luck in the draw continued as they faced Crystal Palace of Division Three in the semi-final, late goals by Paul Gilchrist and David Peach (penalty) clinching a drab but emotional triumph.

Thus the Saints - beaten finalists in 1900 and 1902 and who had never won anything more auspicious than the Third Division title - were at Wembley and, as Mick Channon had announced for those with ears to hear, they were not going along merely for the ride. They were booked into the same Surrey hotel that had catered for Sunderland three years earlier, a happy circumstance for those who believed in omens but McMenemy and company could base their optimism on more solid grounds. Since the identity of the final opposition was known, former long-serving Southampton boss Ted Bates, one of the shrewdest characters in the game, had been watching United's every move, enabling Lawrie to evolve eminently suitable tactics. Defensively, they included the expected ploy of denying space to Hill and Coppell, as well as using Channon and Stokes to block the penetrative supporting runs of United full-backs Alex Forsyth and Stewart Houston. Offensively, they were equally and deceptively simple - knock the ball to a forward, who would touch it back before turning and running into space behind the northerners' rearguard. Docherty, on the other hand, had not bothered his men with a detailed team talk, apparently expecting United's undeniably superior ability to win the day. Time would show the wiser.

The Reds were at full strength, Southampton nearly so, having named Fisher as substitute after he revealed unselfishly that he was not 100 per-cent fit, his place going to semi-final hero Gilchrist. The opening exchanges were much as predicted, with the effervescent favourites swarming goalwards, but there was something missing. Somehow United looked less like calm craftsmen going sensibly about their business than eager schoolboys straining to claim some long-promised treat. Crosses were misplaced, openings were snatched at and squandered and Saints 'keeper Ian Turner, who had looked jittery in failing to take a Coppell cross early on, grew in confidence. As the first half progressed and the Red Devils' feverish strivings were to no avail, the frustration of both players and fans was palpable. All the while the underdogs were assuming new stature, with Mel Blyth and Jim Steele coping comfortably with the central threat of Pearson and Sammy McIlroy,

Above: Mick Channon in the Stamford Bridge dressing-room after the semi-final win over Crystal Palace. On May Day at Wembley, United found there was grit behind the grin.

Below: United flier Steve Coppell is the slight favourite in this race for the ball with Saints full-back David Peach.

Saint Peter goes for goal. Here Southampton's Osgood is squeezed out by United's Stewart Houston (centre) and Brian Greenhoff, but on an afternoon when experience counted for a great deal, Peter exerted a telling influence against the young Red Devils.

Below: United skipper Martin Buchan fails to block a shot from Jim McCalliog, a former team-mate at Old Trafford. Jim was returning to Wembley ten years after his first Cup Final appearance, for Sheffield Wednesday.

and the experience of former Old Trafford man Jim McCalliog and the cultured Peter Osgood proving a creative match for United's untypically uninspired midfield think-tank. Most crucially, though, the Southampton full-backs, skipper Peter Rodrigues and David Peach, were not only obliterating the much-vaunted menace of Coppell and Hill, they were finding time to drive forward on the overlap, making unexpected inroads into United territory. Indeed, for all Macari and company's huffing and puffing - though it should be pointed out that Lou played with a broken toe for most of the match - the most clear-cut chance of the first period fell to Channon, who found himself with only Stepney to beat but was unable to evade the 'keeper's courageous smothering challenge.

However, the Doc's side had not risen to eminence for nothing and they began the second period in purposeful mode. Though there was a distinct impression of anxiety about them, something of their customary crispness was in evidence and after 59 minutes they might have won the match. Hill's corner was back-headed by Pearson to McIlroy, who nodded against the angle of post and bar. Had that gone in, Southampton would have been forced to adjust their patient approach and the whole tenor of the game must have changed. As it was, the ball was cleared and United's desperation grew. Soon Hill, who was enduring a veritable stinker of a game, was replaced by 18-year-old substitute David McCreery, but if Gordon's guile was not going to undo the Saints, then neither was the startling acceleration that had earned the little Ulsterman the tag of 'Road Runner'. As the Saints stood fast, the Red Devils became ever more frenetic; imperceptibly, the inevitability of victory was

Left: Sammy McIlroy was one of many potential match-winners for United but the nearest he came to a breakthrough was when his header bounced back off the woodwork after 59 minutes. Here he is frustrated by Saints captain Peter Rodrigues.

Right: Moment of destiny. Bobby Stokes (out of picture to the left) has hit an awkward shot across 'keeper Alex Stepney and into the opposite corner of United's net.

Above: Stokes (second from right) wheels away to frolic with his team-mates after scoring the most important goal of his life. The rest of Bobby's career was not to be especially eminent but nothing could ever mar the lustre of his golden day.

receding to be replaced by mushrooming doubt.

It was on 83 minutes that the young men of Manchester United met their moment of truth. A goal-kick from Turner soared high above the Wembley stands before falling to Channon on the right flank. Mick hooked the ball to the edge of the centre circle where McCalliog dispatched an instant, curling pass over the Reds' defence. Stokes peeled away from his marker in the inside-left channel, ran on to the bouncing ball and hit an awkward volley that bounced three times on its way past Stepney into the far corner of the net. Some reckoned Bobby was offside and television replays failed to settle the argument but, of course, it didn't matter. Southampton played out the remainder of time with an apparent composure they could hardly have been feeling and the giants had been slain.

At the end there were tears from several United players, who a month earlier had cherished dreams of the League and Cup double. For Docherty, who had already lost finals as a player with Preston in 1954 and manager with Chelsea in 1967, it was a bitter pill, but he found dignity in defeat. As soon as the final whistle sounded, he offered hearty congratulations to McMenemy and found time for a special word with Osgood, who served under him at Chelsea. Then Tommy told the press: 'My lads are crying now, but that's good. It shows they care. They have the resilience and youth to throw off the setback and learn from it. As for Southampton, this success couldn't have happened to nicer people.' That evening, at what was to have been a celebration for conquering heroes, he sang a sad Irish song, then rang the Saints at their victory banquet to add further praise for their performance. The fans, too, took the reverse in good part, and fears of widespread hooliganism if United lost proved groundless. Indeed, the police offered unqualified approbation for the supporters' behaviour and one coach operator even compared them to old folks out for a picnic.

But what had gone wrong for the team that had ventilated English football with a breath of invigorating air? Perhaps, quite simply, the occasion had been too big

for them. Extremely inexperienced as most of the players were, maybe they were unable to cope with the distractions of media attention and commercial deals in addition to maintaining a keen performing edge. While Southampton - whom, it should never be forgotten, had played exceedingly well - had relaxed and enjoyed the run-up to the final, the Reds had been embroiled in a hectic and disappointing climax to their League season. On the big day, wise heads such as Osgood, Rodrigues and McCalliog, all veterans of previous FA Cup Finals, knew a little too much for them. Three days later, when United closed their campaign with a victory over Manchester City, the Stretford End sang: 'We'd rather win the derby than the Cup.' Of course, they were not serious. Meanwhile the Doc mouthed the age-old platitude: 'We'll be back next year.' As Liverpool were to discover, he *was* serious.

Two men with vividly contrasting memories of Wembley 1976. Southampton's Bobby Stokes, the unlikely hero, and Gordon Hill of Manchester United, much touted as a key figure but utterly anonymous on the day.

MANCHESTER UNITED 2

Pearson 50, J Greenhoff 55

LIVERPOOL 1

Case 52

Half-time 0-0

MANCHESTER UNITED	○	LIVERPOOL
Alex Stepney	**1**	Ray Clemence
Jimmy Nicholl	**2**	Phil Neal
Arthur Albiston	**3**	Joey Jones
Sammy McIlroy	**4**	Tommy Smith
Brian Greenhoff	**5**	Ray Kennedy
Martin Buchan *(captain)*	**6**	Emlyn Hughes *(captain)*
Steve Coppell	**7**	Kevin Keegan
Jimmy Greenhoff	**8**	Jimmy Case
Stuart Pearson	**9**	Steve Heighway
Lou Macari	**10**	David Johnson*
*Gordon Hill	**11**	Terry McDermott
* (subDavid McCreery)		(sub Ian Callaghan)*

Attendance: 100,000

Referee: R Matthewson, Bolton

IT HAPPENED THIS YEAR

Millions mourned the death of Elvis Presley.

The Queen celebrated her Silver Jubilee.

Red Rum won the Grand National for the third time.

Virginia Wade lifted the Wimbledon ladies' title.

The Kerry Packer circus split the world of international cricket.

Geoff Boycott notched his 100th hundred, against Australia at Headingley.

There was so much more than the FA Cup at stake when Liverpool and Manchester United locked horns on a stiflingly hot Wembley afternoon. The Merseysiders had secured the League Championship already and four days later in Rome would take on the might of Borussia Moenchengladbach in the European Cup Final; for Bob Paisley's men, there was an unprecedented, hitherto unthinkable treble in prospect. Meanwhile Tommy Docherty's Red Devils were under fearful pressure of their own. Still smarting from their shock defeat by Southampton a year earlier and having trailed in a disappointing sixth in the First Division, they were desperate not to dash the hopes of their vast army of fans again. Add to that the intense natural rivalry between followers of the north-western giants - not yet as senselessly, unhealthily bitter as it was to become in subsequent decades, but ferocious enough - and the scale of the confrontation is apparent. On paper it was sure to be a classic match, in reality it wasn't, though in context of the priceless bounty awaiting the winners, there was as much drama and tension, elation and despair, as anyone had a right to expect from 90 minutes of football.

Below: United boss Tommy Docherty applauds his 'Red Army' during the pre-match walkabout. Come the end of the afternoon he had plenty to celebrate, but a storm of controversy was about to break around his head.

Both clubs had been forced to battle on the road to Wembley, United almost all the way, Liverpool at the outset and climax of their journey. The Liverpudlians' first opponents were Terry Venables' sparky Crystal Palace, destined for promotion from the Third Division and self-confident enough to force a draw at Anfield, then yielding only by the odd goal in five at Selhurst Park. The Liver Bird's feathers remained unruffled through the next three rounds, comfortable home victories being secured at the expense of Carlisle United, Oldham Athletic and Middlesbrough, but in the last four came the clash that all Merseyside had hoped would be reserved for the final - Liverpool against Everton. In a thrilling tussle at Maine Road - during which the Reds' Terry McDermott won a TV goal of the season award with an exquisite chip - the Blues excelled themselves, earning a creditable draw and all but carrying off the spoils. Indeed, to this very day many Evertonians maintain that they were robbed when referee Clive Thomas controversially disallowed Bryan Hamilton's second-half 'winner' for alleged handball. The rematch proved a demoralising anti-climax for the Toffeemen, who lost 3- 0.

The Mancunians, meanwhile, had been forced to scrap it out almost every step of the way. Having reached the fifth round by way of single-goal Old Trafford triumphs over Walsall and Queen's Park Rangers (this on an icy pitch that made the outcome a lottery), they were faced with . . . Southampton. The opportunity for revenge was inviting but, against such spirited opposition, there was the distinct possibility of a second severe embarrassment. Predictably, the Saints resisted nobly at The Dell, forcing a replay in which they were bested 2-1 by Jimmy Greenhoff's double strike. Next United won a tight quarter-final against Aston Villa by the same score, before being paired with old adversaries Leeds United in the semi. Twice before, in 1965 and 1970, the Elland Roaders had unseated the Red Devils at this stage, but now early goals by Greenhoff and Steve Coppell established an immutable superiority which a second-half Allan Clarke penalty could not shake.

Thereafter the League form of both finalists was poor. Liverpool beat Ipswich Town and then United in a Wembley dress rehearsal before three draws and a defeat saw their eventual title-winning margin over runners-up Manchester City clipped to a single point; in similar mode, the Doc's side managed only two wins in seven games. In mitigation, both managers had a lot on their mind. Paisley was

Opposite page: The Manchester United faithful fill Wembley with their fervour for the second successive year.

Below: Arthur Albiston, the young full-back who was perceived as a possible weak link yet made a telling contribution to United's victory. Of course, Arthur went on to become a model professional in a long and successful Old Trafford career.

giving thought to finding a replacement for Kevin Keegan, the England star who had announced he would be heading overseas that summer and whose honesty in revealing his plans early had exposed him to understandable but unwarranted resentment from some Liverpool fans. Also, Bob was expending energy in opposing unsuccessfully the FA's decision to hold a replay, if one was necessary, on June 27, just two weeks before the players reported back for the new season! It seemed a combination of the Reds' own European commitments and international matches made an earlier date impossible and while the Merseysiders would have been happy to settle the issue on penalties on the day, both the FA and Manchester United demurred. Meanwhile Tommy Docherty, while still giving his all to his professional duties, was wrestling with a personal problem that soon would be splashed across the nation's front pages.

As the teams lined up for the Wembley kick-off, there were three notable absentees from the Liverpool ranks and one immensely significant figure was present and correct at the heart of United's rearguard. Already deprived of long-term casualty Phil Thompson in defence, Paisley had opted to leave out carrot-topped striker David 'Supersub' Fairclough, who had played in both Everton matches, in favour of David Johnson, and preferred McDermott to 35-year-old Ian Callaghan in midfield. 'Cally', just back after injury and perhaps being saved for Rome, had the consolation of a seat on the bench. Docherty's only selection doubt had involved the immaculate Martin Buchan, on whose knee physiotherapist Laurie Brown had expended much effort and expertise during the preceding week, and to the vast relief of the Old Trafford party he was pronounced fit. His fellow Scot, left-back Stewart Houston, was not so lucky, being confined to crutches after breaking his ankle in a recent game with Bristol City. Consequently 19-year-old Arthur Albiston stepped up to make his FA Cup debut on the grandest of stages.

When the action got under way, Liverpool - who having lost the toss for choice of strip were wearing white shirts and black shorts - were quicker to settle and for most of the first period played the more composed football.

They created most openings, too, though there was nothing clear-cut until the 42nd minute, when Jimmy Case crossed from the right and Ray Kennedy rose to head against the base of a post via Alex Stepney's boot. Then, from the ensuing corner, left-back Joey Jones shot narrowly over the bar. However, come the interval

Above: Liverpool's Ray Kennedy leaves Jimmy Nicholl standing but his header was touched on to a post by Alex Stepney and United escaped.

United could be satisfied with the first stage of a job well done. Buchan had nullified the threat of Keegan in majestic manner, Albiston had made nonsense of notions that he would be a weak link by making a series of cool and timely tackles, and fellow defenders Brian Greenhoff and Jimmy Nicholl had been equally firm. With the security of such a solid barrier behind them, it was reasonable to expect a more telling second-half display from a six-man attack that, on its day, could lay waste to any defence in the land.

If Messrs Pearson, J Greenhoff and company were in any doubt about how to proceed, they were shown the way two minutes after the interval by none other than the rookie Albiston, whose 50-yard left-flank dash left Phil Neal and Tommy Smith for dead but was marred by a wild cross. Sure enough, three minutes later

*Scouser Jimmy Case,
whose goal was one of the
most spectacular seen in
modern finals.*

the hint was taken. Sammy McIlroy headed on to Jimmy Greenhoff, who in turn nodded precisely into the path of Pearson. Without breaking stride, 'Pancho' rode a challenge, surged into the penalty box and beat Ray Clemence at his near post with a low 15-yard drive. The shot was hit passably well but the England 'keeper, presumably expecting a far-post effort, allowed the ball under his body in wholly uncharacteristic fashion. The beaming Pearson, fist clenched in trademark style, was duly submerged by ecstatic team-mates, but their joy was to be short-lived. Two minutes later, Jones sidestepped Coppell on the left flank and delivered a high, deep pass to Case, lurking on the edge of United's area with his back to goal. The combative Scouser stunned the ball on his thigh, swivelled adroitly and delivered a pulverising half-

Left: Seconds after this picture was taken, Stuart Pearson was punching the air with characteristic glee. The popular 'Pancho' had just given United the lead with a firm shot but one that Ray Clemence might have been expected to save.

Below: Strictly not the product of practice! Lou Macari (to the right of the post) has shot wildly and the ball has rebounded from the chest of Jimmy Greenhoff to arc tantalisingly into the Liverpool net. 'Keeper Ray Clemence looks back in despair, Phil Neal is helpless on the line and United are 2-1 up.

volley which the gallant Stepney touched unavailingly as it tore past him into the top corner of his net. It was a breathtaking goal, one fit to grace any occasion, and the feeling was that the tide would now turn in Liverpool's favour.

So much for hunches! A mere 180 seconds further had elapsed when Macari headed on to Jimmy Greenhoff, who tussled for possession with Smith, before the ball ran loose. It fell to the onrushing Lou who, some ten yards out and to the right of goal, swung his foot and the ball caromed off Jimmy's chest before looping gently and unstoppably beyond Clemence and Neal into the net. It was one of those almost surreal sequences that seem to take place in slow motion, and even as the Merseysiders were kicking off again, it seemed difficult to absorb what had taken place. Still there were 35 minutes left to play, ample time for another comeback, but it never happened. Soon Callaghan replaced Johnson, with Case moving up front, after which most of the exchanges took place in the Manchester half, yet without placing Stepney's goal in undue peril. Alex played splendidly, retrieving his only mistake by beating Keegan to the ball after letting a mishit Case shot slip through his fingers, and the only moment of real danger came two minutes from time when Kennedy's 20-yard left-footer clipped the crossbar.

Thus the 'Treble Buster' prophecies on the banners of the travelling Stretford Enders had come to pass; the Red Devils had prospered in the unaccustomed role of underdogs and made up for the debacle of 1976. In timeless FA Cup Final tradition, there were scenes of starkly contrasting emotions. Alex Stepney fell to his knees in an attitude of prayer; the Greenhoff brothers embraced, two blond clean-cut heroes grinning delightedly; Gordon Hill gambolled, this time not as tetchy at being replaced late on by David

McCreery as he had been the previous season. Then, the faces of defeat: Liverpool skipper and Footballer of the Year Emlyn Hughes led his men on a well-earned lap of honour, yet looked tragic enough to be on his way to a funeral; Ray Clemence cut a lonely figure trudging towards the dressing room, too dejected to join his colleagues in saluting the fans. The Kopites themselves were more generous, applauding their opponents, acknowledging that it had been a memorably sporting contest. There was a marvellous gesture, too, from Arthur Albiston, who offered his medal to the limping Houston; poor Stewart, though much moved,

declined with thanks.

And what of Tommy Docherty? Having finally won at Wembley on his eighth visit as player or manager, one of soccer's larger-than-life, volatile personalities capered around with the FA Cup's lid on his head, but close observers noticed that he was unnaturally quiet at that night's celebration dinner. Having presided over such a famous victory and, even more important, having engineered Manchester United's swashbuckling renaissance of recent years, surely there could be no doubts about *his* future. But life was never simple for the Doc. Before long news broke of his romance with Mary Brown, wife of club physio Laurie, and, sensationally, he was sacked.

As for Liverpool, their period of mourning was short-lived. After a couple of miserable hours assimilating the truth that their treble dream was over, they revived their spirits with a convivial journey back to Merseyside before hitting the road to the Eternal City. There, on a night of sheer magic, they pulled off the most glorious triumph in the club's history, a 3-1 victory over Borussia Moenchengladbach. Thus, with Championship and European Cup at Anfield, and FA Cup at Old Trafford, everyone was happy.

Faces of joy and despair. Top: The brothers Greenhoff, Jimmy (left) and Brian, are on cloud nine. Above: Emlyn Hughes looks gutted as he is consoled by United 'keeper Alex Stepney.

IT HAPPENED THIS YEAR

World's first test-tube baby was born in Oldham.

A Polish Cardinal became Pope John-Paul II, the first non-Italian pontiff since 16th century.

BBC started regular broadcasts from Parliament.

Argentinians won World Cup on their home soil.

Muhammad Ali beat Leon Spinks, becoming first fighter to win world heavyweight crown for third time.

Weak at the knees but deliriously happy, Roger Osborne (centre) is about to faint after scoring the only goal of the match. Clive Woods, Arsenal's chief tormentor, advances for a congratulatory bearhug while skipper Mick Mills offers a supportive arm.

There is a story about Lady Blanche Cobbold, the venerable and much-loved president of Ipswich Town from 1965 until her death in 1987, that does much to explain the high regard in which the East Anglians are held by football folk the length and breadth of the land. It seems that Lady Blanche was sitting in the stand at Wembley on the afternoon of the 1978 FA Cup Final when she was asked if she wanted to meet Tory leader Margaret Thatcher, who was among assorted dignitaries gathered for the gala occasion. With a twinkle in her eye, the admirable octogenarian replied: 'I'd rather have a gin and tonic!' It was a response encapsulating spirit and humour, honesty and down-to-earth practicality, qualities which have characterised the Portman Road club down the years. Small wonder, then, that the Town's triumph over mighty Arsenal will always occupy an affectionate niche in the memories of not only Ipswich supporters, but of almost every soccer fan whose premier allegiance is not to the Gunners. It should be added, perhaps, that an element of this widely-felt warmth was down to the ludicrous, rather patronising portrayal by certain tabloid newspapers of Bobby

IPSWICH TOWN 1

Osborne 77

ARSENAL 0

Half-time 0-0

IPSWICH TOWN		ARSENAL
Paul Cooper	1	Pat Jennings
George Burley	2	Pat Rice *(captain)*
Mick Mills *(captain)*	3	Sammy Nelson
Brian Talbot	4	David Price
Allan Hunter	5	David O'Leary
Kevin Beattie	6	Willie Young
*Roger Osborne	7	Liam Brady*
John Wark	8	Alan Sunderland
Paul Mariner	9	Malcolm Macdonald
David Geddis	10	Frank Stapleton
Clive Woods	11	Alan Hudson
*(sub Mick Lambert)		(sub Graham Rix)*

Attendance: 100,000

Referee: D Nippard, Bournemouth

Robson's men as 'country cousins', an image fuelled by the gentle, open demeanour of match-winner Roger Osborne. In fact, they were a group of superbly-drilled professionals, including five internationals - England's Mick Mills, Kevin Beattie, Paul Mariner and Brian Talbot, and Allan Hunter of Northern Ireland - and though a season of League struggle qualified them for the tag of underdogs, to class them as giant-killers was spurious in the extreme.

Indeed, the previous term Ipswich had finished third in the League and at the outset of the new campaign had been among the title favourites. However, the Suffolk club have always lacked the resources of the big battalions and were unable to cope with a debilitating sequence of injuries. It seemed that no sooner was one casualty restored to fitness than someone else was on the treatment table. Accordingly, a disappointing first half-term slid into a potentially disastrous second half as the Town nosedived, eventually ensuring their top-flight survival with three matches to spare. As Robson laid plans for Wembley, he was hampered by the knee problems of key central defenders Hunter and Beattie, and already

255

Below: David Geddis, who replaced the injured Trevor Whymark and did himself and Ipswich proud.

resigned to being without striker Trevor Whymark, whose season had been ruined by ligament trouble after making his England debut in the autumn. In the event, both Kevin and Allan played - the last-mentioned after a late fitness test on the lawn of the team hotel - and there were mutterings from the direction of North London that Ipswich had been 'crying wolf'. The fact was that Arsenal, too, were in the midst of a dire injury crisis. Causing most concern was the sore ankle of Irish play-maker Liam Brady and centre-forward Malcolm Macdonald's knee, which was showing an alarming tendency to lock. In addition, skipper Pat Rice, his fellow full-back Sammy Nelson, stopper Willie Young and midfielder Alan Sunderland were all playing win pain and it's possible - though the Gunners didn't seek excuses - that the fitness factor had an effect on the destination of the trophy.

After heavy rain had soaked the pitch, the sun shone brightly if intermittently

Left:: The race is on between Arsenal's Frank Stapleton and Allan Hunter of Ipswich. The East Anglians' centre-half was cleared to play only after a late fitness test on the lawn of the team's hotel, but he appeared in fine fettle once the action began.

Inset left: A tussle for possession between two men whose Wembley fortunes could hardly have been more different. Roger Osborne of Ipswich (left) emerged as the hero of the hour, while Arsenal's star striker Malcolm Macdonald laboured throughout with the knee injury that was to end his career.

for Wembley's 50th, Ipswich's first and Arsenal's ninth FA Cup Final. Terry Neill's team started the sprightliest with David O'Leary going close following a corner by Alan Hudson. But soon the East Anglians began to impose themselves, radiating confidence from a rearguard in which Beattie and Mills were outstanding, through the midfield in which Talbot slaved unceasingly and on to a swift-moving attack of which all three prongs exuded potency. Mariner combined power and touch to telling effect; winger Clive Woods roamed from flank to flank, at times seemingly able to waltz past opponents at will; David Geddis, deputising for Whymark and normally an out-and-out striker, patrolled the right side with commendably penetrative verve, while fulfilling the secondary yet crucial function of blocking the marauding runs of Sammy Nelson.

During the course of an enjoyable match, Arsenal's goal was to have a succession of narrow escapes, the first coming after only ten minutes when a cross from the ubiquitous Woods was touched on by Osborne to Mariner and the centre-forward's shot rebounded from the crossbar. Meanwhile Paul's opposite number, the unfortunate Macdonald, was no more effective than he had been for Newcastle in that unhappy performance of four years earlier, though this time the

Below: A typically enterprising display by Arsenal 'keeper Pat Jennings was a major factor in making Ipswich wait so long a their breakthrough. Here the prone Ulsterman has foiled Paul Mariner.

state of his knee - which was to be operated on three days after the final, yet ultimately would bring his career to a premature end - offered much in mitigation. However, with Frank Stapleton holding up the ball skilfully, the Gunners were not devoid of menace, though when acceptable openings were created they were spurned, first by Sunderland, then Nelson.

Come the second period, the blue tide continued to flow inexorably towards Pat Jennings' goal, but the shovel-handed Ulsterman - who had come close to joining Ipswich when Spurs made the shock decision to part with him the previous summer - was in his customary magnificent form. Indeed, one save from a George Burley header had the young Scottish right-back gasping in disbelief, his

Inset above: Roger Osborne swings his left leg and at last Ipswich take the lead their superiority has deserved.

Left: Big Willie Young is horror-struck as Roger Osborne's shot passes Pat Jennings on the way into the Gunners' net. There would be no way back for Arsenal now.

expression mirroring that of his countryman John Wark on two earlier occasions when the midfielder had beaten Jennings with fierce shots only to see them cannon back off the woodwork. With 25 minutes remaining, the lame Brady had been replaced by Graham Rix who, with Hudson ineffective, represented Arsenal's best chance of unlocking the East Anglians' formidable defence. However, at this late stage it would have been a travesty if the North Londoners had broken through, and justice was done on 77 minutes. The thrust came from Geddis, who strode past Nelson before crossing hard and low into the goalmouth, where an unsighted Young could only block the ball into the path of Osborne some ten yards out. For the industrious, slightly ungainly midfield forager, the moment of a lifetime had arrived: drawing back his favoured left foot, he buried his shot emphatically in the heart of the net, then capered up and down on the spot like some oversized schoolboy set loose in a chocolate factory.

In the blink of an eye he was surrounded, then submerged by cavorting colleagues. But there was something amiss: though Roger's features were creased in an enormous grin, his head was swimming. A combination of euphoria, exhaustion and relief, the effect heightened by the stifling humidity of the airless stadium, proved too much and he sank to his knees in a faint. Clearly Roger could not continue and he was led from the pitch in a daze, being replaced by substitute Mick Lambert. The goal might have been the signal for a late, desperate assault by the erstwhile favourites, but with Jennings and O'Leary the only Gunners who did themselves full justice on the day, the momentum was not there and Ipswich sailed on, almost serenely, to victory.

There was no doubt about who was the hero of the hour. Having recovered

Above: The groggy Roger Osborne gets the sponge-and-cold-water treatment from Ipswich trainer Cyril Lea. Roger took no further part in the match, but his final kick had been decisive.

to collect his medal from Princess Alexandra, Osborne radiated engagingly wholesome joy as he told the press: 'I suppose when I scored the goal I had gone over the top emotionally. I had put everything into the game, and I knew at that moment that we had won the Cup.' It was the climax of a season of contrasting fortunes for a 28-year-old whose career would never again scale such heights. On the debit side he had been plagued with knee trouble which had limited him to 24 League starts; and, less painful but more embarrassing, he lost his false teeth when his jacket was stolen from the dressing room at Old Trafford! Against that, he had earned rave reviews for the close-marking job he did on Barcelona superstar Johan Cruyff in the UEFA Cup - and now came Wembley. Unfortunately, Roger was to be dogged by fitness worries in the years ahead, playing only a handful of further games for the Town before switching to Colchester in 1981. Happy to report, at Layer Road he confounded the pessimists who reckoned he was on his last legs by playing more than 200 games in five years' sterling service with the Essex club. Roger's presence in the final - along with that of Burley, Beattie, Talbot, Wark, Woods and Geddis - bore shining testimony to Bobby Robson's youth policy, which was as efficient as the way he ran the club in general. Having been sacked by Fulham in 1969, he was given a fresh start by one of the most enlightened of boards who stood by him through a traumatic initial three-year period of team reconstruction, even apologising to him for insults by impatient supporters. In return, when Ipswich became a force in the land, Robson repaid their loyalty by turning down lucrative offers to join Everton, Leeds and Derby. The win over Arsenal offered deserved tangible reward for the type of sane, moral policy that had become all too rare in the success-at-all-costs atmosphere that pervaded the modern game.

Bobby Robson, who repaid the faith of his far-sighted board.

In the afterglow of triumph, knowing that it all came right in the end, fans find a perverse pleasure in recalling odd moments when their campaign came close to derailment. In Ipswich's case, there had

been only one instance of dire peril: after disposing comfortably of Cardiff and Hartlepool, the Town found themselves at Eastville, the now-sadly-defunct home of Bristol Rovers. It was a perishing February day, the surface was frostbound and the ebullient Pirates, who had had a Bobby Gould 'goal' disallowed in controversial circumstances, were 2-1 up with only four minutes to play. Enter another of the East Anglians' unsung performers, reserve striker Robin Turner, to net for the second time that afternoon to set up a comparatively routine replay win. There was drama of a less savoury kind in the 6-1 quarter-final annihilation of Millwall at The Den. With the result beyond doubt, there was an ugly pitch invasion and the game was held up for 18 minutes while the playing area was cleared. On a happier note, Paul Mariner's hat-trick that day brought his Cup tally to seven for the season. In the last four at Highbury, blood was spilt as Brian Talbot clashed heads with West Bromwich Albion's John Wile in the act of opening the scoring in a 3-1 victory. Both men suffered nasty wounds, Talbot's forcing him off but Wile continued with a gory bandage which gave photographers a field day. Arsenal's progress had been a little less eventful, though they were given a sixth-round fright by Third Division champions-elect Wrexham, who yielded 3-2 only after a titanic struggle. Back at the Racecourse Ground 14 years later, the Robins were to extract sweet revenge, more of which anon. The Gunners had experienced one of those what-might-have-been seasons, finishing fifth in the First Division, second in the FA Cup and losing a League Cup semi-final, but they wouldn't have long to wait for Wembley glory. In the meantime, for one lucky man, Ipswich's triumph had a profitable aftermath. Two days after the final a bumper crowd, eager for a glimpse of the trophy, turned up at Portman Road for Mick Lambert's testimonial match. Perfect timing, indeed.

Above: Ipswich captain Mick Mills in time-honoured pose.

Left: Delighted Suffolk bunch. Left to right are Kevin Beattie, Paul Cooper, reserve Robin Turner - whose two goals had rescued the Town at Eastville - and David Geddis.

IT HAPPENED
THIS YEAR

Margaret Thatcher
became Britain's first
female prime minister.

Rubbish piled up on
British streets as
industrial unrest
escalated.

Boxing Day invasion
of Afghanistan by
Soviet troops.

Shah of Iran driven into
exile by supporters of
Ayatollah Khomeini.

Trevor Francis became
Britain's first £1
million footballer,
then helped new club
Nottingham Forest
win European Cup.

12 May 1979

ARSENAL 3
Talbot 12; Stapleton 43; Sunderland 89

MANCHESTER UNITED 2
McQueen 86; McIlroy 88

Half-time 2-0

ARSENAL	○	MANCHESTER UNITED
Pat Jennings	1	Gary Bailey
Pat Rice *(captain)*	2	Jimmy Nicholl
Sammy Nelson	3	Arthur Albiston
Brian Talbot	4	Sammy McIlroy
David O'Leary	5	Gordon McQueen
Willie Young	6	Martin Buchan (captain)
Liam Brady	7	Steve Coppell
Alan Sunderland	8	Jimmy Greenhoff
Frank Stapleton	9	Joe Jordan
*David Price	10	Lou Macari
Graham Rix	11	Mickey Thomas
*(sub Steve Walford)		

Attendance: 100,000
Referee: R Challis, Tonbridge

Opposite: Head and shoulders above the rest. Liam Brady, the architect of all three Arsenal goals, out-manoeuvres United's Joe Jordan (left) and Lou Macari.

For sheer heart-in-the-mouth melodrama, there hadn't been an FA Cup Final like it since that golden afternoon in 1953 when a national hero had held the sporting world in thrall. And, arguably, the annual showpiece had not thrown up a more mesmeric individual performance since Stanley Matthews' finest hour. Like his illustrious predecessor, this modern magician was slim, elusive and exercised uncanny command over a football. His name was Liam Brady, his team was Arsenal, his wretched victims were Manchester United. The bare bones of the contest reveal that the Gunners were two up with four minutes to go, the Red Devils were level some 120 seconds later and - their mood having catapulted from despair to elation - looked likely to complete a phenomenal comeback. But then, with barely a minute remaining, the North Londoners snatched back the prize with a conclusive, demoralising strike. Like Matthews 26 years earlier, Brady didn't score; but he fashioned all three of his side's goals in the course of a sublime creative display that touched world-class. Liam's artistry and the spellbinding finale rendered irrelevant the undoubted truth that the match as a whole was unremarkable; but more of that later.

First it is appropriate to recall the extraordinary outset to Arsenal's Cup campaign. If all goes well, a top club can reach Wembley in five matches, but in 1979 the Gunners needed that number of games to get past the third round - and it took them most of January to do it! Though Sheffield Wednesday were in the Third Division at the time, they boasted considerable tradition and were managed by the formidable Jack Charlton, so the North Londoners would not have been too disappointed with their 1-1 draw at Hillsborough on the 6th. But on the 9th, when the Owls went ahead at Highbury and only a late-ish equaliser from Liam Brady kept his side in the competition, matters were getting beyond a joke. That draw necessitated a meeting at neutral Filbert Street on the 15th, but still Big Jack's dogged battlers would not give in and the game finished at two-apiece. Come the 17th, at the same venue, Arsenal and Wednesday shared six goals, and it was not until the 22nd - by which time Leicester City must have had visions of their pitch being worn out - that strikes by Steve Gatting and Frank Stapleton settled the affair in the Gunners' favour. A total of nearly 144,000 fans had watched 540 minutes of football, including three sessions of extra time, and a little matter of 16 goals. Of course, in this age of the penalty shoot-out - understandably reviled by so many people in the game - such a marathon could never be repeated, thus removing one of the distinctive quirks that made the Cup endearingly special for more than 100 years. The fourth round brought a return to normality, with Arsenal making routine progress at the expense of Second Division Notts County, but clearly those other Trentsiders, League Champions Nottingham Forest, constituted a more daunting hurdle in the fifth. Brian Clough's men were undefeated for more than 50 matches at the City Ground, and sure enough, they poured forward ceaselessly. However, a Stapleton breakaway goal saw the Gunners into the quarter-finals, where they disposed of Southampton after a replay. Next came Wolves in the last four, and Alan Sunderland had the satisfaction of scoring the clincher against his former club to put Arsenal into their second successive final.

Manchester United, meanwhile, were heading towards their third in four years. Well off the pace in the title race, an unhappy position they shared with the North Londoners, Dave Sexton's team were eager to atone on the Wembley trail. A quartet of southern opponents had been bested - Chelsea easily, Fulham narrowly after a replay, gallant little Colchester luckily and Spurs competently, again after a rematch - when they were confronted with the toughest possible semi-final opposition, Liverpool in the process of romping away with the Championship. The Anfield Reds were favourites, but it was as if the outcome was as important to United as life itself and in a passionate encounter at Maine Road during which fortunes fluctuated dramatically, honours were even. Now the wise money was on Liverpool - Graeme Souness tempted fate by proclaiming to the press that United had blown their

Above: United's Steve Coppell (left) is in full flight but David O'Leary of Arsenal looks favourite to nick the ball away.

chance - but that took no account of the Red Devils' desire. Accordingly, on a night of high emotion in the replay at Goodison Park, Jimmy Greenhoff grabbed his fifth goal of the Cup run to set up the showdown with Arsenal.

A pair of old friends and colleagues found themselves in confrontation for the final. Gunners boss Terry Neill and Old Trafford number-two Tommy Cavanagh had worked in harness at Hull City, Neill's first managerial posting before the Irishman had headed for Highbury via White Hart Lane. Terry was an urbane charmer, very different to Tommy's current boss, Dave Sexton, but not such a contrast as Tommy himself. Where Dave was quiet and reserved, happy to let his team do his talking for him, 'Cav' was a raging extrovert who thrived on the cut and thrust of verbal sparring. He liked to have the last word and did so frequently, much to his charges' dismay on the pre-match journey from their hotel to Wembley when he insisted that a 'lucky' Max Bygraves tape be played on the coach stereo. In the event, Max's musical merits notwithstanding, the ritual produced little in the way of luck for United, and neither did a trio of Sexton's match-day superstitions - donning the same suit he had worn when leading Chelsea to FA Cup triumph in 1970, having a haircut and visiting his mother in Brighton.

The Gunners' tireless target-man Frank Stapleton (left) chases back to block a cross from United's Mickey Thomas, who beavered bravely all afternoon and outshone some of his side's more famous names.

Arsenal, wearing a change strip that earned them the tag of 'Terry's All Gold', were at full strength for the final, while United took something of a gamble on their top scorer Jimmy Greenhoff, who played despite suffering from a pelvic strain and was never at his most effective. For 12 minutes the two sides enjoyed vigorous equality, with subtlety very little in evidence, until Liam Brady started to rewrite the script. Picking up possession in the centre circle, the nimble-footed Irishman danced past Lou

Below: Brian Talbot wins the race with team-mate Alan Sunderland to prod home Arsenal's opener. Brian would finish the day as the only man this century to win the Cup with different clubs in successive seasons. As for Alan, his moment would come . . .

Macari, shook off Mickey Thomas and Sammy McIlroy and pushed the ball to Stapleton, who had roamed to the right touchline. The tall target-man slipped an incisive pass to blond mid-fielder David Price, inside and to the right of the penalty box; he evaded United skipper Martin Buchan and crossed crisply to the edge of the six-yard area, where Brian Talbot pipped Alan Sunderland to stab the ball into the net. For the next half-hour there was virtual parity until, two minutes before the break, that man Brady seized the game by the scruff of its neck for the second (but not last) time. Squirming beguilingly through the inside-right channel, he slipped past Arthur Albiston, left Buchan in a heap and found himself deep in the penalty area near the byline. Then, offering eloquent justification for his nickname of 'Chippy', he flighted a perfect cross to the head of the unmarked Stapleton, who made no mistake from six yards.

Two up at the interval, Arsenal seemed to be in a well-nigh impregnable position, an opinion confirmed as the second half wore on. Though United

Above: When hemmed in by opponents Frank Stapleton could nod a goal out of nothing; when given time and space by the United defence, scoring Arsenal's second goal proved a routine task.

enjoyed more of the possession and their centre-forward Joe Jordan had the edge in his muscular confrontation with Gunners stopper Willie Young, the North Londoners carried more penetration thanks to the central combination of Brady and Talbot. The former Ipswich dynamo, who had helped the East Anglians beat Arsenal a year earlier and was now on his way to becoming the first man this century to pocket winners' medals with different clubs in successive seasons, seemed to be everywhere. Whether breaking up United attacks or starting raids of his own, the £450,000 England international exerted a mammoth influence and, barring the presence of Brady, must have been man of the match. Nevertheless, the Mancunians pressed on and left-flanker Mickey Thomas, who had overcome a severe case of pre-match nerves to be his side's most dangerous attacker on the day, began to put pressure on the Gunners' back line with a series of telling crosses. Accordingly, in a bid to stem the flow some 20 minutes from time, Neill

Above: A neglected gem. Having squirmed past two Arsenal defenders, Sammy McIlroy slips the ball beyond the grounded Pat Jennings for United's equaliser. Because of what happened a minute later, Sammy never garnered due credit for an inspired effort.

Centre right: Gordon McQueen, whose late goal created a chink of light for United and their frustrated supporters.

Right: The sweetest moment in Alan Sunderland's footballing life, and one of the low points of United's entire history. Goalkeeper Gary Bailey has been bypassed and the Arsenal number-eight tucks in the winner.

withdrew Price and sent on an extra defender, Steve Walford. However, the new arrangement seemed to suit United, who grew stronger as the minutes ticked by. In retrospect, Young remarked that at that stage 'in our heads we were already halfway up the steps to the royal box', an attitude for which they almost paid dearly.

Even so, 86 minutes had passed and the match seemed to be going through its final rites before that

complacency - if such it was - had an effect. Steve Coppell took a free-kick on the right, it ran to Jordan on the left, who turned it back inside for Gordon McQueen to sweep into the net from seven yards. Still, most observers saw it as a mere consolation, but only for another two minutes. Then Coppell sent McIlroy scurrying into the Arsenal area, the Ulsterman jinked past David O'Leary, nutmegged Walford and squeezed the ball past Pat Jennings as he dived. It was a magnificent individual goal, all the more sensational for its timing, and it seemed to have turned the FA Cup Final on its head. Suddenly United were consumed with glee and relief; the North Londoners were rocking, extra time seemed inevitable and every last ounce of impetus was now with the Red Devils. But out of this potential holocaust of Highbury hopes strode a man apart, a fellow whose ability to keep his head in this moment of crisis spoke as eloquently as his twinkling feet of his footballing greatness. It was Brady, surging into United territory, accelerating on aching legs between Macari and Thomas and delivering a deft left-foot pass to Graham Rix on the left. First time the blond midfielder met it, and the ball sailed over the head of 'keeper Gary Bailey to the far post, where Albiston waited to head it to safety. But suddenly it dipped in flight and Alan Sunderland, lurking behind the full-back, stretched out a foot and poked the ball into the empty net before wheeling

To the Gunners the glory. Left to right are skipper Pat Rice, Sammy Nelson, Brian Talbot and David O'Leary.

away to begin understandably extravagant celebrations. At the inevitable inquest, some blamed the rookie custodian - who had done exceptionally well since making his debut in November - but others more experienced than he should have defused the threat long before it reached him.

Later Dave Sexton, unable to conceal his devastation but as dignified as ever, said it was a cruel way to lose a final, going on to admit that a few of his players had lost their concentration. Typically decent, though, he refused to blame them, pointing out that their reaction had been only human. Brady, wearing the red

shirt he had swapped for his own golden one with Jimmy Nicholl, spared a sympathetic thought for the losers, and conceded that immediately after McIlroy had scored, Arsenal would have been happy to settle for extra time. Sammy himself, who described that equalising moment as the most magical of his career, spoke graphically of his emotions as the Gunners had plundered their winner: 'It was like winning the pools only to find you hadn't posted your coupon.' But no one summed up the United viewpoint more succinctly than one of the greatest names in their history, Bobby Charlton, when he said with feeling: 'It shouldn't happen to a dog.'

WEST HAM UNITED 1

Brooking 14

ARSENAL 0

Half-time 1-0

WEST HAM UNITED		ARSENAL
Phil Parkes	1	Pat Jennings
Ray Stewart	2	Pat Rice *(captain)*
Frank Lampard	3	John Devine *
Billy Bonds *(captain)*	4	Brian Talbot
Alvin Martin	5	David O'Leary
Alan Devonshire	6	Willie Young
Paul Allen	7	Liam Brady
Stuart Pearson	8	Alan Sunderland
David Cross	9	Frank Stapleton
Trevor Brooking	10	David Price
Geoff Pike	11	Graham Rix
		(sub Sammy Nelson)*

Attendance: 100,000

Referee: G Courtney, Spennymoor

Talk has abounded down the years of the Upton Park footballing 'academy', yet tributes to the Hammers' attractive, flowing style have tended to be accompanied by the same old reservations. The skill and panache are fine on their day, the argument goes, but what West Ham lack is commitment, application, single-mindedness. Those who took that line in 1980 when the FA Cup Final brought John Lyall's Second Division outfit into confrontation with Arsenal, a club renowned for adherence to the work ethic, were in for a resounding shock. The outcome of the third all-London final was decided as much by sweat and will-power as by poise and pizazz, and the greater will on the day belonged to the Hammers. That said, the Gunners were out-thought as much as out-played, the Highbury management team of Terry Neill and Don Howe apparently failing to combat Lyall's intelligent tactics. In truth, for a match in which each side boasted a top-notch schemer, there was little sustained creativity from either side, but with Trevor Brooking outshining Liam Brady the result was an eminently fair reflection of play.

1980

IT HAPPENED THIS YEAR

John Lennon was murdered in New York.

Ronald Reagan won United States Presidential election.

SAS men stormed Iranian embassy in London, which was occupied by terrorists.

Britain debated 'Who shot JR?' as American soap Dallas topped the TV ratings.

Steve Ovett, Sebastian Coe, Allan Wells and Daley Thompson won Olympic gold for Britain in Moscow.

Memories of the event are dominated by two figures: the splendid Brooking, who scored the only goal and contributed to the majority of the game's most eye-catching movements, and his fellow midfielder Paul Allen, who at 17 years 256 days was deemed at the time to be the youngest player in an FA Cup Final. Subsequent research has revealed that one James Prinsep of Clapham Rovers, who lost to Old Etonians in 1879, was younger still, but that does not detract from a stirring all-round display by the latest member of the footballing family Allen to spring to prominence (following uncle Les and cousin Clive). Paul it was who chased and harassed Brady out of effective contention, then went on to win the nation's admiration and sympathy when he became the victim of the most notorious so-called professional foul in recent history.

The protagonists arrived at Wembley having enjoyed vividly contrasting fortunes during the season. West Ham, relegated in 1978, had dismayed their supporters by failing for the second time to regain the top flight. Arsenal had challenged for the League Championship (fourth would be their eventual

The game's three principal figures in the thick of the action. West Ham's Paul Allen, the youngest man this century to take part in an FA Cup Final, looks on as Willie Young of Arsenal battles for possession with Trevor Brooking, scorer of the only goal. Towards the end Young provoked widespread outrage by his foul on Allen.

Right: Arsenal's David O'Leary, one of ten Arsenal players appearing in a third consecutive FA Cup Final, launches a long ball out of defence.

position) and had reached the final of the European Cup Winners' Cup, which they would contest with Valencia in Brussels just four days hence. Accordingly the Hammers were hungry while the Gunners had every excuse if they seemed a trifle jaded. Between April 2 and May 1 they had endured a four-match FA Cup semi-final saga against the most demanding of all opponents, Champions-elect Liverpool, also five League games (including one at Anfield), and as if that wasn't enough they had faced and beaten mighty Juventus in the two-legged European semi-final. In fact, Terry Neill's men had been made to labour throughout most of their FA Cup campaign, which began with a draw at Cardiff. The Bluebirds - whose 1927 triumph over Arsenal makes them the only non-English winners of the trophy - did not capitulate easily at Highbury, either, going down only to the odd goal in three. Brighton offered more comfortable passage, but then Bolton earned a replay and Watford mounted noble resistance before the Gunners were through to meet Liverpool. The Reds were favourites to lift the League and FA Cup double and poured forward for much of the 420-minute marathon. Ironically it was a hero of Arsenal's 1971 double-winning side, Ray Kennedy, who made the mistake which led to Brian Talbot's headed winner at Highfield Road in the third replay. Thus the North Londoners became the first club this century to contest three consecutive finals and equalled Newcastle's record of appearing in 11 in all.

West Ham had begun their Wembley pilgrimage at the Hawthorns, where only a stupendous display by Phil Parkes held West Bromwich Albion to a draw. Flamboyant Throstles boss Ron Atkinson, never a man prone to understatement, reckoned the goalkeeper's performance was worth 12 marks out of ten! The fourth-round star was another defender, Ray Stewart, who was switched to midfield in an injury-induced reshuffle for the Brisbane Road encounter with Orient. Ray, whose £430,000 move from Dundee United in August had made him British football's most expensive teenager, scored twice in a 3-2 win. Late goals by Paul Allen and David Cross ousted Swansea, then 'Tonker' Stewart struck again with the penalty that defeated Aston Villa in the quarter-final at Upton Park. Everton, though struggling in the League, offered a stern last-four test, a draw at Villa Park being followed by a narrow victory at Elland Road in which midfielder Alan Devonshire was outstanding. The winner was headed by full-back Frank Lampard, who celebrated with an extravagant waltz with a cornerflag, the memory of which is said to have embarassed him for years afterwards. The Hammers were the fourth Second Division club in eight seasons to reach the final and, coincidentally, both their successes in the competition to date - against Preston in 1964 and Fulham in 1975 - had been achieved over second-flight opposition.

Below: Are you watching Cloughie? Even apart from his goal, Trevor Brooking (second left) exerted a huge influence on the match, making a mockery of doubts expressed by the Nottingham Forest manager.

Only three players survived from the class of '75, and at one point there were fears that skipper Billy Bonds would be unable to join Brooking and Lampard for their second FA Cup Final. The inspirational defender had been sent off along with Birmingham's Colin Todd in a League match and suspension loomed. Fortunately for the East Londoners' cause, the FA ruled that the automatic one-match ban was punishment enough. Arsenal's starting line-up showed only one change from that which beat Manchester United in 1979, John Devine coming in for Sammy Nelson at left-back, though the experienced Ulsterman was to replace his Republic of Ireland counterpart after an hour. The pre-match analysis had thrown up one particularly contentious point, not surprisingly as it was raised by Brian Clough. The Nottingham Forest boss had criticised Trevor Brooking, questioning his competitive attitude and likening him to a butterfly. If the England star had needed extra motivation - which surely he didn't - Clough had provided it. The final, played in sweltering heat for the fifth successive year, offered conclusive evidence that Brooking could, when necessary, supplement his silky skills with hard graft, though maybe the lion's share of credit for the Hammers' victory should go to the 'think-tank' of John Lyall and coach Eddie Baily. With Arsenal so well-drilled at the back, it was decided that something different was needed to disrupt their pattern, so striker Stuart Pearson was withdrawn into a deep-lying role. This ploy meant that David Cross had to forage on his own at the front and left the hugely influential David O'Leary seemingly confused with no one to mark. For the underrated Cross - who like an earlier West Ham Cup hero, Alan Taylor, had begun his career at Rochdale - the upshot was a staggering workload and limited

Alan Devonshire (left), a gem the Hammers had unearthed from non-League football, was one of the most thrilling runners with the ball on the contemporary scene. But here he shows that, despite his slight physique, he was not afraid to get involved in the midfield maelstrom. Also pictured, left to right, are Arsenal's Brian Talbot, and Frank Lampard and Paul Allen of West Ham.

possession, but he set to selflessly and fulfilled his manager's requirements to the letter. Meanwhile the quick and skilful Pearson made an extra passing option wherever he was needed and his freedom to roam played a telling part as the action unfolded. Indeed, there was an early warning when 'Pancho' popped up on the left and crossed for Geoff Pike to bring a save from Pat Jennings, but the Gunners never heeded it. Instead of perhaps pushing O'Leary forward into a more advanced role, they allowed Brady and company to be swamped in midfield and paid the price.

The only goal came after 14 minutes. The admirable Devonshire sprinted down the left, swayed past Pat Rice and Brian Talbot and centred from the byline. Jennings stretched to deflect the ball into the path of Cross, whose half-volley was blocked by Willie Young to Pearson on the right angle of the six-yard box. The former Manchester United marksman responded with a snap-shot which flew across the face of goal to Brooking, who stooped and leant backwards slightly to deflect the ball into the net with his forehead from four yards. It was a quickfire pinball sequence, over in the blinking of an eye, and left Jennings, Devine and David Price no more than helpless spectators on the line. Later Trevor, who had been quoted at 16-1 by bookmakers as scorer of the opening goal, revealed that it was only the third time he had hit the target with his head in his 13-year career to date.

Thereafter West Ham competed for everything, matching the Gunners' famed industry stride for stride and tackle for tackle. Parkes was called on to make few saves - dives to repel efforts from Talbot and Graham Rix come to mind - while centre-backs Bonds and Alvin Martin were in dominant form against Frank Stapleton and Alan Sunderland. Indeed, of all the gold-shirted Gunners, the two strikers appeared most exhausted by their recent exertions; they never stopped trying, but the usual thrust and vitality was missing, momentarily spent in recent draining battles with Liverpool and Juventus. Near the end, with the Hammers 'closing down' the game with a professionalism more habitually associated with their opponents, there seemed little likelihood of further drama. But, with just three minutes left, came the most controversial incident of the afternoon. A beautifully weighted Brooking pass freed Allen for a run on goal, presenting the youngster with a gilt-edged chance to crown the most memorable day of his life. But as he closed on Jennings, little 'Ollie' was scythed down from behind by Willie Young, a cynically calculated manoeuvre that outraged public opinion. The following season it was decreed that such an offence should merit a sending-off, and there is little doubt that Young's tackle - exposed as it was to a worldwide TV audience - played a significant part in the ruling. Meanwhile Allen emerged with vast credit for his mature attitude. Many youths might have reacted petulantly but Paul merely got up, shook hands with the offender and got on with the game, later heightening the effect by telling the press: 'After all, I still had to beat Pat Jennings and that's not easy, is it!'

So West Ham clinched the best possible consolation for failure in the promotion race and, drawing confidence from their success, went on to win the Second Division title handsomely in 1980/81. But for Arsenal there was trauma in store. Even before they had left Wembley, poor Brian Talbot, whose third successive final had yielded his first loser's medal, had collapsed with exhaustion and had to be revived by physio Fred Street. Then, on Wednesday, they lost to Valencia on penalties, Brady and Rix recording the crucial misses. The agony was compounded for Gunners fans by the long-dreaded departure of Brady to Italy and, one year on, of Stapleton to Manchester United. The two stars were not replaced adequately and the Highbury glory days were over until the dawning of the George Graham era. After contesting three FA Cup Finals in four years, Arsenal would wait until 1993 for their next appearance at the climax of English club football's premier knockout competition.

Below: Embarking on a celebratory lap of Wembley are Geoff Pike (left) and Paul Allen. The latter's part in the victory has been well chronicled, but Pike's sterling, unshowy contribution should not be overlooked.

Bonzo's big moment. West Ham captain Billy Bonds lifts the Cup and what had been a disappointing season for the Hammers ends on a note of sheer bliss.

9 May 1981

TOTTENHAM HOTSPUR 1

Hutchison (og) 80

MANCHESTER CITY 1

Hutchison 29

Half-time 0-1 Extra time played

TOTTENHAM HOTSPUR	○	MANCHESTER CITY
Milija Aleksic	1	Joe Corrigan
Chris Hughton	2	Ray Ranson
Paul Miller	3	Bobby McDonald
Graham Roberts	4	Nicky Reid
Steve Perryman *(captain)*	5	Paul Power *(captain)*
*Ricky Villa	6	Tommy Caton
Ossie Ardiles	7	David Bennett
Steve Archibald	8	Gerry Gow
Tony Galvin	9	Steve MacKenzie
Glenn Hoddle	10	Tommy Hutchison*
Garth Crooks	11	Kevin Reeves
*(sub Garry Brooke)		(sub Tony Henry)*

Attendance: 99,500

Referee: K Hackett, Sheffield

The extremes of emotion that football can engender have rarely been depicted more vividly than by the drama that befell Tottenham Hotspur's Ricardo Villa at Wembley in 1981. With some 22 minutes of normal time remaining in the 100th FA Cup Final and his team a goal behind, the gifted but inconsistent midfielder was withdrawn from the fray, bringing to an end a performance of numbing anonymity. With television beaming the match live to his countrymen back home in Argentina, Ricky was not impressed by manager Keith Burkinshaw's decision, and he showed it. Instead of taking a seat on the bench, he made a gesture of disbelief and trudged, slowly and forlornly, towards the dressing rooms at the far end of the stadium. But as he was about to disappear into the tunnel, he paused to watch the 80th-minute Glenn Hoddle free-kick which produced the equaliser. It was the turning point, not only for Spurs but also for Ricky, who slipped back to the bench to witness the extra-time stalemate. Even so, having given such a public demonstration of disenchantment, he can hardly have hoped to retain his place for the replay. Burkinshaw, however, showing admirable restraint and exceptional insight into his player's character, kept faith in the fitfully brilliant 'Dark Horse of the Pampas' and reaped the richest of rewards. The second time around, Ricky Villa set the tone for a far more sprightly display by giving Tottenham an early lead, then he graced Wembley with one of the most glorious individual goals ever seen at a major footballing occasion. In any context, such a strike would have been more than enough to earn redemption for earlier aberrations; as the winner in an FA Cup Final, it stretched the bounds of belief.

Naturally, any mention of Wembley '81 brings forth a flood of reminiscences concerning Spurs and their enigmatic Argentinian, yet Manchester City's substantial - and almost victorious - part in the proceedings should not be forgotten, neither should the fact that their very presence in the final represented the culmination of a remarkably rapid renaissance. Back in mid-October with Malcolm Allison and Tony Book at the helm, the Maine Road club were one place off the foot of the First Division and without a League win. The two managers, having spent as extravagantly as any in British football history, were duly sacked. John Bond assumed the reins and watched his new charges plummet to a home defeat by Birmingham that saw them hit rock bottom; relegation

beckoned menacingly but Bond was not dismayed. He bought winger Tommy Hutchison and defender Bobby McDonald from Coventry and astringent midfielder Gerry Gow from Bristol City and, suddenly, the gloom lifted. City soared to mid-table safety, reached the League Cup semi-final, then went one better in the senior knockout competition. Having put four goals past Crystal Palace, six past Bond's former club Norwich and one past Fourth Division Peterborough United, all without reply, the Mancunians found themselves facing a rather desperate Everton in the quarter-finals. Their boss Gordon Lee was under increasing pressure in the shadow of Liverpool's phenomenal achievements - indeed, he would be dismissed at season's end - and the FA Cup represented the Toffeemen's only remaining interest. Two of the north-west's erstwhile giants shared four goals at Goodison before City prevailed at Maine Road, thanks largely to two strikes by McDonald. At this point John Bond announced that he was beginning to believe in fairy-tales, and his 'born again' team gave further credence to the theory as a goal by skipper Paul Power proved enough to upset Cup favourites Ipswich Town in the semi-final at Villa Park.

Tottenham's Argentinian connection. Ossie Ardiles (centre) is tackled by City skipper Paul Power, but Ricky Villa comes away with the ball.

Tottenham, meanwhile, had been progressing with the aid of a remarkably kind draw. Until their Hillsborough semi-final clash with Wolves, the North Londoners did not have to leave the capital, every game but their goalless third-round encounter with Queen's Park Rangers being played at White Hart Lane. Between that Loftus Road deadlock and the last four, Burkinshaw's side seemed in control of their Cup destiny, winning each tie by two clear goals. After their quarter-final victory over valiant Third Division Exeter, the inevitable media overkill about the club's record of success in calendar years ending with the number one began to intensify. There had been the FA Cup in 1901 and 1921, the title in 1951, the double in 1961, the League Cup in 1971; would the sequence continue in 1981? Certainly, Wolves believed it wouldn't, but the Black Countrymen appeared to have been sunk by an archetypal Hoddle free-kick until a late and hotly-disputed penalty set up a semi-final rematch. The referee Clive Thomas (no stranger to semi-final controversy, having disallowed an Everton 'winner' against Liverpool four years earlier) judged Hoddle to have fouled Kenny Hibbitt and Willie Carr netted from the spot. TV evidence, that bane of the modern referee, appeared to confirm that Glenn's tackle had been clean, and Tottenham fans made the short journey to the replay at Highbury nursing a grievance. However, they need not have worried as two goals by Garth Crooks and a long-range bender from Villa settled the issue.

For Wembley, both Spurs and Manchester City stuck with the combinations that had steered them through the semi-finals, which meant a fascinating confrontation between the North Londoners' prolific £1.5 million strike-force of Steve Archibald and Garth Crooks, and the Blues' inexperienced but promising young central defenders, Tommy Caton and Nicky Reid. Also it meant frustration in his testimonial season for Tottenham goalkeeper Barry Daines, who had been first choice for most of the League campaign. His place went to Milija Aleksic, whose previous Wembley appearance had been nine years earlier, helping Stafford

Veteran Tommy Hutchison (left), whose match was packed with incident, holds off the challenge of Spurs' Chris Hughton.

Rangers beat Barnet to lift the FA Trophy. In truth, neither of the two was a worthy long-term successor to Pat Jennings, whose 1977 transfer to Arsenal still rankled with Spurs supporters and who was not adequately replaced until the arrival of Ray Clemence that summer. One man who had little trouble winning over the White Hart Lane faithful, however, was Graham Roberts, whose meteoric rise up the football ladder qualified even more convincingly for fairytale status than Bond's transformation of City. Little more than a year earlier, Graham had been earning his crust as a fitter in a south-coast shipyard, playing his football for non-League Weymouth after being rejected by the likes of Southampton and Portsmouth. Then former Tottenham manager Bill Nicholson got talking with a friendly stranger at a railway station and received a glowing recommendation for the sturdy central defender-cum-midfield dynamo. Bill took a look for himself, was mightily impressed and here was Graham taking a crucial role in English soccer's most prestigious game.

In the countdown to the match, the managers - Burkinshaw in particular - had their hands full in protecting the players from the ever more intense spotlight directed on them by television and newspapers. But, in fairness, the goggle-box did perform one welcome service, organising a TV link-up between Ossie Ardiles and Ricky Villa and their families in Argentina. Burkinshaw deserved huge credit for his boldness in buying the pair in 1978, and though Ardiles had settled much more effectively than his countryman, both had contributed significantly during a season in which

Spurs had often belied their mid-table position with some sparkling displays. Accordingly, they were clear favourites to preserve their record of never having lost at Wembley, yet this time they were to come perilously close to doing so.

The afternoon was humid, the surface made slightly slippery by early rain and after four minutes the ball deflated. To be honest, much of the early action was equally flat, but while inspiration might have been in scant supply, of effort there was plenty. City, determined not to be over-awed by their classier opponents, poured forward to win a spate of early corners and it was clear that the aristocrats had a fight on their hands. With Hoddle and Ardiles denied time and space by the hustle-and-crunch approach exemplified by the fearsome, hairy Gow, it was no surprise when City scored. The goal came just before the half-hour mark when right-back Ray Ranson crossed from the right and the spindly Hutchison launched himself full-length to net with a brilliant near-post header from ten yards. The lead was as deserved as it was spectacular and was almost doubled soon after when young midfielder Steve MacKenzie - who had been yet to make his League debut when Malcolm Allison paid Crystal Palace £250,000 for his services - hit a post. Though Roberts and Tony Galvin brought fine saves from Joe Corrigan, City continued to hold sway and the match seemed to be drifting away from Tottenham when, after 68 minutes, Villa was substituted for the more zestful Garry Brooke. He came close to scoring in his first attack, but it was not until the 80th minute that Spurs saved the game with a freak equaliser. Gow - who else? - conceded a free-kick on the edge of the box; Hoddle struck his shot crisply, but Corrigan appeared to have it covered when Hutchison, who had inexplicably forsaken his position in the defensive wall, deflected it with his shoulder into the unprotected side of the net. Thus 33-year-old Tommy, oldest player on the pitch, descended from match-winning hero-elect to unwitting saviour of Tottenham and was replaced by Tony Henry. Extra time failed to avert the tenth draw in the century of finals, thus necessitating Wembley's first replay (others had been staged at club grounds).

Above: Tommy Hutchison leaves an indelible mark on the 100th FA Cup Final. First his acrobatic header puts Manchester City into the lead (top); then he deflects Glenn Hoddle's free-kick past Joe Corrigan to gift Tottenham their equaliser (inset).

Right: Whenever he had the ball at his feet, City's Dave Bennett seemed to trouble Spurs' defence.

Above: The bustling style of Tottenham's Tony Galvin (left) keeps City's Ray Ranson on his toes.

Right: If Spurs substitute Garry Brooke (left) thought the mere loss of a boot could curb the aggressive instinct of Gerry Gow, he was probably very much mistaken!

282

14 May 1981

Replay at Wembley

TOTTENHAM HOTSPUR 3

Villa 7, 76; Crooks 70

MANCHESTER CITY 2

MacKenzie 10; Reeves (pen) 49

Half-time 1-1

TOTTENHAM HOTSPUR	○	MANCHESTER CITY
Milija Aleksic	1	Joe Corrigan
Chris Hughton	2	Ray Ranson
Paul Miller	3	Bobby McDonald*
Graham Roberts	4	Nicky Reid
Ricky Villa	5	Paul Power *(captain)*
Steve Perryman *(captain)*	6	Tommy Caton
Ossie Ardiles	7	David Bennett
Steve Archibald	8	Gerry Gow
Tony Galvin	9	Steve MacKenzie
Glenn Hoddle	10	Tommy Hutchison
Garth Crooks	11	Kevin Reeves
		(sub Dennis Tueart)*

Attendance: 92,000

Referee: K Hackett, Sheffield

Above: Graham Roberts - Wembley ball-boy in 1973, part-timer with Weymouth in 1980, Cup winner in 1981. Some rise!

Above: Steve MacKenzie's blast leaves Milija Aleksic helpless and City are level at 1-1 in the replay.

The FA had ruled that if the two teams could not resolve matters at the second attempt they would have to resort to penalties, so it was under threat of that unedifying denouement that battle resumed. This time, though starting line-ups were unchanged, there was infinitely more dash and verve about the whole proceedings. Now Spurs appeared to have come to terms with City's vigour, resuming their normal inventive habits; the game prospered as a result and goals were not long in coming. Tottenham took the lead when Corrigan could only block an Archibald shot to Villa, who netted simply from seven yards. City responded royally only three minutes later when Hutchison nodded into the path of MacKenzie, who blasted home a searing 20-yarder. Now the action switched from end to end, but there was no further score until four minutes into the second period, when winger Dave Bennett was sandwiched by Paul Miller and Chris Hughton, and Kevin Reeves put City ahead from the spot.

Above: A clinical finish from Garth Crooks (grounded right, alongside his strike partner Steve Archibald) restores Tottenham's parity at 2-2.

Opposite: A far cry from the tears of Saturday. Ricky Villa with the trophy he did so much to win.

Below and opposite: 'The Dark Horse of the Pampas' proves his pedigree. This action sequence shows how Villa jinked through the City defence to net his fabulous winner.

For the second time in the match, time was ebbing away from Spurs, but they regained parity with 20 minutes left when Hoddle found Archibald with a long pass, the ball ran free and Crooks rammed it past Corrigan.

Now there remained just one more sting in the tail of an exhilarating game - and it proved fatal to City's hopes. There was no immediate danger as Galvin played the ball to Ricky Villa in the inside-left position some 14 minutes from the end; a blue-shirted barrier blocked the Argentinian's way and a safe, square pass seemed inevitable. But Villa strode forward purposefully, perfectly balanced, his instinct taking him on and on. Dancing to the tune of a gloriously different drum, he weaved past Caton, then Ranson, then Caton again. Corrigan advanced and committed himself courageously, but Villa saw him coming and slipped the ball beyond him for a sublime winner. His Saturday sulkiness forgotten, Ricky had enshrined himself on Wembley legend. Corrigan was voted Man of the Final for his performances over the two matches; there was widespread rejoicing that Spurs skipper Steve Perryman, who had recently overhauled Jennings' club appearance record, marked the achievement by holding aloft the famous trophy. But the name fans will associate forever with Tottenham's 1981 triumph is that of Ricky Villa.

1982

IT HAPPENED THIS YEAR

Britain went to war with Argentina over the Falkland Islands.

Unemployment in Britain topped the three million mark.

Mass protests against nuclear missiles at Greenham Common.

Channel Four took to the air.

Princess Grace of Monaco killed in car crash.

Princess Diana gave birth to her first son, Prince William.

Footballer of the Year Steve Perryman remains characteristically cool in the face of a vigorous challenge from Rangers' Bob Hazell. Already Steve had played more games for Spurs than any man before him, and he was distinctly unlucky that his full England career was limited to 20 minutes as a substitute in Helsinki.

22 May 1982

TOTTENHAM HOTSPUR 1
Hoddle 110

QUEEN'S PARK RANGERS 1
Fenwick 115

Half-time 1-0 Extra time played

TOTTENHAM HOTSPUR	○	QUEEN'S PARK RANGERS
Ray Clemence	1	Peter Hucker
Chris Hughton	2	Terry Fenwick
Paul Miller	3	Ian Gillard
Paul Price	4	Gary Waddock
*Mike Hazard	5	Bob Hazell
Steve Perryman *(captain)*	6	Glenn Roeder *(captain)*
Graham Roberts	7	Tony Currie
Steve Archibald	8	Mike Flanagan
Tony Galvin	9	Clive Allen*
Glenn Hoddle	10	Simon Stainrod
Garth Crooks	11	John Gregory
*(sub Garry Brooke)		(sub Gary Micklewhite)*

Attendance: 100,000

Referee: C White, Harrow

To Tottenham Hotspur the Cup, to Queen's Park Rangers what little glory there was to be garnered from one of the most forgettable of modern finals. Many Wembley showpieces down the decades have been so gripping, so upliftingly entertaining, that there has been a sense of loss when they have ended; when referee Clive White blew his whistle to bring down the curtain on this 210-minute anti-climax there was general relief, tempered with a feeling that the Loftus Road underdogs had not received their just deserts. Somehow, all-London finals usually fail to capture the imagination of the country at large and this fourth such occasion in 16 seasons was no exception. Indeed, when a replay became necessary, it was possible to buy tickets at the gate and there were gaps on the terraces for what is traditionally a sell-out event. The touts had never had it so bad!

HOW THEY GOT THERE

TOTTENHAM HOTSPUR
Round 3:
Arsenal (h) 1-0.

Round 4:
Leeds United (h) 1-0.

Round 5:
Aston Villa (h) 1-0.

Round 6:
Chelsea (a) 3-2.

Semi-final:
Leicester City *at Villa Park*
2-0.

QUEEN'S PARK RANGERS
Round 3:
Middlesbrough (h) 1-1, replay
(a) 3-2.

Round 4:
Blackpool (a) 0-0,
replay (h) 5-1.

Round 5:
Grimsby Town (h) 3-1.

Round 6:
Crystal Palace (h) 1-0.

Semi-final:
West Bromwich Albion *at*
Highbury 1-0.

Both clubs were celebrating their centenaries and both were looking to the FA Cup to provide cheer at the end of campaigns in which they had played plenty of attractive football but with no tangible reward. Yet again Spurs had imposed themselves in the title race, despite having started 1981/82 with genuine hopes of their first League success for 21 years. True, most clubs would have been reasonably satisfied with a fourth-place finish but for the star-studded North Londoners it was palpably not good enough. There had been disappointment at Wembley in March, too, when Keith Burkinshaw's team had been within three minutes of lifting the Milk Cup, only for Liverpool to equalise and then seize the spoils in extra time. And in the European Cup Winners' Cup, Tottenham had been narrowly squeezed out at the semi-final stage by Barcelona, the over-physical Catalans' victory owing much to an uncharacteristic error by Ray Clemence. However, one prize did find its way to White Hart Lane, skipper Steve Perryman being voted Footballer of the Year by the game's writers, a decision as popular as it was justified. Since making his debut as a 17-year-old in 1969, Steve had become one of the most consistent and versatile performers in Spurs' history, shattering the club's appearance record. Yet after starring at under-23 level, he went on to win just one full cap, his England career falling victim to changes of management. After Alf Ramsey had appeared to be preparing him for a long-term international future, neither Don Revie nor Ron Greenwood were ready to give him his chance. This award offered some consolation, both to Steve and to Tottenham, whose season of attacking enterprise was offered further recognition by the fact that Glenn Hoddle was runner-up in the poll.

For Queen's Park Rangers, also, it had been a term of mixed fortunes. Managed by Terry Venables - who had played for Spurs in the 1967 FA Cup Final and who was destined to have such a massive influence on their future - they had been tipped heavily to win promotion to the First Division. Sadly, despite several encouraging runs, they had lacked consistency, eventually finishing two points behind Norwich, who went up in third place. However, most recent media attention to Loftus Road was not lavished on the team but the pitch. In the summer the club had spent £350,000 laying a synthetic surface, which was not against the laws of the game but broke dramatically with tradition. Though the former surface had been extremely poor, the ball tending to flop like a brick into pudding, the new one went too far the other way, with the bounce ridiculously pronounced. Although it placed a high premium on skill, others argued that it gave Rangers an unfair advantage as they were accustomed to it while their opponents were not. The controversy became bitter and at one point, when the FA refused to guarantee it could be used in the Cup, Rangers' forthright chairman Jim Gregory threatened to withdraw from the competition.

Happily, the situation was resolved and it was on plastic that the richly gifted Simon Stainrod - dubbed 'Stainrodney' by fans who lionised the memory of a certain Mr Marsh - scored a brilliant late equaliser against Middlesbrough in the third round. On the more familiar mixture of mud and grass at Ayrsome Park, it was left to a less flamboyant individual, 19-year-old defender Warren Neill, to head the winner three minutes from time. Following two fine displays against Boro, newly-promoted rookie goalkeeper Peter Hucker was to retain his place for the rest of a season which was to culminate in a superb man-of-the-final show at Wembley. Rangers' hero in the fourth round was marksman Clive Allen, who scored four times in the Loftus Road replay demolition of Fourth Division Blackpool. Grimsby were dispatched with relative comfort in the fifth, then Allen struck again in both quarter-final and semi-final, supplying the only goal of each game, against his former club Crystal Palace and West Bromwich Albion respectively. For many supporters the last-four encounter with the Throstles carried echoes of QPR's finest hour, the 1967 League Cup triumph in which Clive's

A citizen's arrest? Rangers substitute Gary Micklewhite apprehends Tony Galvin and seizes the Tottenham forward's left arm in a limpet-like grip. The indomitable Galvin, meanwhile, ploughs on regardless.

father, Les, had played for the Londoners. This time Rangers owed considerably more to luck, with Albion defender Ally Robertson's attempted clearance bouncing into the net off Clive's knee, though his predatory instinct for being in the right place was surely a significant factor.

Spurs' Cup journey commenced with a North London derby which was decided by a rare Pat Jennings clanger, the one-time idol of White Hart Lane allowing a distinctly wan effort from Garth Crooks to creep past him. Another Crooks strike was enough to unseat Leeds in the fourth and Mark Falco's score in the fifth made it a hat-trick of single-goal home wins against top-flight opposition. Amazingly enough, Tottenham would not be required to face another First Division team for the duration of the competition. Not that Chelsea of the Second were easy meat in the quarter-final. Having tasted the blood of Liverpool in the previous round, they feared no one and gave an entertaining account of themselves before bowing out to the odd goal in five at Stamford Bridge, a result that gave Spurs a record 25 senior cup games without defeat. Waiting for the holders in the Villa Park semi-final were Leicester, some of whose fans gave a hard time to Ossie Ardiles over Argentina's recent invasion of the Falklands. It must have been a fraught situation for the little schemer but he responded in a typically positive manner, combining with Hoddle to set up the first goal for Crooks. The second and only other score was bizarre in the extreme, the Filberts' Ian Wilson executing a perfect chip over his own 'keeper when under no apparent pressure.

Thus Spurs, who had won all six of their previous FA Cup Finals, were through to a seventh, giving them the chance to equal Aston Villa's record number of triumphs, though recent history indicated that little could be taken for granted. Rangers, who had never before ventured beyond the sixth round, were the fifth

The bounteously gifted Tony Currie, ever ready to try the unorthodox, attempts to catch the Tottenham rearguard flatfooted with a surprise lob.

club from the Second Division to reach the final in the last ten years and three of them had gone home with the trophy. Certainly, Venables could approach the match knowing that he had players capable of winning it. The front-line double-act of Mike Flanagan and Allen, the subtle, silky promptings of former England play-maker Tony Currie, the cultured defensive contribution of skipper Glenn Roeder, they could all be decisive on the day. Meanwhile Spurs, who had employed psychologists to relax the players during a season of hyperactivity, now had new anxieties. With British forces arriving in the Falklands ready for war, how did that affect the position of the club's two Argentinian stars? In fact, Ardiles had been due to return to Buenos Aires to link up with his national side anyway, and now he did so. The case of Ricky Villa, not required by his country, was less straightforward and it was not until the morning of the match that Burkinshaw

decided it would be wisest to exclude him from his plans. Accordingly, Ricky remained at home and watched the final on television.

Nevertheless with Clemence, Perryman and flankman Tony Galvin all recovering from injury in time to play, the Spurs boss was able to field a formidable team, which took the field in their change strip of all yellow, Rangers switching from their familiar blue-and-white hoops to red shirts and black shorts. The game was only two minutes old when the underdogs suffered a severe setback, the prolific Allen twisting his ankle and losing mobility to such a degree that he would be replaced by Gary Micklewhite soon after the break. Spurs buzzed forward purposefully and Hucker made a good save from Crooks, the first of half-a-dozen excellent stops. However, if that implies a contest packed with exciting incident then it is misleading. For the most part, particularly in the second half, the jaded favourites spluttered and misfired, and with Rangers further handicapped by injuries that left centre-half Bob Hazell and midfielder Currie limping, there was little for the fans to admire. The most inviting chances fell to Tottenham's striker Steve Archibald, who failed twice with only Hucker to beat and then, summing up a dismal day, when he did find the net the 'goal' was disallowed for offside. Late in normal time Rangers might have stolen the prize but

Below: Groggy goalkeeper Peter Hucker, QPR's outstanding player over the two matches, holds on to physio Dave Butler for support. Hucker recovered to resume between the posts, his form unimpaired by the knock.

Clemence made a smart save from Stainrod, then extra time saw the spotlight back on Hucker, who did especially well to deny substitute Garry Brooke.

What seemed certain to be the decisive goal arrived with only ten minutes remaining, Hoddle exchanging passes with Graham Roberts before deceiving the faultless Hucker with a 20-yard daisy-cutter that took a deflection off Currie's leg. A reply seemed out of the question, but five minutes later Rangers stilled the Laneites' celebrations when a long throw from Stainrod was nodded by Hazell to Fenwick, who flung himself forward to head home powerfully from close range. So Spurs found themselves in a second successive FA Cup Final replay.

This time they faced a side weakened by the absence of Allen, nursing his ankle, and Roeder, who was suspended, their deputies being Micklewhite and Neill. Only six minutes had elapsed when Tottenham took the lead in ironic fashion, Currie the artist fouling Roberts the cruncher and Hoddle obliging from the penalty spot. The early breakthrough might have signalled a relaxing of tension and a consequent exhibition of skills from Burkinshaw's men, but it was not to be. Instead it was Rangers who seized the initiative, and for their efforts during the rest of the game they deserved to win the Cup. Micklewhite was woefully unlucky to see his 43rd-minute strike ruled out for marginal offside against Fenwick, Hoddle was reduced to the indignity of heading off his own line from a John Gregory chip, then Crooks felled Fenwick in the box and no penalty was given. But the moment that gallant Rangers must have realised it was not going to be their day came midway through the second half when Gregory hit the bar with a magnificent volley. After that, Currie and company continued to strive but the match petered out to its inevitable conclusion. In the last minute Archibald hit the post, but a two-goal win would have been monstrously unfair. For their form over the season as a whole, Tottenham had merited both a reward and a showcase for their talents. Sadly, though they claimed their reward, they failed utterly to make the most of their showcase.

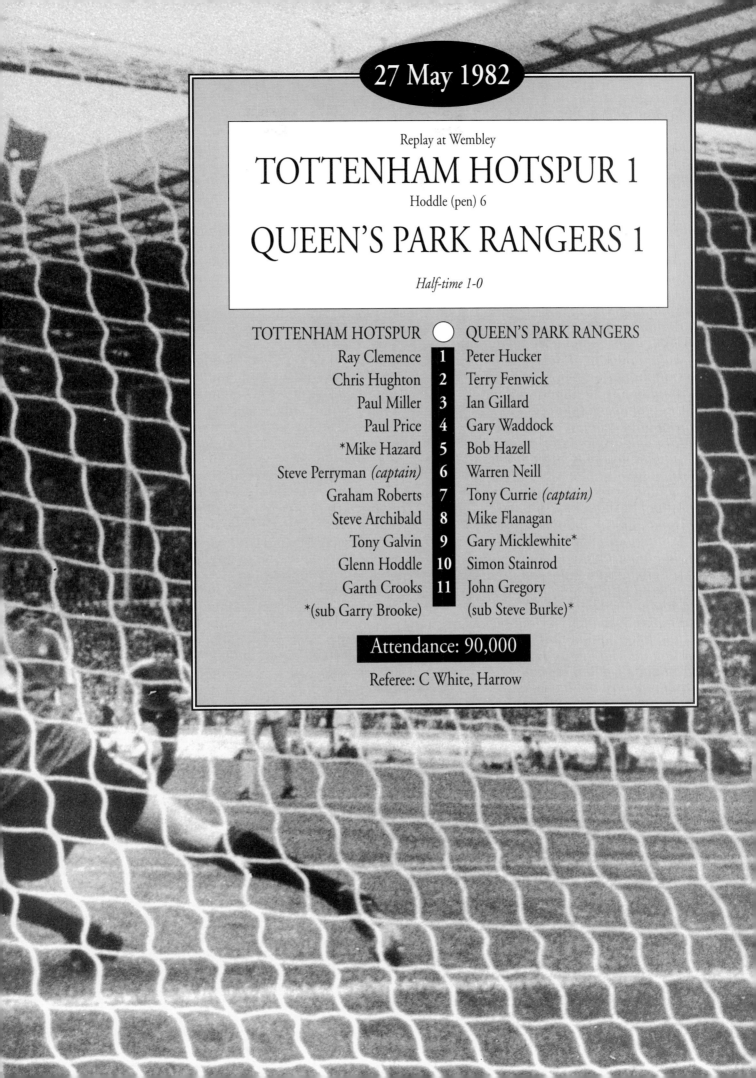

27 May 1982

Replay at Wembley

TOTTENHAM HOTSPUR 1

Hoddle (pen) 6

QUEEN'S PARK RANGERS 1

Half-time 1-0

TOTTENHAM HOTSPUR		QUEEN'S PARK RANGERS
Ray Clemence	1	Peter Hucker
Chris Hughton	2	Terry Fenwick
Paul Miller	3	Ian Gillard
Paul Price	4	Gary Waddock
*Mike Hazard	5	Bob Hazell
Steve Perryman *(captain)*	6	Warren Neill
Graham Roberts	7	Tony Currie *(captain)*
Steve Archibald	8	Mike Flanagan
Tony Galvin	9	Gary Micklewhite*
Glenn Hoddle	10	Simon Stainrod
Garth Crooks	11	John Gregory
*(sub Garry Brooke)		(sub Steve Burke)*

Attendance: 90,000

Referee: C White, Harrow

IT HAPPENED
THIS YEAR

Margaret Thatcher
returned to power in
election landslide for
Tories.

Neil Kinnock replaced
Michael Foot as
Labour leader.

Cecil Parkinson
resigned from
Government after jilt-
ing pregnant mistress.

Breakfast TV took to
the air in Britain.

Car seatbelts became
compulsory, first use
of wheel-clamps.

Derby winner Shergar
was kidnapped in
Ireland.

21 May 1983

MANCHESTER UNITED 2
Stapleton 55, Wilkins 73

BRIGHTON 2
Smith 14, Stevens 87

Half-time 0-1 Extra time played

MANCHESTER UNITED	○	BRIGHTON
Gary Bailey	1	Graham Moseley
Mike Duxbury	2	Chris Ramsey*
Arthur Albiston	3	Graham Pearce
Ray Wilkins	4	Tony Grealish *(captain)*
Kevin Moran	5	Gary Stevens
Gordon McQueen	6	Steve Gatting
Bryan Robson *(captain)*	7	Jimmy Case
Arnold Muhren	8	Gary Howlett
Frank Stapleton	9	Michael Robinson
Norman Whiteside	10	Gordon Smith
Alan Davies	11	Neil Smillie
		(sub Gerry Ryan)*

Attendance: 100,000

Referee: A Grey, Great Yarmouth

'And Smith Must Score . . .' If no television commentator uttered those precise words as plucky Brighton frightened the life out of Manchester United in the dying seconds of extra time at Wembley, then it scarcely matters now. Somehow the phrase sums up one of the most entertaining FA Cup Final clashes of the modern era, and whoever chose it as the title of a Seagulls fanzine deserves a winner's medal of their own. Replete with irony, devoid of self-pity, happy to recall what might have been . . . it is perfect. Of course, Gordon Smith *should* have scored from the clearest opening of the match to give Brighton - commendably feisty despite being freshly relegated from the top flight - an improbable 3-2 victory. But he was foiled by Reds goalkeeper Gary Bailey and Jimmy Melia's men, after enjoying the better of exchanges in the first 20 minutes of the replay, were steamrollered by a hungry United team that would not be denied.

The story of every final is crowded with fascinating characters, this one more than most. For Brighton there were Steve Foster, Jimmy Case, Gary Stevens, Melia himself; then there were United's Norman Whiteside, Bryan Robson, Steve

Coppell and Alan Davies. They all played their part (or not, as in the case of poor Coppell), they will all get their mention, but first let's place their Wembley meeting in context by noting the clubs' vividly contrasting fortunes during a dramatic season. In their second term under the flamboyant Ron Atkinson, United had finished third in the First Division and already had paid one unhappy visit to Wembley, losing 2-1 to Liverpool after extra time in the Milk Cup Final. Having won only one major trophy in 15 years, United felt the reverse

exceptionally keenly, especially after they had led for most of the match against their bitter Merseyside rivals. Meanwhile Brighton had problems of their own at the bottom of the table. In December they had switched managers, replacing Mike Bailey with chief scout Melia, and although that didn't bring about a climb to League safety, it did coincide with an uplifting FA Cup campaign. From the crown of his shining pate to the tip of his elegant footwear, Jimmy Melia was a Scouser, with all the humour and street-wisdom that implies. One of 11 children, he grew up as a Liverpool player and was the schemer in Bill Shankly's first side, only for his Anfield career to lose impetus through injury. Eventually he moved into management, but always in the lower divisions until he got his chance at the Goldstone. There, at last, Jimmy had a suitable stage on which to parade his belief in neat, flowing football and his Brighton became an attractive combination whose enterprise was rewarded on a thrilling surge to Wembley.

It all began with two matches against Newcastle, a Peter Ward goal securing progress after two would-be equalisers by the Magpies were disallowed in a tumultuous finale at St James' Park. Next came crushing victory over Manchester

Neither Liverpool nor Everton were at Wembley but there was no shortage of Scousers. Both managers - United's Ron Atkinson (above left) and Jimmy Melia of Brighton - and Seagulls midfielder Jimmy Case (left) all hailed from Merseyside.

City, with Michael Robinson relishing the satisfaction of scoring twice against his former club and Jimmy Case also finding the net. For Case, however, who was to be on the scoresheet at four successive stages of the competition, the fifth round was going to be even sweeter. Like his manager, he had served nobly in Liverpool's midfield and now experienced the joy of returning to Anfield to net with a spectacular 25-yarder as the Seagulls won 2-1 in the season's biggest upset. Jimmy supplied the only goal of the quarter-final against Norwich - this despite predictions of gloom by a fortune-teller Melia consulted before the game - and then delivered another long-range scorer in the semi-final victory over Sheffield Wednesday. As the next ten years would show, Jimmy Case was one of the few players to reach his zenith after leaving Liverpool; indeed, even the Seagulls didn't reap the benefit of Jimmy's prime, which followed his 1985 move to Southampton.

While Brighton had been enjoying the Cup as light relief from their relegation battle, United might have viewed it as compensation for their unavailing chase of Liverpool in the League. The Red Devils dealt competently with West Ham and

Luton, then won well at Derby despite being limited to a late Whiteside winner, before they encountered stern quarter-final resistance from Everton at Old Trafford. In fact, the Toffeemen had been demonstrably the better side when Atkinson decided in injury time that a substitution might help. So on went Lou Macari to lay on a brilliant goal for Frank Stapleton and Merseyside's interest in the FA Cup was terminated. That set up a titanic semi-final clash at Villa Park against Arsenal, who were eager for revenge after United had thrashed them at the same stage of the Milk Cup. This time Tony Woodcock put the Gunners ahead, but classic strikes by Robson and Whiteside deservedly booked the Old Trafford men's return ticket to Wembley.

By now Robson was England captain, arguably the most influential footballer in the land and was improving all the time, yet the emergence of Whiteside ensured that he had no monopoly of headlines. The husky Ulsterman, just 18 but going on 30, was a phenomenon. A year earlier he had taken the record of Pele, no less, as the youngest player to appear in the World Cup Finals; since then he had scored in the Milk Cup Final and the FA Cup semi-final, and boasted an all-round game in which delicate skills fused with fearsome strength to suggest an awesome future. But United supporters' delight in the potential of these stars, indeed of their whole promising team, was tempered by the plight of popular England winger Steve Coppell. He would miss the final through a knee injury which, come September, would force his retirement at the chronically premature age of 28. In view of Steve's condition, Atkinson had taken the precaution of acquiring another England flankman, Lawrie Cunningham, from Real Madrid, but he too was unfit and stepped aside in favour of young Alan Davies, called up for only his fourth senior start.

Much of the pre-match discussion concerned suspensions, with United midfielder Remi Moses and Brighton's defensive bulwark and captain, Steve Foster, condemned to miss the action. Foster was outraged, refusing to accept the decision and even attempting to overturn it in the High Court. He failed, but his part in proceedings was far from done. In Foster's absence, Melia made gutsy midfielder Tony Grealish his captain - Steve even lent Tony his trademark headband for the afternoon! - and paired Gary Stevens and Steve Gatting in central defence. Of course, United were white-hot favourites but as they had found to their cost seven years earlier, that carried no guarantee of success.

On a heavy pitch and under brooding skies, the game began brightly, but the Reds' initial slickness and confidence were to receive an early jolt. Young Gary Howlett's cross from the right was met by Gordon Smith's back-post downward header and the ball bounced beyond Bailey and into the corner of the net. Thereafter United pressed, with Gordon McQueen and Robson going close, but never dominated and ten minutes of the second half had elapsed before Mike Duxbury centred from the right, Whiteside touched it on and Stapleton shot high into goal from close range. Now, though the Seagulls continued to play controlled football, the Reds began to get on top and it was no surprise when they took what

Above: Young Gary Howlett of Brighton offers a dummy to fellow Dubliner Kevin Moran as the Seagulls push forward.

Above: Ray Wilkins, out of shot to the right, bends home perfectly from outside the box to give United what seems likely to be a decisive lead . . .

Left: . . . but Gary Stevens (second right) strides forward to smash in a late equaliser.

seemed like a decisive lead with only 17 minutes to go. Fed expertly by Arnold Muhren, Ray Wilkins sidestepped a defender, cut inside from the right and scored with a majestic 20-yard left-foot curler. It was a goal worthy of winning the Cup, but the Seagulls had other ideas. They began to pin United back and after 87 minutes their spirit and persistence paid off. Case's low corner-kick found Grealish unmarked on the edge of the box, the skipper turned the ball into the area where Stevens controlled it with one touch and drove home emphatically from eight yards. Thus, deservedly, Brighton had forced an extra period, which

Right: Brighton carve the opening from which they could - and should - have won the Cup. Michael Robinson (number nine) has gulled Gordon McQueen and slides the ball square to the unmarked Gordon Smith.

Above: Smith (right), perhaps overawed by the enormity of the responsibility, has shot weakly and Gary Bailey makes a scrambling save. The sequence is etched in stark detail on the memories of every Brighton fan who lived through that moment.

produced deadlock until there was time for just one more attack - and that from the underdogs. The strong-running Robinson tricked his way past Kevin Moran and McQueen and pushed the ball across the box to Gordon Smith, on his own ten yards from goal and with only Bailey to beat. But the tall Scot, seemingly transfixed by the enormity of the occasion, shot feebly; Bailey blocked, the ball squirmed away but as Smith stretched forward to deliver the killer blow, the 'keeper gathered safely, thus removing the last vestiges of the unfair stigma attached to him since Arsenal's late winner in 1979. Atkinson described it as 'the moment we died a thousand deaths'. More accurately, it was the moment Brighton lost their best chance of lifting the Cup.

Replay at Wembley

MANCHESTER UNITED 4

Robson 24, 44; Whiteside 28; Muhren (pen) 62

BRIGHTON 0

Half-time 3-0

MANCHESTER UNITED	○	BRIGHTON
Gary Bailey	1	Graham Moseley
Mike Duxbury	2	Steve Gatting
Arthur Albiston	3	Graham Pearce
Ray Wilkins	4	Tony Grealish
Kevin Moran	5	Steve Foster *(captain)*
Gordon McQueen	6	Gary Stevens
Bryan Robson *(captain)*	7	Jimmy Case
Arnold Muhren	8	Gary Howlett
Frank Stapleton	9	Michael Robinson
Norman Whiteside	10	Gordon Smith
Alan Davies	11	Neil Smillie

Attendance: 100,000

Referee: A Grey, Great Yarmouth

Below: Brighton skipper Steve Foster, back for the replay after missing the first encounter through suspension, was a butt for the wicked jibes of United fans.

Nevertheless, having enchanted every uncommitted fan in the country, the Seagulls were not going to give it all up without a fight in the rematch. Supposedly fortified by the return of Foster - Gatting moved to right-back in place of Chris Ramsey, laid low by a Whiteside tackle - they began in some style, passing fluidly and threatening to expose a certain lack of pace at the heart of the Manchester rearguard. The Brighton fans were ebullient, informing the rather subdued United contingent they only sang when they were winning. However, before long they were winning, and they never stopped singing for the rest of the night. After 24 minutes the excellent Arthur Albiston crossed from the left to Davies, who pushed the ball back to Robson some 20 yards out. Without breaking stride, 'Captain Marvel' hit the ball low and true with his left foot into the far corner, and that proved the point of no return. Four minutes later it was Davies again, chipping into the box from the left for Whiteside to elude Foster

United's Norman Whiteside, whose personal fairy story continued.

with an ease he had never managed against Gatting on Saturday, before heading powerfully past 'keeper Graham Moseley. Thus West Ham's Johnny Sissons joined Pele in losing a record to the Reds' own Roy of the Rovers - at 18 years and 19 days, Norman had become the youngest scorer in FA Cup Final history.

A few minutes later, Bailey made an acrobatic back-pedalling save from a deflected Case thunderbolt before the game was ended as a meaningful contest. A minute before the break, Robson glanced a Muhren cross to Stapleton, who nodded back across the area for the skipper to drive in from one yard. In truth Brighton,

Right: This is one United triumph that Graham Moseley, a Red Devils fan as a boy, is in no mood to celebrate after failing to reach Muhren's coolly-dispatched spot-kick.

who had managed five goal attempts to United's six, did not deserve to be 3-0 down, but now there was no way back. Muhren completed the scoring with his first penalty in English football, after Stevens had pulled back the rampant Robson, then Moseley pushed a Whiteside shot against the bar. Even then Brighton, who had contributed fully to Wembley's third successive FA Cup Final replay, did not give up and Bailey was forced to make a fine double save from Gatting and Robinson.

United fans, ever expectant of winning trophies but so often disappointed in recent years, indulged themselves with an extensive repertoire of chants, ranging from a joyous 'Happy Birthday' in honour of Sir Matt Busby - who was celebating his 74th - to the cruelly derisive 'What a difference you have made', directed at Steve Foster. The Man of the Final award went to Gary Stevens, outstanding in the first match and very good in the second, though Case, Robson and Davies would all have been worthy choices. Jimmy and Bryan, of course, were showered with honours throughout long careers, but for Alan this was to be his greatest achievement. Just as he seemed on the verge of a great future, he broke his leg and never regained momentum. Nevertheless, he went on to play for Wales and serve several clubs faithfully before his untimely and horrendous death in 1992. His fate put the importance of football into proper proportion; no one who knew Alan Davies well would be likely again to use the term 'tragedy' in a sporting context.

Born to lead. Captain Bryan Robson, who selflessly spurned the chance of a hat-trick by insisting that Arnold Muhren took United's penalty.

Below: Alan Davies, for whom life appeared to hold so much after he excelled for United in both Wembley outings. Yet he was to die by his own hand while still a young man.

IT HAPPENED
THIS YEAR

Millions died in
Ethiopian famine.

Pickets and police did
battle during British
miners' strike.

Four killed as IRA
bombed Tory Party
Conference at
Brighton.

York Minster
devastated by fire
after lightning struck.

Assassination of Indian
Prime Minister Indira
Gandhi.

Ronald Reagan won
his second term as
United States
President.

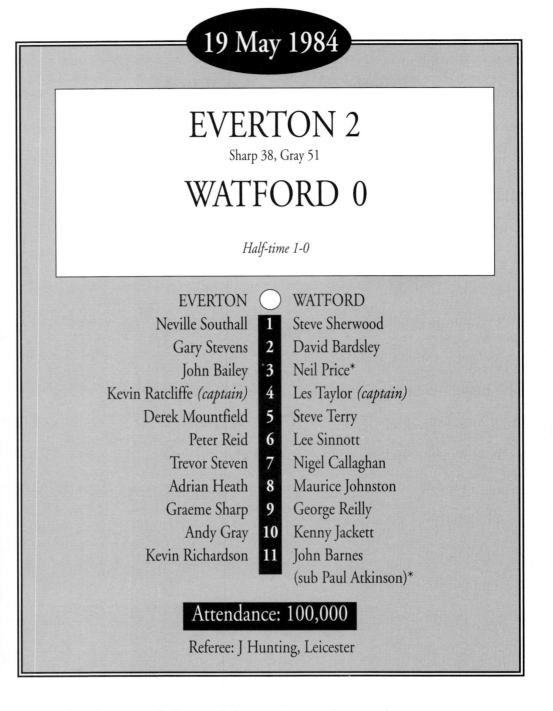

19 May 1984

EVERTON 2
Sharp 38, Gray 51

WATFORD 0

Half-time 1-0

EVERTON		WATFORD
Neville Southall	1	Steve Sherwood
Gary Stevens	2	David Bardsley
John Bailey	3	Neil Price*
Kevin Ratcliffe *(captain)*	4	Les Taylor *(captain)*
Derek Mountfield	5	Steve Terry
Peter Reid	6	Lee Sinnott
Trevor Steven	7	Nigel Callaghan
Adrian Heath	8	Maurice Johnston
Graeme Sharp	9	George Reilly
Andy Gray	10	Kenny Jackett
Kevin Richardson	11	John Barnes
		(sub Paul Atkinson)*

Attendance: 100,000

Referee: J Hunting, Leicester

It was the day one of the world's trendiest and most famous pop stars was transformed into an engagingly eager, ingenuous schoolboy; the day an historically unfashionable but delightfully friendly club experienced a richly deserved taste of the high life. Yet in terms of footballing significance, the occasion of Watford's Wembley debut will be recalled most widely as the day on which their opponents, a team that was to emerge as England's finest of the mid-1980s, put a period of trauma behind them to produce the first tangible evidence of approaching eminence. In short, it was the day Howard Kendall's Everton came of age.

But so frequently do the Toffeemen crop up in the pages that follow - in 1985, 1986 and 1989, albeit in defeat each time - that it seems reasonable at this point to dwell for a bit upon the Hornets. Eight years earlier the aforementioned pop star, Elton John, had taken over as chairman and in 1977 Watford appointed as manager an ambitious 32-year-old named Graham Taylor. It was to prove a dream ticket for the homely Vicarage Road club, who became Fourth Division champions in Taylor's first season. Since then they had progressed to the top flight, their meteoric progress culminating with the runners-up spot behind Liverpool in 1983, a passport to Europe which would have been dismissed as pure fantasy had it been predicted during the mid-1970s. Admittedly, 1983/84 had got off to a disappointing start but new players had been drafted in and by the turn of the year the Hornets began the surge that was to see them improve to finish in the top half of the table and - in the wake of Queen's Park Rangers and Brighton - become the third successive first-time FA Cup finalists.

Graham Taylor, whose fielding of criticism about Watford's style was to stand him in good stead for subsequent trauma as England manager.

Though Taylor's team were subjected to considerable flak from leading figures in the game for their long-ball tactics and so-called 'wild dog' readiness to chase and harry, they were victims of decidedly unfair generalisation. Workaholics are needed at every club, especially those with limited budgets, but Watford's contingent was leavened by two performers of outstanding flair. On the left wing was John Barnes, oozing talent and destined to become one of the most captivating entertainers of his generation, and up front was a young man snatched from under the noses of Everton and other top clubs in November. When Taylor

failed to persuade Leicester to part with a certain Gary Lineker, he switched his attention to Maurice Johnston, relatively unknown south of the border but whose prolific goal-scoring exploits for Partick Thistle marked him out as a golden prospect. 'Mo', who would move eventually to Goodison Park but not until after seven years of wandering, was blessed with sharp reflexes and a predatory instinct that provoked some observers into comparisons with the young Denis Law - extravagant, maybe, but even to be mentioned in such company spoke volumes for the Johnston potential. Sure enough, the blond, baby-faced Scot took a prominent role in the Hornets' march on Wembley, scoring in each of the first three ties, the

Above: Watford strikers Maurice Johnston and George Reilly, here being tackled by Everton's John Bailey. The Hornets' pair had enjoyed a prolific season but both drew a blank at Wembley.

most dramatic contributions coming in the third round against Luton. At Kenilworth Road, Watford went two down and it was a Johnston penalty that earned a replay. Then, in a pulsating seven-goal thriller at Vicarage Road, Maurice nodded the winner in the 108th minute. After that, victories over Charlton and Brighton (conquerors of Liverpool for the second year running) were accomplished without too much ado, at least on the part of the team if not the chairman. Elton was on honeymoon in New Zealand at the time of the Seagulls clash and got up in the early hours of the morning to listen to his club's hospital radio broadcast by phone. In the quarter-final Watford gave arguably their most convincing performance of the competition, winning 3-1 at Birmingham with Barnes in scintillating form. That set up a last-four meeting with Plymouth Argyle, struggling in the lower reaches of the Third Division but determined to sell their lives dearly. So they did, too, but one goal from big George Reilly was enough to wipe out the memory of Watford's only previous FA Cup semi-final, which had ended in a 5-1 thrashing by Chelsea in 1970.

Above right: Andy Gray, the spark that re-lit the Goodison flame just as many fans were preparing to sweep out the ashes.

And so to Everton, whose winter had been one of dark travail which had lightened into a spring of renewed hope. So chronic were the Blues' early-season form and results that manager Howard Kendall had been subjected to an unprecedented campaign of vilification. There were leaflets calling for him to be sacked, an unkind slogan was painted on his garage doors, members of his family were harassed and he was under constant fire in the press. At one stage he offered his resignation but the board, to their vast credit, kept faith with the man they had hired and, almost imperceptibly at first, the tide began to turn. As in most such situations, the change in fortunes must have been due to myriad factors, but ostensibly the most telling was the signing that November of Andy Gray from Wolves. To many of the wiseacres revelling in the Toffeemen's distress, the acquisition of the injury-prone marksman smacked of sheer desperation. But they reckoned without the courage, determination and, above all, the effervescent personality of a player who, in effect, stood the ailing club on its head. His larger-than-life presence banished tension and doubt among his new team-mates, replacing them with confidence and sheer *joie de vivre*. Standing shoulder-to-shoulder with the warrior-like Scot, it was impossible not to respond with like boldness. And it should not be forgotten that Gray was an experienced, top-quality international striker in his own right, a man who but for fitness problems would have been well-nigh priceless. Thus inspired, Everton took twin roads to salvation, and both of them were via Wembley. First they reached the final of the Milk Cup, only to lose after a replay to none other than Liverpool, in whose shadow they had languished for so long. But this was no ignominious reverse; the Toffeemen held their own throughout the two meetings and the manner of their single-goal defeat gave rise to genuine optimism. That was in late March, by which time Everton had already reached the FA Cup semi-finals at the expense of Stoke, Gillingham, Shrewsbury and Notts County, a quartet of whom the Third Division Gills had proved by far the most testing. Indeed, Kendall's team needed three matches and large quantities of luck to go through, the Kentishmen hitting Neville Southall's woodwork in each of the first two goalless encounters before succumbing 3-0 in the third. Notts County, too, put up doughty resistance and were overcome thanks only to a typical diving effort by Gray, the Scot seeming to half-volley the ball with his head while apparently ploughing a furrow through the mud with his nose! When little Adrian Heath got the only goal of an excruciatingly tight semi-final against Southampton, it was the signal for a great outpouring of pent-up emotion from the Goodison camp. So low had spirits sunk earlier in the season that now there was an understandable desire to savour every moment of success and the coach driver was instructed to take his time on the journey home from Highbury while the achievement sunk in.

Of course, there remained a considerable job of work if the Blues were to win their first major honour for 14 years, a period in which their Anfield rivals had lifted no fewer than 18 trophies, to which would be added a fourth European Cup in 11 days time. Many in the media appeared to think a victory for resurgent Everton was a foregone conclusion, but there were only four positions between the finalists in the First Division table and, in reality, the outcome was anybody's guess. Admittedly, the absence of key men tipped the odds a little in favour of the Merseysiders. Though they had lost schemer Kevin Sheedy to an injury sustained in the Milk Cup Final and centre-half Mark Higgins had been sidelined by a pelvic disorder that would end his Blues career, the Hornets - with a smaller squad - were even more troubled by the fitness problems which ruled stopper Steve Sims and midfielder Kenny Jackett out of contention. And probably even more debilitating was the suspension of their attacking full-back and captain Wilf Rostron, whose duty of leading the team out passed to midfielder Les Taylor. Even so, Elton John - whose touring commitments had prevented his attendance at any of the earlier rounds - was not going to let it spoil his day. The man who had performed before countless thousands of adoring fans the world over was unashamedly moved by the Cup Final scene. Resplendent in fedora and opulent double-breasted suit, he emerged from the tunnel in gregarious mood but clearly soaking up the unique atmosphere like some wide-eyed youngster. For all his years in another branch of the entertainment industry, he had never before been granted privileged access to this very special occasion and, charmingly, it showed, notably when he was moved to tears by the communal singing of Abide With Me.

As the game got under way, it seemed that soon Elton's cup of happiness might be over-flowing. Watford were first into their stride and in the second minute Lee Sinnott's gargantuan throw was flicked on by Reilly only for Barnes to

The Yellow Brick Road had nothing on this! The endearingly enthusiastic Watford chairman Elton John revels in that Wembley feeling.

Above: Graeme Sharp, granted too much room in the Watford box, shoots Everton into the lead after seizing on a miscued effort by Trevor Steven.

Right: Despite pressure from Watford's John Barnes and George Reilly, Everton's Kevin Ratcliffe makes a timely clearance. A little later the 23-year-old Welshman became the youngest captain to receive the FA Cup since Bobby Moore 20 years earlier.

misdirect his goal attempt with only Southall to beat. The Hornets continued to buzz and after 17 minutes the Everton 'keeper was forced to throw himself at Barnes' feet, the ball rebounded to Les Taylor with the defence wrongfooted but somehow the chance went begging. Then Maurice Johnston went close with a header and a volley, but gradually the Blues settled to their task, openings began to appear and seven minutes before the interval they went ahead. The instigator was Kevin Richardson, who played a smooth one-two passing interchange before crossing from the left flank. The ball was headed out to Trevor Steven who, under heavy challenge, mishit a first-time shot from the edge of the 'D'. It flew to Graeme Sharp near the penalty spot, who controlled it neatly before swivelling and shooting low into the net off a post. The finish had been clinical, even if there had been an element of fortune about the build-up.

Thereafter, Everton retained the edge against a Watford side in which there was perhaps not enough accumulated experience for the big occasion. Accordingly, it was no surprise when the lead was doubled early in the second half, although the manner of the strike raised more than a few eyebrows. The splendid Steven eluded Barnes and Neil Price on the right before dispatching a hanging cross towards the far post. 'Keeper Steve Sherwood - the

Above: Two men raise their arms, one in celebration of the goal that clinched the Cup, the other in vain supplication to the referee. The joy is being radiated by Everton's Andy Gray, the protest lodged by Les Taylor of Watford. Gray's controversial strike brought back memories of 1958.

only Hornet to have made every step of the club's journey from the League's basement - appeared to gather the leather a split second before Andy Gray's bullet head made contact and the ball dropped into the goal. Many observers compared it to Nat Lofthouse's infamous charge in 1958 but TV evidence was nothing like as clear-cut this time, and it should be remembered that Nat's strike was allowed, too! Perhaps Andy headed the back of Steve's hand, maybe he nodded the ball, undoubtedly his arms were down and there was no push; certainly it happened so quickly that the referee could hardly be blamed, whichever way his decision went. That goal was the fatal blow to Watford, who never mustered sufficient fire or self-belief to trouble the Merseysiders unduly for the remaining 39 minutes. Evertonian joy was unalloyed, with extrovert left-back John Bailey - wearing a giant blue-and-white top hat and enormous joke specs - leading the antics. So Howard Kendall, twice an FA Cup Final loser as a player - with Preston in 1964 and Everton in 1968 - emerged from a personal nightmare. The next year of his life was to be more like a dream come true.

Above: Everton's impressive Trevor Steven shoots for goal, despite the close attentions of Neil Price.

Left: Party time for the Toffeemen. Back row (left to right): Derek Mountfield, John Bailey (note the discreet headgear), Peter Reid, Kevin Ratcliffe, Alan Harper (unused substitute), Andy Gray. Front: Trevor Steven, Kevin Richardson, Neville Southall, Graeme Sharp, Adrian Heath, Gary Stevens. After Spurs in 1982 and Manchester United in 1983, Everton were the third successive club to make up for losing the League Cup by winning the FA Cup in the same season.

1985

IT HAPPENED THIS YEAR

Live Aid rock concerts raised more than £40 million for famine victims.

Mikhail Gorbachev became the new Soviet leader.

Earthquake killed thousands and destroyed much of Mexico City.

The disease Aids reached epidemic proportions in parts of the world.

The moment of truth for Kevin Moran (left). Unmoved by the protests of the animated Irishman, referee Peter Willis points emphatically towards the touchline. Most neutrals thought Moran was unlucky, yet the real sympathy should go to team-mate Graeme Hogg, who had been first choice in Kevin's central defensive position for much of the season before injury removed him from contention at a crucial time.

MANCHESTER UNITED 1

Whiteside 110

EVERTON 0

Half-time 0-0 Extra time played

MANCHESTER UNITED	○	EVERTON
Gary Bailey	1	Neville Southall
John Gidman	2	Gary Stevens
*Arthur Albiston	3	Pat Van den Hauwe
Norman Whiteside	4	Kevin Ratcliffe *(captain)*
Paul McGrath	5	Derek Mountfield
Kevin Moran	6	Peter Reid
Bryan Robson *(captain)*	7	Trevor Steven
Gordon Strachan	8	Graeme Sharp
Mark Hughes	9	Andy Gray
Frank Stapleton	10	Paul Bracewell
Jesper Olsen	11	Kevin Sheedy
*(sub Mike Duxbury)		

Attendance: 100,000

Referee: P Willis, County Durham

There was no way, surely, that Everton against Manchester United could fail to be a classic. The Toffeemen, having won the League with five matches to spare and then lifted the European Cup Winners' Cup, were the most accomplished and well-balanced side in England; the Red Devils, never more dangerous than in sudden-death confrontations, were arguably the best of the rest. Of the 22 players who would start the final, only Everton centre-back Derek Mountfield was not a full international; stars and thoroughbreds abounded; the table was laid for a soccer feast. Yet for the bulk of its 120-minute duration, the game was gruesomely, perplexingly dull, the two teams locked in a stifling defensive stalemate that might have been filmed as an effective last resort for chronic insomniacs. However, when the contest finally came alive it did so with a vengeance, producing two moments of undiluted sensation that will endure longer in most memories than countless hours of fine football in more worthy finals. The pure melodrama of Kevin Moran's sending-off and the exquisite execution of Norman Whiteside's winner made certain of that.

In the three days grace after Everton's European victory against Rapid Vienna in Rotterdam, they were able to reflect ecstatically on the most triumphant season in their history. Not only were two major prizes in the bag and a third in prospect, but midfield general Peter Reid had been voted players' player of the year, goalkeeper Neville Southall had received a similar accolade from the football writers, and Howard Kendall was manager of the year. But what made it sweeter still for Goodison fans was that across Stanley Park at Anfield, the trophy cupboard was bare. Similarly, it had not escaped the Blue legions that while Liverpool had dominated for so long, they had never claimed the League and FA Cup double. So here was another march to steal. As to their Wembley rivals, what was there to fear from United? Hadn't they finished a mere fourth in the title race, 14 points adrift? And hadn't they been annihilated 5-0 in the gala display of Everton's League season? And what about the Toffeemen's Milk Cup victory at Old Trafford back in October? More cautious counsels feared that Kendall's men could become victims of their own success, pointing out that the final would be the 63rd game of a gruelling campaign. Throughout their FA Cup run, the Merseysiders had given admirable value for money, entertaining marvellously but also showing resilience at need. Neither Leeds nor Doncaster posed serious problems in the early rounds, but that was not true of Telford United in the fifth. For more than an hour they held the Blues goalless at Goodison before a late and rather flattering flurry saw the favourites run out 3-0 winners. Howard Kendall paid tribute to the precocious Salopians as 'one of the best non-League sides I have ever seen.' In the quarter-final, however, the going got tougher and it took a late Derek Mountfield equaliser to survive at home to Ipswich. That was after a remarkable demonstration of dead-ball expertise by Kevin Sheedy, whose fifth-minute free-kick over the defensive wall to the right of 'keeper Paul Cooper was ruled out because the referee had not signalled for it to be taken. While the supporters moaned, the unflappable Irishman replaced the ball, then coolly lifted it over the wall and into the net to Cooper's *left!* However, there was to be a tragic ending to the day when former Everton boss Harry Catterick collapsed and died in the stand after the match. A Graeme Sharp penalty was enough to win the Portman Road replay, then Sheedy and Mountfield were heroes again in the Villa Park semi-final. A goal up with five minutes left, Luton looked Wembley-bound, but Kevin's free-kick saved the day. Then, in extra time, yet another Sheedy free-kick landed on Mountfield's head and a stirring comeback was complete.

United, too, had shown convincing form. Bournemouth were dispatched emphatically in the third round - revenge for shock defeat at the Cherries' hands a year earlier - and both Coventry and Blackburn were overcome without undue fuss. A Whiteside hat-trick was the centrepiece of an exhilarating quarter-final demolition of West Ham, which earned the dubious pleasure of a last-four meeting with Liverpool. Even by the standards of past battles royal between the north-

west giants, this was an enthralling confrontation. At Goodison United led twice, only for Joe Fagan's side to equalise first on 90 minutes, then repeat the dose at the end of extra time. The rematch at Maine Road saw Liverpool nose in front when Paul McGrath put through his own goal, before spectacular strikes by Bryan Robson and Mark Hughes carried the day.

Thus both finalists had reached Wembley in circumstances of intense excitement and, with so much talent on display, it was not unreasonable to expect more of the same. However, the proceedings began on a sombre note, with a minute's silence in memory of the 52 people who had lost their lives in the Bradford City fire a week earlier. No one could know it, but a few days hence the soccer world would be stunned by another disaster, this time at Heysel. For the moment, though, football occupied the emotions of a mostly shirtsleeved crowd on a sunlit afternoon. Early exchanges were undistinguished, to say the least, before Peter Reid almost kick-started the game into life after 15 minutes. Right-back Gary Stevens took a long throw from the right, United 'keeper Gary Bailey punched to the edge of the box where Reid met the dropping ball with a full-blooded volley. His shot was arrowing inside a post when ex-Evertonian John Gidman lunged at it, got the slightest deflection and the ball hit the woodwork before bouncing to safety. The only other incident of note in a stultifying first half was the booking of Robson for a foul; suffice it to say that Everton had the best of it, but that was not saying

Shoulder to shoulder, a pair of footballing gladiators make for the heart of the fray. Andy Gray (centre) prepares to clash with Bryan Robson, while Paul McGrath awaits developments.

Below: An early let-off for United as a desperate John Gidman makes minimal contact with Peter Reid's shot, but just enough to turn it on to the post.

Battle of the wingmen. Jesper Olsen, United's diminutive Dane, throws himself into a challenge on Trevor Steven of Everton.

Two men who just aren't going to agree. Discussion hots up between Kevin Moran and Peter Willis.

much. After the break, the deadlock persisted, with each side creating one clear-cut opening. For Everton, Reid pulled the ball back from the byline to Sheedy, whose flick reached Gray, only for the Scot to blaze wide from 12 yards. In the opposite direction, Hughes freed Whiteside with a sweet through-ball only for Southall to make the best save of the match, diving bravely at the muscular Ulsterman's feet.

It remained only for Everton skipper Kevin Ratcliffe to escape a booking for a hideously clumsy body-check on Frank Stapleton before the game's pivotal incident occurred on 77 minutes. United centre-half Paul McGrath made a rare error, losing the ball to Reid just inside his own half. But as the Blues' diminutive dynamo set off towards goal, Kevin Moran closed in with a lunging tackle from the side, missing the ball but catching Reid, who tumbled spectacularly, like a small boy somersaulting over the handlebars of his bike. Policeman Peter Willis, a well-respected referee but one whose bearing was strikingly officious, lectured the culprit, who then turned to walk away only to be called back.

Then, in what the Irishman later described as the worst moment of his life, the tall man in black pointed imperiously towards the dressing room, and the awful truth dawned that Moran was the first player to be sent off in an FA Cup Final. Skipper Robson registered his outrage and a disbelieving Kevin appeared to beseech the implacable Willis for a reprieve, eventually being restrained by Stapleton for fear of incurring further penalty before plodding off, clearly dumbstruck. As television evidence was to show, Moran's challenge had been low and missed the ball by the merest whisker. There was nothing to suggest intention to clatter his opponent, who had joined the chorus requesting leniency. When he told pressmen after the match: 'I went for the ball, that was all I could see, it was definitely playable,' it was difficult not to feel sympathy with one of football's most honest characters. Of course, it must be remembered that Willis had made his decision without the benefit of protracted TV replays and under all the pressure that a Cup Final brings, so it would be wrong to pillory him.

However, nothing was going to alter the fact that United must fight on with ten men, surely the decisive factor in favour of an Everton side who, in boxing parlance, were already marginally ahead on points. Not so. Now a sense of anger at perceived injustice ran through the Red Devils; suddenly their work was crisper, more incisive; despite the obvious logic that they should dig in for a replay, they began to blossom. Stapleton moved effectively into the back four, and after 88

Below: Neville Southall dives in vain as Norman Whiteside (out of picture to the right) deposits an exquisite bender just inside the far post. It was a goal of the highest quality, worthy of settling any contest, and stands as the crowning moment of a glorious but all-too-short career. Ironically, Whiteside was an Everton player when injury forced his premature retirement.

minutes they nearly lifted the Cup without recourse to extra time when Gidman galloped forward, played a one-two with Whiteside and was foiled only by a desperate challenge from Pat Van den Hauwe. Even so, the additional period began ominously for the Mancunians with Bailey being forced to save smartly from Paul Bracewell's firm 25-yarder, then an unmarked Mountfield setting up Van den Hauwe for a close-range effort. Soon, Everton came even closer when Robson nodded against his own bar from a corner, but with only ten minutes remaining, the game's one flash of genuine inspiration produced a breakthrough at the other end. Jesper Olsen found Hughes near halfway, the Welshman back-tracked into Red Devil territory before turning, gliding past Bracewell and splitting the Blues' defence with a glorious, outside-of-the-foot pass into space on the right flank. Ignoring fatigue, oblivious to tension, Whiteside pounded after it, took possession and, as Van den Hauwe stood off, he entered the corner of Everton's area. With Gordon Strachan unmarked on the left, a crossfield pass was the obvious option but Norman, as recorded elsewhere in this book, was

Right: It's United's day and their players milk the moment to the full. Left to right are Jesper Olsen, Gary Bailey, Kevin Moran and Norman Whiteside.

accustomed to writing his own scripts. Thus with Van den Hauwe still blocking his path and Southall having wandered towards his near post, the Irish prodigy executed his own version of the Ali Shuffle, drew back his left foot and curled a sublime cross-shot inches inside the far post. Some thought it was a fluke, but it wasn't; Norman had done it a hundred times in training and now he had done it when it mattered. Behind the goal BBC commentator Tony Gubba waved his heels in the air (giving rise to certain questions about his neutrality); on the bench Moran embraced Arthur Albiston, who had been replaced by Mike Duxbury after 90 minutes; meanwhile Ron Atkinson gave a fair impression of the Cheshire Cat. But if they thought it was over, it wasn't yet. First McGrath had to head a Trevor Steven cross over his own bar, then Mountfield found himself unmarked six yards from goal only for Bailey to gather his back-header. Soon, though, it *was* all over and Atkinson engulfed Moran in a bear-hug, then sprinted on to the pitch, pausing suddenly and almost comically for the ritual handshake with Kendall. As they contemplated the end of their treble dream, the Everton boss and Reid found time to commiserate generously with Moran for his dismissal. Kevin listened, apparently woebegone, until they moved on; then his mask of tragedy dissolved as he whooped and threw himself into Whiteside's arms. Rules being rules, Moran was barred from collecting his medal, and there was even talk that he would be deprived of it permanently. However, good sense and mercy prevailed and within a few days he received his hard-earned gong. As for Everton, they could reflect on a wonderful season while pondering how achingly close they had come to a once-in-a-lifetime achievement.

Above: Bryan Robson lifts the FA Cup for the second time in three years, but as his fellow Red Devils wait in line, one man is missing. Because of his dismissal, Kevin Moran was not allowed to collect his medal.

Left: Neville Southall leads the gallant losers on a lap of honour. Like Liverpool in 1977, they had fallen victim to 'Treble-Busters' United, but could still look back on a brilliant season in which they had won the League and a European trophy.

1986

IT HAPPENED THIS YEAR

Chernobyl nuclear explosion sent radio-active fall-out over vast areas of Europe.

The United States' Challenger space shuttle exploded, killing the crew.

American planes bombed Libya in retaliation for terrorist acts.

Mike Tyson became the youngest world heavyweight boxing champion.

Prince Andrew married Sarah Ferguson.

Every picture tells a story. The final whistle has blown and Liverpool have won the League and Cup double while Everton have finished with nothing. Jubilant Reds Jan Molby, Kenny Dalglish and Craig Johnston are in a world of their own, while Blues midfielder Peter Reid looks understandably morose.

10 May 1986

LIVERPOOL 3

Rush 57, 84; Johnston 63

EVERTON 1

Lineker 28

Half-time 0-1

LIVERPOOL		EVERTON
Bruce Grobbelaar	1	Bobby Mimms
Mark Lawrenson	2	Gary Stevens*
Jim Beglin	3	Pat Van den Hauwe
Steve Nicol	4	Kevin Ratcliffe *(captain)*
Ronnie Whelan	5	Derek Mountfield
Alan Hansen *(captain)*	6	Peter Reid
Kenny Dalglish	7	Trevor Steven
Craig Johnston	8	Gary Lineker
Ian Rush	9	Graeme Sharp
Jan Molby	10	Paul Bracewell
Kevin MacDonald	11	Kevin Sheedy
		(sub Adrian Heath)*

Attendance: 98,000

Referee: A Robinson, Portsmouth

Life had dealt some cruel blows to Evertonians in the quarter of a century or so since Bill Shankly had revived their ailing neighbours, just a short stroll away across Stanley Park at Anfield. But even languishing until the mid-1980s in the shadow of Liverpool's ever-growing mountain of silverware was as nothing compared to the stark soccer nightmare that descended on them in the late spring of 1986. After looking, by common consent, the best side in the League since Christmas, they forfeited their First Division leadership in the home straight and lost the title . . . to Liverpool. Then a week later, they dominated the first hour of the FA Cup Final, led 1-0, squandered chances to make it safe and then saw the trophy snatched from their grasp . . . by Liverpool. Had they been deprived of the most coveted English club prize of them all, the League and FA Cup double, by Manchester United or Arsenal or Spurs it would have been monstrous enough. But for the sackcloth and ashes to be dispensed by their fellow Scousers was utterly beyond belief. In a city where football allegiance could pit brother against brother, father against son, even husband against wife in some cases, the significance was not easy to exaggerate. However, the calamitous late derailment of the Blues' glory train must not be allowed to obscure yet another great Anfield achievement, one which would have been remarkable at any point of the Shankly-Paisley-Fagan success story, but which was all the more stupendous for being attained in Kenny Dalglish's first season as player-manager. When the taciturn Scot had accepted the job, he had inquired of those who questioned his inexperience 'Why not start at the top?' though even he could hardly have expected quite such an illustrious beginning to his new career before ringing down the curtain on his old one.

By the time the top clubs were due to commence their Cup campaigns, the battle for the Championship was unfolding in somewhat bizarre fashion. Back in August, Cup holders Manchester United had shot out of the blocks as if their Wembley victory had been a mere appetiser for their first League triumph in 19 years. Ron Atkinson's men won their opening ten games and remained unbeaten in 15, at which point they were ten points clear of Liverpool and no less than 17 better off than Everton. But then, in what was a staggering collapse even when measured against previous title traumas endured by Old Trafford fans, United nosedived abruptly out of contention. Incredibly, come February the first, Howard Kendall's Blues had ascended to the First Division summit and were playing the same brand of exciting but beautifully controlled football that had seen them lift League and Cup Winners' Cup a year earlier. Indeed, when Everton won at Anfield in late February the outcome of the Championship race seemed cut and dried but, as is their wont, the Reds refused to give up, hanging on to the Toffeemen's shirt-tails throughout March. But even when Liverpool took over the top spot for the first time on the last day of the month, the clever money was on the Blues, with a game in hand and oozing class, to carry the day. Yet it never happened: Dalglish and company took 34 points from a possible 36 - a fantastic feat at that stage of a draining season - and they were the Champions.

It was against this background and unhampered by Continental commitments - English clubs were serving a European ban in the wake of the Heysel tragedy - that the Merseyside pair marched on Wembley. Liverpool began in a blizzard,

Everton's walking wounded, Neil Pointon (left) and Neville Southall.

obliterating Second Division leaders Norwich City 5-0 at Anfield, then encountered sterner opposition at Stamford Bridge. Chelsea fought spiritedly, despite being reduced to ten men by injury for much of the match, before capitulating 2-1, yet they never came as close to toppling the mighty Reds as did little York City in the fifth round. The Minstermen, whipped 7-0 in a replay in front of the Kop a year earlier, again held Liverpool to a draw at Bootham Crescent, this time taking the lead only to be pegged back by a Jan Molby penalty. Still defiant, they were holding their hosts to 1-1 at Anfield when they netted again, and midfielder Craig Johnston confessed later that he had thought the Reds were doomed. But the referee spotted an infringement, the 'goal' was disallowed, and extra-time strikes by Molby and Dalglish won the day. In the quarter-final, Liverpool were frustrated by a superb Anfield display from Watford 'keeper Tony Coton, setting up a Vicarage Road rematch which saw John Barnes frighten his future employers by putting the Hornets ahead. Once more, Molby came to the rescue with a penalty and Ian Rush got the winner in extra time. The Welshman was the hero again in the last four, his two goals seeing off Southampton in the third consecutive tie in which the Reds had required the additional period to win through.

The best of buddies. Everton's Howard Kendall (left) and Kenny Dalglish of Liverpool lead their teams out at Wembley for the first all-Merseyside FA Cup Final.

Everton's progress was slightly more straightforward in that they needed just the regulation 90 minutes to dispose of each of their first three opponents, Exeter, Blackburn and Spurs. The going got tougher in the sixth round on Luton's much-criticised synthetic surface, though, and the Blues had to come back from two down to force a replay. At Goodison, a single goal from Gary Lineker was enough to see them safe, underlining for the umpteenth time that term what a bargain the former Leicester striker had been at £800,000 plus a percentage of any sell-on price. At first he was not the most popular man on Merseyside, having replaced folk hero Andy Gray and taken several outings to get into his customary prolific stride, but as nets began to bulge with increasing regularity he won the hearts of the Gwladys Street sceptics as surely as later he would capture the affection of practically the entire football world. Nevertheless, Everton managed without Lineker in the semi-final, defeating Sheffield Wednesday 2-1 thanks to a sweet floater from the unsung Alan Harper and a volley from Graeme Sharp.

Now the scene was set for the first all-Merseyside FA Cup Final and one of the most soccer-conscious communities on the planet was consumed with fervour as never before. Twice previously the teams had resolved differences at Wembley - both in 1984, Liverpool winning the Milk Cup, Everton the Charity Shield - but neither occasion had approached this one in import. Several unfortunates were out of contention for a place in the historic clash. Liverpool had been deprived of midfielder John Wark since March with a broken leg, then defender Gary Gillespie fell victim to a virus in final week. Everton were without Neville Southall, Britain's finest goalkeeper, who had also missed the semi-final after dislocating his ankle playing for Wales in Dublin, but Kendall expressed confidence that England under-21 international Bobby Mimms would deputise capably. There had been fears, also, that centre-back Derek Mountfield would be unfit, but a late test cleared him to play.

When the action got under way the opening exchanges were surprisingly one-sided with the Blues dominating from midfield, where Paul Bracewell and

Peter Reid were in outstanding form. The pressure mounted on the Liverpool goal and a breakthrough might have come after 18 minutes when Sharp appeared to be impeded in the Reds' box by Steve Nicol. However, to Everton's consternation, referee Alan Robinson refused to uphold what had seemed to be a watertight claim for a penalty. Six minutes later Lineker exchanged passes smartly with Reid only to be foiled by a last-ditch tackle from Mark Lawrenson, but soon the England pair combined to fashion a well-merited lead. Dalglish lost possession in midfield and Reid loosed a 30-yard through-ball for Lineker to chase; the Goodison greyhound outpaced Alan Hansen with ease, Bruce Grobbelaar parried the shot, but Gary followed up to bundle the ball home. At this point, Kendall's men looked every inch the likely winners as they pushed the ball around slickly and incisively. Liverpool must have been relieved to reach half-time no further in arrears but there was no let-up after the break, with Trevor Steven shooting wide with Grobbelaar beaten, then Kevin Sheedy leaving three defenders in a heap before missing the target. Bruce was looking increasingly shaky and after dropping one cross he was involved in an altercation with team-mate Jim Beglin, the volatile 'keeper pushing the astonished left-back out of his area.

But after 57 minutes an England

Below: Watch that man! Everton's potential match-winner Gary Lineker (centre) is policed by Liverpool's Jan Molby (left) and Kevin MacDonald. Lineker gave the Blues the lead, but it didn't last.

player committed a ghastly error and the match lurched on its axis. Everton right-back Gary Stevens, under no immediate pressure, attempted to thread a pass through an unlikely gap along the touchline, but his execution was sadly lacking and Liverpool's Ronnie Whelan intercepted. The Irishman found Molby - he of hefty girth but exquisite vision - who freed Ian Rush; the predatory Welshman bore down on Mimms, sidestepped nimbly and slid the ball into the empty net for an equaliser that had not seemed remotely likely to arrive. Suddenly, ominously, the Reds were going about their business with

renewed purpose, but the Blues had not reached their current eminence without large quantities of resilience, which they now displayed. Indeed, they came close to regaining the lead on 61 minutes when Hansen misplaced a clearance and Sharp headed towards the unguarded goal from the edge of the box. But the cries of exultation from the Everton contingent were still-born as the back-pedalling Grobbelaar arched his back in a graceful salmon leap to tip the ball over his bar. What a crucial contribution that turned out to be. Two minutes later Rush found Molby on the left, the Dane brushed aside an inadequate challenge from Stevens and crossed. Dalglish failed to make contact and the ball ran to the unmarked Johnston, who stabbed home from close range. Now Kendall was desperate. Off went defender Stevens, on came attacker Adrian Heath, and the Blues operated with a three-man rearguard as they strove to regain parity in a match in which they had reigned supreme for so long. But now there was an inevitability about Liverpool's grip on proceedings, which tightened still further six minutes from time. Rush found the ever-more influential Molby, Whelan took up possession, then delivered a lovely chip to Ian's feet and the master marksman drilled his second goal. Near the end the undisputed man of the match might have claimed a

Above: A craftsman at work. Ian Rush rounds grounded Everton 'keeper Bobby Mimms before slipping home the equaliser (inset), then grabs Liverpool's third (main picture) to clinch the double.

323

hat-trick, shooting limply with only Mimms to beat, but that would have been appalling justice on a demoralised Everton side who had contributed so much. Afterwards the two teams flew home on the same plane, then the next day Reds and Blues boarded a bus together and set off on an 18-mile celebratory tour of the city. It was a well-meant exercise, aimed at fostering togetherness among fans, and offered a euphoric experience to Dalglish and his men. But for the Evertonians it was excruciating, the last thing they wanted after losing League and Cup to their close rivals in the same week. Indeed for one man, it was all too much. Peter Reid, gutted by defeat, failed to turn up for 'personal reasons', though there were rumours that he had been negotiating a move to a foreign club. If so, it never materialised, although team-mate Gary Lineker *was* on the verge of departure, joining Barcelona later that summer for £2.5 million. The last word, though, should be devoted to Liverpool, who had become the fifth club to do the double. Amazingly, they had clinched the honour without one Englishman in their side and with a rookie manager at the helm. Just wait until Kenny learned the ropes . . .

Who said it was impossible to be a successful player-manager? The cares of office have slipped from the shoulders of Kenny Dalglish as he celebrates Liverpool's fabulous achievement.

Reds rejoice. Back row (left to right): Grobbelaar, Dalglish, Gillespie, Molby, Walsh, Hooper, Lee, Lawrenson, Rush, MacDonald, Whelan, Wark. Front: McMahon, Johnston, Beglin, Hansen, Nicol.

Victory parade. Jim Beglin (left) and Alan Hansen show the fans Liverpool's latest item of silverware.

COVENTRY CITY 3

Bennett 9; Houchen 63; Mabbutt (og) 96

TOTTENHAM HOTSPUR 2

Allen 2; Mabbutt 40

Half-time 1-2 Extra time played

COVENTRY CITY		TOTTENHAM HOTSPUR
Steve Ogrizovic	1	Ray Clemence
David Phillips	2	Chris Hughton*
Greg Downs	3	Mitchell Thomas
Lloyd McGrath	4	Steve Hodge
*Brian Kilcline (captain)	5	Richard Gough (captain)
Trevor Peake	6	Gary Mabbutt
Dave Bennett	7	Clive Allen
Micky Gynn	8	Paul Allen
Cyrille Regis	9	Chris Waddle
Keith Houchen	10	Glenn Hoddle
Nick Pickering	11	Ossie Ardiles †
*(sub Graham Rodger)		(sub Nico Claesen)*
		(sub Gary Stevens)†

Attendance: 98,000

Referee: N Midgley, Salford

When Jimmy Greaves disagrees with Old Moore's Almanack, just who is a poor punter to believe? Well, throughout the 1987 FA Cup campaign there was compelling evidence in favour of the time-honoured and widely revered publication. The fact was that the record-breaking former Spurs marksman turned media pundit had been predicting the downfall of Coventry City, one of the leading local sides on the patch of his employers, Central TV, since January. He reckoned they would come unstuck against Manchester United at Old Trafford in the fourth round and nominated Second Division Stoke City to beat them in the fifth. At the quarter-final stage Jimmy didn't believe the Sky Blues could cope with Sheffield Wednesday, then he added insult to injury by backing another second-flight team, Leeds United, to reach Wembley at City's expense. Finally, despite having been wrong every time, he could hardly tip Coventry on the big day itself, paired as they were with Tottenham, the club he had served so brilliantly in his 1960s heyday. Meanwhile, the all-seeing eye of Old Moore had glimpsed the treasured trophy going to a team wearing blue-and-white stripes. Central TV themselves were in no doubt, taking a full-page advertisement in the Wembley programme to detail the Sky Blues' achievements and inquire in huge type: Are You Watching Jimmy Greaves?

It was all splendid fun, which matched precisely the ambience given off by the buoyant Highfield Road outfit as their season moved towards its euphoric climax. The credit for this feel-good atmosphere went to the charismatic management team of George Curtis and John Sillett. George, who as an 'iron-man' centre-half between 1956 and 1970 had established the club's appearance record, was a breezy, outgoing disciplinarian who concentrated on the business side; John, another former Sky Blue and even more extrovert by nature, bore chief responsibility for the football. The chemistry between them appeared to be perfect and as their success began to snowball, they inspired spontaneous affection far beyond the boundaries of an increasingly Cup-crazy Coventry. Though City were undeniably one of the less fashionable clubs in the First Division, the fact remained that they had been among the elite for 20 years, only Arsenal, Everton and Liverpool boasting a longer current run. Now, after scraping to safety in four successive relegation battles - the most recent of them with Curtis at the helm and Sillett as his lieutenant - they had finished in

If it's true there's no fun left in football, then nobody told Coventry City. George Curtis doffs his sky-blue topper, John Sillett puts his right leg in and his left arm out, while goal-scorer Dave Bennett adopts a more traditional pose.

the top half of the table. More glamorously, of course, they had reached the first FA Cup Final in their 104-year history. The improvement had been achieved without a galaxy of stars; indeed, centre-forward Cyrille Regis, a £300,000 acquisition from West Bromwich Albion in 1984, was the most expensive as well as the best-known player. It should be pointed out, too, that the Highfield Road double-act had forged their success principally by getting the best out of footballers signed by previous bosses Bobby Gould and Don Mackay, who both deserved a portion of the praise.

What a contrast to the situation at Tottenham, both in terms of tradition and in money spent. Bulging with costly talent, the North Londoners were going for a record eighth FA Cup triumph, having won all seven of their finals to date. They too had a comparative newcomer at the helm, David Pleat having been recruited a year earlier, since when he had fulfilled his pledge to ensure that the White Hart Lane faithful should be treated to attractive fare. Much had been made of his five-man midfield - featuring such luminaries as Glenn Hoddle, Ossie Ardiles and Chris Waddle - which had proffered exquisite service to lone striker Clive Allen.

Full-back Brian Borrows, who missed only one match in Coventry's Cup campaign. Sadly, it was at Wembley.

He had responded royally, arriving at Wembley having scored 48 times in senior competition, a record which had helped Spurs finish third in the First Division and reach the semi-final of the Littlewoods Cup. On a personal level, there had been even richer reward for Allen, who won player of the year awards from his fellow professionals and the nation's soccer writers. Not that all had been sweetness and light at the Lane, however. Spurs' conquerors in the Littlewoods had been deadly local rivals, Arsenal, who had gone on to lift the trophy, increasing the pressure on Pleat's men to make no mistake on their own visit to the Twin Towers. And the club's premier play-maker, Hoddle, was leaving after the final to join the French club Monaco, a decision bitterly regretted by the majority of Tottenham fans. He, and they, were anxious that he should bid farewell with a memorable flourish.

Both sides had made straightforward progress to Wembley, neither needing a replay along the way, though there had been plenty of close contests. In fact, Spurs experienced difficulty at the first hurdle, slipping through by the odd goal in five against Fourth Division Scunthorpe. Crystal Palace were removed from their path by a rather flattering four-goal margin, then Newcastle succumbed following a controversial penalty decision. In the quarter-final, Tottenham moved up a gear, giving their most impressive performance to date in eliminating Wimbledon 2-0 with Waddle and Hoddle scoring spectacular goals. It was a particularly satisfying victory in view of brash predictions some of the Dons had made in the press, but the day had its poignant side, too. Spurs full-back Danny Thomas had been seriously injured in a recent League meeting with QPR - as it transpired, he would never play again - and in a TV interview, Hoddle dedicated his goal to his sidelined team-mate. Poor Danny, universally liked throughout football, was in tears as he watched from his hospital bed. Now only Watford stood between Tottenham and Wembley, and the Hornets' challenge was brushed aside 4-1 in a Villa Park encounter that was as one-sided as the score suggests. Coventry, who prepared at the same 'lucky' hotel near Bournemouth throughout their Cup run, had started comfortably against Bolton, only to be dispatched to Old Trafford in the fourth round. They prevailed, though, by means of Keith Houchen's scrambled effort, then shaded a one-goal thriller at Stoke thanks to Micky Gynn. Hillsborough was the venue for the Sky Blues' next two encounters, a Houchen brace helping to sink Sheffield Wednesday in the quarter-final, then Keith chipping in again with a fine goal in a seesawing semi-final thriller against Leeds. At that stage the well-travelled frontman had scored only one League goal but struck four times in the FA Cup - and he hadn't finished yet! Throughout that spring, Cup fever had been breaking out all over in Coventry; now, with City the first Midlands club to reach the final since Leicester in 1969, it assumed epidemic proportions. Though 14,500 was the

average home gate at Highfield Road, some 20,000 fans had headed north for the semi-final and demand for Wembley tickets was phenomenal. People began queueing for two days before the club's allocation of 25,000 were due to go on sale, and in the event they were sold 24 hours early so everyone could go home. The unluckiest man in the Coventry camp was right-back Brian Borrows, injured in the season's last League match and out of the final. City would miss his enterprising overlaps, but Sillett did much to make good the deficiency by handing the number-two shirt to the versatile David Phillips and drafting little Gynn into midfield. Otherwise the Sky Blues were at full strength, as were Spurs, though there was a shock in store for their sponsors. As the game began it was noticed that half the Tottenham team were wearing shirts bereft of the Holsten legend - apparently there had been a kit cock-up in all the pre-match excitement. As a rival brewer might have put it, someone needed to refresh the parts that a certain lager presumably didn't reach.

However, such commercial niceties were quick to recede as the match got off to a sensational start. In the second minute the ball was hacked desperately out of Coventry's area and fell to Waddle on the Tottenham right. The crew-cut wingman of lackadaisical bearing but explosive talent wrongfooted two defenders with a wicked body-swerve before crossing precisely to set up Allen for an unstoppable

Above: The day of 49. Clive Allen beats Trevor Peake to give Spurs a second-minute lead, but the match and the season was to end with the ace poacher still one short of his half-century.

Left: Are we playing for the same team? Tottenham's Steve Hodge bears the sponsor's name on his shirt, while Glenn Hoddle's chest carries only a cockerel.

bullet of a header at the near post. That was the predatory Londoner's 49th senior strike of the season and, at that stage, it would have been a rare bookie to offer generous odds against his reaching the half-century before the afternoon was over. But Coventry were not dismayed and they piled forward, their pressure paying off seven minutes later when Houchen nodded a left-wing cross from Greg Downs into space; the Spurs defence reacted sluggishly but that nippy raider Dave Bennett was on his toes, sidestepping Ray Clemence, then netting left-footed with a smart cross-shot. In 1981 Tottenham had condemned Bennett, then with Manchester City, to a loser's medal and he had no intention of allowing a repeat.

Nevertheless, with the smooth skills of Hoddle and Waddle becoming ever more influential, Spurs appeared to be gaining ground, though they received another reminder of City's menace when a long throw from Phillips was headed on by Houchen for Regis to glance it past Clemence. The 'goal' was ruled out, apparently for pushing, and though some fans were mystified, the players took it in good part, Houchen even enjoying a joke with referee Neil Midgley. There followed a double let-off for Coventry when 'keeper Ogrizovic lost possession on an adventurous dribble outside his box and Hoddle's 30-yard shot towards an empty goal was intercepted by Trevor Peake; then, in the ensuing confusion, Allen hit the side netting. As the action ebbed and flowed, Gynn burst through but was blocked by Clemence, but there was no further score until shortly before the break when Hoddle floated a free-kick from the right which fell to the feet of Coventry's Brian Kilcline and Spurs' Gary Mabbutt. They challenged for the ball, which rebounded into the net for a scruffy goal which was later credited to Mabbutt.

Again the Sky Blues were unbowed, attacking brightly after the interval and

Above: Gary Mabbutt (centre) had an eventful afternoon, first putting Spurs in the lead, then deflecting Coventry's winner past his own goalkeeper.

Left: A safe pair of hands. Coventry custodian Steve Ogrizovic, one of the stars of the Sky Blues' campaign, clasps the ball to his chest to frustrate Tottenham's Richard Gough. In the middle of a rather msucular sand-wich is City striker Keith Houchen, who has tracked back to block Gough's forward surge.

Poor Gary Mabbutt is on his knees after Lloyd McGrath's cross had rebounded from his knee and into Spurs' net for the decisive goal.

regaining parity with the goal of the game on 63 minutes. Houchen fed Bennett on the right, the winger bent his cross beyond Richard Gough and the slim striker threw himself horizontal to head home from six yards. Shortly after, Keith came close to giving Coventry the lead with another header, but Clemence saved alertly at the foot of a post. As extra time loomed, the balance appeared to swing towards the North Londoners when 'Killer' Kilcline fell victim to his own ferocious late challenge on Mabbutt and limped off the pitch to be replaced by Graham Rodger. But the additional period was to spark off carnival time in Coventry. Young Rodger made a neat interception, moved confidently into the Spurs half and freed Lloyd McGrath on the right. The little ball-winner steamed into the Tottenham

Left: Happiness is . . . netting at Wembley and lifting the FA Cup. Coventry marksmen Dave Bennett (left) and Keith Houchen register their delight.

Below: Horizontal hero. Keith Houchen dives full length to level matters at 2-2.

box and released a cross which caught Mabbutt on his left knee, sending the ball looping agonisingly over the stranded Clemence and into the net. Now Pleat sent on forward Nico Claesen for defender Chris Hughton but it was too late; indeed, it was the Midlanders who came closest to adding to their tally, but Clemence foiled Gynn again. Soon captain Kilcline was limping up the steps to the royal box to receive the FA Cup, which he hoisted with all the snarling relish of a wounded tiger brandishing its prey. Back at pitch level Curtis and Sillett were cavorting joyously, George sporting a sky-blue topper and 'Snozz' indulging in his own version of the hokey cokey. That was the lasting image of the 1987 FA Cup Final - and it was a happy one, indeed.

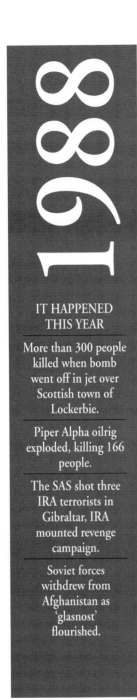

More than 300 people killed when bomb went off in jet over Scottish town of Lockerbie.

Piper Alpha oilrig exploded, killing 166 people.

The SAS shot three IRA terrorists in Gibraltar, IRA mounted revenge campaign.

Soviet forces withdrew from Afghanistan as 'glasnost' flourished.

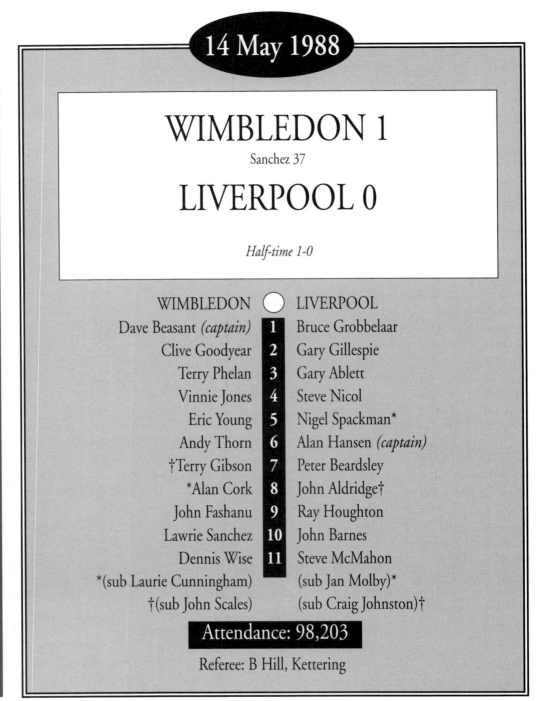

14 May 1988

WIMBLEDON 1
Sanchez 37

LIVERPOOL 0

Half-time 1-0

WIMBLEDON		LIVERPOOL
Dave Beasant *(captain)*	1	Bruce Grobbelaar
Clive Goodyear	2	Gary Gillespie
Terry Phelan	3	Gary Ablett
Vinnie Jones	4	Steve Nicol
Eric Young	5	Nigel Spackman*
Andy Thorn	6	Alan Hansen *(captain)*
†Terry Gibson	7	Peter Beardsley
*Alan Cork	8	John Aldridge†
John Fashanu	9	Ray Houghton
Lawrie Sanchez	10	John Barnes
Dennis Wise	11	Steve McMahon
*(sub Laurie Cunningham)		(sub Jan Molby)*
†(sub John Scales)		(sub Craig Johnston)†

Attendance: 98,203

Referee: B Hill, Kettering

A vast amount of unmitigated bunkum has been written about the 1988 FA Cup Final between Liverpool and Wimbledon, and at the risk of being accused of adding to the pile, this writer has an opinion to venture. The match, between arguably the most entertaining side ever to come out of Anfield and the widely denigrated purveyors of the so-called hump'n'bump style, was described in some quarters as 'the battle for the future of English football'. The contention was that if the artistic Reds were defeated by long-ball tactics in the season's showpiece then a gradual descent into Stone-Age methods at all levels of the game was inevitable. The theory produced column after column of melodramatic copy, but did not deserve to be taken seriously. Quite simply, managers have *always* cut their coat according to their cloth, producing attractive teams when they have had players of sufficient ability at their disposal, slogging their way combatively to whatever success they could achieve when they did not. That will not, cannot change, and the outcome of Liverpool v Wimbledon was never going to have sinister long-term significance. On a more cynical note, it was fascinating to note how the tenor of

The impossible dream has come true for the Dons. Manager Bobby Gould is happy with his unconventional headgear, while scorer Lawrie Sanchez, goal-keeper-cum-skipper Dave Beasant and little Terry Phelan wave to Wimbledon's heavily outnumbered supporters.

certain press coverage changed when the Dons emerged victorious. Suddenly the team vilified hitherto as little less than Sons of Satan were transformed into 'those wonderful Wombles'!

It was true, of course, that the two finalists offered inescapably vivid contrasts in background, resources and method. Indeed, the rise and rise of Wimbledon was the stuff of unadulterated fantasy. Back in 1975, when as giant-killing amateurs they had knocked top-flight Burnley out of the FA Cup, then drew with mighty Leeds, it would have been dismissed as so much romantic tripe if anyone had predicted that 13 years on they would have entered the Football League, rocketed to the First Division, then capped it all by lifting the game's most hallowed senior prize. In the process successive managers Dario Gradi, Dave Bassett and now Bobby Gould had assembled for peanuts a squad known popularly as 'The Crazy Gang', whose motto was along the lines of 'one for all and all for one'. Their number included centre-forward John Fashanu, tagged 'Fash the Bash' for obvious reasons; midfielder Vinnie Jones, a former hod-carrier whose unbridled aggression symbolised the club's rough-and-ready image; giant goalkeeper and skipper Dave 'Lurch' Beasant; midfielder Lawrie Sanchez, a Bachelor of Science and man of the people; winger Dennis Wise, an effervescent jack-in-the-box; and, rather incongruously, Alan Cork, a striker with a subtle aerial touch reminiscent of that soccer aristocrat Alan Gilzean. The Gang were identified with effort, enthusiasm and muscle, and rarely complimented for the ability that many of them possessed. They were based in ramshackle headquarters at Plough Lane and subsisted on miniscule support. When not being castigated as 'bully-boys' they were pigeon-holed as working-class heroes and, to be fair, they played up to this role, glorying in carrying the banner for the under-privileged everywhere.

What made Wimbledon's presence at Wembley all the more enticing was the identity of their opponents, the fabulous Liverpool side that had already lifted the League title and, after one recent performance against Nottingham Forest, had moved no less a judge than Tom Finney to remark that he had never seen a finer footballing exhibition. It was Kenny Dalglish's third season in charge, and after two terms of making the most of a golden legacy from Bob Paisley and Joe Fagan, he had put his own personal stamp on the team. This had been achieved principally by buying bounteously gifted forwards John Barnes and Peter Beardsley, and replacing marksman Ian Rush with the less lauded but equally prolific John Aldridge. The result was pure delight, a combination of all the game's most attractive qualities, and it was no surprise when Barnes was voted player of the year by both his fellow footballers and the soccer writers. It was no surprise, either, that in one poll he was trailed by team-mates Steve McMahon and Beardsley and in the other by his skipper Alan Hansen, with 96 per-cent of the vote going to Liverpool men. Dalglish wondered drily who on earth could have received the other four per-cent!

In such a heady atmosphere, Reds fans were savouring the prospect of putting down the upstarts from SW19, heading for Wembley as though for a public execution. However, the Dons *had* finished seventh in Division One - albeit 33 points adrift of Liverpool - and some of the travelling Merseysiders were unwisely

Dons' substitute Lawrie Cunningham (left) chats with John Barnes of Liverpool before the match.

cocky. They might have done well to ponder the fine form Wimbledon had displayed on the way to the final, starting with a crushing victory over Ron Atkinson's West Bromwich Albion. There followed a narrow win against Mansfield - courtesy of a Beasant penalty save that would not be his last of the competition - before three triumphs over top-flight opposition, Newcastle at St James' Park (where Vinnie Jones blotted out a young midfielder name of Paul Gascoigne), Watford at Plough Lane (coming back from a goal down with ten men after defender Brian Gayle was sent off), and Luton in the semi-final at White Hart Lane (again overturning a one-goal deficit). For their part, the Reds had progressed shakily at the expense of Stoke (after Mike Hooper's late save at the Victoria Ground had earned a replay), comfortably against Second Division Aston Villa, narrowly against Everton (thanks to a Ray Houghton header) and crushingly against Manchester City, the fourth successive tie in which they had been drawn away.

Though everything in the Anfield garden appeared to be rosy after two Aldridge goals - including a penalty - had seen off Nottingham Forest in the semi-final at Hillsborough, Liverpool's peace of mind was disturbed on two counts during the

Wimbledon defender Clive Goodyear fails to block a cross from John Barnes, but like all Liverpool's attacks on the day, this one came to nothing.

run-up to the final. First defender Gary Gillespie and midfielder Nigel Spackman clashed heads in a League game at home to Luton, both needing stitches and raising doubts about their availability for Wembley. In the event both played, in padded bandages. Then, even more disruptively, forward Craig Johnston announced that he was homesick for Australia and disillusioned with football, and soon would be off to start a new life Down Under. The Reds reacted by reminding him of his contractual obligations and he was named as a Cup Final substitute. It was to be Craig's last senior game and he duly emigrated, becoming a professional photographer.

With all the hype that had surrounded the clash between Kenny Dalglish's 'Beauties' and Bobby Gould's 'Beasts', supporters might have been forgiven for expecting the underdogs to emerge with fangs bared, ready for blood, and if subsequent claims by centre-half Andy Thorn were anything to go by, that was not a million miles from the truth. He told the press how the Dons had shouted and screamed in the tunnel: 'We looked at them and they had never heard anything like it . . . they were lost.' However, no such unseemliness was witnessed by the public, who watched the Reds begin as the brighter side only for the verve, dash and imagination that had characterised their performances all season to desert them. Whether the alleged 'psyching out' had any bearing on proceedings, it is not clear; suffice it to say that Wimbledon's desire appeared to burn the stronger.

Nevertheless, on a sweltering afternoon it was the Merseysiders who made the early running with both Houghton and Aldridge forcing Beasant to make enterprising saves at the second attempt. Aldridge, especially, had been well placed but the 'keeper somehow scooped the ball away for Jones - already booked for a foul on McMahon - to clear. Though the Dons' attack was sprightly enough to underline the necessity for alertness in the Reds' rearguard, the favourites

continued to threaten and after 34 minutes they were woefully unlucky not to take the lead. The darting Beardsley took a long pass from Gillespie and rode a foul by Thorn before chipping neatly beyond Beasant into the net. However, referee Brian Hill had blown instantly for the unfair challenge, neglecting to play the advantage rule that would have seen justice done. Later Mr Hill conceded that, with hindsight, he might have reacted differently, but that didn't save him from a barrage of criticism. It was unfortunate but sadly inevitable treatment of an able and honest referee who appeared to have made a mistake in the heat of the contest.

The incident doubled in significance just two minutes later when Steve Nicol fouled Terry Phelan on the Wimbledon left flank. Eschewing the obvious option

of going for the lanky Fashanu and Eric Young on the far side of the box, Wise glided his free-kick cunningly to the near post, where Sanchez rose unmolested to glance a looping header high into the net past Bruce Grobbelaar. The Liverpool fans, who heavily outnumbered those of the Dons', bayed for reprisal, then hurled abuse at Mr Hill as he turned down a penalty appeal after a clash between Young and Aldridge. At the other end Terry Gibson shot narrowly wide after Grobbelaar had dropped a cross, but soon the magnificent Beasant was back in action, denying Houghton and Hansen with fine saves as the half drew to a close. After the break former England winger Laurie Cunningham replaced the tired Cork, but the Reds exerted further pressure which, on the hour, seemed on the point of paying off. Aldridge dashed into the box, Clive Goodyear made what appeared to

Above: Dave Beasant's brilliant save from John Aldridge's penalty.

Back at Plough Lane, the FA Cup in the joyful custody of Alan Cork (left) and Terry Gibson.

Opposite: Spirit of the Crazy Gang - Vinnie Jones and medal.

be a fair tackle, but Mr Hill thought otherwise and pointed to the spot. With a minumum of fuss, 'Aldo' placed the ball, strode forward and struck it firmly to Beasant's left, only for Dave to dive full-length and paw it to safety. John, who had been due to be substituted anyway, sank to his knees in despair and minutes later retired to the bench in tears, to be replaced by Johnston. Thereafter, the Reds brought on Jan Molby for Spackman and did most of the attacking but the Dons were not to be denied, surviving with more ease than might have been expected to claim their prize.

Man of the match for the performance of a lifetime was the gangling Beasant, excelling himself in his 351st consecutive outing for the club. Dave, watched by his father for the first time in his career, had made history as the first man to save a penalty in an FA Cup Final and the first goalkeeper to hold aloft the trophy as captain. But perhaps the individual most responsible for clipping the Liver Bird's wings was that wiliest of coaches, Don Howe. As late as the evening before the game, he had made tactical changes - switching Cork to the left so the workaholic Wise could move to the right and play deep alongside Jones, thus taking up the space that Barnes and Beardsley adored to exploit. Also he stressed the need to deny room to the Liverpool back four, cutting off the supply of creative passes and reducing Grobbelaar to long kicks down the ground. Howe paid tribute to his charges for their single-minded adherence to his instructions and they honoured him for his nous, exemplified by his presence of mind in ordering iced towels to cool them down at the interval. The next day, some 25,000 people turned out to welcome home a team that attracted average gates of 6,500. It was pointed out that their Plough Lane HQ was a 'wooden hut' not safe to house the famous trophy. And many who feared a plague of Wombles clones predicted doom for English football. But the snipers could whine as much as they liked, it didn't matter to Wimbledon. They had cocked the ultimate snook at the soccer elite; they had won the FA Cup. Power to the people . . .

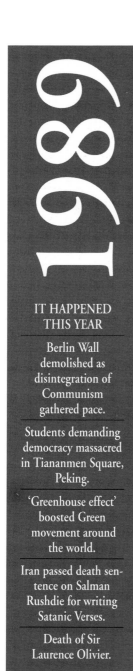

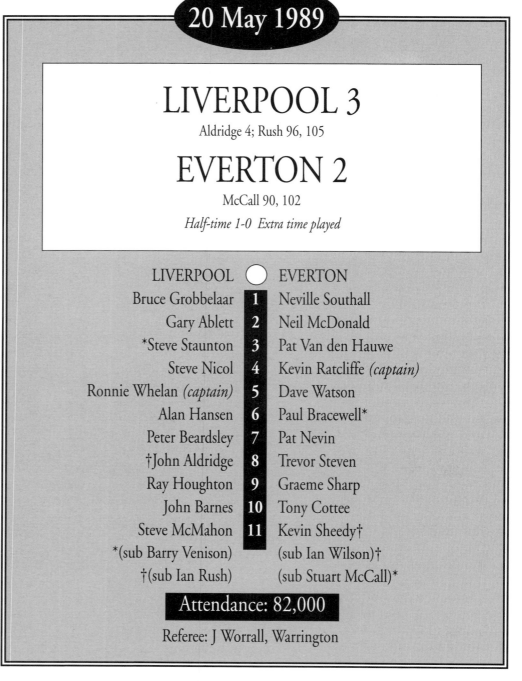

IT HAPPENED
THIS YEAR

Berlin Wall
demolished as
disintegration of
Communism
gathered pace.

Students demanding
democracy massacred
in Tiananmen Square,
Peking.

'Greenhouse effect'
boosted Green
movement around
the world.

Iran passed death sen-
tence on Salman
Rushdie for writing
Satanic Verses.

Death of Sir
Laurence Olivier.

20 May 1989

LIVERPOOL 3

Aldridge 4; Rush 96, 105

EVERTON 2

McCall 90, 102

Half-time 1-0 Extra time played

LIVERPOOL	⚪	EVERTON
Bruce Grobbelaar	**1**	Neville Southall
Gary Ablett	**2**	Neil McDonald
*Steve Staunton	**3**	Pat Van den Hauwe
Steve Nicol	**4**	Kevin Ratcliffe *(captain)*
Ronnie Whelan *(captain)*	**5**	Dave Watson
Alan Hansen	**6**	Paul Bracewell*
Peter Beardsley	**7**	Pat Nevin
†John Aldridge	**8**	Trevor Steven
Ray Houghton	**9**	Graeme Sharp
John Barnes	**10**	Tony Cottee
Steve McMahon	**11**	Kevin Sheedy†
*(sub Barry Venison)		(sub Ian Wilson)†
†(sub Ian Rush)		(sub Stuart McCall)*

Attendance: 82,000

Referee: J Worrall, Warrington

The emotion was overwhelming, the game was dramatic and the arguments were complex; but whatever the viewpoint about pressing on with the FA Cup Final in the wake of the Hillsborough disaster, there is no doubt that it was a unique and unforgettable occasion, by turns uplifting and moving, bizarre and - it must be said - with aspects that were downright distasteful. Before the game between Liverpool and Everton, the main question was not 'Who will win?' It was 'Should it be played at all?' Every conventional footballing consideration had been rendered irrelevant by the tragic events which unfolded a few minutes after the start of Liverpool's semi-final against Nottingham Forest in Sheffield. Ninety-five people died in an overcrowded section of the Leppings Lane end amid hellish scenes that will remain forever vivid in the minds of eye-witnesses. One of them was photographer Steve Hale, a Merseysider who had lived through the trauma of Heysel four years earlier. This is not the place for a minute-by-minute exposition of what took place on that black afternoon, but a sense of the sheer horror is important to place subsequent developments in context. Steve recalls: 'Peter

Above: Kenny Dalglish, whose humanity and dignity in the wake of the Hillsborough disaster was an inspiration to many. What personal toll the resulting stress might have exacted, none can say.

Left: Some of the floral tributes which engulfed Anfield.

Beardsley had just hit the bar and as the shouts of excitement died away, they were replaced by something different, a sound I had heard before only at Heysel - the sound people make when they are being crushed to death. Confusion reigned. Behind the railings I saw the dead and the dying. The shouting and screaming was unbearable . . .'

In the days that followed, Merseyside was gripped by a gargantuan outpouring of grief which, it is no exaggeration to say, grew into an all-encompassing religious experience. Anfield itself was turned into an altar of remembrance, the pitch and goalposts submerged in a sea of flowers, the Kop terrace draped in red-and-white scarves and mementoes. A week on from Hillsborough a human chain stretched around Goodison Park, across Stanley Park and into Anfield, where a service took place. Through it all manager Kenny Dalglish and his players displayed colossal dignity and humanity, giving unstintingly of themselves in an effort to comfort the bereaved. Dalglish, in particular, shouldered a huge burden, seemingly never away from the ground, always on hand to offer support. No man could have done more. All this time, of course, Liverpool were not playing football and no resumption date had been announced. Meanwhile a great debate built up over whether or not the Reds should withdraw from the FA Cup. Many maintained that it would be indecent to continue with the campaign. Their theory went that to persist with a comparative triviality in the current catastrophic circumstances was to lose sight of life's true values. Others contended that the most fitting memorial to the dead would be for Liverpool to win the Cup, adding that it would also afford succour to the grieving relatives. Crucially, the majority of the bereaved families left the players in no doubt that they wanted the Reds to carry on. The FA had set a new semi-final date of May 7 at Old Trafford, but Liverpool commendably refused to be hurried and it was not until two weeks after the disaster - on the day they returned to action in a friendly against Celtic - that they put an end to speculation by announcing that they *would* meet Forest.

Despite Hillsborough, Brian Clough's men were determined - and quite rightly - to reach their club's first FA Cup Final for 30 years, but as well as a very fine Liverpool side they had to overcome a huge groundswell of popular emotion. Quite simply, it was never on and it was somehow appropriate that two of the goals in the Reds' 3-1 victory were scored by John Aldridge. A Scouser himself, he had been moved as profoundly as anyone by recent events and had read the lesson at the first funeral. In an agony of despair, he had even pondered giving up the game, but now had come to terms with the future and his stirring comeback was a symbolic tonic for fans and team-mates alike.

Thereafter, though nothing would be quite the same again, footballing considerations began to re-emerge. For a start, Liverpool's opponents in the final were to be none other than Everton, opening the way for one of the most affecting of all Wembley occasions. Then there was the little matter of tilting for their second League and FA Cup double in four seasons. Dalglish's team were still in with a great chance of winning their title race with Arsenal, who had to visit Anfield for a

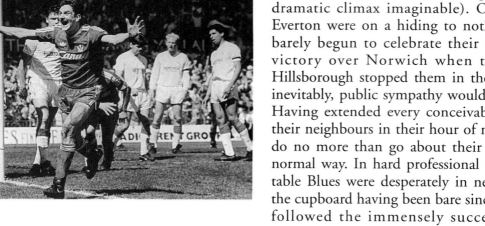

Scouser John Aldridge scores in Liverpool's semi-final victory over Nottingham Forest. So upset was John by Hillsborough that he considered retirement.

last-game showdown. (In the event, Liverpool were to miss out when the Gunners snatched the Championship with a late, late goal in the most dramatic climax imaginable). Of course, poor Everton were on a hiding to nothing. They had barely begun to celebrate their own semi-final victory over Norwich when the news from Hillsborough stopped them in their tracks. Now, inevitably, public sympathy would be all one way. Having extended every conceivable assistance to their neighbours in their hour of need, they could do no more than go about their business in the normal way. In hard professional terms, the mid-table Blues were desperately in need of a trophy, the cupboard having been bare since Colin Harvey followed the immensely successful Howard Kendall into the manager's seat two years earlier. Their progress to the final had been quiet rather than spectacular. They had needed a replay before disposing narrowly of West Bromwich Albion, were distinctly fortunate to get a second chance against Second Division Plymouth, then saw off Barnsley, holders Wimbledon and Norwich with consecutive 1-0 victories. By contrast, in all but one tie Liverpool had something to spare, starting with away wins at Carlisle and Millwall. Then came their closest call, conquering Second Division Hull 3-2 at Boothferry Park, before Brentford and Nottingham Forest were beaten with comparative ease.

Of course, the final represented far more than the culmination of a mere Cup campaign, taking on in the minds of many the stature of a crusade to honour the dead. With Everton providing the opposition, there was also an atmosphere of togetherness in the face of tragedy, a feeling heightened by the pre-match community singing. Led by Liverpool's own Gerry Marsden, Reds and Blues - and, surely, every soul in the stadium - joined together for a heart-rendingly touching rendition of You'll Never Walk Alone, followed by Abide With Me. Sadly the national anthem was marred by fans who drowned it out with their own song, an act interpreted widely as a snub to the Royal Family for not sending a 'major' member to the Hillsborough memorial service. With the Duke and Duchess of Kent, who *had* attended the service, at Wembley that day, the protest was both poor-spirited and inappropriate.

On the hottest afternoon of the year, the game began at frantic pace and, untypically of what was to follow, the first notable incident occurred at the Liverpool end when Steve McMahon was forced to clear off his line from a misplaced clearance by Steve Nicol. But before long Nicol was justifying his newly-acquired Footballer of the Year tag with a penetrating through-pass that freed McMahon on the right. The blond former Evertonian delivered a low cross into the path of John Aldridge, who sprinted beyond a flat-footed Blues defence before sweeping a sweet first-time shot into the top left-hand corner of Neville Southall's net. It was a superb strike which offered consolation for Aldo's missed penalty a year earlier and capped a term in which he had risen so brilliantly to the challenge of Ian Rush's return from Italy that the Welshman was confined to a seat on the Wembley bench. Of course, Ian would make his own decisive contribution before the afternoon was over.

After 16 minutes Pat Nevin climaxed a rare Everton assault with a shot that

*An emotional Gerry Marsden leads the singing of 'You'll Never Walk Alone'.
Below: John Barnes surges between Kevin Ratcliffe (left) and Dave Watson as Liverpool gain an early ascendancy.*

Inset above: Stuart McCall (right), who brought a new sense of urgency to Everton's approach, squeezes home his first equaliser in the dying moments of normal time.

went narrowly wide but there was no disguising the truth of Liverpool's almost total dominance. It was most marked in midfield, where Ray Houghton, Ronnie Whelan and McMahon did as they liked while Paul Bracewell, Kevin Sheedy and, to a lesser extent, Trevor Steven seemed powerless to intervene. Accordingly, chances came the Reds' way regularly, but a combination of inspired goalkeeping by Southall and inaccurate finishing kept the score at 1-0. When an on-song John Barnes capped a surging run past three defenders with a shot that just missed the target after 56 minutes, it seemed that the floodgates must not be long in opening, but then the balance was significantly redressed by an Everton substitution. Off went the ineffective Bracewell and on came flame-haired Stuart McCall, whose aggressive enterprise gave the Blues renewed impetus. In response to this partial

interruption in the flow of one-way traffic, Dalglish replaced the drained Aldridge after 77 minutes, bringing on an Ian Rush burning to prove he was still a potent force, while Harvey exchanged Sheedy for Ian Wilson. Now the Toffeemen forced the pace, but the game seemed beyond them when, inside the last minute of normal time, Dave Watson hit a cross-cum-shot from the right, Bruce Grobbelaar parried and the ball fell to McCall, who slid it in at the far post.

At this point and after all they had been through, a less resilient side than Liverpool might have caved in. However, they began extra time purposefully and were not long in regaining the ascendancy. Nicol bore down from the left, finding Rush inside the box with his back to goal and closely marked by Ratcliffe; the lean opportunist feinted one way, swivelled the other and shot high past Southall.

Above: Some substitute! Ian Rush, his dummy having duped Kevin Ratcliffe (number four), lashes the ball past Neville Southall to put Liverpool 2-1 up. The goal broke Dixie Dean's scoring record in Merseyside derbies.

Now, surely, it was all over, but no! Six minutes later a Ratcliffe free-kick was headed out by Alan Hansen to McCall who, cool as you like, stunned the ball on his chest before hitting a looping 20-yard volley just inside Grobbelaar's left-hand post. Thus did the Scot become the only substitute to score twice in an FA Cup Final, a distinction he held for all of three minutes. Liverpool swarmed forward for the umpteenth time, Barnes found space on the left and dispatched a perfectly angled cross to the head of Rush, who had wormed free of Ratcliffe once more. He stooped to direct it with almost uncanny precision past Southall for what, this time, really was the winner. The scoreline did not reflect the

Main picture: Ian Rush, never more lethal than when he has a point to prove, turns away in exultation after laying waste the Blues' defence.

Inset left: Stuart McCall, who held a Wembley record for just three minutes.

Below: Everton just could not cope with Ian Rush. Here he guides a subtle header into the Blues' net for the winner. Having taken the Cup, Liverpool were favourites to win the double, but six days later they lost the title when Arsenal grabbed a late goal at Anfield.

John Barnes, supplier of the tantalising cross from which Ian Rush glanced home the decisive goal, is greeted by the scorer with outstretched arms.

superiority that Liverpool had exerted throughout most of a match in which they had played beautifully. But that didn't matter. What did matter was the manner in which an oafish minority of supporters tarnished the moment for players and the vast majority of fans alike. In recognition that Hillsborough made this day a special case, the authorities had removed the perimeter fencing, but that gesture of trust had been boorishly betrayed. In the last 40 minutes of action there had been no less than six pitch invasions. All but one of them - in which Trevor Steven had been threatened - were good-humoured, but in the light of Sheffield such behaviour was crassly irresponsible. Then, as the game ended, spectators poured on to the arena making it impossible for the players to perform the lap of honour that - in this of all years - would have meant so much. There was no violence but the selfishness and disrespect were an affront; what should have been a supremely emotional finale disintegrated into sorry confusion that sent entirely the wrong message, both to the British Government and European football chiefs looking for evidence that we were fit to return to the fold after Heysel. Wembley chairman Brian Wolfson told the press the decision to remove the fences (which went back up immediately) had been vindicated, but added: 'We got away with it by the skin of our teeth'. If the calamity of Hillsborough could not teach the idiots a lesson, then what could?

Opposite: An absence of taste. Left to right, Barry Venison, Steve McMahon and Ronnie Whelan lament the behaviour of the boorish minority who prevented the lap of honour.

**IT HAPPENED
THIS YEAR**

Iraq invaded Kuwait,
the prelude to the
Gulf War.

Nelson Mandela
released from prison
in South Africa after
28 years.

Margaret Thatcher
ousted as Prime
Minister, replaced by
John Major.

Mass rally in London
against poll tax
turned into
full-scale riot.

Beef sales
plummeted over mad
cow disease scare.

12 May 1990

MANCHESTER UNITED 3

Robson 35; Hughes 62, 113

CRYSTAL PALACE 3

O'Reilly 18; Wright 72, 92

Half-time 1-1 Extra time played

MANCHESTER UNITED		CRYSTAL PALACE
Jim Leighton	**1**	Nigel Martyn
Paul Ince	**2**	John Pemberton
*Lee Martin	**3**	Richard Shaw
Steve Bruce	**4**	Andy Gray*
Mike Phelan	**5**	Gary O'Reilly
† Gary Pallister	**6**	Andy Thorn
Bryan Robson *(captain)*	**7**	Phil Barber †
Neil Webb	**8**	Geoff Thomas *(captain)*
Brian McClair	**9**	Mark Bright
Mark Hughes	**10**	John Salako
Danny Wallace	**11**	Alan Pardew
*(sub Clayton Blackmore)		(sub David Madden)*
†(sub Mark Robins)		(sub Ian Wright)†

Attendance: 80,000

Referee: A Gunn, Sussex

Old Trafford was in a slough of despond. As the 1990s dawned, the awful truth was that Bobby Charlton's 'theatre of dreams' had become a place of nightmares for an audience that was growing increasingly restive. Despite boasting a talent-laden team, Manchester United were alarmingly close to the foot of the First Division and, worse still, their football was drab. In such circumstances, it is traditional to demand the manager's head on a plate and there was no shortage of fans ready to sharpen the axe for Alex Ferguson. They argued that Ron Atkinson had been sacked after winning two FA Cups *and* producing an attractive side; if, after three years and £13 million in transfer fees, Alex could not equal that, much less improve on it, then he should go. The tabloids took up the chant of 'Fergie Out' and popular wisdom had it that if United suffered a third-round FA Cup exit at Nottingham Forest, then the strong-willed Scot would be seeking employment elsewhere. Three years and four trophies later, chairman Martin Edwards declared the manager's job had never been in danger; he had not said so at the time as it would have seemed like the traditional vote of 'confidence' that precedes the dagger between the shoulder-blades. If that is the case - and there is no reason to doubt Edwards' word - Ferguson was lucky to have such an enlightened boss, and the oft-vilified chairman deserves huge credit for standing by his man. Neverthless, had Brian Clough's side triumphed that Sunday afternoon at the City Ground, it is hard to see how United's board could have resisted what must have been overwhelming public pressure for a change. In the event, Mark Hughes bent an exquisite pass into the path of Mark Robins, the young striker executed a deft header and, though it was not immediately obvious, a long-term renaissance was under way.

A day earlier at Selhurst Park, an 89th minute penalty by Andy Gray was enough to end the Wembley dreams of Portsmouth for another year, while setting Crystal Palace on the trail towards their first FA Cup Final. Like United, the Eagles were struggling in the First Division, though of course they were not burdened with such high expectations. However, even the most understanding fan

Alex Ferguson, for whom the 1990 FA Cup marked a turning point. Before that, though his chairman denied it, Fergie's job must have been on the line; afterwards United lifted a succession of trophies and the Scot looked set for a lengthy reign at Old Trafford.

must have baulked in September when Liverpool had drubbed them by *nine* clear goals. Manager Steve Coppell, a former Old Trafford star, reacted positively, making Nigel Martyn of Bristol Rovers Britain's first £1 million 'keeper and acquiring combative defender Andy Thorn from Newcastle, two signings which steadied the boat. Palace's subsequent form proved good enough to preserve their top-flight status - they finished in 15th place, behind United on goal difference - while the Cup offered welcome diversion. Huddersfield, Rochdale and Cambridge, all from the lower divisions, were overcome on the way to a semi-final clash with . . . Liverpool. The scars left by that autumn humiliation were far from healed yet the hope of revenge seemed hardly realistic; in their hearts, most Selhurst supporters surely would have settled for respectability. Their apprehension was heightened when Coppell announced a debilitating injury list but, on a sunny spring Sunday lunchtime at Villa Park, the sweet uncertainty of football was manifested in all its glory. By using dead-ball expertise to exploit the Merseysiders' one glaring flaw - aerial weakness at the back - the Eagles came from behind to win a seven-goal thriller. The shock sparked bitter recriminations in the Reds' dressing room and in truth, although the Liverpool went on to win the title, from that day until the time of writing they were never to be quite the same force. Meanwhile Manchester United were inching along the tortuous route to recovery via close Cup calls on a Hereford mudheap, against Newcastle in a gripping encounter on Tyneside and in a taut contest with Second Division pacemakers Sheffield United at Bramall Lane. That set up a semi-final confrontation with their neighbours, Joe Royle's Oldham Athletic, who despite their ultimate failure to reach the top flight that term were arguably the most watchable side in the League. Having been away in every round, United fans were grateful that the venue was Maine Road, which took on a carnival atmosphere when news of Liverpool's demise came through (the semis were played one after the other to facilitate blanket TV coverage). The attitude was that with the old enemy out of contention, who could stop their resurgent team - now not such an endangered First Division species after two recent wins - from lifting the Cup? However, the Latics were swift to prick the Reds' balloon, taking an early lead, playing superbly and grabbing a deserved equaliser to cap a pulsating 3-3 draw. Oldham maintained the tempo in the

replay, too, performing even more stirringly, and were unlucky to lose 2-1. United's winner owed nothing to fortune though, young Mark Robins justifying Alex Ferguson's belief that he was the best finisher at the club with a perfect, clinical placement deep in extra time.

That gave the Mancunians the chance to equal the record of seven FA Cup victories - held by Aston Villa and Spurs - in their 11th final; Wembley rookies Crystal Palace would try to frustrate them as they did Liverpool. To that end they put in extra set-piece practice, which included delaying their kicks to create confusion and doubt in the opposition ranks. The two teams were destined to meet twice, the first game a seesawing, edge-of-the-seat affair in which dashing attackers frequently embarrassed a pair of creaky defences, the second a sour, ill-tempered confrontation decided by a single goal.

The first all-seated FA Cup Final crowd - which had paid more than £2 million for the privilege - had seen little to suggest the excitement that was to follow when Palace drew first blood in inevitable manner. Gray was fouled by Danny Wallace on the right, Phil Barber bent his free-kick expertly to the edge of the six-yard box and United were undone. Two giant Garys, the Eagles' O'Reilly and Pallister of the Reds, threw their heads at the ball, the Eagle got the important touch and the ball looped towards the net. 'Keeper Jim Leighton (whose trauma had scarcely begun) was caught in no-man's land, Steve Bruce's lunge was to no avail and the underdogs were in front. Any lingering hint of complacency among the Red Army of supporters was removed almost instantly when Geoff Thomas found himself unmarked in front of goal, only to hit a tame shot into Leighton's arms. United picked up and pushed forward, but it was not until ten minutes before the break that they gained parity. Brian McClair and Wallace exchanged passes on the right, the Scot crossed invitingly and Bryan Robson, legs planted like stalwart oaks, leaned forward to head in from seven yards, the ball taking a slight but crucial deflection off John Pemberton. Three minutes later, McClair should have given his side the lead, but sent a free header wide from four yards after good work by Mike Phelan.

Below: A study in battle-hardened resolve, Bryan Robson takes a breather.

Thereafter the game remained evenly balanced until just after the hour, when the Reds edged in front, the ball rebounding conveniently from a penalty-box skirmish to Mark Hughes, who buried an emphatic left-foot cross-shot just inside the far post from eight yards. Now United might have seized the moment, but Thorn cleared off the line from McClair and Robson sliced wide when well placed, misses that were to prove costly. Three minutes after coming on as substitute, the exuberant Ian Wright - a non-starter as his recuperation from injury was deemed incomplete - received the ball on the left and rode a tackle from Phelan before cutting inside Pallister and threading a pinpoint shot into Leighton's far corner from 12 yards. There followed chances at either end, the

Opposite top: United 'keeper Jim Leighton is stranded hopelessly as Gary O'Reilly's header sails over his head for Palace's first goal.

Opposite below: In typically ferocious style, Mark Hughes slams United into a 2-1 lead with Gary O'Reilly powerless to intevene.

Jim Leighton's nightmare continues. The United 'keeper is floundering as Ian Wright outstretches Steve Bruce to volley the Eagles into a 3-2 lead early in extra time.

Right: Mark Hughes (white-shirted, right) has just turned the ball past Nigel Martyn and the Palace 'keeper can only watch in frustration as it progresses inexorably towards the corner of his net to level the contest at 3-3. United's Brian McClair and Richard Shaw of Palace look on with contrasting emotions.

nearest to a goal being Robson's header against a post, but 2-2 after 90 minutes was a true reflection of play. Extra time began dramatically. A long pass from Thomas found John Salako to his left near the corner flag, he beat Phelan and dispatched a deep centre. The ball sailed over the head of the ill-positioned Leighton for Wright to elude Bruce and volley home from close range. The celebrations, understandably unrestrained, were interrupted by referee Alan Gunn, mindful of the possible effects on crowd control. Now the favourites were up against it. After Gray had missed a chance to clinch it for Palace, United attacked relentlessly, but Martyn tipped over a 25-yarder from Paul Ince, a subtle Phelan chip landed on top of the net and time was running out. Indeed, only seven minutes remained when Wallace passed cleverly between two defenders to meet Hughes' diagonal run and the Welshman turned the ball adroitly past the advancing Martyn for the equaliser. Even then, either side might have stolen it, Reds' substitute Clayton Blackmore going close from 25 yards, Robson heading marginally over and Palace winning two late corners. But, as they drew breath at the end of a stirring contest, few fans would have argued at the outcome.

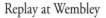
Replay at Wembley

MANCHESTER UNITED 1
Martin 59

CRYSTAL PALACE 0

Half-time 0-0

MANCHESTER UNITED	○	CRYSTAL PALACE
Les Sealey	1	Nigel Martyn
Paul Ince	2	John Pemberton
Lee Martin	3	Richard Shaw
Steve Bruce	4	Andy Gray
Mike Phelan	5	Gary O'Reilly
Gary Pallister	6	Andy Thorn
Bryan Robson *(captain)*	7	Phil Barber †
Neil Webb	8	Geoff Thomas *(captain)*
Brian McClair	9	Mark Bright
Mark Hughes	10	John Salako*
Danny Wallace	11	Alan Pardew
		(sub David Madden)*
		(sub Ian Wright)†

Attendance: 80,000

Referee: A Gunn, Sussex

The ebullient Les Sealey, called up to replace Jim Leighton between United's posts for the replay, gave a brave and competent display. Later he offered the unhappy Scot his winner's medal, but Jim declined with thanks.

Top: Steve Coppell applauds the Palace fans at the end of a replay in which his team did themselves no favours with their muscular methods.

Come replay night, Alex Ferguson dropped a bombshell. Jim Leighton, whose uncertainty on Saturday had been the culmination of a run of poor form, was dropped in favour of Les Sealey, on loan from Luton and with only two senior games behind him all term. For Ferguson, it was an agonising decision, having known Leighton for 15 years (with Aberdeen and Scotland before United), and also it was a gamble; for Jim himself it was a savage reverse, one from which his career was never to fully recover; and for the extrovert Sealey, expecting a free transfer from Kenilworth Road at season's end, it was a once-in-a-lifetime bonus. From the outset of the rematch, Palace adopted a physical approach that rendered good football hard to play, but if they were out to bully United into submission, their plans went badly awry. Bryan Robson and company met might with might, the outcome being a spoiling game and a dismal spectacle. Palace set the tone in the second minute when Mark Bright clattered Sealey and was rightly booked.

Whatever Les's faults, timidity was not one of them, and he responded with a brave, competent display. His finest moment came in the 22nd minute when he blocked with his legs a thunderous low free-kick from Gray. In the subsequent confusion United were lucky not to concede a penalty, McClair's foul clearly *inside* the box, the ensuing free-kick awarded *outside*. Thereafter the game dragged on in unimaginative fashion until the 59th minute when United launched a lovely, sweeping attack that began with Ince in the left-back position, moving via McClair and Wallace to Webb in the inside-right channel. Calm as ever, the England midfielder spotted young full-back Lee Martin surging towards the left side of the Palace box, and delivered an inch-perfect crossfield pass. Without breaking stride, the unlikely hero chested it down, then thumped it gleefully under the crossbar in one smooth blur of action.

Sadly, the goal brought precious little improvement to an appalling match. Each side managed one more noteworthy attack, Gray squeezing the ball against a post in a goalmouth melee and Robson heading against the bar from a Webb free-kick. So the Red Devils took the trophy they deserved on the night, having contributed what little decent football there had been, and Eagles fans were left to wonder why their men had not continued in Saturday's exciting vein. 'Captain Marvel' became the first skipper to receive the Cup three times, and though this contest offered precious little evidence of it, United were on the verge of something big. They went on to win the European Cup Winners' Cup, League Cup and FA Premier League in consecutive seasons and begged the burning question: have we seen the best of a very good team, or the early stirrings of a great one?

Above: United's man of the moment, Lee Martin, with the trophy his goal (left) had secured. Alex Ferguson dubbed the young left-back his player of the season and a bright future beckoned. But injuries caused loss of impetus the following term and the quiet local boy could not regain a regular place.

IT HAPPENED
THIS YEAR

Gulf War ended with
Allied victory but
Saddam Hussein still
in power.

Slovenia and Croatia
declared
independence,
Yugoslavia broke up.

IRA launched mortar
attack on 10
Downing Street.

Publisher Robert
Maxwell died
mysteriously at sea.

Yeltsin in, Gorbachev
out, as political
change swept Russia.

18 May 1991

TOTTENHAM HOTSPUR 2

Stewart 54; Walker (og) 94

NOTTINGHAM FOREST 1

Pearce 15

Half-time 0-1 Extra time played

TOTTENHAM HOTSPUR	○	NOTTINGHAM FOREST
Erik Thorstvedt	1	Mark Crossley
Justin Edinburgh	2	Gary Charles
Pat Van den Hauwe	3	Stuart Pearce *(captain)*
Steve Sedgley	4	Des Walker
David Howells	5	Steve Chettle
Gary Mabbutt *(captain)*	6	Roy Keane
Paul Stewart	7	Gary Crosby
† Paul Gascoigne	8	Garry Parker
*Vinny Samways	9	Nigel Clough
Gary Lineker	10	Lee Glover†
Paul Allen	11	Ian Woan *
*(sub Paul Walsh)		(sub Steve Hodge)*
†(sub Nayim)		(sub Brian Laws)†

Attendance: 80,000

Referee: R Milford, Bristol

Not since 1953 had so much been expected of one man in an FA Cup Final. On that most magical of Wembley occasions 38 years earlier, Stanley Matthews had responded in heroic fashion, inspiring Blackpool's late and melodramatic victory. But there was to be no such storybook ending for Paul Gascoigne. Though his team, Tottenham Hotspur, beat Nottingham Forest to lift the trophy, Gazza's most meaningful contributions on the day were a brace of frenzied fouls before he left, disgraced in the eyes of many, on a stretcher. To be fair, the two stars were very much men who epitomised their own wildly contrasting eras, and there were similar gulfs in experience and temperament. Stan cut a mature, thoughtful figure, a genius dedicated to his art, universally respected, even loved. For him in final week there were no real distractions beyond a niggly knee; yes, there was intense public interest in his performance, but he was granted an acceptable degree of privacy and could devote himself principally to footballing considerations. Paul, on the other hand, was a brash, naive young man of simple tastes, condemned by the times he lived in to a goldfish-bowl existence that he could not quite handle.

A natural clown who could be endearing or gross or petulant as the mood took him, he was prone to the outrageous and a prime target for controversy. On Stan's off-days - and he had them like anyone else - he might expect the degree of understanding due to any craftsman who was doing his level best. Whenever Gazza's standard dipped, he was crucified. His fans were crazy about him but there were too many others who gloried in finding fault; the build-'em-up-knock-'em-down brigade had never been more rampant. What these two great players shared, of course, was truly wondrous talent. Gazza had displayed his with a series of fabulous performances throughout Spurs' Cup run; to expect him to top the lot at Wembley was unreasonable in the extreme but nothing less, it seemed, would suffice. As if one larger-than-life character was not enough for any football match, the 1991 final boasted two - in charge of Nottingham Forest was a certain Brian Clough. There is no doubt that as the Forest manager led his team out at Wembley, he was carrying with him the best wishes of most neutral fans. Clough was the domestic game's Great Eccentric, lauded widely as a courageous maverick and the unbending champion of a classical style which involved passing the ball along the ground. A familiar face even to those with no interest in sport, he was the people's perennial choice for the England job but was destined never to get it. Though he could charm the birds off the trees in nearby Sherwood Forest, Brian was also egotistical, authoritarian and downright rude at times, inspiring awe and fear as well as loyalty among his players. During his career, he had presided over two European Cup triumphs, two League titles and three League Cups, making him by far the most successful Englishman currently plying his management wares. Yet after 38 years as player and boss he had failed to win the FA Cup, and this was his best chance to date.

Above: On the edge. Court jester and genius Paul Gascoigne, perhaps too hyped-up for his own good, exhorts the Spurs fans to greater pre-match vocal effort.

Left: On the threshold of a dream. Terry Venables, who had more than football on his mind.

To add a further dramatic dimension to proceedings, the final was to be played against the soap-like backdrop of the Tottenham takeover saga. Here the intriguing figure was Spurs boss Terry Venables, who was dividing his time between preparing the team for Wembley and getting together a consortium to buy out the owners. It was all part of his dream to run a club from top to bottom - 'Tel' was nothing if not ambitious. Rumours and counter-rumours

circulated daily but it was pretty clear that the prime asset, Paul Gascoigne, would have to be sold to help keep Tottenham in business and he was expected to join the Roman club, Lazio, for £8.5 million that summer. It was a traumatic situation for the long-suffering White Hart Lane faithful, whose nerves were shredded further by stories that their other England star, Gary Lineker, was being hawked around foreign clubs in a bid to raise money and that Paul Stewart, a revelation since his switch from centre-forward to midfield, might also be up for grabs. To their credit, some of the fans managed to dredge some black humour from their plight, singing 'We're so broke it's unbelievable' as they marched towards the Twin Towers.

Of the finalists, Tottenham had enjoyed by far the more convincing Cup campaign. They began in a gale at Fourth Division Blackpool, where Stewart scored the only goal of a scrappy game against his old club. Thereafter it had been Gazza, Gazza, all the way. Though handicapped by a groin injury that needed an operation between quarter- and semi-final, Paul produced scintillating contributions to see off - as near to single-handedly as any footballer could contrive - Oxford in the fourth round (he scored two goals), Portsmouth in the fifth (two more) and Notts County in the sixth (merely the winner!). But in the last-four meeting with Arsenal, which took place at Wembley to accommodate extra fans and to avoid travel problems, there was something special in store, even by the hyperactive Geordie's amazing standards. Just five minutes into the contest, Gazza hit a 30-yard free-kick high into the net with prodigious power, and little heed should be paid to churlish observers who reckoned David Seaman was at fault. Wembley had witnessed few such majestic strikes, and the Gunners' 'keeper

did well to get a finger to Paul's projectile. Five minutes later, the Great Man played a leading part in a second goal, and continued to torment his markers until concern for his groin forced him to withdraw after an hour. As victory was clinched, the hitherto beleaguered Spurs support chanted 'Where's your Double gone?' at their Arsenal counterparts, whose confidence that their team would win the League was soon to be vindicated.

There had been no such heady moments on the Forest path to the final, which had been long and hard, featuring nine games to Tottenham's five. It had taken three attempts to see off Crystal Palace, then Clough's men had to come back from two down to force a replay against Newcastle, with the boss's son, Nigel, supplying the equaliser. Next, at Southampton, only a late goal from Steve Hodge, who had played for Spurs in the 1987 FA Cup Final, kept Forest alive. Come the quarter-final at Norwich (the Trentsiders were drawn away for the fourth successive time) a new hero emerged in the form of 19-year-old midfielder Roy Keane, a recent £25,000 bargain from the Irish club Cobh Ramblers, who netted the only goal. Semi-final opponents West Ham were outraged at the sending off of centre-half Tony Gale for a professional foul at Villa Park, an incident that proved to be the turning point of the match. When Gale went the scoreline read 0-0; in the end the Hammers were tanned 4-0. During the run-up to Wembley, Forest showed the more impressive form, beating Liverpool (to end their title hopes) and Leeds, while Spurs lost at Anfield. Meanwhile the tabloids concentrated on Gazza from every conceivable angle, reported the latest lurid details of Tottenham's financial travail, not forgetting to point out that there was a 'one' at the end of the year so the North Londoners were sure to win.

If the big day itself was grey, the action most certainly wasn't, though the early drama was of the inglorious kind. The game was barely a minute old when Gazza, already the recipient of a crunching challenge from Stuart Pearce, planted his boot

Left: The Great Eccentric. Nottingham Forest boss Brian Clough, who referred to himself as 'Old Big 'Ead', walks out alongside Spurs' Terry Venables, hoping for a first FA Cup Final success after 38 years of trying. Following their managers are the respective captains, Forest's Stuart Pearce and Gary Mabbutt of Tottenham.

Left: The Young Man. Nigel Clough, the subtle, richly-talented fulcrum of the Forest attack, who did not enjoy one of his more effective days at Wembley.

Above: Stuart Pearce draws back that lethal left foot and the ball is on its way through Spurs' defensive wall for the opening goal.

Right: Writhing in self-inflicted agony, Paul Gascoigne receives treatment to the knee injury that is to put him out of football for a year and jeopardise his multi-million pound move to Italy.

in the solar-plexus of Garry Parker. Lucky to get away without a booking, Paul had begun to pick up the pace of the game when, after 15 minutes, he committed his second and most catastrophic bloomer, perpetrating a wild tackle on Gary Charles. This time it was amply clear that he was in more trouble than his victim as he hobbled off to help defend against the free-kick he had so needlessly conceded on the edge of the 'D'. If there was anyone in the land as fearsome from this position as Gazza himself it was the powerhouse Pearce, and so it proved. Up he stepped, the ball was cracked brutally into the net and referee Roger Milford, perhaps mesmerised by the sheer force of the strike, failed to notice that the ball passed through a gap in the wall opened by Lee Glover's nudge on Gary Mabbutt. The Trentsiders celebrated but soon all eyes were back on Gascoigne, who was in severe pain with what turned out to be appalling damage to his knee. On came a stretcher, off went the Likely Lad, and many believed he took Tottenham's hopes of victory with him.

Ironically, with Nayim brought on to patrol the left side of midfield, Spurs looked a brighter side and after 25 minutes they deserved to equalise when Paul Allen set up Lineker, who slipped the ball past Mark Crossley only to be judged offside, a decision with which neither the North Londoners' fans nor the TV cameras agreed. Nothing daunted, Tottenham continued to show enterprise and Allen had failed to make the most of a header on goal when Lineker broke

through again and rounded Crossley, only to be brought to earth by the 'keeper's hand. Though Milford saw no professional foul, he did give a penalty, only for Crossley to guess Lineker's intentions from the spot and make a fine save. At this stage, Forest might have been expected to assume control, but with creator-in-chief Nigel Clough well martialled by the underrated David Howells and every Spur working overtime to make up for the absence of Gascoigne - not least Vinny Samways, who had a splendid match - it never happened. Thus when the equaliser arrived after 54 minutes, it came as no surprise. Nayim found Allen, who moved purposefully through the inside-right channel before releasing the ball with perfect timing to Stewart on his right. The burly forager, growing in influence as the game went on, hit a sweet, low cross-shot from 12 yards that bypassed Crossley to enter the net just inside the far post. Thereafter Forest improved slightly when

Below: Forest 'keeper Mark Crossley demonstrates his agility, but has no hope of reaching Paul Stewart's crisp shot and Spurs are level.

Provider Paul Allen (left) congratulates scorer Paul Stewart, whose goal capped a splendid personal display. Since moving from centre-forward to midfield, Stewart had improved immeasurably and soon would earn an England call-up which, before his switch, would have been deemed out of the question.

Right: Despair for Des Walker as the England defender (number four) heads the ball into his own net to settle the match.

Hodge replaced the inexperienced Ian Woan while Paul Walsh gave Spurs, still looking the better bet, a little extra impetus after coming on for the tiring Samways.

However, there were no more goals in normal time, and as the teams drew up in separate huddles to lay their plans for the extra period, it was noticeable that Brian Clough - ever his own man - remained on the bench, leaving it to his assistants to motivate his players. Three minutes after the re-start, Forest escaped when Walsh sent a looping header against the bar, but the reprieve lasted only some 60 seconds. Nayim's corner was touched on by Stewart and Des Walker, attempting to head the ball for a corner, instead nodded into the roof of his own net. That Tottenham deserved the lead was unarguable, but that the cool England centre-back should drop such a mortifying clanger towards the end of a characteristically assured display was hard lines, indeed. As the last minute drew nigh, Forest pushed forward but, to a crescendo of whistling from the Spurs contingent,

Keane's shot was saved comfortably by Erik Thorstvedt and it was all over. Forest had suffered their first defeat in three FA Cup Finals, Tottenham had triumphed for a record eighth time. That evening the famous nine-pint pot was taken to the Princess Grace hospital for the inspection of the court jester, who was yet to learn the full extent of his injury. In fact, it was to keep him out of action for a year, slashing his transfer fee from £8.5 million to a mere £5 million. It was a bizarre, anti-climactic finale to Gascoigne's initial tenure in English football, though it would be surprising if he does not return at some stage. As for the other principals in the Wembley 1991 show, Clough was destined to retire two years later without landing his coveted Cup, while Venables was to achieve part-ownership of Spurs and become chief executive. But only for a while: he was ousted in messy circumstances in 1993, though it was hard to believe he would be out of the game for long.

Happy Hotspurs. Left to right are Paul Stewart, Gary Lineker, Paul Allen, Vinny Samways, Erik Thorstvedt, Pat Van den Hauwe, Gary Mabbutt, David Howells, Nayim, Steve Sedgley and Paul Walsh.

Below: At the final whistle, Gary Lineker spares a thought for distraught England chum Des Walker, whose slip cost Forest so dear.

IT HAPPENED
THIS YEAR

Britain reeled
under effects of severe
recession

Separations of Prince
Charles and Princess
Di, Duke and
Duchess of York.

John Major led Tories
to election victory.

Bill Clinton defeated
George Bush
in American
Presidential poll.

Linford Christie and
Sally Gunnell won
Olympic gold.

Nigel Mansell became
world motor racing
champion.

9 May 1992

LIVERPOOL 2

Thomas 47; Rush 68

SUNDERLAND 0

Half-time 0-0

LIVERPOOL		SUNDERLAND
Bruce Grobbelaar	1	Tony Norman
Rob Jones	2	Gary Owers
David Burrows	3	Kevin Ball
Steve Nicol	4	Gary Bennett
Jan Molby	5	Anton Rogan
Mark Wright *(captain)*	6	David Rush †
Dean Saunders	7	Paul Bracewell *(captain)*
Ray Houghton	8	Peter Davenport
Ian Rush	9	Gordon Armstrong*
Steve McManaman	10	John Byrne
Michael Thomas	11	Brian Atkinson
		(sub Warren Hawke)*
		(sub Paul Hardyman) †

Attendance: 79,544

Referee: P Don, Middlesex

Uniquely gripping off-the-pitch drama and the timeless romance of underdogs tilting at unlikely dreams; a bevy of fascinating characters and all the passion that Merseyside and Wearside could engender; even a couple of splendid goals . . . the 1992 FA Cup Final had the lot, yet still won't go down as anything like a classic contest. Somehow it was a fitting climax to a curiously lacklustre season. Leeds had pipped Manchester United in a title race that never *really* caught the imagination, now a non-vintage Liverpool side overcame Second Division strugglers Sunderland to win the Cup in a manner which, though not without a certain flourish on the day, was hardly convincing when viewed in the context of the earlier rounds.

Begging Sunderland's pardon, but undeniably the central figure was Graeme Souness, who had succeeded Kenny Dalglish in the Reds' hot seat only to endure a first full season of sheer trauma, both professional and personal. As if it wasn't harrowing enough to see his squad sorely stretched by the most debilitating of

injury crises, he presided over an alarming slide from the perennial position of Championship challengers and garnered only meagre European consolation as the Reds bowed out in the UEFA Cup quarter-finals. But then, just as a place in the FA Cup Final had been secured in particularly tense and stressful fashion, Souness announced that he was suffering from heart disease which demanded immediate surgery. Accordingly, 32 days before the final, he underwent a triple-bypass operation and was advised not to work for three months. Complications and further treatment followed, but come May the 9th and the showdown with Sunderland, an understandably gaunt Graeme was led to the Wembley bench flanked by two medical 'minders', club doctor Bill Reid and physio Paul Chadwick. Not only was he fretting over a game while still in the early stages of recuperation from life-threatening illness; he had been hit, also, by controversy over selling the story of his heart condition to the Sun newspaper, despised on Merseyside over its coverage of the Hillsborough disaster. As a result, many fans

Walking back to happiness? Liverpool boss Graeme Souness (second right), having recently undergone a heart operation, was not to be kept away from Wembley. Here he appears for the second half with his lieutenant Ronnie Moran (second left) and two medical men in case of emergency. On the left is physio Paul Chadwick, on the right club doctor Bill Reid.

wanted him sacked and had not been slow to voice their feelings. Yet here was Souness, supremely defiant, refusing to bow his head before anything life could throw at him. Courageous? Foolhardy? Plain crazy? Everyone had a view, but patently, he was not for turning.

Now let's peer into the Roker Park camp, which had been beleaguered all term with turmoil of its own. After Christmas, manager Denis Smith had been dismissed following dire results and coach Malcolm Crosby - an unassuming local man with an entirely misleading physical resemblance to manic American comedian Robin Williams - had been placed in temporary charge. He responded by leading Sunderland to three straight League wins and a third-round FA Cup victory over Crewe, a record which won him instant recognition as Manager of the Month. Thereafter the Rokerites slumped back towards the foot of the table, but with continuing Cup exploits to buoy them up, they managed to avoid relegation. It seemed inconceivable that Malcolm's efforts would not be rewarded with a full-time appointment and, somewhat grudgingly as it seemed to the outside world, between semi-final and final he was given a one-year contract. For the moment, at least, the new boss was lionised on Wearside, while elsewhere his image of a home-

John Byrne, to whom Sunderland looked for goals at Wembley.

spun innocent abroad earned him plenty of affection but not always the respect he was due. In truth, as their League position reflected, Sunderland were a moderate outfit. There was no shortage of solid workers, but they were blessed with only two likely sources of inspiration on the pitch, skipper Paul Bracewell and striker John Byrne. Bracewell, both the brains and engine of the side in midfield, had been an unlucky individual, seeing a promising England career torpedoed by injury and finishing as a loser in three FA Cup Finals with Everton. The flamboyant Byrne had proved one of the bargains of the season after arriving from Brighton for £225,000 in October. After a taxi-driver who doubled as a York scout 'discovered' him having a kickabout with his mates as a teenager, he served City, Queen's Park Rangers, then French club Le Havre, before checking in at the Goldstone, winning caps for the Republic of Ireland along the way. But never before had he won national renown as he had done in Sunderland's Cup run, scoring against Port Vale, Oxford, West Ham and Chelsea before netting the only goal of the semi-final against much-fancied Norwich. If he could hit the mark against Liverpool, he would be the tenth man to score in every round of the competition and the first since Peter Osgood in 1970.

Of the Wearsiders' victories, the last three had been against top-flight opposition and all of them close (two of them after replays) and they attested to the battling spirit with which Crosby had imbued his team. But if Sunderland had been forced to work their passage, then so too had Liverpool. Crewe at Gresty Road had been a doddle but then the Reds were fortunate to

escape with a draw against Bristol Rovers at Twerton Park and were forced to come from behind to win the replay. Ipswich pushed the Reds to extra time in another Anfield rematch, then Aston Villa gave as good as they got before losing to the only goal in the quarter-final. But it was Portsmouth, their third opponents from the Second Division, who came closest to unseating Souness' men, leading through a Darren Anderton strike until the dying moments of the Villa Park semi-final only for Ronnie Whelan to equalise. Then, five minutes from the end of normal time in the goalless replay, Pompey rattled Liverpool's crossbar, but could not break through and the issue was settled by penalties. After more than matching the favourites for four hours, it was an excruciating method of elimination for the south-coast side and one that was vilified widely afterwards. Shoot-outs favour teams with big-time experience and are thus contrary to the traditional ethos of the FA Cup, but with modern policing problems and fixture congestion, it is unlikely that more than single replays will ever be sanctioned again.

As the finalists prepared for Wembley, neither club had the luxury of a settled team. Ronnie Moran, standing in for Souness, was reconciled already to the absence of several regulars when he lost John Barnes with a thigh strain and drafted in 20-year-old Steve McManaman for his first senior game since a knee operation. As events turned out, that was not a bad decision! Liverpool had difficulties, also, with 'keeper Mike Hooper, who was so outraged that he was not preferred to Bruce Grobbelaar that he refused to attend the match. On a happier note, young Rob Jones, who had started the season with Crewe but had already played for England after joining the Reds in October, was following in family footsteps. His grandfather, Bill Jones, had kept Bob Paisley out of Liverpool's final line-up against Arsenal in 1950. Meanwhile Sunderland were without one defender, John Kay, with injury and surprisingly left another, Paul Hardyman, on the bench, opting to use the versatile Gary Owers and Anton Rogan as full-backs.

To Moran fell the honour of leading out Liverpool, Souness emerging behind the players and enjoying a chat with the Duchess of Kent after she had dispensed with the formalities. Seated between Moran and Phil Boersma, but with the medicos close behind him, he was under strict instructions to remain calm and as the game began he seemed, on occasions, to be gritting his teeth in an effort to do so. The first test arrived in the third minute when the immaculate Jan Molby

Left: Out with the old. The excellent Ray Houghton, as busy as ever in what was to prove his last game for the Reds before he left for Aston Villa. Many a Liverpool fan bemoaned his departure.

Below: In with the new. Steve McManaman, a leading light of Anfield's new generation, who shredded Sunderland's defence at Wembley after switching flanks.

A long way from Gresty Road. Liverpool's splendid young right-back Rob Jones (left), who had started the season with Crewe and finished it as an England international, shadows Sunderland raider Gordon Armstrong.

Right: Reds skipper Mark Wright (left) attempts to poke the ball away from Sunderland's Peter Davenport. Wright ended his first term at Anfield by collecting the FA Cup.

combined with Ray Houghton to send Michael Thomas in on goal, only for the former Arsenal midfielder - whose strike had deprived the Reds of the title at the last gasp in 1989 - to scoop the ball over the bar. Then, alarmingly for Souness, Sunderland began to push his men back and chances began to fall the way of the outsiders. After 13 minutes, Rogan's shot was turned away by Grobbelaar; the resulting corner fell invitingly to the unmarked Byrne eight yards out but he miskicked wildly. Four minutes later Molby put Jones in trouble with a casual lay-off, Bracewell won possession and his shot was destined for the net until it took a deflection off Mark Wright and wormed past the outside of a post. As the pressure continued, Jones felled Peter Davenport and although no penalty was given, Souness must have been fearing the worst and on one occasion eluded his guardians to rise to his feet for purposes of remonstration.

But now Molby, that corpulent yet endlessly creative schemer, began to come into his own and the Reds were resurgent. McManaman headed over, then was brought down by Bracewell for what looked even more like a penalty than the earlier incident, and there was a feeling that maybe the Rokerites had shot their bolt. Sure enough, shortly after an interval during which Souness had summoned the energy to give his players a rocket, and with McManaman far more dangerous having been switched from left wing to right, the deadlock was broken. The lean flankman went past Brian Atkinson and, under heavy challenge from Gordon Armstrong, delivered a delightful flick into the box with the outside of his foot. On the end of it was Thomas, who swivelled to volley home exquisitely from 15 yards, a goal worthy of any stage. Back on the bench Dr Reid encased Souness in a respectful headlock, while the boss permitted himself a brief smile. His words had had the desired effect! Though 43 minutes still remained, there was now only one team in it. Liverpool were rampant as rain poured down and Molby strolled through centrefield, spraying forth immaculate passes when and where he chose while the admirable McManaman picked his precocious path past any number of desperate tackles. The tide flowed all one way: after 52 minutes Sunderland 'keeper Tony Norman made the save of the match from Molby's magnificent 25-yarder, a quarter of an hour later Dean Saunders headed against the bar from Steve Nicol's

Above: Another Reds new boy, Michael Thomas, whose goal for Arsenal had dashed the Championship champagne from Liverpool's lips in 1989. Now he redeemed himself in Kopites' eyes with his sweet strike (inset) at Wembley.

*Liverpool scorers Ian
Rush (left) and Michael
Thomas share the glory.*

*Above: Victory is magical
for Dean Saunders (left),
while Steve Nicol has seen
it all before!*

cross, then within a minute the elusive Welshman, whose quick-stepping running style was so reminiscent of Kevin Keegan, had played his part in the goal that removed the last vestige of Wearside hope. 'Deano' passed to Thomas, whose contact on the ball was indecisive but it ran on to arch predator Ian Rush, who sidefooted clinically inside a post from 12 yards. That was the signal for Moran, till then as sergeant-majorish as ever, to dance an uncharacteristic jig and, no doubt, for Graeme Souness to relax a little. Thereafter chances proliferated for Liverpool, Saunders missing two and Houghton one, though the game was played out in an atmosphere of almost polite restraint. There were red faces among FA officials after Sunderland were given winners' medals - they joked about making off with them but soon handed them to their rightful owners - though for Bracewell, a Wembley loser for the fourth time, it was all too much and he headed for the dressing room without waiting for the lap of honour.

Thus Liverpool had survived a first-half spell in which they might have been sunk to record their fifth win in ten finals. For Sunderland, who could not quite conjure up the magic of '73, it was the first defeat in three. Both bosses hoped for better in 1992/93, but neither achieved it: Souness, apparently fit and well, could do little to lighten the Reds' most disappointing term for more than three decades, then kept his job after an embarrassingly protracted saga which was expected widely to end with his sacking; Crosby was not so lucky, receiving the axe as the Rokerites floundered once more. The money might be good, but the long-term prospects stink; who would be a football manager?

*Left: The Executioner.
Ian Rush sidefoots
Liverpool's second goal
with unerring accuracy.*

*Above: Paul Bracewell,
now a four-time loser in
FA Cup Finals.*

*Below: That old bush
fighter Bruce Grobbelaar
in typically irrepressible
mood. No matter what
the critics reckoned, it
was going to take a good
man to oust him from the
team.*

375

15 May 1993

ARSENAL 1

Wright 21

SHEFFIELD WEDNESDAY 1

Hirst 62

Half-time 1-0 Extra time played

ARSENAL			SHEFFIELD WEDNESDAY
David Seaman	1	1	Chris Woods
Lee Dixon	2	2	Roland Nilsson
Nigel Winterburn	3	3	Nigel Worthington
Andy Linighan	5	4	Carlton Palmer
Tony Adams *(captain)*	6	5	David Hirst
Kevin Campbell	7	6	Viv Anderson *(captain)**
† Ian Wright	8	8	Chris Waddle†
Paul Merson	10	9	Paul Warhurst
*Ray Parlour	11	10	Mark Bright
Paul Davis	14	11	John Sheridan
John Jensen	17	15	John Harkes
*(sub Alan Smith)	9	17	(sub Graham Hyde)*
†(sub David O'Leary)	22	14	(sub Chris Bart-Williams)†

Attendance: 79,347

Referee: K Barratt, Coventry

Jaded, sterile, muscular . . . not the adjectives one would hope to employ in reporting an FA Cup Final, particularly one in which such gifted entertainers as Chris Waddle and Paul Merson were on parade. Yet, in truth, each of those damning descriptions was depressingly apt as Arsenal and Sheffield Wednesday played on . . . and on . . . and on. The action continued for close on 260 minutes (in cluding two extra periods and eight chunks of stoppage time) as two evenly-matched sides cancelled each other out. Part of the problem was that having clashed in the Coca-Cola Cup Final and a recent League game, every strength and weakness was known to the opposition and there were no surprises left. Equally, though such an explanation carries little credibility with the average working man, many of the players were suffering from fatigue. Not the sort of tiredness that comes from expending too much effort in a day or a week, but the cumulative stress on arguably over-trained bodies that gives rise to deep-seated, long-standing injuries of the type that was expected to mean a groin operation for Gunners skipper Tony Adams in the summer. Having said that, however, the fans had a right to expect better value for money than this marathon exercise in mediocrity.

Arsenal had won the Coca-Cola, and there was a theory that Wednesday would be all the hungrier for the one that really mattered. After all, Trevor Francis had moulded them into one of the most attractive sides in the land, and in a season when Manchester United, Aston Villa and Norwich City had set a compelling standard, that was a compliment worth its salt. But could they make their undoubted flair count against the attritional Gunners, whose clam-like defence, stifling midfield and speedy forwards ever-eager to chase the long ball made them deucedly formidable opponents? That is not to dismiss George Graham's men as 'Wimbledon in red', as one soccer correspondent dubbed them unkindly and rather inaccurately. Perhaps the most frustrating aspect of their game - and there are a few ! - is that they do possess the fluency to build beautifully from the back, yet so often choose not to do so. In the event, over the two matches they played as much enjoyable football as the Owls, though that was not saying a great deal.

In their bid to win the FA Cup for the fourth time, Wednesday had overcome three teams from the new First Division - Cambridge, Sunderland and Southend - at the first attempt and another, Derby, after a six-goal quarter-final thriller had necessitated a replay. That set up the last-four confrontation that all Sheffield had prayed would be reserved for the final, a showdown with Dave Bassett's United.

George Graham, now the first man to win all three major domestic honours as both player and boss, was also the first manager to go up for an FA Cup winner's medal. Other innovations in 1993 were the introduction of players' names on shirts and the use of squad numbers.

All sorts of venues were mooted before the Sheffield rivals got their wish to meet at Wembley, thus not allowing the winner of the other semi-final an unfair advantage. It turned out to be a game fit to grace the national stadium, Waddle in particular lighting it up with a wonderful free-kick and sparkling all-round display as Wednesday prevailed 2-1. Those canny folk from the Steel City had been right, it would have made a smashing final!

Arsenal, too, had offered splendid fare on their Cup journey, beginning at Huish Park, the sumptuous, custom-built home of

Above: Paul Merson of Arsenal, one player whose flair might have lifted a dour contest from its rut, skips past the challenge of Wednesday's Roland Nilsson. Unfortunately, Merson spent most of his time in a negative midfield role.

Yeovil Town, where an Ian Wright hat-trick had halted but not humbled the ambitious Vauxhall Conference outfit. Next came a two-match test against champions Leeds, the Gunners going through 3-2 at Elland Road after being held at Highbury. Nottingham Forest, struggling sadly in what was to be Brian Clough's final term, were the victims in the fifth round, then captain Adams made light of 29 stitches in a head wound to lead a successful quarter-final fightback against Ipswich to open the way for a second local derby in the semis. In the Wembley clash with Spurs, Arsenal survived heavy first-half pressure, then gained revenge for their 1991 semi-final knockout through a late Adams winner.

Shortly before the final, Chris Waddle was named as Footballer of the Year and much was expected of the man England boss Graham Taylor persisted in omitting from his World Cup plans despite the north-easterner's exhilarating form for the Owls. Waddle's subtle prompting had had plenty to do with the amazing success of defender Paul Warhurst's conversion to prolific marksman. The pity was, though, that injuries removed Nigel Pearson and Peter Shirtliff from central defence, which meant the reversion of Paul (himself forced to play with strapping on a broken wrist) to the rearguard and a consequent loss of firepower up front, where England's David Hirst was still well short of optimum fitness. Arsenal were deprived of David Hillier in midfield, though the springtime return of the quietly influential Paul Davis was a plus.

As kick-off time approached, one man at least was assured of a winner's medal. Gunner Steve Morrow had scored the crucial goal in the Coca-Cola final, but then had fallen victim to the boisterous after-match celebrations of his skipper, breaking his elbow so badly he had been unable to collect his gong. Now came Steve's postponed moment of glory, and his lone climb to the royal box, his arm in a sling, was a happy curtain-raiser to the main business of the day. That began with a misleading flourish as Wednesday attacked, John Sheridan took a corner and a backheader from Carlton Palmer brought a hurried tip-over from David Seaman. Then it was the Gunners' turn and Andy Linighan missed with a free header, before the Owls retaliated and Seaman was forced into his most spectacular action of the entire final, producing a flying one-handed save to keep out Waddle's 30-yard free-kick. But ominously, any flowing movement by either side was being smothered at birth, with both Waddle and Merson being employed as little more than midfield nullifiers. Thus it was no surprise either that the opening goal arrived courtesy of a set piece, or that it fell to Arsenal. Davis floated in a free-kick from the right, Andy Linighan nodded it across the box to Wright, who eluded Warhurst to direct his header past a helpless Chris Woods from six yards. Now the Gunners assumed the ascendancy and by the interval it was difficult to see them relinquishing their grip.

However, the Trevor Francis team talk must have been eloquent indeed, the Owls beginning the second half with a wave of attacks in which Waddle was prominent. Now roaming more freely to the flanks, he began to make life difficult for his markers and one step-over and pirouette that duped the combative John Jensen was sheer poetry. Twice Hirst went close and a Mark Bright effort was disallowed for offside before Wednesday's pressure culminated in a deserved equaliser. Sheridan delivered from the right, Bright glanced on to the underrated John Harkes, whose selfless and intelligent headed knockback was buried - low, left-footed and with enormous relish - by Hirst from six yards. Nearly half an hour of normal time remaining and everything to play for; there was still time for the game to save itself, but it wasn't to be. Arsenal brought on target-man Alan Smith for midfielder Ray Parlour, but the ensuing unimaginative exchanges proved inconclusive. After 85 minutes, Wednesday's attacking options were weakened when they lost centre-half and skipper Viv Anderson with a knee injury and were forced to move Palmer, the most potent midfielder on display, into the back four, bringing on busy little Graham Hyde as his replacement. In all honesty, no one had earned the right to brandish the Cup, but in injury time Arsenal came close to victory when a clearance dropped to Wright, who spun and volleyed from eight yards to force a fine save from Woods. Extra time, for which David O'Leary replaced Wright - whose broken toe had prevented him from training for three weeks - was eminently forgettable, so it was back to the drawing board for Thursday night.

Above: Chris Waddle, of whom so much was expected, struggles in vain to escape from the clam-like attention of Arsenal's Nigel Winterburn and John Jensen. Only rarely did he break free to hint at the form which had earned him the Footballer of the Year accolade.

Top: Ian Wright is perfectly positioned to head Arsenal into the lead, and when he scores, the England striker knows how to celebrate! (main picture).

Right: David Hirst cracks home the equaliser following a clever and unselfish piece of work by John Harkes.

Replay at Wembley

ARSENAL 2

Wright 33; Linighan 120

SHEFFIELD WEDNESDAY 1

Waddle 68

Half-time 1-0 Extra time played

ARSENAL	○		SHEFFIELD WEDNESDAY
David Seaman	1	1	Chris Woods
Lee Dixon	2	2	Roland Nilsson*
Nigel Winterburn	3	3	Nigel Worthington
Andy Linighan	5	4	Carlton Palmer *(captain)*
Tony Adams *(captain)*	6	5	David Hirst
Kevin Campbell	7	7	Danny Wilson†
*Ian Wright	8	8	Chris Waddle
Alan Smith	9	9	Paul Warhurst
Paul Merson	10	10	Mark Bright
Paul Davis	14	11	John Sheridan
John Jensen	17	15	John Harkes
*(sub David O'Leary)	22	14	(sub Chris Bart-Williams)*
		17	(sub Graham Hyde)†

Attendance: 62,267

Referee: K Barratt, Coventry

Arsenal personified. Captain Tony Adams, a born winner, hoists the FA Cup. The big centre-half has endured plenty of flak in recent years but, significantly, it does not come from within the game.

Wednesday were facing the most pressing problems. With Anderson now their third unavailable central defender, Palmer had to remain at the back, depriving the side of its midfield power base. Though the gangling beanpole would never win prizes for elegance, his strength and ceaseless running between penalty areas would be sorely missed and Danny Wilson, for all his skill, was a pallid replacement. Francis was also concerned about the stamina of right-back Roland Nilsson, who had captained Sweden in a World Cup qualifier on Wednesday, not linking up with the Owls until one o'clock on replay morning. As for Arsenal, they opted to retain the experienced Smith, not even giving Parlour a place on the bench and thus depriving him of a medal.

On a miserable, drizzly night, kick-off was put back half an hour after delays on the M1 had held up Sheffield supporters, yet there were plenty of empty seats, the game attracting the lowest ever gate (62,267) for a Wembley FA Cup Final. Nevertheless, there was a feeling that the match could only be better than Saturday's, and it was - but only just. Waddle began brightly but his enterprise provoked immediate and brutal reprisal from Jensen, whose horrible foul, directly in front of the referee, was punished only by a free-kick. Wednesday bristled visibly and the tackling from both teams grew increasingly immoderate as the game was compressed mainly into a crowded midfield. Once again, openings were few, the first falling to Paul Merson after 16 minutes when Smith put him clear on the left. The England dasher moved menacingly into the box, slipped past Palmer but then struck the feeblest of shots with only Seaman to beat. The next incident of note was of the unsavoury variety, Bright breaking Linighan's nose with his elbow, and the Wednesday man was lucky to escape with a booking. The Gunners' big defender, whose finger was also broken in the collision, was not deterred, however, and soon moved forward to head wide from Lee Dixon's tempting cross.

Now Arsenal were looking ever more dangerous and took the lead on 33 minutes when a delightful nudge from Smith reached Wright, who outpaced Palmer and Warhurst, drew Woods from his goal and dinked the ball expertly inside a post from 14 yards. Then, four minutes from the break, Smith almost doubled

Ian Wright opens the scoring in the replay with a quicksilver piece of opportunism, though some observers criticised Owls 'keeper Chris Woods for hesitating as he came off his line. The helpless Wednesday defender is Roland Nilsson.

the lead when he sidefooted wide from close-range after a nod-on from Kevin Campbell. Had that gone in the Gunners would have been in the home straight, but as the second half wore on Wednesday were resurgent, reducing George Graham to near apoplexy on the touchline. The Owls deserved parity, but achieved it in slightly fortunate fashion. Harkes, giving another fine personal display, crossed from the right, the ball brushed Linighan, slid off Dixon and ran to Waddle on the left. Chris hit it first time and Seaman might have had it covered, but a slight deflection off Dixon's heal defeated him - 1-1. Three minutes later the Owls could, and should, have gone ahead when the ball bounced to the unmarked Bright, 12 yards out and with half the goal at his mercy, but he scuffed his shot against the outside of a post. Soon O'Leary - whose testimonial and so-called farewell match after 20 years at Highbury had been played three nights earlier - came on once more for the flagging Wright, and after Merson, Dixon and Hirst had all missed chances, extra time commenced. With the added period producing further stalemate, the dreadful spectre of a penalty shoot-out loomed

Above: Paul Warhurst, the stopper-turned-striker who was forced to revert to his original role by the Owls' injury crisis.

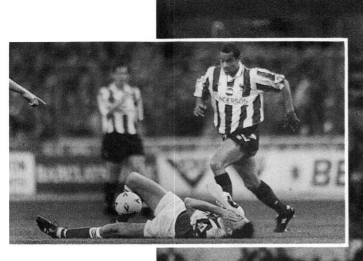

Above: Arsenal stopper Andy Linighan is prostrate after getting the elbow from Mark Bright. The Wednesday striker must have been relieved when the referee produced a yellow card.

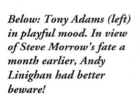

Below: Tony Adams (left) in playful mood. In view of Steve Morrow's fate a month earlier, Andy Linighan had better beware!

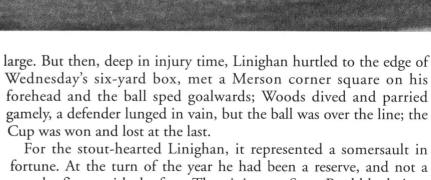

large. But then, deep in injury time, Linighan hurtled to the edge of Wednesday's six-yard box, met a Merson corner square on his forehead and the ball sped goalwards; Woods dived and parried gamely, a defender lunged in vain, but the ball was over the line; the Cup was won and lost at the last.

For the stout-hearted Linighan, it represented a somersault in fortune. At the turn of the year he had been a reserve, and not a popular figure with the fans. Then injury to Steve Bould had given him his chance, he had come in and played well and, having more than paid his dues, he was now experiencing the sweet side of football life. His manager, the first man to win all three major domestic honours as both player and boss, told reporters he hadn't consid-

Left: Andy Linighan's bullet header wins the FA Cup for the sixth time in Arsenal's history. Coincidentally, with the Gunners now qualified for the Cup Winners' Cup, the result enabled Andy's former club Norwich to enter the UEFA Cup.

Below: What a way to go. David O'Leary finishes his 20th and last season as a Gunner with yet another honour.

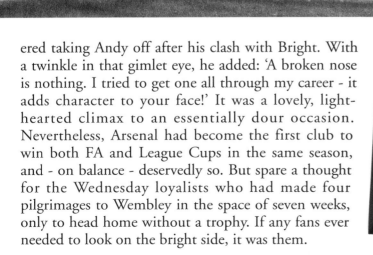

ered taking Andy off after his clash with Bright. With a twinkle in that gimlet eye, he added: 'A broken nose is nothing. I tried to get one all through my career - it adds character to your face!' It was a lovely, light-hearted climax to an essentially dour occasion. Nevertheless, Arsenal had become the first club to win both FA and League Cups in the same season, and - on balance - deservedly so. But spare a thought for the Wednesday loyalists who had made four pilgrimages to Wembley in the space of seven weeks, only to head home without a trophy. If any fans ever needed to look on the bright side, it was them.